Positive Youth Development in Global Contexts of Social and Economic Change

The youth of the world are our most important assets. When youth develop positively, they have the power to benefit themselves and their families, communities, and societies. These tremendous benefits accrue for many generations, so investments in youth represent a highly cost-effective opportunity for positive change. This is the first volume to focus globally on the effects of social and economic change on youth, and on the opportunity to support youth through policy, programs, and interventions to develop positively despite challenges.

The chapters in this volume highlight research demonstrating youth assets and resilience, as well as programs and interventions that increase the likelihood that youth will thrive. Many chapters also draw attention to opportunities for youth leadership, helping youth to develop their strengths as they benefit their communities. Additional chapters focus on promoting optimal youth development in the presence of adversity, risk, or challenge, taking into consideration the potential and capacity of the young person. Finally, the ecological system theory is a strong influence in many chapters that examine the interrelationship of different social contexts such as family, peers, school, and work.

Positive Youth Development in Global Contexts of Social and Economic Change is both a vision for the future and an ideology supported by a new international vocabulary for engaging with youth development. Developed by researchers across interdisciplinary fields, the volume has enormous policy implications for lawmakers given the surge in youth population in many parts of the world.

Anne C. Petersen is Research Professor at the University of Michigan, USA and Founder/President of the Global Philanthropy Alliance.

Sílvia H. Koller is Professor of Psychology at the Universidade Federal do Rio Grande do Sul, Porto Alegre, Brazil.

Frosso Motti-Stefanidi is Professor of Psychology at the National and Kapodistrian University of Athens, Greece.

Suman Verma is the former Head of the Department of Human Development and Family Relations in the Government Home Science College, Panjab University, Chandigarh, India.

POSITIVE YOUTH DEVELOPMENT IN GLOBAL CONTEXTS OF SOCIAL AND ECONOMIC CHANGE

Edited by Anne C. Petersen,
Sílvia H. Koller,
Frosso Motti-Stefanidi, and
Suman Verma

Routledge
Taylor & Francis Group

NEW YORK AND LONDON

First published 2017
by Routledge
711 Third Avenue, New York, NY 10017

and by Routledge
2 Park Square, Milton Park, Abingdon, Oxon, OX14 4RN

Routledge is an imprint of the Taylor & Francis Group, an informa business

© 2017 Taylor & Francis

The right of Anne C. Petersen, Sílvia H. Koller, Frosso Motti-Stefanidi, and Suman Verma to be identified as the authors of the editorial material, and of the authors for their individual chapters, has been asserted in accordance with sections 77 and 78 of the Copyright, Designs and Patents Act 1988.

Library of Congress Cataloging in Publication Data
A catalog record for this book has been requested

ISBN: 978-1-138-67080-8 (hbk)
ISBN: 978-1-138-67081-5 (pbk)
ISBN: 978-1-315-30727-5 (ebk)

Typeset in Bembo
by HWA Text and Data Management, London

CONTENTS

PART II
Interventions to Support and Promote Positive Adaptation and
Development

PART III
Research, Interventions, and Policy Needs

LIST OF FIGURES

LIST OF TABLES

ABOUT THE EDITORS

Anne C. Petersen is Research Professor at the University of Michigan, USA and Founder/President of the Global Philanthropy Alliance. She has also been a faculty member/academic administrator at Stanford University, University of Minnesota, Pennsylvania State University, and the University of Chicago; leader in philanthropy at the Kellogg and the MacArthur Foundations; as well as in the federal government at the National Science Foundation. She has published 13 books and over 300 articles, holds many honors, and leads/serves on many boards/committees.

Sílvia H. Koller is Professor of Psychology at the Universidade Federal do Rio Grande do Sul, Porto Alegre, Brazil and an Extraordinary Professor at North-West University, Vanderbijlpark, South Africa. Currently she is Visiting Scholar at Harvard Graduate School of Education, USA. She is former president of the Brazilian Association of Developmental Psychology. Her research focus is on positive youth development and social policy. Her research interests are related to the study of street populations, sexually abused victims, and at-risk families. She has published 10 books and over 200 articles, holds many honors, and serves on many international committees.

Frosso Motti-Stefanidi is Professor of Psychology at the National and Kapodistrian University of Athens, Greece. She is former President of the European Association of Developmental Psychology and of the European Association of Personality Psychology. She is currently serving on the Governing Council of the Society for Research in Child Development. She studies immigrant and non-immigrant youth adaptation and well-being during the economic recession from a risk and resilience perspective.

Suman Verma is the former Head of the Department of Human Development and Family Relations in the Government Home Science College, Panjab University, Chandigarh, India. She is a developmental psychologist whose research with an advocacy component focuses on child work, daily ecology of adolescent family life, school stress, abuse, life skills interventions, and social policy.

CONTRIBUTORS

Amina Abubakar, Pwani University, Kenya and KEMRI/Wellcome Trust Research Programme, Kenya

Itziar Alonso-Arbiol, University of the Basque Country UPV/EHU, Spain

Arzu Aydnili-Karakulak, Bahçeşehir University, Turkey

Bernadine Brady, National University of Ireland, Ireland

Marlis Buchmann, University of Zurich, Switzerland

Patricio Cumsille, Pontificia Universidad Católica de Chile, Chile

Radosveta Dimitrova, Stockholm University, Sweden

Pat Dolan, National University of Ireland, Ireland

David L. DuBois, University of Illinois-Chicago, USA

Stephen F. Hamilton, Cornell University (Emeritus), USA

Mary Agnes Hamilton, Cornell University, USA

Ingrid Holsen, University of Bergen, Norway

Venzislav Jordanov, University of World and National Economy (UWNE), Bulgaria

Jennifer E. Lansford, Duke University, USA

Torill Larsen, University of Bergen, Norway

James Lester, North Carolina State University, USA

Carolina Lisboa, Pontifícia Universidade Católica do Rio Grande do Sul, Brazil

Angela Helena Marin, Universidade do Vale do Rio dos Sinos, Brazil

M. Loreto Martínez, Pontificia Universidad Católica de Chile, Chile

Virginia Martinez-Fernandez, Miguel Hernandez University, Spain

Stefanos Mastrotheodoros, National and Kapodistrian University of Athens, Utrecht University, the Netherlands

Pasquale Musso, University of Palermo, Italy

Moses Kachama Nyongesa, KEMRI/WTRP, Kenya

Elizabeth M. Ozer, University of California-San Francisco, USA

Emily J. Ozer, University of California-Berkeley, USA

Nancy Papathanasiou, National and Kapodistrian University of Athens, Greece

Vassilis Pavlopoulos, National and Kapodistrian University of Athens, Greece

Amber Akemi Piatt, University of California-Berkeley, USA

Juliana Pureza, Pontifícia Universidade Católica do Rio Grande do Sul, Brazil

Susana Núñez Rodriguez, Federal University of Rio Grande do Sul, Brazil

Katariina Salmela-Aro, University of Helsinki, Finland; University of Jyväskylä, Finland

Maja Schachner, Universität Potsdam, Germany

Barbara Schober, University of Vienna, Austria

Ingrid Schoon, University College London, UK; WZB – Berlin Social Science Center, Germany

Deborah E. Sellers, Cornell University, USA

Halimu Shauri, Pwani University, Kenya

Rainer K. Silbereisen, University of Jena, Germany

Iva Polackova Solcova, The Czech Academy of Sciences, Czech Republic

Christiane Spiel, University of Vienna, Austria

Delia Stefenel, Lucian Blaga University of Sibiu, Romania

Peter Tavel, Palacky University, Czech Republic

Fitim Uka, Private Bearer of Higher Education "qeap-heimer", Kosovo

Katja Upadyaya, University of Helsinki, Finland; University of Jyväskylä, Finland

Manuel C. Voelkle, Humboldt University Berlin, Germany; Max Planck Institute for Human Development, Germany

Alice J. Wuermli, University of California-Davis, USA

Hirokazu Yoshikawa, New York University, USA

Skerdi Zahaj, University of Tirana, Albania

FOREWORD

Lonnie R. Sherrod
EXECUTIVE DIRECTOR, SRCD

This volume resulted from a Society for Research in Child Development (SRCD)-sponsored meeting on the same topic, held in Prague in October, 2014. It was the second round of a program of smaller topically focused meetings begun by SRCD in 2012 to complement its much larger Biennial meeting. I was especially enthusiastic about this meeting because it was SRCD's first international meeting held outside North America. Now I am even more pleased that the meeting has produced the current outstanding volume, which is supported by SRCD's past and current strategic plans.

Internationalizing Developmental Science

As many of you know, for the past ten years, SRCD has been pursuing a strategic plan, one goal of which is to become more international in both membership and program. This goal reflects the realization that children are increasingly growing up in a global context, meaning that it is impossible to fully understand children's development within national boundaries. Transnational comparative research such as that represented at this meeting and covered in this volume is crucial. Furthermore, it is critical to include in our research the majority world of children as well as those in the industrialized world. A developmental science built on studies of 5% of the world's children is not adequate. To fully achieve this goal of internationalizing developmental science, organizations like SRCD have to attend to building research capacity across the full globe. We have begun to work with other similar organizations such as the Society for Research on Adolescence (SRA), the International Congress on Infant Studies (ICIS), and the International Society for the Study of Behavioral Development (ISSBD) to make this happen. Meetings such as the Prague one and volumes such as this one are one means to that goal. SRCD's International Committee, chaired by Anne C. Petersen and Frosso Motti-Stefanidi, the organizers of the Prague meeting (along with Sílvia H. Koller), have launched a series of other activities to pursue this goal, e.g., a collaboration with UNICEF on early childhood development. We urge interested SRCD members and readers of this volume to work with us to continue to pursue these goals.

Promoting Positive Youth Development

The second reason for my enthusiasm for this volume and the meeting on which it is based is its topic, positive youth development (PYD) in the global context of social and economic change. This volume has three unusual foci: youth in the second and third decades of life, positive development, and the global economic and social context of development. My research interests across the past couple of decades have been on youth civic engagement. The PYD approach has been especially important to this topic, completely changing our orientation to both research and policy. The third decade of life has also become an increasingly important topic as the transition to adulthood has been delayed worldwide. Finally, youth have been particularly hard hit by the global economic recession and other social contextual changes addressed in this volume. For example, many young people are trapped in endless cycles of unemployment, underemployment, and/or of being forced back to education because of lack of job opportunities. The tools of developmental science sorely need to be applied to this topic. Other social contextual changes such as immigration are equally important to youth development. What are the effects of the economic downturn and other social contextual changes such as immigration for youth's adaptation and development? What makes a difference for those who are able to more successfully navigate through the current global situation? How can we support youth to become the engines of hope and change in their countries? What can scientists from different countries learn from each other? Sections of this volume address these topics.

Growing Up During Rapid Social Change

Across the past year, SRCD has developed a new strategic plan which maintains the main ingredients of the former plan, such as building a global developmental science, but adds a concern for the need for innovation in the field and as a result for SRCD, given the rapidly changing nature of today's global context. The rise of digital media is one example of today's changing global context for children's development. The global economic and social context addressed by this volume is of course another example. Hence, this volume is perfectly in line with this new focus, and I am delighted that this volume is emerging just as we are unfolding and implementing this new strategic plan. This rapidly changing global contexts presents both challenges and opportunities to our field. This volume does an outstanding job of addressing those challenges and opportunities and as a result offers guideposts for further field development.

International Consortium of Developmental Science Societies (ICDSS)

I have already mentioned that SRCD wishes to partner with other developmental science societies to internationalize developmental science. As one important example of this effort, in 2012, SRCD joined eight other developmental science societies to form a consortium oriented to promoting collaborations across the topics and age groups represented by the member organizations and to provide an international resource for bring developmental science to global policy affecting children and their development. Since 2012, ICDSS has held several meetings and is planning a consensus conference in 2016 or 2017. Two other organizations have since joined the consortium so that it now represents 11 associations. This consortium, like this volume, reflects the increasing internationalization of developmental science. Many of the same scientists are involved in both. Furthermore, the consensus conference will address three topics of global developmental science, all relevant to this volume: Migration, disasters, and global climate change. Interested SRCD members and readers of this volume are encouraged to get involved in our efforts at internationalization.

As Executive Director of SRCD, I am delighted that we are playing a role in bringing this important volume to fruition.

1

GLOBAL POSITIVE YOUTH DEVELOPMENT

Framing the Issues

Anne C. Petersen, Suman Verma,
Sílvia H. Koller, and Frosso Motti-Stefanidi

We have three goals for this framing chapter for the volume: (1) provide a
rationale for the topic of the volume, (2) describe the origins of the volume
which emanated from a conference on this topic, and (3) provide an overview
of the volume contents. The concepts driving this volume – global perspective
especially in developmental science, an emphasis on youth and particularly
positive youth development, and the importance of youth action or interventions
supporting youth in the face of social change – continue to have urgency for
the world. The economic crisis, deepest in the US and minority world with
shockwaves globally, was the original impetus for this effort. While the economic
crisis has now abated in many regions, the context of social change with its
effects especially on youth has continued to be salient globally.

Why Focus Globally?

Globalization is a reality, affecting challenges and opportunities for all. Global
epidemics have been especially powerful in demonstrating that no nation can
pretend to remain isolated. Terrorism is similarly ubiquitous and, like epidemics,
worse in some places than others. Both of these examples leave nations with little
control but with an imperative to establish as least preventive approaches such
as educating the public and providing structures for response. Globalization
has primarily expanded business and trade beyond national boundaries but
some nations attempt to exert some control over trade. Technology has been
more difficult to limit but some nations have attempted restrictions. In general,
globalization has extended communication broadly, making it easy and fast to

share ideas, making global thinking and behaving a reality. For the purposes of this chapter, globalization has had significant effects on youth (e.g., Silbereisen & Chen, 2010; Thompson, 2012).

In discussing global issues, we use the terms majority and minority world, following the convention established by the World Bank for the 15% of countries who are wealthier (minority world) compared with all others (World Bank, 2015.) These terms replace older terms with more pejorative meaning, such as developed/developing worlds.

Challenges of Globalization

Globalization presents major challenges to nations in terms of controlling business, trade, and communications within their boundaries. Consequently, it presents a challenge for national policies and institutional structures. In addition, globalization may threaten national identity and culture for some countries. At the individual level, globalization may be experienced as a threat because of reducing predictability for the future in terms of jobs and other social realities. The challenges of globalization have been repeatedly articulated, and have generally represented a source of fear to nations and their populations.

One challenge is that benefits of globalization are not uniform and to a large extent globalization has increased inequality between rich and poor nations, as well as between lower-skilled workers and higher-skilled within nations, contrary to expectations for "free trade" (Goldberg & Pavcnik, 2016). For example, minority world countries have moved businesses and especially manufacturing plants to majority world countries to take advantage of lower wages and less regulation. This movement of businesses or plants creates more jobs but also burdens countries with higher pollution, causing health and other problems. Further, this process has created more unemployment for lower-skilled workers in minority world countries.

Further, growth has been uneven (World Bank, 2013). For example, in the past two decades, China and India have grown faster economically than minority world nations. Similarly, the average of all countries (including failed states) in Africa is higher than minority world increases. Majority world countries, of course, are beginning from low starting levels. For example, many countries in Africa still have the highest poverty rates (World Bank, 2015).

Another way to consider progress with globalization is to examine changes in the human development index which combines income, life expectancy, and education for countries (*The Economist*, 2015). From 1990 to 2015, the best performers were Rwanda (remarkable since the genocide of 1994), China (which is now at the level of South Korea in 1990), Singapore, Iran, and Mozambique. These countries also made major investments in social or health institutions as well as other infrastructure. The worst performers on this index were Swaziland, Zimbabwe, Lesotho, Tajikistan, and Central African Republic, all with near-zero growth (*The Economist*, 2015).

Opportunities of Globalization

At the same time, globalization brings opportunities such as economic progress, technical development, political influence, health systems, social and natural environment awareness, and improvements. Globalization has also created new opportunities in majority world countries for new jobs, roles, and ideas, especially for individuals. It has also created an interdependence between the minority and majority world countries, with resources and technology coming from the minority world and raw material, food, and oil increasingly supplied by the majority world. The impact of globalization is also evident in areas of health and education systems, with increased exchange of information. A greater demand for higher-skill jobs has resulted in youth pursuing higher education and skill training.

There has also been slow but steady growth in economies, living standards, and life expectancies in the majority world, with improved services for health care and education for the poor. Many of these improvements received a huge boost from the UN Millennium Development Goals (UNDP, 2015). The information and communication technology (ICT) boom has had its share of impact on culture with the emergence of a global culture. Nations are slower to act and are still seeking opportunity, primarily through trade deals and alliances. The young, more than older people, are likely to be enthusiastic about new opportunities and ideas. Young people have especially embraced the internet for educational and occupational information (among other purposes such as social communications.) Unfortunately, too many in the majority world are limited in access to the internet because of unreliable power and, also in some areas, limited connectivity. Nonetheless, growth of internet resources and applications to use them effectively are expected to continue to increase exponentially (International Telecommunications Union, 2015).

Global Science

Science is already global (Suresh, 2012), especially in terms of global communication of scientific information. Global collaborations are increasingly being pursued, though not as quickly as is needed. The existence of global challenges and threats has brought a rapid increase in global science. For example, global climate change stimulated the Intergovernmental Panel on Climate Change established formally in 1988 (www.ipcc.ch). The United Nations and other global bodies (e.g., World Bank) have increasingly been hosting research on global topics over the last few decades, including those related to human development (e.g., Lundberg & Wuermli, 2012).

Developmental science must also become global. At this point, publications in developmental science, like related fields of behavioral or social science, are almost entirely dominated by research based on minority world populations conducted by minority world researchers (e.g., Arnett, 2008). Research conducted by majority world researchers with their populations sometimes finds markedly different results from those in the minority world, especially when the prevailing theories are grounded in specific cultures (e.g., Serpell, 2011; Tchombe, Nsamenang, & Keller, 2013). Understanding of human development requires its study with all major populations, cultures, and contexts.

Geography has played a role in the challenges of creating global science, including developmental science. In addition to geographic distance, the global south tends to have poorer populations, compounding distance. The fact that English has become the language of global science adds further challenge to minority world researchers. As developmental scientists, we must continue to find ways to create partnerships and collaborations that reduce these challenges so we can all benefit from the rich diversity of ideas and innovations from our colleagues globally.

Scientific societies have a role to play with engaging researchers globally. The International Society for the Study of Behavioral Development (ISSBD) is the oldest developmental science society with a global focus and a strong history of active global engagement of both scientists and students, and was established in 1972. The Society for Research in Child Development (SRCD) is the oldest developmental science society, formally established in the US in 1933 but engaging in activities earlier. SRCD now has a priority on global science engagement in its recent strategic plan, as do other developmental science societies. The newly formed International Consortium of Developmental Science Societies (ICDSS) is further aiming to globalize developmental science, with a particular focus on global policy.

Why Youth?

Youth are highly significant globally for many reasons, grounded in challenges and opportunities. One seldom-discussed challenge is the neglect or even resistance toward youth in many countries. Perhaps because of their energy, young people may be regarded as threats on a political level or trouble makers on a social level. This stance by elders leads to policies in many countries that ignore youth needs, including supportive pathways for them to become constructive and productive citizens. Extant research on youth demonstrates that those who are most energetic and talented will find outlets for their efforts; if positive outlets are not provided, negative ones involving criminal activity will be pursued (e.g., Catalano et al., 2004). Young people globally who navigate through these unhealthy pathways are often those who find lucrative employment using the internet to engage in theft, as well as more traditional forms of criminal activity with drugs or human trafficking. The internet is also used to appeal to youth idealism (among other motivations) by engaging in acts of terror. These negative routes represent a waste of young human capital.

Conversely, there is increasing evidence for youth as assets to any society (e.g., Diers, 2013). Minority world research has found that youth who live in contexts that support their positive academic, social, and psychological development feel better about themselves and their contexts (such as families and peers), and both the young people and their meaningful social groups benefit from these (e.g., Jelicic et al., 2007). When nurtured and supported, and sometimes even without any help, young people globally demonstrate remarkable energy, motivation, and creativity on behalf of their families and communities (e.g., Souza, et al., 2011; Sharma & Verma, 2013). Further, the bravery and commitment of young people globally are demonstrated in biographies of young people such as the "lost boys" of Sudan (Baker, 2008; Loming & Tabb, 2012) as well as Malala Yousafzai (Yousafzai & Lamb, 2013), the girl who championed education in Pakistan and was recognized with a Nobel Prize.

Gender Issues

In addition to increased uncertainty about employment pathways and opportunities globally, young people in the majority world experience major disjunctions in the transitions from school to work. In addition, gendered distribution of resources at both the community and individual level offers new opportunities for young women, yet constraints persist. While communities value education and career options for girls, they do not always grant autonomy to females in taking decisions about their life choices (whether marriage, child bearing, or careers.) The pervasiveness of social norms that curtail freedoms for women and are based on undervaluation or devaluation of what women do can lead young women themselves to internalize negative self-perceptions and doubt their own abilities. There are stark gender differences in favor of males in adaptation to the changing societal demands. The combined effect of economic development, rising education among women, and declining fertility goes a long way to explain changes in work force participation rates. However, despite significant progress in female labor force participation, pervasive and persistent gender differences remain in productivity and earnings across different sectors and jobs. For instance, women are more likely than men to work in jobs that offer flexible working arrangements (such as part-time or informal jobs) so that they can combine work with child care responsibilities at home. For many, coping with high levels of stress accompany their socioeconomic and psychological adaptation to social change. In situations of economic adversity, intense competition for limited resources may result in altering education or career goals and aspirations. Individuals and groups may perceive, interpret, and respond to macro-level societal and economic changes differently. For many young people, adapting to a changing environment with multiple demands may result in failure to cope. For instance, a mismatch in employment requirements and skill deficit among the youth results in frustration thus increasing the possibilities of adopting negative pathways to earning money. In today's globalized digital world, youth can play an active role in their own adaptation, mainly through the creation of new social and cultural environments for their activities and social interactions. To foster positive youth development, we need to build on assets in youth's ecology that will enhance their capability to navigate through the current global economic stress that countries are experiencing.

Youth Bulge

Demographic change is another important factor to consider with youth, specifically the youth bulge. The birth rate in the global south, and more generally in the poorest regions, is predicted to drive a 4% increase in children by 2025 (You & Anthony, 2012). Further, by 2050, one-third of all children will be African. Some nations, such as China, will have decreased resources for children because of dramatically increasing old-age populations. The working-age population will increase dramatically over the same period of time, with the most dramatic increases in Africa and decreases in Europe and China (Lam & Liebbrandt, 2013).

While some have termed this a demographic disaster, we prefer Diers' (2013) framing as a demographic dividend. These young people constituting the youth bulge can provide an economic boost to their countries *if* they are provided with education and training. Countries in the global south must invest in their young to capitalize on this opportunity; and multinational financial organizations should support such efforts. In addition, the World Bank (2015) has also urged higher income countries to consider changing their immigration policies to facilitate in-migration of youth to balance their net work force losses. This has happened to a small degree with Syrian refugees but most of these have migrated to other lower-income countries.

We have never before had a greater opportunity to invest in the future of the world by supporting youth. Efforts must be undertaken by all to realize a demographic dividend from the youth bulge. There is ample evidence that youth can be a solution for global challenges (e.g., Catalano, 2004, Diers, 2013). Programs that engage youth assets demonstrate that young people thrive when supported to play helpful roles for their families and communities. There are many programs that support youth playing economic roles. Other programs engage youth capacity for service and community engagement generally, as leaders and change agents. Even youth who have had problematic childhoods can find a second chance in adolescence and young adulthood (i.e., youth) and become productive adults. Fortunately, we have many effective programs available to capitalize on youth assets.

Why Positive Youth Development?

We use the term positive youth development because it succinctly captures an emphasis on positive development for youth. As we will review, the emphasis on youth problem behavior failed to lead to any improvement in behavior. There are other terms or especially constructs for positive development, all useful in some circumstances.

In this case, the Wikipedia definition (https://en.wikipedia.org/wiki/Positive_ Youth_Development) says it well:

> Positive Youth Development (PYD) refers to intentional efforts of other youth, adults, communities, government agencies, and schools to provide opportunities to enhance their interests, skills, and abilities. PYD is used in scientific literature and by practitioners who work with youth to refer to programs designed to optimize developmental progress.
>
> (Catalano et al., 2004)

This entry identifies programs globally that use this framework. Since our interest is with global programs and interventions supporting youth, this term fits well.

As mentioned earlier, youth research in the latter half of the 20th century (as usual, dominated by the minority world) focused on adolescent and youth problem behavior in research (e.g., Petersen, 1988), with research on minority youth almost exclusively focused negatively (Garcia-Coll, 2013; McLoyd, 1990). With increased interest in interventions to address problems, two major transitions occurred: (1) evaluations of programs to reduce problem behaviors, including prevention research showed limited success, at best, and (2) developmental science results of longitudinal studies demonstrated positive pathways through adolescence as well as predictors of negative pathways (Catalano, et al., 2004). Based on developmental science, health promotion more generally (focusing on multiple outcomes) came to be seen as a more effective approach to addressing adolescent development (e.g., Coates, Petersen, & Perry, 1982). By the 1990s in the US, practitioners, policy makers, and prevention scientists adopted a broader focus for addressing youth issues (e.g., Millstein, Petersen, & Nightingale, 1993). A comprehensive review of youth interventions in the US has demonstrated that the positive youth development framing is the most effective one for achieving better outcomes for youth (Catalano, et al., 2004). These interventions must include some of the key constructs: promotes bonding competence (social, emotional, cognitive, behavioral, moral); fosters self-determination, resilience, spirituality, self-efficacy, clear and positive identity, belief in the future, and prosocial norms; provides recognition for positive behavior and opportunities for prosocial involvement (e.g., Catalano et al., 2004; Koller et al., 2015).

Positive development perspectives were heard in many meetings toward the end of the 1990s. Larson (2000) probably had the first major publication on positive youth development, yet Lerner (e.g., Lerner et al., 2005) is typically credited with promoting the PYD framework, with an emphasis on the potential of each child to achieve optimal development. This framework is organized around the "five Cs": competence, confidence, connection, character, and caring as constructs. Informed by Bronfenbrenner's ecological systems theory (Bronfenbrenner, 1979, 2005), PYD programs recognize contextual variability in youth experience for what is considered developmentally appropriate in different settings and cultures (Catalano et al., 2004). It is important to note that *The Lancet* global review of effective programs in adolescent health (Catalano et al., 2012) recommends the positive youth development perspective.

Other Constructs

The positive youth development framework as it has come to be used globally is the one we intend here: a broad model to signify focusing on positive rather than negative outcomes. The framing for this volume is not focused on a specific theory. We recognize, however, that most research does articulate a particular theory with processes and measures. So we here mention some of the more specific constructs that also are used to focus on positive outcomes.

There are many specific constructs that are used in identifying positive outcomes for youth but we only mention a few here. The risk and resilience framework (e.g., Masten, 2014a) is probably the dominant construct used in this research. (We note that Lerner includes resilience in his positive youth development framework.) This framework explicitly requires evidence of having experienced a significant risk or adversity as well as currently is functioning and developing well in spite of adversity. Developmental progress is indexed as positive adaptation on developmental tasks (Masten, 2014a). Masten's broader theoretical approach of developmental cascades is important to this framework as well (Masten & Cicchetti, 2010).

Masten (2014b) discussed the similarities and differences between resilience and positive youth development as articulated by Lerner, noting that the perspectives are similar in being grounded in developmental systems theory, targeting positive outcomes, and in being translational or seeking also to promote positive development. Masten (2014b) also notes the research that is embedding resilience in global cultural processes and contexts and notes that similar work is needed with PYD to assure cross-cultural validity to all measures. We note that PYD has been used as a broad concept globally for at least a decade now, and hope that attention is being paid to assuring that measures are valid in local cultures and contexts.

Another dominant framework for positive outcomes is that of coping and adaptation (e.g., Petersen, Susman, & Beard, 1989; Petersen, Kennedy, & Sullivan, 1991). Coping/adaptation is an older framework considered primarily from a mental health and general stress perspective; it is used globally. Silbereisen (this volume) uses adaptation as a major construct in his research on managing massive social change. To some extent, the way Silbereisen and others use adaptation is similar to the risk and resilience perspective in that adaptation is measured only in the context of a significant social change.

Competence is another construct used to measure positive development, and is centrally incorporated into the PYD framework described above. Thriving is sometimes mentioned as a construct of PYD in the sense of optimal development but we have found few studies that use it as a measure.

Conclusions About Positive Youth Development

While there are many ways to consider developing positively for young people, we have chosen to use the phrase without adhering to a single set of measures or theoretical framework, much as global prevention researchers have now done (Catalano et al., 2012). Since the concept has been embraced by policy makers, practitioners, and researchers globally, it is highly appropriate for our general framework. We emphasize again that any constructs must be valid for the target context and culture.

Youth Action and Interventions Supporting Youth

As suggested by earlier sections, the emphasis on positive youth development is driven by interest in supporting youth to bring to adulthood their strengths and energy for the good of themselves as well as their communities and societies. Increasingly in global research, developmental science is being integrated with intervention science (Wuermli et al., 2015). While this integration is newer for developmental science, it builds from the behavioral science tradition of better understanding behavior by trying to change it (e.g., Bandura, 2006). Much of the impetus for understanding youth globally comes from the recognition that youth are important for national development, especially with the youth bulge (e.g., Diers, 2013). The research demonstrating the positive role that young people can play (e.g., Souza et al., 2011) as well as the now voluminous body of research evaluating interventions that yield positive outcomes for youth globally (e.g., Catalano et al., 2004; Catalano et al., 2012) makes it clear that the youth bulge can yield demographic dividends and that everywhere, youth bulge or not, youth should be supported to be positive agents for change.

Stimulus for Global Developmental Science

As we noted earlier, developmental science must become global in populations studied and researchers engaged in the effort. This book is a product from a conference generated by the International Affairs Committee of the Society for Research in Child Development (SRCD). The International Affairs Committee of SRCD has focused on global issues for about a decade, now supported by the SRCD strategic plan.

SRCD together with the Jacobs Foundation provided funding for the conference, held in Prague, Czech Republic in October 2014. This was the first meeting of SRCD outside North America. The title of the conference, whose planning began in 2012, was "Positive Youth Development in the Context of the Global Recession." The global recession was still at crisis point in much of the minority world in 2012 but had begun to abate by the time of the conference. At the same time, economic issues continue to affect most populations globally. We also note that data now show that the global recession affected the economies of the majority world to a lesser extent than the minority world; at the same time, any negative impact on the poorest countries of the majority world has much more devastating consequences because they have no cushion or alternative funding sources for their economies.

The conference was framed in terms of the effect of the global recession on youth, especially on employment opportunities but also on future aspirations. The recession stimulated some migration, with a "brain drain" effect on the departed countries. The primary questions of the conference were: (1) what are the effects of the economic downturn on youth's development and adaptation? and (2) what are the contexts or supports as well as personal characteristics of those who are able to more successfully navigate through this situation? The conference program was designed to examine the extant research on the questions, to learn from effective intervention research, and to learn best methods for examining the issues. We invited 11 expert speakers and two symposia. From the many proposals submitted for the conference, the five program review panels selected eight submitted symposia as well as five poster symposia and a large individual poster session. The early career scholar organizations of SRCD and the European Association of Developmental Psychology collaborated on hosting "meet the scholar" tables at lunch time on the first two days of the meeting. In addition, the early career scholars organized the summary session on the last morning and did an excellent job of reviewing the conference. The participants of the conference were drawn from 35 countries around the world.

The conference defined "youth" as the second and third decades of life, from ages 10–30 years. We intended to cast a broad net while also capturing the period involved with the transition from schooling to work. This age span does not fully capture that transition for all youth in all countries. But we believed that it was both broad enough to include most of the relevant phenomena and targeted enough on the appropriate band of the life course.

This Volume

The major result of the conference is the learning from presentations and discussions engaged by participants, which the evaluations reported were highly valuable. A secondary result of the conference, intended to benefit all those who could not be present, is this volume. We have framed this volume now in terms of social and economic change rather than solely on the economic recession, since the recession has abated in most countries and economic change is one of the kinds of social changes. We note, however, that all social change is much less frequent and dramatic in terms of human effects than natural disasters (with the biggest effects) and political conflict/violence (Lundberg & Wuermli, 2012).

The structure of the volume follows to a great extent from that of the conference: framing the issues (three chapters including this one), PYD in diverse contexts experiencing change (eight chapters), interventions promoting positive development (three chapters), and concluding thoughts on research, intervention, and policy (three chapters.) We are grateful that Lonnie Sherrod, Executive Director of SRCD, has written a Foreword to this volume. And we are especially grateful to have a wonderfully diverse, global set of authors for this volume.

Conclusions

We hope that this volume will begin to stimulate research on the issues and approaches for studying youth globally, and especially intervening on their behalf, with both programs and policy. We know that a book is simply a communication device, and one that is only accessible to those who can obtain it. A major issue with global research is that too many in the world who might be interested in studying these issues, or even simply learning about them, cannot obtain this information. Major efforts are needed especially by scientific societies but also universities and research consortia to develop research infrastructure globally. Technology can be a significant aid to this effort but researchers themselves must engage in these issues. Research collaborations between north and south, minority and majority worlds are needed to build knowledge and understanding as well as to share research infrastructure and engage in joint training of students and early career scholars. We welcome continued discussion on how to engage all interested researchers and professionals.

We also want to mention one effort to carry these ideas forward. The International Consortium of Developmental Science Societies now has 11 member societies to study issues of global significance for human development with the primary purpose of achieving policy impact. A consensus conference is scheduled for February 2017 to prepare a policy research agenda addressing effective responses to global crises – natural (e.g., climate change) and human disasters (e.g., political conflict/violence) – benefitting human development. Issues such as migration and trauma will have primary focus.

References

Arnett, J. J. (2008). The neglected 95%: Why American psychology needs to become less American. *American Psychologist, 63*(7), 602–614.

Baker, M. (2008). *The lost boys of Sudan: An American story of the refugee experience.* Athens, GA: University of Georgia Press.

Bandura, A. (2006). Toward a psychology of human agency. *Perspectives on Psychological Science, 1*(2), 164–180.

Bronfenbrenner, U. (1979). *The ecology of human development: Experiments by nature and design.* Cambridge, MA: Harvard University Press.

Bronfenbrenner, U. (2005). Ecological systems theory. In U. Bronfenbrenner (Ed.), *Making human beings human: Bioecological perspectives on human development* (pp. 3–15). Thousand Oaks, CA: Sage.

Catalano, R.F., Berglund, M.L., Ryan, J.A.M., Lonczak, H.S., & Hawkins, J.D. (2004). Positive youth development in the United States: Research findings on evaluations of positive youth development programs. *Prevention and Treatment, 5,* 1–111.

Catalano, R. F., Fagan, A. A., Gavin, L. E., Greenberg, M. T., Irwin, C. E., Jr., Ross, D. A., & Shek, D. T. (2012). Worldwide application of prevention science in adolescent health. *The Lancet, 379*(9826), 1653–1664.

Coates, T. J., Petersen, A. C., & Perry, C. (Eds), (1982). *Promoting adolescent health: A dialog on research and practice.* New York: Academic Press.

Diers, J. (2013). Why the world needs to get serious about adolescents: A view from UNICEF. *Journal of Research on Adolescence, 23*(2), 214–222.

Garcia-Coll, C. (2013). Minority children: The future majority of the USA. *Social Policy Report, 27*(2), 23.

Goldberg, P. K. & Pavcnik, N. (2016). *Distributional effects of globalization in developing countries.* National Bureau of Economic Research Working Paper #12885. www.nber. org/digest/aug07/w12885.html. Accessed March 30, 2016.

International Telecommunications Union. (2015). ICT facts and figures. www.itu.int/en/ITU-D/Statistics/Documents/facts/ICTFactsFigures2015.pdf. Accessed January 13, 2016.

Jelicic, H., Bobek, D, Phelps, E. D., & Lerner, R. M. (2007). Using positive youth development to predict contribution and risk behaviors in early adolescence: Findings from the first two waves of the 4-H study of positive youth development. *International Journal of Behavioral Development, 31*(3), 263–273.

Koller, S. H., Dutra-Thomé, L., Nieto Silva, C. J., Morais, N. A., & Santana, J. P. (2015). Work in adolescence: Home, villages, streets, and armies. In L. A. Jensen (Ed.), *Oxford handbook of human development and culture: An interdisciplinary perspective* (pp. 456–470). New York: Oxford University Press.

Lam, D. & Liebbrandt, M. (2013). Post-2015 UN MDG development agenda employment and economic growth: Global demographic trends and their implications for employment. Retrieved December 2015 from http://www.post2015hlp.org/wp-content//uploads2013/05/Lam-Liebbrandt_Global_Demographic_Trends_and_their_Implications_for_Employment.pdf.

Larson, R.W. (2000). Towards a psychology of positive youth development. *American Psychologist, 55,* 170–183.

Lerner, R. M., Almerigi, J., Theokas, C., & Lerner, J. V. (2005). Positive youth development: A view of the issues. *Journal of Early Adolescence, 25*(1), 10–16.

Loming, L. & Tabb, M. (2012). *Running for my life: One lost boy's journey from the killing fields of Sudan to the Olympic Games.* Nashville, TN: Nelson Thomas.

Lundberg, M. & Wuermli, A. J. (Eds). (2012). *Children and youth in crisis: Protecting and promoting human development in times of economic shocks.* Washington, DC: World Bank.

Masten, A. S. (2014a). Global perspectives on resilience in children and youth. *Child Development, 85*(1), 6–20.

Masten, A. S. (2014b). Invited commentary: Resilience and positive youth development frameworks in developmental science. *Journal of Youth and Adolescence, 43*(6), 1018–1024.

Masten, A. S. & Cicchetti, D. (2010). Developmental cascades. *Development and Psychopathology, 22*(3), 491–495.

McLoyd, V. C. (1990). Minority children: Introduction to the special issue. *Child Development, 61*(2), 263–266.

Millstein, S. G., Petersen, A. C., & Nightingale, E. O. (1993). Adolescent health promotion: Rationale, goals, and objectives. In S. G. Millstein, A. C. Petersen, & E. O. Nightingale (Eds), *Promoting the health of adolescents: New directions for the twenty-first century* (pp. 3–10). New York: Oxford University Press.

Petersen, A. C. (1988). Adolescent development. *Annual Review of Psychology, 39,* 583–607.

Petersen, A. C., Kennedy, R., & Sullivan, P. (1991). Coping with adolescence. In M. E. Colten, & S. Gore (Eds), *Adolescent stress: Causes and consequences* (pp. 93–110). New York: Aldine de Gruyter.

Petersen, A. C., Susman, E. J., & Beard, J. L. (1989). The development of coping responses during adolescence: Endocrine and behavioral aspects. In D. S. Palermo (Ed.), *Coping with uncertainty: Behavioral and developmental perspectives* (pp. 151–172). Hillsdale, NJ: Lawrence Erlbaum.

Serpell, R. (2011). Social responsibility as a dimension of intelligence, and as an educational goal: insights from programmatic research in an African society. *Child Development Perspectives, 5*(2), 126–133.

Sharma, D. & Verma, S. (2013). Street girls and their fight for survival across four developing countries. *Psychological Studies, 58*(4), 365–373.

Silbereisen, R.K. & Chen, X. (Eds.) (2010). *Social change and human development: Concepts and results.* Sage: Thousand Oaks, CA.

Souza, A. P. L., Dutra-Thomé, L., Schiró, E. D. B., Aquino-Morais, C., & Koller, S. H. (2011). Criando contextos ecológicos de desenvolvimento e direitos humanos para adolescentes [Building ecological context for human rights and development for adolescents]. *Paidéia, 21*(49), 273–278.

Suresh, S. (2012). Cultivating global science. *Science, 336*(6084), 959.

Tchombe, T., Nsamenang, B., & Keller, H. (2013). *Cross-cultural psychology: An Africentric perspective.* Limbe, Cameroon: Design House Publisher.

The Economist (2015). The world's fastest developing countries: A quarter century of progress. www.economist.com/news/21684038-quarter-century-progress-worldu2019s-fastest-developing-countries. Accessed March 30, 2016.

Thompson, R. (2012). Changing societies, changing childhood: Studying the impact on child development of globalization. *Child Development Perspectives, 6,*187–192.

UNDP (2015). The Millennium Development Goals Report 2015. www.undp.org/content/undp/en/home/librarypage/mdg/the-millennium-development-goals-report-2015.html. Accessed March 30, 2016.

World Bank (2013). *The winners and losers of globalization: Finding a path to shared prospects.* www.worldbank.org/en/news/feature/2013/10/25/The-Winners-and-Losers-of-Globalization-Finding-a-Path-to-Shared-Prosperity. Accessed March 30, 2016.

World Bank (2015). New country classifications. http://data.worldbank.org/news/new-country-classifications-2015. Accessed March 30, 2016.

Wuermli, A. J., Tubbs, C. C., Petersen, A. C., & Aber, J. L (2015). Children and youth in low- and middle-income countries: Toward an integrated developmental and intervention science. *Child Development Perspectives, 9*(1), 1–6.

You, D. & Anthony, D, (2012). Generation 2015 and beyond. (Occasional papers no, 1), UNICEF. New York, NY. Retrieved December 9, 2015 from http://www.unicef.org/media/files/Generation_2015_and_beyond_15_Nov2012_e_version.pdf.

Yousafzai, M. & Lamb, C. (2013). *I am Malala: The story of the girl who stood up for education and was shot by the Taliban.* New York: Little, Brown and Company.

2

DEVELOPMENT IN THE CONTEXT OF SOCIAL AND ECONOMIC CHANGE

The Jena Model

Rainer K. Silbereisen

Social change denotes gradual or rapid change of political institutions, economic systems, technological solutions, cultural orientations, and similar characteristics of societies. The change of belief systems is an instance of the gradual variant that is not necessarily part of all people's own conscious experience. A recent model case for the rapid variant is the social revolutions associated with the breakdown of the communist rule in Europe in the early 1990s, comprising radical political and economic reforms, including reconfiguring of all major societal institutions.

Explanatory Principles of Social Change and Research Methodologies

There are many explanations by social science broadly speaking; one is the lack of economic modernization, characterized by technological backwardness and deficiencies of central planning (Zapf, 1996). Another one is the profound gap between the officially propagated ideological priority of humanity and the everyday deprivation of human rights and civil liberties (Schmidt, 2010). In psychological terms, such challenges often result in breaking apart of citizen's overarching tendency for justification of the established political system's status quo on the one hand (Cichocka & Jost, 2014), and on the other hand attempts at reforms by the authorities resulting in a gradual loss of control that promotes reactance and protest (Laurin, Kay, & Fitzsimons, 2012).

Since the early 1990s, the political situation in the "transformation societies" is characterized by an amalgamation of the changes by manifestations of globalization, worldwide economic shocks, ongoing population ageing, and demographic shifts due to transnational migration. Our science was badly prepared to study such macro-level social change, as can be exemplified for psychology.

Positive was that models of dealing with economic adversities, borrowed from sociology, seemed to be adequate for generalization to the situation of social change. Research in the Elder-Conger tradition (Elder & Conger, 2000) emphasizes individual manifestations of dire economic circumstances as antecedents of psychological mechanisms that cope with the strains and result in new adaptations. This induces psychological studies on linkages between social change and adjustment at the individual level. Negative was that the connection between the big societal changes and individual experiences were not detailed in terms of the various layers of ecologies that first undergo change, like the system of law, the economic order, or even the political-administrative units of a country. Here psychology was badly prepared because of its traditional emphasis on individuals and their micro contexts. Consequently, one needed to revitalize buried traditions and profit from the new efforts at analyzing the interplay between multiple layers of cultures and ecological contexts (Oishi & Graham, 2010).

In recent years, with reference to social change, this linkage became a vivid domain of research by cultural anthropologists (Gelfand et al., 2011; Greenfield, 2009) and behavioral economists (Thalhelm et al., 2014), demonstrating pathways from changed cultural and social traditions over social institutions to behavior. In this way, Titma and Tuma (2005) showed that differences in old cultural traditions predating socialism in successor states of the former Soviet Union were promoted by differences in effects on young people's behavior after the breakdown, in spite of their joint socialization in the past times.

Principles of Effects of Social Change

Research over the last two decades established a number of empirically validated principles for the consequences of social change. First, especially the political changes in Europe showed a particular syntax. The initial rapid transition from one system to another was followed by a gradual transformation whereby more and more social institutions became adjusted, and that led after several years to a post-transformation that corrects for "overshooting" adaptations. An example is the privatization of entire industries, resulting in economic concentrations that undercut competition and needed to be corrected (Kollmorgen, 2013).

Second, social change implied a devaluing of social capital and social reproduction, especially during the transition. Old professional achievements and social positions turned precarious under the new system. Instead, human capital such as personal agency and exploration as personality attribute became more relevant for adaptation. With the consolidation of the new political system, established pathways to success, like advanced education, regained their power in social stratification (Titma & Tuma, 2005).

Third, old cultural informal institutions, apparently buried in the past, underwent revitalization and even were accentuated, whereas new formal rules were quickly taken over. The surprisingly strong prevalence of entrepreneurial activities in regions of former East Germany that used to be centers of such business before WW II but had no incentive for self-employment at all during the 40 years of communist time, is an instance of such revitalization, pointing to the hidden innovation capital in regions (Fritsch & Wyrwich, 2014). An example for the quick adaptation is the change of the school-to-work transition from a state-guided system to a personal choice scenario in former East Germany. When comparing times still reminiscent of the communist rule with a few years later when the new order was established, the timing of first occupational choice was in the beginning at a lower age in the East compared to the West, but only a few years after unification at about the same age (Silbereisen, 2000).

Fourth, rising inequality and rising poverty seem to be characteristic of the transition, but subsequently moderates during the transformation (Galbraith, Krytynskaia, & Wang, 2004). This hazard to social cohesion varied a lot in Europe, but it is a concern for all.

Fifth, and possibly related to the rising inequality, there are clear relationships to well-being. A case in point is the decrease in life-satisfaction without full recovery in these countries (Easterlin, 2009), and the increase in the prevalence of mental disorders in transformation countries after 1990 (Orosa, 2013). Research on mass privatization programs showed a clear effect on increasing mortality rates, net of the effects of many possible confounders like trade liberalization or income change. A likely mediator is the rising unemployment following privatization (Stuckler, King, & McKee, 2009).

Sixth, under the influence of all principles mentioned, the time since the early 1990s was characterized by growing perceived uncertainties concerning the resolution of developmental tasks in major life domains, such as work, family, and civic life. Certainly social change in Eastern Europe also has benefits, starting with the famous freedom of movement across borders, and including appreciation of human rights, self-determination as a guiding principle of public life, everyday availability of advanced technologies, and in general democratic rules and an economy based on socially regulated competition. Nevertheless, in the current situation uncertainties prevail, especially among those less well-off due to social background, human capital, or age-related differences like seniority in occupational contexts (Silbereisen, Reitzle, & Pinquart, 2005).

Prototypic Methodologies

Research on social change followed a number of different approaches. All are worthwhile and have helped to form the overall picture as described. One possibility is to analyze archived cohort data spreading over decades, and compare post-hoc periods that turned out to be different in terms of social change. For instance, the British Cohort Studies enabled comparing periods differing in economic prosperity. A result was that young people's job aspirations predicted success in economically stable times, whereas it was educational preference in economically precarious times that demanded specially skilled workers to balance the challenges facing industries (Schoon & Silbereisen, 2015). Likewise, period comparisons can be organized prospectively subsequent to a particular instance of social change, such as German unification. As Silbereisen, Reitzle, and Juang (2002) reported, biographical transitions like family formation changed in their timing in conjunction with changing social institutions that serve as pacemakers. A later timing occurred after unification in the former East of the country due to the difficult labor market especially for women and because of reduced family supports by employers. Other transitions unrelated to changing social institutions, such as the timing of puberty or the timing of the first romantic involvement, were unaffected.

Another approach in the analysis of social change recently used was the comparison of samples from countries representing different periods (like transition vs. post-transformation) in a longer term process of social change and economic and political transformation. The research by Kohn (2006) is the quintessential example. Research in the US decades ago showed that a higher position in the stratification hierarchy provides greater opportunity for self-directed work, with implications to higher flexibility of personality. Research in Poland under the old socialist regime showed the same except for differences in the association between well-being and class position – due to higher job protection, workers' well-being in Poland was higher than that of managers in the US. Further research in Poland and other Eastern European transformation countries after 1990, however, showed that the similarity to the US results grew due to the change in the economy toward the Western mold of market capitalism.

Furthermore, this line of research was expanded to the emerging reforms in China, and revealed a clear distinction between the cosmopolitan centers and rural regions. In the centers, the effect of work on personality was comparable to the new developments in Eastern Europe; in the countryside, the old communist background of China prevailed. We found similar distinctions between regions, with a much more positive appraisal of social change to a market-driven economy among urban samples. The rapidity of change revealed by such a series of country comparisons is impressive. Other research demonstrated that in parallel to the economic transformation parents and teachers changed their habit toward traditional Chinese behavior patterns – being restrained in emotional expression and self-presentation was no longer appreciated in favor of a more Western-style outgoing behavior (Chen et al., 2005).

All strategies mentioned above were more or less characterized by the belief that especially in the transition periods, the societal changes are so overwhelming that they would basically affect everybody. This is not true – depending on the scale of manifestations of change people experienced, their behaviors vis-à-vis the new system differed. For instance, we showed that the size of change in the timing of transitions between periods after German unification could be explained in part by constraints like unification-related re-training or housing problems within the families (Reitzle & Silbereisen, 2000).

In other words, social change affects individuals in a possibly highly differentiated way, first, depending on the structural circumstances because there are always niches that the changed ideologies in social institutions do not directly affect. Differential effects were also due, second, to individual conditions because people in general vary in their susceptibility to environmental change as a function of many biopsychosocial functions (Belsky & Pluess, 2009). Self-efficacy is a case in point – those higher in this attribute suffered less from negative effects of system change in Germany, even if they had been closely affiliated with the old political system (Pinquart, Juang, & Silbereisen, 2004).

The Jena Approach in the Analysis of Perceived Social Change

These observations lead us to a new research strategy that focused on the differential experience of changes in life circumstances related to social change. Such new "demands" as we call them are basically perceived uncertainties, but sometimes also benefits, concerning the resolution of important developmental tasks in the domains of work, family, and civic life. Great variation in such uncertainties across the population is typical for the transformation or post-transformation period of social change. Take the change in the labor market and on the job as an example – ownership changed repeatedly, entire plants were closed, jobs became less secure, globalization made professions obsolete, etc. The demands are "filtered" by various social and personal conditions, such as social capital or personality attributes, and then the filtered demands influence how people deal with them (Hofaecker, Buchholz, & Blossfeld, 2010).

Jena Model of Social Change and Human Development

We are not the first to address perceptions of social change. For instance, Kim (2008) assessed subjective appraisals of negative change in various domains, like politics or economy, in South Korea. The instances of change were identified by focus group methods, and in contrast to our approach referred to the society at large, not to the individual experience of negative change. Likewise, Kubicek, Paškvan, and Korunka (2014) have developed an instrument that addresses in great detail new demands affecting jobs, such as intensification of work. The theoretical background was Rosa's (2013) claim that in recent time social change has accelerated with respect to technologies, social roots, and pace of life more generally.

Our list of demands instead was based on a careful analysis of societal trends concerning globalization, individualization, and demographic change, in the domains of work, family, and civic life. The demands referred to the situation in the mid-2000s in Germany, and were obviously rooted in objective changes as to public statistics and conceptual analyses (Tomasik & Silbereisen, 2009). Demands referred to the last five years and were formulated as statements which people had to endorse on a scale from 1 to 7, such as "it has become more difficult to plan my career path", "the knowledge and experience of my parents now provides less sense of direction in my life." The demands imply less than complete knowledge about the future course of affairs, and can thus be considered an aversive psychological state (Westerhof & Keyes, 2006) that requires action to overcome the situation. They also implicate the possible loss of resources that produces stress (Hobfoll, 2001).

To bring the various prior insights on how people process manifestations of social change together, we formulated the Jena Model of Social Change and Human Development, shown in Figure 2.1. It is conceived based on inspirations from the Elder-Conger tradition (Elder & Conger, 2000) in analyzing the effect of societal challenges, like economic hardship on individual adaptation, which addresses the internal cognitive-motivational processing of demands, leading to psychosocial outcomes such as well-being.

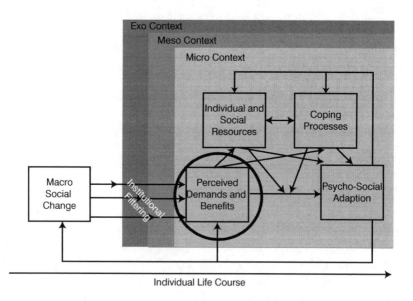

FIGURE 2.1 Jena Model of Social Change and Human Development

Adapted from Tomasik, M.J. & Silbereisen, R.K. (2014). Negotiating the demands of active ageing: Longitudinal findings from Germany. *Ageing and Society*, 34: 790-819.

Details of the model will be described when reporting exemplary research results below. One particular feature, however, should be mentioned upfront. Various contextual layers from the most abstract ideologies and beliefs of a society, over various distal social institutions to the more proximal conditions in the neighborhood, are thought to be influenced by social change first – forces and effects of change arrive at the individual through a series of interrelated changes in the system of interconnected contexts (Hedström & Swedberg, 1996).

The emphasis on the moderating role of contexts has two main reasons. First, scientifically speaking, it is the too often overlooked role of the ecology in shaping behavior and development, eloquently expressed by Oishi and Graham (2010), and for years a guideline of our research ("Development as Action in Context" was the title of Silbereisen, Eyferth, and Rudinger, 1986). Second, for the purpose of helping societies in facing the ubiquitous effects of social change, the emphasis on contexts has a particular advantage – after all, social policies usually cannot target individuals but they are dealing with collectives by providing or shaping opportunities for action. Opportunities usually rest in contexts, like the promotion of entrepreneurial minds in a region by offering financial support, providing training facilities, or allowing tax exemptions. If our science can demonstrate that psychological processes of relevance for dealing with uncertainties of social change are moderated by particular contextual opportunities, then this is the necessary epistemological prerequisite for the planning of interventions.

Our ecology-mindedness was recognized in the choice of two countries for the research. Originally we investigated large random samples from the East and West of post-unification Germany, in the age range between 16 and 42 years, beginning around 2005, with several annual follow-ups. This was the time of rising unemployment rates and upward trends in divorce rates, to give examples of objective uncertainty-inducing conditions, both indicating destabilization of the work and partnership situation. We compared the results with comparably designed samples from the East and West of Poland, a few years later. The rationale was to see whether differences in the cultural orientation (higher uncertainty avoidance in Poland; Hofstede 1991), and differences in the type of government (much less welfare support in Poland, representing the post-socialist welfare regime in contrast to German regulations; http://ec.europa.eu/eurostat) can explain probable differences in how people deal with uncertainties. Furthermore, in both countries we had organized the samples such that several dozen of political-administrative territorial units could be compared (NUTS-2 regions, comparable to counties, and NUTS-3 regions, comparable to districts within counties, as represented in European statistics; NUTS means Nomenclature des Unités Territoriales Statistiques), for which public statistics on a large number of social indicators like unemployment rates or welfare recipient rates are available, and can be used as proxies to moderating influences.

Demands and their Appraisals in Adults and Youth

We concentrate on a series of findings that demonstrate the role of political and other contexts on how people deal with demands of social change, and that at the same time illustrate the Jena Model. Thereby adults beyond the period of education and training will be compared to youth who are before the transition to traditional adult roles.

Addressing adults, the first question was whether the filtering of demands works as expected. The simple answer is yes – the "load" of demands (load is the cumulative index of highly endorsed statements, a convenient way to represent the potential for overtaxing the coping capabilities, but other ways such as means or factor scores are possible and show similar results) showed predicted effects. People reported lower demands if employed or married (or otherwise cohabitating), likewise if highly educated; conversely those living in the East of Germany had higher loads of uncertainties. Demand loads operated similarly with the domains of work and family. Our interpretation was that those sociodemographic characteristics such as being employed or married conveyed higher levels of resources and consequently shielded individuals from uncertainties. The effects were in part quite remarkable: 50% lower demand load among people in employment compared to those unemployed (Tomasik & Silbereisen, 2009). More or less the same applied to Poland, although the absolute load was a bit lower, probably related to the fact that the trends toward part-time and other non-traditional forms of employment were less advanced (European Foundation for the Improvement of Living and Working Conditions, 2011), and thus could not affect uncertainties to the same degree.

The above description refers to adults beyond the usual time for education and training and thus is likely to reflect personal experiences of growing uncertainties on the job and in partnerships. As additional analyses on youth revealed, the personal encounter with the circumstances described in the demands may not be crucial for being worried, because for the young the demands may indicate trends for the worse they will have to face in the future The publicly available information on the precarious labor market for young people or the communication within the families when approaching the time to plan for a career may be triggers enough to become concerned. Note that across the European Union, youth unemployment rates (15–24 years) in 2014 ranged from as low as 8% in Germany to as high as 60% in Greece, twice as high than among adults. Against this backdrop we analyzed separately the young in our samples still in education and training. The main difference to the adults was not in the demand level that was comparable to those in employment among the adults. Rather, they appraised the demands more as challenge than threat. We deem this an indication of anticipatory socialization with a positive undertone – young people are aware of risks but they deem them more as challenges and consequently manageable – whether this is a consequence of inexperience or characteristic of youthful optimism, we cannot decide (Lechner, Tomasik, & Silbereisen, 2016).

Effects on Well-being

According to the Jena Model, the uncertainties are associated with well-being because of the stressful nature of the demands. Before we can go into the intricacies of the cognitive-motivational and the contextual conditions, this relationship needed to be confirmed. Here the issue is that the relationship may go in both ways, that is, people low in well-being may experience a higher demand load to begin with. We used three annual assessments and found that both directions were of about the same strength, meaning that change in well-being is possible under the influence of demands, but that the demands as perceived uncertainties themselves are also a function of how well one feels (Koerner, Silbereisen, & Cantner, 2014).

This result was no surprise and encouraged us to consider whether the effects are constrained to "soft" outcomes like life satisfaction or depressive mood, or whether the experience of demands of social change is also associated with "hard" facts, like becoming unemployed or experiencing income decline. As Koerner et al. (2015) reported, this was indeed the case thus confirming again that the demands signal serious hazards to life success.

Coping and its Correlates

A series of other studies addressed the coping component of the Jena Model. We considered two basic types of "regulation strategies" that were conceived as modes of dealing with challenges of developmental tasks (Heckhausen, 1999), and seemed particularly suitable for the present purpose. First, *engagement* means the investment of time and energy in dealing with the demands, attempts to increase motivation and in case of obstacles, detour and search for support. In turn, *disengagement* concerns self-protection and discounting the demands or ignoring them. Here is an example for dealing with uncertainties in the career planning field. Realizing that one's career perspective becomes clouded, a person may undertake engagement of many activities and invest a lot of motivation into recurrent training; because of difficulties encountered, the person ultimately decides to detour to a different field with better chances. In contrast, disengagement means a devaluing of goals in face of obstacles or a total change in direction.

We found in Germany and Poland for adults and youth that engagement was always more endorsed than disengagement, reflecting a shared cultural orientation in dealing with developmental tasks one cannot avoid. Concerning the appraisal of the demands as challenge or threat and as gain or loss, however, there was a difference between the countries. Whereas engagement was higher in Germany in the case of challenge and gain, these evaluations played no role in Poland (Tomasik et al., 2013; Lechner, Tomasik, & Silbereisen, 2016). We deemed this a reflection of the difference in welfare provision in case of financial and other trouble. The Poles can count on about one-seventh of what is available in Germany, and thus they have no choice other than to act irrespective of the appeal of the demands.

Control beliefs concerning the demands, in contrast, played the same role in both countries. Further, we expected that regulation strategies would show congruence with opportunities to protect well-being in spite of the demands. *Congruence* means the combination of high engagement and high controllability, and vice versa. This is what Gruemer, Silbereisen, and Heckhausen (2013) found – the usual relationship between demands and life satisfaction was less negative under congruence than otherwise. Sense of control seems to be highly relevant and leads us to the role of resources in looking for benefits as to the Jena Model.

Personal Resources

As an instance of personal resources we investigated basic personality attributes because according to the Jena model they may influence the entire process of dealing with demands and benefits. *Exploration* is a disposition to scrutinize context and embrace novelty for personal growth (Kashdan, Rose, & Fincham, 2004). Benefits of social change, such as "having easy access to social media," like the uncertainties addressed thus far, are not always obvious – in order to influence well-being, they first need to be extracted from the offerings in the world around us in order to influence well-being. Here people higher in exploration should have an advantage because they reap benefits more easily, such as increased freedom to choose a personalized lifestyle or enrich one's knowledge via new media and education opportunities. Due to the role of contexts as conceived in the Jena Model, however, this was to be expected especially when living in political-administrative regions that were prone for such exploration-driven people. Indeed, Lechner, Obschonka, and Silbereisen (in press) found that regions with higher divorce rates were apparently conducive for new lifestyles and regions with higher internet domain registration rates were conducive for perceiving the benefits of new learning opportunities, if and when exploration was high.

Interplay with Contexts

We could address many more results on personal resources, but want to constrain this report to analyses that brought all the elements of the Jena Model together in a multi-level format. Pinquart, Silbereisen, and Koerner (2009, 2010) reported the moderating role of the contexts on the entire process comprising demands, coping, and well-being. As proxy for living in a region characterized by many obstacles, we used the variation in the unemployment rates across the political-administrative regions. Had we first read the economic literature on the motivation of the effects of individual unemployment on mental health by the aggregate unemployment in the region, we would have been less surprised by our results. What Clark (2003) called the "social norm" effect (and what psychologists might have called downward social comparisons) was revealed – the negative effect of demands on well-being was less (!) negative when living in economically precarious regions. Further, the effect of engagement was less positive than otherwise. In other words, among individuals living in regions characterized by economic duress, probably due to self-enhancing social comparisons, well-being was higher than that of those in better-off regions facing the same demand load, although the engagement in duress regions was less effective for well-being. The downside of this may be that they do not feel encouraged to deal with the demands required of those in other regions. This is perhaps a self-serving illusion of invulnerability that hurts longer term.

What about disengagement? If our reasoning applies we should expect that it has a benign effect because withdrawing from the challenges may provide relief. This exactly is what we found. For people who lived in regions with higher unemployment rates, demands had a less negative effect on well-being if they showed disengagement. Additional analyses among those who were really hit hard by high demand loads revealed the moderating role of contexts even more clearly. Whereas disengagement had a negative effect on satisfaction with work in the upper two-thirds of economically prosperous regions, it was a rather strong positive association in the lower third. Because of the factual divide in Germany between the former two countries in the degree to which people attribute their economic fate to either the government (East) or themselves (West), we were especially satisfied when we realized that the opposing trends of disengagement on well-being did occur in both parts of the country (Tomasik, Silbereisen, & Heckhausen, 2010).

People resolve the difficulties around developmental tasks in challenged times against the embedding of their own life in the broader context. The political-administrative regions are the preferred loci of policy intervention, and consequently they are of higher relevance for the application of our science. From a merely scientific point of view, we would have liked to demonstrate that the effects of the broader context are moderated by jeopardy in the narrower neighborhoods where people live, such as data on features like many buildings available for lease, closed shops and businesses, reduced public services, signs of neighborhood conflict, and vandalism. Nevertheless, simply looking at local newspapers shows the prominence of reporting on differences in unemployment ratios and their trends even across regions of a Federal State. So, our interpretation of the results as driven by knowledge and not just circumstance is probably right.

Outlook

The Jena Model encourages future research efforts in various directions. One is to look for demands of social change, either in more detail as Kubicek, Paškvan, and Korunka (2014) did concerning changes on the job that reflect "societal acceleration" (Rosa, 2013), or in other fields like the growing expectations for "active ageing" (WHO, 2002) that may be perceived as challenges or, more likely, threat (Pavlova & Silbereisen, 2012). Further, we have to realize that in reality, demands and benefits may come in tandem. We have reason to believe that benefits may discount demands. Higher work intensity has fewer negative effects if combined with greater decision latitude on the job (Obschonka, Silbereisen, & Wasilewski, 2012), but this principle is likely to apply more broadly. Often the demands are more prominent than the benefits, and the latter thus requires more exploration. Although we have only few data on other countries (China and Ghana are an exception: Chen et al. 2010; Mahama, Silbereisen, & Eccles, 2013), the Jena Model is probably applicable to other transition or transformation countries or regions, like the Korean Peninsula or the Middle East.

Social change and the new demands and benefits are ubiquitous experiences of life in our times, and as such cannot be avoided. The main insights we gained through the line of research reported are that people prefer to engage with the challenges under most circumstances, but that this is especially successful when conducted in congruence with control beliefs. Moreover, the load of demands or benefits is filtered (aggravated or diminished) by sociodemographics and by personality attributes such as exploration. Finally, the broader environmental context plays an intriguing role by reducing the strength of association between demands and well-being, as well as between engagement and well-being. Against cultural stereotypes on engagement as the proper way of action, disengagement can have positive effects when the circumstances in the broader environment are poor in opportunities.

As mentioned at the outset, the social evil hitting Europe the most is youth unemployment and part of the solution is strengthening capabilities of dealing with demands (or promoting an "entrepreneurial mindset" as the political phrase of the day goes). The cause of youth unemployment in the minds of many is obviously related to social change more broadly speaking – lack of economic growth, missed labor market reforms, and weak negotiation power due to low social capital (Eichhorst, Hinte, & Rinne, 2013). As the social costs are so tremendous (shaken system identification, lower well-being, threatened health status, low future job satisfaction, scarring effects on future employment prospects; Schmillen & Umkehrer, 2013), scientific and political action is required. A range of projects funded by the European Union (http://ec.europa.eu/research/participants/portal/desktop/en/opportunities/h2020/topics/young-4-2015.html) attempts to develop models for empowering young people by promoting talents, strength, interest, and future potential, all indicators of positive youth development (Damon, 2004). As to our results, habitual engagement ("initiative" as Larson, 2000 would call it) together with guarded disengagement, further adequate control beliefs and personality characteristics like expectation, are crucial for such an endeavor. From a policy point of view, it is also mandatory to realize that "one size fits all" is too simple – the opportunity structures in the regions where people live are important moderators and need to be the target of policies.

References

Belsky, J., & Pluess, M. (2009) Beyond diathesis stress: Differential susceptibility to environmental influences. *Psychological Bulletin*, *135*(6), 885–908.

Chen, X., Cen, G., Li, D., & He, Y. (2005). Social functioning and adjustment in Chinese children: The imprint of historical time. *Child Development*, *76*(1), 182–195.

Chen, X., Bio, Y., Xin, T., Wang, L., & Silbereisen, R.K. (2010). Perceived social change and childrearing attitudes in China. *European Psychologist, 15,* 260–270.

Cichocka, A., & Jost, J. T. (2014). Stripped of illusions? Exploring system justification processes in capitalist and post Communist societies. *International Journal of Psychology, 49*(1), 6–29.

Clark, A. E. (2003). Unemployment as a social norm: Psychological evidence from panel data. *Journal of Labor Economics, 21*(2), 323–351.

Damon, W. (2004). What is positive youth development? *The ANNALS of the American Academy of Political and Social Science, 591*(1), 13–24.

Easterlin, R. A. (2009). Lost in transition: Life satisfaction on the road to capitalism. *Journal of Economic Behavior & Organization, 71*(2), 130–145.

Eichhorst, W., Hinte, H., & Rinne, U. (2013). *Youth unemployment in Europe: What to do about it?* (IZA Policy Paper No. 65). Bonn: Institute for the Study of Labor.

Elder, G. H., & Conger, R. D. (2000). *Children of the land: Adversity and success in rural America.* Chicago, IL: University of Chicago Press.

European Foundation for the Improvement of Living and Working Conditions (2011). *European company survey 2009: Part-time work in Europe.* Luxembourg: Publications Office of the European Union.

Fritsch, M., & Wyrwich, M. (2014). The long persistence of regional levels of entrepreneurship: Germany 1925 to 2005. *Regional Studies, 48*(6), 955–973.

Galbraith, J. K., Krytynskaia, L., & Wang, Q. (2004). The experience of rising inequality in Russia and China during the transition. *The European Journal of Comparative Economics, 1*(1), 87–106.

Gelfand, M. J., Raver, J. L., Nishii, L., Leslie, L. M., Lun, J., Lim, B. C., & Aycan, Z. (2011). Differences between tight and loose cultures: A 33-nation study. *Science, 332*(6033), 1100–1104.

Greenfield, P. M. (2009). Linking social change and developmental change: shifting pathways of human development. *Developmental Psychology, 45*(2), 401.

Gruemer, S., Silbereisen, R. K., & Heckhausen, J. (2013). Subjective well-being in times of social change: Congruence of control strategies and perceived control. *International Journal of Psychology, 48*(6), 1246–1259.

Heckhausen, J. (1999). *Developmental regulation in adulthood: Age-normative and sociostructural constraints as adaptive challenges.* New York: Cambridge University Press.

Hedström, P., & Swedberg, R. (1996). Social mechanisms. *Acta Sociologica, 39*(3), 281–308.

Hobfoll, S. E. (2001). The influence of culture, community, and the nested-self in the stress process: Advancing conservation of resources theory. *Applied Psychology, 50*(3), 337–421.

Hofaecker, D., Buchholz, S., & Blossfeld, H. P. (2010). Globalization, institutional filters and changing life course. Patterns in modern societies: A summary of the results from the GLOBALIFE-project. In R. K. Silbereisen, & X. Chen (Eds), *Social change and human development: Concept and results* (pp. 101–124). London: Sage.

Hofstede, G. (1991) *Cultures and organizations: Software of the mind.* London: McGraw-Hill.

Kashdan, T. B., Rose, P., & Fincham, F. D. (2004). Curiosity and exploration: Facilitating positive subjective experiences and personal growth opportunities. *Journal of Personality Assessment, 82*(3), 291–305.

Kim, J. (2008). Perception of social change and psychological well being: A study focusing on social change in Korea between 1997 and 2000. *Journal of Applied Social Psychology, 38*(11), 2821–2858.

Koerner, A., Silbereisen, R. K., & Cantner, U. (2014). Work-related demands emanating from social change and their relation to trait-like and occasion-specific aspects of subjective well-being. *Social Indicators Research, 115*(1), 203–222.

Koerner, A., Lechner, C. M., Pavlova, M. K., & Silbereisen, R. K. (2015). Goal engagement in coping with occupational uncertainty predicts favorable career-related outcomes. *Journal of Vocational Behavior, 88,* 174–184.

Kohn, M. L. (2006). *Change and stability: A cross-national analysis of social structure and personality.* Greenbrae, CA: Paradigm Press.

Kollmorgen, R. (2013). Theories of postcommunist transformation. Approaches, debates, and problems of theory building in the second decade of research. *Studies of Transition States and Societies, 5*(2), 88–105.

Kubicek, B., Paškvan, M., & Korunka, C. (2014). Development and validation of an instrument for assessing job demands arising from accelerated change: The intensification of job demands scale (IDS). *European Journal of Work and Organizational Psychology, 24*(6), 898–913.

Larson, R. W. (2000). Toward a psychology of positive youth development. *American Psychologist, 55*(1), 170–183.

Laurin, K., Kay, A. C., & Fitzsimons, G. J. (2012). Reactance versus rationalization: Divergent responses to policies that constrain freedom. *Psychological Science, 23*(2), 205–209.

Lechner, C. M., Obschonka, M., & Silbereisen, R. K. (in press). Who reaps the benefits of social change? Personality and its socioecological boundaries. *Journal of Personality.*

Lechner, C. M., Tomasik, M. J., & Silbereisen, R. K. (2016). Preparing for uncertain careers: How youth deal with growing occupational uncertainties before the education-to-work transition. *Journal of Vocational Behavior,* 90–101.

Mahama, S., Silbereisen, R.K., & Eccles, J.S. (2013). Perceived work uncertainties and expectancies as predictors of postgraduate intentions. *Journal of Psychology in Africa, 23,* 401–408.

Obschonka, M., Silbereisen, R.K., & Wasilewski, J. (2012). Constellations of new demands concerning careers and jobs: Results from a two-country study on social and economic change. *Journal of Vocational Behavior, 80*, 211–223.

Oishi, S., & Graham, J. (2010). Social ecology lost and found in psychological science. *Perspectives on Psychological Science, 5*(4), 356–377.

Orosa, F. J. E. (2013). Psychosocial wellbeing in the Central and Eastern European transition: An overview and systematic bibliographic review. *International Journal of Psychology, 48*(4), 481–491.

Pavlova, M. K., & Silbereisen, R. K. (2012). Participation in voluntary organizations and volunteer work as a compensation for the absence of work or partnership? Evidence from two German samples of younger and older adults. *The Journals of Gerontology, Series B: Psychological Sciences and Social Sciences, 67*(4), 514–524.

Pinquart, M., Juang, L. P., & Silbereisen, R. K. (2004). Changes in psychological distress among East German adolescents facing German unification: The role of commitment to the old system and of self-efficacy beliefs. *Youth and Society, 36*(1), 77–101.

Pinquart, M., Silbereisen, R. K., & Koerner, A. (2009). Perceived work-related demands associated with social change, control strategies, and psychological well-being. *European Psychologist, 14*(3), 207–219.

Pinquart, M., Silbereisen, R. K., & Koerner, A. (2010). Coping with family demands under difficult economic conditions: Associations with depressive symptoms. *Swiss Journal of Psychology, 69*(1), 53–63.

Reitzle, M., & Silbereisen, R. K. (2000). The timing of adolescents' school-to-work transition in the course of social change: The example of German unification. *Swiss Journal of Psychology, 59*(4), 240–255.

Rosa, H. (2013). *Social acceleration: A new theory of modernity.* New York: Columbia University Press.

Schmidt, S. (2010). A challenge-response model in research on social change. In R. K. Silbereisen, & X. Chen (Eds), *Social change and human development: Concept and results* (pp. 31–49). London: SAGE Publications.

Schmillen, A., & Umkehrer, M. (2013). *The scars of youth. Effects of early-career unemployment on future unemployment experience* (IAB Discussion Paper 6). Nuremberg: Institute for Employment Research.

Schoon, I., & Silbereisen, R. K. (2015). *Transitions from school to work: Globalization, individualization, and patterns of diversity.* Cambridge: Cambridge University Press.

Silbereisen, R. K. (2000). German unification and adolescents' developmental timetables: Continuities and discontinuities. In L. Crockett, & R. K. Silbereisen (Eds), *Negotiating adolescence in times of social change* (pp. 104–122). Cambridge, MA: Cambridge University Press.

Silbereisen, R. K., Eyferth, K., & Rudinger, G. (Eds) (1986). *Development as action in context: Problem behavior and normal youth development.* New York: Springer.

Silbereisen, R. K., Reitzle, M., & Juang, L. (2002). Time and change: Psychosocial transitions in German young adults 1991 and 1996. In L. Pulkkinen, & A. Caspi (Eds), *Paths to successful development: Personality in the life course* (pp. 227–254). Cambridge, MA: Cambridge University Press.

Silbereisen, R. K., Reitzle, M., & Pinquart, M. (2005). Social change and individual development: A challenge-response approach. In K. W. Schaie, & G. E. Elder, Jr. (Eds), *Historical influences on lives and aging* (pp.148–165). New York: Springer.

Stuckler, D., King, L., & McKee, M. (2009). Mass privatisation and the post-communist mortality crisis: a cross-national analysis. *The Lancet, 373*(9661), 399–407.

Thalhelm, T., Zhang, X., Oishi, S., Schmin, C., Duan, D., Lan, X., et al. (2014). Large-scale psychological differences within China explained by rice versus wheat agriculture. *Science, 344*, 603–608.

Titma, M., & Tuma, N. B. (2005). Human agency in the transition from communism: Perspectives on the life course and aging. In K. W. Schaie, & G. Elder (Eds), *Historical influences on lives and aging* (pp. 108–143). New York: Springer.

Tomasik, M. J., & Silbereisen, R. K. (2009). Demands of social change as a function of the political context, institutional filters, and psychosocial resources. *Social Indicators Research, 94*(1), 13–28.

Tomasik, M., Silbereisen, R. K., & Heckhausen, J. (2010). Is it adaptive to disengage from demands of social change? Adjustment to developmental barriers in opportunity-deprived regions. *Motivation and Emotion, 34*(4), 384–398.

Tomasik, M. J., Silbereisen, R. K., Lechner, C. M., & Wasilewski, J. (2013). Negotiating demands of social change in young and middle-aged adults from Poland. *International Journal of Stress Management, 20*(3), 222–253.

Westerhof, G. J., & Keyes, C. L. (2006). After the fall of the Berlin Wall: Perceptions and consequences of stability and change among middle-aged and older East and West Germans. *The Journals of Gerontology Series B: Psychological Sciences and Social Sciences, 61*(5), 240–247.

World Health Organization (WHO). (2002). *Active ageing: A policy framework.* Retrieved from http://apps.who.int/iris/bitstream/10665/67215/1/WHO_NMH_NPH_02.8.pdf (accessed August 28, 2016).

Zapf, W. (1996). Zwei Geschwindigkeiten in Ost- und Westdeutschland [Two paces in East and West Germany]. In M. Diewald, & K. U. Mayer (Eds), *Zwischenbilanz der Wiedervereinigung: Strukturwandel und Mobilität im Transformationsprozess* (pp. 317–328). Opladen, Germany: Leske + Budrich.

3

SOCIOECONOMIC STATUS, PARENTING, AND POSITIVE YOUTH DEVELOPMENT IN GLOBAL PERSPECTIVE

Jennifer E. Lansford

To understand positive youth development, researchers often adopt an ecological perspective that encompasses several levels of influence, including proximal familial influences as well as more distal cultural influences. Throughout the world, parents strive to promote their children's positive growth and development, but the desired outcomes as well as how parents try to promote these outcomes vary, as do the resources available to promote positive youth development. Many resources are contingent upon country-level socioeconomic factors such as prevalence of poverty as well as family-level socioeconomic factors such as parental education that affect the social capital available to promote positive youth development. This chapter adopts a global perspective to understand links among socioeconomic status (SES), parenting, and positive youth development. It begins by reviewing different indicators of SES, as well as how appropriate indicators may differ across countries. It then reviews research on links between different indicators of SES and parenting, links between SES and positive youth development, and links between parenting and positive youth development. The chapter next turns to reviewing evidence regarding parenting as a mediator of the link between SES and positive youth development. The chapter concludes by considering policies and interventions that alter SES or parenting to enhance positive youth development.

Indicators of Socioeconomic Status

The most common indicators of family socioeconomic status are parents' level of completed education, parents' occupational status, and household income

(Bornstein & Bradley, 2003). The three indicators are usually significantly correlated, as more educated parents typically attain more prestigious and better paying jobs. Yet, the meaning of these different indicators varies somewhat across countries. For example, graduating from high school in a country where even attendance at secondary school is for the privileged may confer more status than graduating from high school in a country in which college attendance is more common. Nevertheless, together, these indicators represent both economic and social capital that parents bring to their families.

All of these indicators of family SES are situated within broader community and national socioeconomic contexts. For example, on the basis of gross national income per capita, the World Bank (2015a) classifies entire countries as being low-income (US$1,045 or less), middle-income (US$1,046–12,735), or high-income (more than US$12,735). Worldwide, 12.7% of the population lives on less than US$1.90 per day, but poverty is unequally distributed around the globe (World Bank, 2015b). In sub-Saharan Africa, 42.7% of the population is below this global poverty threshold of less than US$1.90 per day, compared to 18.8% in South Asia, and only 2.1% in Europe and Central Asia (World Bank, 2015b). Educational attainment also varies widely across countries. For example, nearly 100% of secondary school-age youth in Western Europe attend school, compared to fewer than 30% of youth in the Central African Republic, Mozambique, Niger, and Uganda (World Bank, 2015c). In low-income countries, families often cannot afford to send adolescents to school both because of the direct costs as well as the indirect costs in terms of lost income from child labor (Chudgar & Shafiq, 2010).

National- and family-level indicators of SES are important because they are closely tied to many other predictors of health and well-being. For example, compared to low-income countries, high-income countries have lower rates of infant and child mortality and higher average life expectancies, in large part because of greater access to clean water, vaccines, and health care. Just as between-country differences in socioeconomic resources are related to standards of living, so too are within-country differences. For example, compared to low-income families within a given country, high-income families can afford to live in safer neighborhoods and access more resources such as healthier food and better health care.

Indicators of socioeconomic status can be conceptualized in relative or absolute terms. Absolute poverty, for example, refers to an income level below a standardized threshold such as US$1.90 per day to define the international poverty line. Individual countries also have poverty thresholds determined by country-specific factors such as the cost of living in that place. In contrast to absolute poverty, relative poverty relies not on where a family stands in relation to a preset threshold but rather how a family compares to other families, either objectively or subjectively.

Countries differ not only in their overall designation as low-, middle-, or high-income but also in the distribution of resources within the country.

The Gini coefficient is a measure of inequality within a country (World Bank, 2015d). Some countries are more egalitarian in the distribution of wealth across individuals than others, which have large discrepancies between the wealthiest and poorest individuals. Both absolute and relative poverty are important but may differ in salience depending on the country. For example, in a low-income country such as Togo, where 54% of the population falls below the international poverty line of living on US$1.90 per day (World Bank, 2015b), absolute poverty may be quite salient while relative poverty is less so. However, in a high-income country characterized by large disparities in wealth, relative poverty may be more salient than absolute poverty. In particular, poverty may be less stigmatizing in a country in which the majority of the population is poor than in a country with wide disparities in poverty. Because socioeconomic factors vary both between and within countries, understanding how SES is related to parenting and youth development is enhanced by considering the broader cultural and national contexts in which families are situated.

Links between Socioeconomic Status and Parenting

Socioeconomic status is related to parenting, both directly and indirectly through its effects on parents' stress and adjustment. In terms of direct effects, SES affects parents' ability to provide material resources and social experiences for their children (Hoff, Laursen, & Tardif, 2002). Economic resources enable parents to afford housing in safer neighborhoods, which generally provide access to better schools, and to afford better health care. More highly educated parents provide more cognitive stimulation to their children in the form of reading to them, having conversations that advance verbal skills, and providing enriching extracurricular opportunities such as music lessons and visits to museums (Bradley & Corwyn, 2005). In addition, lower-SES parents treat their children more harshly than do higher-SES parents, generally using more corporal punishment and less reasoning (Scaramella, Neppl, Ontai, & Conger, 2008).

One of the most notable links between SES and parenting involves language. By the age of two years, children from low-income families already show a six-month lag in language acquisition compared to children from high-income families (Fernald, Marchman, & Weisleder, 2013). Hart and Risley (1995) found that early in life, American children with parents on welfare heard, on average, 616 words per hour in comparison to 1,251 words per hour in working class families and 2,153 words per hour in professional families. By extrapolation, by the time of school entry, children with professional parents have heard 30 million more spoken words than children with parents on welfare. This language exposure is related to measures of children's own vocabulary and comprehension (Hart & Risley, 2003). The quality of parents' speech also differs, with college-educated parents more likely to use a varied vocabulary and to converse with children in ways that more closely approximate the kinds of interactions children are exposed to in school (Rowe, 2012).

SES continues to affect parents' ability to support their children's education as they progress through school. For example, more highly educated parents have more knowledge about the college application process and are better able to advise their children on the logistics of admissions and attendance (Lareau & Weininger, 2003). Indeed, high-income American youth in the lowest quartile of performance on standardized math tests in eighth grade were as likely to attend college as low-income youth in the highest quartile of math performance (Fox, Connolly, & Snyder, 2005).

Another notable link between SES and parenting involves the types of attitudes and beliefs parents hold about children. Parents who have completed more years of formal education typically hold attitudes about children that encourage more questioning and independent exploration, which parents foster through verbal reasoning, as opposed to attitudes endorsing obedience and conformity that are more likely to be held by less educated parents (Davis-Kean, 2005). Parents' attitudes about desired child characteristics may mirror characteristics that parents encounter in their own jobs, with more educated parents holding jobs that require more independent thought and decision-making than those held by less educated parents (Conger & Donnellan, 2007). In diverse countries, parents who believe that children are equal partners in the parent–child relationship behave in more responsive and stimulating and less punitive ways than do parents who believe that children should show absolute obedience to parents (Zevalkink & Riksen-Walraven, 2001).

Differences between high-SES and low-SES parents are found even in low-income countries (Bradley & Corwyn, 2005). For example, in Cameroon, educated and more financially resourced parents of the Nso people were more likely to use praise and rewards rather than only corporal punishment, whereas less educated and financially resourced Nso parents were more likely to use corporal punishment (Bradley & Corwyn, 2005). In both high- and low-income countries, higher-SES parents are more responsive and less punitive toward their children and provide them with more material possessions, enriching experiences, and a higher quality physical environment (Bradley & Corwyn, 2005). In many countries, poverty is related to harsh and inconsistent discipline, lack of monitoring, and less cognitive stimulation of children (Deb, 2009; McLoyd, 1998; Ricketts & Anderson, 2008; Scaramella et al., 2008; Shek, 2005).

In addition to direct links between SES and parenting, SES may have indirect effects on parenting through parents' stress and well-being. Parental stress is higher when parents are worried about not having enough money to pay for basic living expenses, and this stress can spill over into harsher parenting (McLoyd, 1998), including harsh and inconsistent discipline (e.g., Conger, Ge, Elder, Lorenz, & Simons, 1994), less provision of cognitive stimulation (e.g.,

Furstenberg, Cook, Eccles, Elder, & Sameroff, 1999), and less nurturing and warm parenting (e.g., Kotchick & Forehand, 2002). Indirect effects of SES on parenting through parents' well-being have been found in both developed and developing countries (Patel, Rahman, Jacob, & Hughes, 2004).

However, links between poverty and parenting stress are not universal. For example, middle-class mothers in a small city in the Dominican Republic reported experiencing more parenting stress than did mothers in extremely poor villages, perhaps because the middle-class mothers reported having less social support within their community than did the mothers in the poor villages (Foucault & Schneider, 2009). Despite these differences in social support and stress, the middle-class mothers valued exploration and self-direction in their children more than did the mothers from the poor villages, who were more likely to value obedience and conformity (Foucault & Schneider, 2009), replicating SES differences in American parents' values (Kelley, Power, & Wimbush, 1992). Therefore, the broader context of poverty within a particular country appears to affect some, but not all, links between SES and parenting (Dyson, Gorin, Hooper, & Cabral, 2009).

Socioeconomic factors may affect parenting not just at the individual level but also at the level of an entire community. For example, in the United States between 2000 and 2009, increases in 90-day mortgage delinquency rates were linked to increases in child abuse requiring hospital admission and of traumatic brain injury allegedly caused by child abuse (Wood et al., 2012). Similarly, from 2007 to 2010, decreases in consumer confidence were related to increases in frequent maternal spanking of children (Brooks-Gunn, Schneider, & Waldfogel, 2013). Thus, links between SES and parenting appear to depend not only on factors within individual families but also on factors that operate at the level of the entire community.

Links between Socioeconomic Status and Positive Youth Development

Socioeconomic status is related not only to parenting but also to youth development from infancy into adulthood. The infant mortality rate in the United States is three times higher for children whose mothers dropped out of high school than for children whose mothers have a college education (Chen, Oster, & Williams, 2014). In India, poor children under the age of five were nearly twice as likely to be underweight and had nearly twice as high rates of mortality than did non-poor children, in large part because of differences in access to nutrition and immunizations (Agarwal & Srivastava, 2009). Discrepancies in morbidity and mortality persist beyond infancy and early childhood, with lower-SES children and adolescents more likely to develop chronic and acute health problems, sustain serious injuries, and die than those from higher-SES families (Evans, Chen, Miller, & Seeman, 2012).

Brain imaging and neuroendocrinology research reveal ways in which poverty elevates stress responses and impedes coping (Evans et al., 2012). SES is related to brain development in ways that can affect both academic achievement and socioemotional adjustment through executive functioning, making it more difficult for individuals exposed to chronic poverty to self-regulate and manage their emotions (Evans et al., 2012). Namely, in lower-SES individuals, the prefrontal cortex (which is related to controlling attention, inhibiting behaviors, and regulating emotions) is smaller than in higher-SES individuals and has less developed connections with the amygdala (which controls emotional reactivity; Evans et al., 2012). Lower-SES individuals also have poorer working memory than higher-SES individuals (Tine, 2014). Each of these factors is related to positive development by affecting the way that youth cognitively and emotionally process and react to their environments.

Beyond better physical health and neurocognitive functioning, higher SES (at both the country level and individual family level) also predicts better access to education and academic achievement. At the country level, literacy rates and primary and secondary school enrollment rates approach 100% in high-income countries, but in low-income countries access to formal education and literacy are much lower. For example, in Burkina Faso, Ethiopia, Guinea, Mali, and Niger, adult literacy rates are less than 30% (United Nations Development Programme, 2010), and free public education is available only in urban areas and for a limited number of years. Low-income families in these countries may not be able to afford supplies and transportation to send their children to school, even if the school itself is free. Primary school enrollment in sub-Saharan Africa is only 57% (African Union, 2006). Gender differences in access to education are profound in some countries. In South Asia (which includes Afghanistan, Bangladesh, Bhutan, India, Maldives, Nepal, Pakistan, and Sri Lanka), 86% of boys but only 61% of girls complete primary school (World Bank, 2004). As a result, 40% of females aged 15 to 24 years in South Asia are illiterate (World Bank, 2004). Cycles of poverty are perpetuated across generations in part by keeping girls out of school in favor of having them at home to care for younger siblings and do housework.

Although rates of school attendance based on family SES are not as pronounced in high-income as in low-income countries (with the exception of dropping out of secondary school and college attendance), achievement in school differs by family SES. Children from lower-SES families have poorer academic achievement than do children from higher-SES families, even controlling for IQ (Frederickson & Petrides, 2008). The effects cannot be explained solely by genetics, because adoptive parents' SES is significantly related to school achievement of their adopted children, although more weakly than to school achievement of biological children (Johnson, McGue, & Iacono, 2007). This achievement gap is present when children start school and widens over time (Lee & Burkam, 2002). During the summer, higher-SES children are exposed to more enriching experiences such as summer camps, vacations, and lessons that help them maintain academic skills from the school year; in contrast, lower-SES children lose ground over the summer and typically start the next school year behind where they left off at the end of the previous year (Alexander, Entwisle, & Olson, 2007).

Just as community-wide economic factors are related to parenting, so too are community-wide economic factors related to youth adjustment. Youth are affected not only by their own parents' job loss, for example. Children and adolescents whose parents remain employed but live in communities where many other adults have lost jobs are negatively affected through strain on social networks, structural changes such as less tax revenue to spend on public schools, and economic and psychological effects such as uncertainty about the future that affect even individuals who remain employed (Gassman-Pines, Gibson-Davis, & Ananat, 2015).

Understanding positive youth development has been guided by the Five Cs theory, which describes positive youth development in terms of competence, connection, character, confidence, and caring (Lerner, Almerigi, Theokas, & Lerner, 2005a). With the exception of academic competence, there has been less attention in the literature to how socioeconomic status is related to these aspects of positive development than to behavior problems. However, there is some evidence that the relation between socioeconomic status and well-being may be curvilinear, with both the lowest-SES and highest-SES youth at risk, albeit for different reasons (Luthar & Latendresse, 2005). Compared to middle-class youth, youth from affluent families feel more pressure to succeed academically and to excel in their extracurricular activities, as well as more disconnected from their parents, all of which have been related to more anxiety, depression, suicidal ideation, and substance use among affluent than middle-class youth (Luthar, Barkin, & Crossman, 2013). Thus, positive development may be maximized for middle-class youth rather than those at either extreme of the socioeconomic distribution.

Links between Parenting and Positive Youth Development

A number of aspects of parenting have been found to be related to positive youth development. For example, monitoring (Li, Fang, Stanton, Su, & Wu, 2003), behavioral control (Hillaker, Brophy-Herb, Villarruel, & Haas, 2008), modeling and encouraging prosocial behaviors (Eisenberg, Eggum-Wilkens, & Spinrad, 2015), coaching social skills (Bandy & Moore, 2011), involvement (Hill et al., 2004), and love and acceptance (Khaleque & Rohner, 2002) have been related to youths' academic achievement, social competence, and other aspects of positive development (Napolitano et al., 2011). Some of these links may be relatively universal, whereas others may depend on both socioeconomic and cultural contexts. In a study of mothers' perceptions of children's competence, mothers of 5- to 18-year-olds in a poor village in the Philippines, in a poor village in St. Vincent in the Caribbean, and in an inner-city homeless shelter in the United States all described child competence in terms of obedience, good behavior, helpfulness, and friendliness (Durbrow, Peña, Masten, Sesma, & Williamson, 2001). In addition, mothers in all three groups said that parents could promote child competence through encouragement, attention, and discipline. Some perceptions differed across contexts, however. Compared to Filipino and Caribbean mothers, American mothers were more likely to define child competence in terms of academic achievement, perhaps because of better access to education in the United States. In addition, American mothers were more likely than Filipino and Caribbean mothers to say that child competence was promoted by parental affection, perhaps because praise and physical affection are more common ways of demonstrating love in the United States, whereas love is expressed more through discipline and attention in the Philippines and St. Vincent. Mothers in the Philippines and St. Vincent also were more likely than American mothers to believe that child competence is innate.

Specific parenting strategies used to promote positive youth development depend on broader socioeconomic and cultural contexts because such contexts provide a reference point for norms and expectations both about parents' behaviors and children's adjustment (DeLoache & Gottlieb, 2000). For example, Yoruba parents in Nigeria use food as a way of instilling the importance of delaying gratification, being thrifty, and showing proper etiquette, all of which are important to socialization as competent members of their society (Babatunde & Setiloane, 2014). Because this part of West Africa has a rainy season and a dry season, the availability of food fluctuates throughout the year. Because of periodic scarcity in food, parents teach children to wait patiently for food, not to visit other families during mealtimes, and to leave meat and fish (which are rare and valuable) untouched until the end of the meal.

Parents' expectations regarding their children's behavior and the obligations parents place on children also have the potential to contribute to positive youth development. For example, Gikuyu children of Ngecha, Kenya demonstrate the most prosocial behaviors in situations involving family obligations, such as caring for younger siblings, doing household chores, and engaging in other types of labor for the benefit of the family; they demonstrate fewer prosocial behaviors in situations that involve free play, leisure, or caring for themselves (de Guzman, Edwards, & Carlo, 2005). Parents in different cultural groups have different expectations regarding children's family obligations (Lansford et al., 2016), suggesting that this route to positive youth development might also differ across cultural groups.

Aspects of parenting that promote positive youth development also are likely to change as children develop, in ways that may depend on socioeconomic and cultural contexts (e.g., Darling, Cumsille, Peña-Alampay, & Coatsworth,

2009). In a study of American and Chinese adolescents' life satisfaction, positive and negative emotions, self-esteem, and anxiety, increases in autonomy over decision-making were more predictive of working- and middle-class adolescents' adjustment in the United States than China, in part because autonomy in decision-making is more normative during adolescence in the United States than in China (Qin, Pomerantz, & Wang, 2009). These differences in autonomy extend to other ways that parents try to promote children's success.

Parenting as a Mediator of the Link between Socioeconomic Status and Positive Youth Development

Cultural and socioeconomic contexts in which families are situated have implications both for parenting and for youth adjustment, and parenting may serve as a mediator of links between socioeconomic status and positive youth development, both at a societal level and within individual families. At a societal level, parents in low-income countries often focus on promoting children's survival, which is more often taken for granted in higher income countries. Yet, even in low-income countries, most children survive, and promoting their positive development entails more than caring for just their physical needs. Postpartum depression and other parental mental health problems contribute significantly to children's stunting and underweight in South Asia, suggesting that children's survival would be promoted not just through nutrition supplements but also from improving maternal mental health (Patel et al., 2004). Societal levels of poverty (including absolute and relative poverty) also have implications for understanding associations among poverty, parenting, and youth adjustment. In low-income countries in which nearly everyone is poor, there may be little personal blame or negative self-appraisals associated with being poor, in contrast to countries with less absolute poverty when relative poverty might be more salient and associated with personal blame (Garbarino & Kostelny, 1993), thereby increasing parents' and adolescents' distress.

At an individual level, low SES can lead to parental distress (e.g., from uncertainty about whether one can pay for basic living expenses and strains associated with living in dangerous neighborhoods), leading to harsher, less consistent, and less responsive parenting, which in turn leads to poorer youth adjustment (McLoyd, 1998). In this way, parenting mediates the link between SES and youth adjustment. It is not just the presence of more negative parenting but the absence of more positive parenting that mediates this link (Bradley & Corwyn, 2002). For example, African American mothers experiencing economic hardship were less likely to set high goals for their children and less likely to engage in activities that would promote their children's competence, both of which related to their children's lower self-regulation and less psychosocial and academic competence (Brody, Flor, & Gibson, 1999). If low-SES parents are themselves resilient and well-functioning, this may protect their children from the otherwise detrimental effects of low SES (see Brody et al., 1994).

Interventions and Policy Implications

Understanding positive youth development within a framework that incorporates both socioeconomic and parenting factors suggests at least three intervention points to enhance positive youth development. First, one could intervene to change SES. This approach is codified as the first of the Sustainable Development Goals guiding the international development agenda through 2030: to end poverty in all its forms everywhere (United Nations, 2015). A number of policies and programs have been implemented to try to change SES and eradicate poverty. For example, between 2000–2009 more than 120 cash transfer programs were implemented in sub-Saharan Africa (Garcia & Moore, 2012). Some of these programs provided one-time transfers in emergency situations; others provided long-term transfers to specific vulnerable groups. Reviews of the effectiveness of these programs have suggested improvements in children's nutrition, access to health care, and education; indeed, receipt of cash is sometimes conditional on school attendance (Garcia & Moore, 2012). The United Nations has deemed cash transfer programs as essential to disrupting intergenerational continuity of poverty and inequality (Hailu & Soares, 2008).

Countries vary widely in the types of social safety nets they provide to families. In high-income countries, tax and social expenditure polices reduce child poverty by as much as 20% and as little as 5% (UNICEF, 2000). To illustrate, 23.4% of Swedish children and 26.7% of American children live below these two countries' respective national poverty lines before taking into account taxes and transfers (UNICEF, 2000). After adjusting for taxes and transfers, however, only 2.6% of Swedish children live below the national poverty line, compared to 22.4% of American children (UNICEF, 2000). The social safety net in Sweden (and other countries such as Denmark, Finland, and Norway, where child poverty is also rare) incorporates polices such as universal access to child care and paid parental leave, which support parents' employment as well as children. In countries with substantial social safety nets, individual family income may be less meaningfully related to parenting and youth adjustment than in countries without social safety nets.

The second intervention point within this framework is to change parenting. Recognizing that parents who are harsh, unresponsive, and uninvolved have less well-adjusted adolescents, many interventions attempt to improve youth adjustment by improving parenting. For example, multisystemic therapy has been rigorously demonstrated to increase adolescents' prosocial behavior and positive relationships with their parents and to decrease problem behavior by enhancing parenting skills and providing family therapy (Henggeler, Schoenwald, Borduin,

Rowland, & Cunningham, 2009). Parenting interventions are more effective when they are culturally sensitive, suggesting the need to adapt interventions to the specific contexts in which they will be used (Holleran Steiker et al., 2008).

The third intervention point involves bypassing SES and parenting and attempting to enhance positive youth development directly. Youth development programs such as 4-H, Boy and Girl Scouts, religious youth groups, band and orchestra, sports, student government, and other school and extracurricular clubs are examples of programs that attempt to have (and often do have) a positive effect directly on adolescents, even if they are not billed as interventions per se (Lerner et al., 2005b). Youth who participate in extracurricular activities have better grades, self-esteem, and social integration, even controlling for SES and other confounds; prospectively, youth extracurricular involvement predicts future civic engagement and occupational attainment, in part by increasing agency and initiative (see Larson, 2000). Some youth serving organizations specifically target at-risk youth. For example, the Boys and Girls Clubs of America's (2015) mission is "To enable all young people, especially those who need us most, to reach their full potential as productive, caring, responsible citizens," which clearly aligns well with the goal of promoting positive youth development. A review of 46 studies of youth development programming in low-income countries revealed that most programs adopted a holistic, cross-sectoral approach to building skills and connecting youth to opportunities that encompassed education, civic engagement, and vocational and life skills training (USAID, 2013). Although few of these programs have been evaluated rigorously, those that have been show promise. For example, gang-involved youth in Central America who participated in a program that taught life skills and provided vocational training and job matching services had higher rates of employment, better self-esteem, more social inclusion, and better interpersonal relationships than the control group (USAID, 2013). Thus, although both SES and parenting affect positive youth adjustment, youth adjustment can also be promoted by factors external to the family.

Conclusions

Socioeconomic conditions such as poverty and how much education most parents complete vary widely among countries. The SES context matters because of its implications for access to resources such as clean drinking water and safe neighborhoods that directly promote health and well-being, as well as because families' own socioeconomic circumstances are often understood in relation to the circumstances of others in their community. Socioeconomic status at both the country level and the family level is related to positive youth development in important ways. At the country level, socioeconomic differences are reflected in disparities between countries in morbidity and mortality, education, and job opportunities. At the family level, both absolute poverty and relative poverty have implications for the resources that youth can access to promote positive development. SES is related to youth development both directly and indirectly, via parenting, as socioeconomic factors affect parents' own well-being and the types of behaviors that characterize their interactions with their children. Interventions have attempted to change socioeconomic factors and parenting as means to promote positive youth development. The challenge moving forward will be to use culturally grounded knowledge of local communities, parenting, and desirable youth outcomes to understand how to foster positive development in ways that do not merely avoid negative outcomes but promote thriving.

References

African Union (2006). *The state of the African population 2006.* Addis Ababa, Ethiopia: Department of Social Affairs, African Union Commission.

Agarwal, S., & Srivastava, A. (2009). Social determinants of children's health in urban areas in India. *Journal of Health Care for the Poor and Underserved, 20,* 68–89.

Alexander, K. L., Entwisle, D. R., & Olson, L. S. (2007). Summer learning and its implications: Insights from the Beginning School Study. *New Directions for Youth Development, 114,* 11–32.

Babatunde, E. D., & Setiloane, K. (2014). Changing patterns of Yoruba parenting in Nigeria. In H. Selin (Ed.), *Parenting across cultures: Childrearing, motherhood and fatherhood in non-western cultures* (pp. 241–252). New York: Springer.

Bandy, T., & Moore, K. A. (2011). What works for promoting and enhancing positive social skills: Lessons from experimental evaluations of programs and interventions. Child Trends fact sheet, Publication #2011-07. Accessed 28/08/2016, available at www.childtrends.org/wp-content/uploads/2011/03/child_trends_2011_03_02_RB_WWSocialSkills.pdf

Bornstein, M. H., & Bradley, R. H. (Eds). (2003). *Socioeconomic status, parenting, and child development.* Mahwah, NJ: Erlbaum.

Boys and Girls Clubs of America (2015). Our mission. Accessed 28/08/2016, available at www.bgca.org/whoweare/Pages/Mission.aspx

Bradley, R. H., & Corwyn, R. F. (2002). Socioeconomic status and child development. *Annual Review of Psychology, 53,* 371–399.

Bradley, R. H., & Corwyn, R. F. (2005). Caring for children around the world: A view from HOME. *International Journal of Behavioral Development, 29,* 468–478.

Brody, G. H., Flor, D. L., & Gibson, N. M. (1999). Linking maternal efficacy beliefs, developmental goals, parenting practices, and child competence in rural single-parent African American families. *Child Development, 70,* 1197–1208.

Brody, G. H., Stoneman, Z., Flor, D., McCrary, C., Hastings, L., & Conyers O. (1994). Financial resources, parent psychological functioning, parent co-caregiving, and early adolescent competence in rural two-parent African-American families. *Child Development, 65,* 590–605.

Brooks-Gunn, J., Schneider, W., & Waldfogel, J. (2013). The Great Recession and the risk for child maltreatment. *Child Abuse and Neglect, 37,* 721–729.

Chen, A., Oster, E., & Williams, H. (2014). *Why is infant mortality higher in the US than in Europe?* National Bureau of Economic Research Working Paper 20525.

Chudgar, A., & Shafiq, M. N. (2010). Family, community, and educational outcomes in South Asia. *Prospects, 40,* 517–534.

Conger, R. D., & Donnellan, M. B. (2007). An interactionist perspective on the socioeconomic context of human development. *Annual Review of Psychology, 58,* 175–199.

Conger, R. D., Ge, X., Elder, G. H., Jr., Lorenz, F. O., & Simons, R. L. (1994). Economic stress, coercive family process, and developmental problems of adolescents. *Child Development, 65,* 541–561.

Darling, N., Cumsille, P., Peña-Alampay, L., & Coatsworth, D. (2009). Individual and issue-specific differences in parental knowledge and adolescent disclosure in Chile, the Philippines, and the United States. *Journal of Research on Adolescence, 19,* 715–740.

Davis-Kean, P. E. (2005). The influence of parent education and family income on child achievement: The indirect role of parental expectations and the home environment. *Journal of Family Psychology, 19,* 294–304.

Deb, S. (2009). Child protection: Scenario in India. *International Journal of Child Health and Human Development, 2,* 339–348.

de Guzman, M. R. T., Edwards, C. P., & Carlo, G. (2005). Prosocial behaviors in context: A study of Gikuyu children of Ngecha, Kenya. *Journal of Applied Developmental Psychology, 26,* 542–558.

DeLoache, J. S., & Gottlieb, A. (2000). *A world of babies: Imagined childcare guides for seven societies.* Cambridge, UK: Cambridge University Press.

Durbrow, E. H., Peña, L. F., Masten, A., Sesma, A., & Williamson, I. (2001). Mothers' conceptions of child competence in contexts of poverty: The Philippines, St. Vincent, and the United States. *International Journal of Behavioral Development, 25,* 438–443.

Dyson, C., Gorin, S., Hooper, C.-A., & Cabral, C. (2009). Bangladeshi families living in hardship: Findings from research using a life-history approach. *Child & Family Social Work, 14,* 362–371.

Eisenberg, N., Eggum-Wilkens, N. D., & Spinrad, T. L. (2015). The development of prosocial behavior. In D. A. Schroeder & W. G. Graziano (Eds), *The Oxford handbook of prosocial behavior* (pp. 114–136). Oxford, UK: Oxford University Press.

Evans, G. W., Chen, E., Miller, G., & Seeman, T. (2012). How poverty gets under the skin: A life course perspective. In V. Maholmes & R. B. King (Eds), *The Oxford handbook of poverty and child development* (pp. 13–36). New York: Oxford University Press.

Fernald, A., Marchman, V. A., & Weisleder, A. (2013). SES differences in language processing skill and vocabulary are evident at 18 months. *Developmental Science, 16,* 234–248.

Foucault, D., & Schneider, B. H. (2009). Parenting values and parenting stress among impoverished village and middle-class small city mothers in the Dominican Republic. *International Journal of Behavioral Development, 33,* 440–450.

Fox, M. A., Connolly, B. A., & Snyder, T. D. (2005). *Youth indicators 2005: Trends in the well-being of American youth.* Washington, DC: U.S. Department of Education, National Center for Education Statistics.

Frederickson, N., & Petrides, K. V. (2008). Ethnic, gender, and socio-economic group differences in academic performance and secondary school selection: A longitudinal analysis. *Learning and Individual Differences, 18,* 144–151.

Furstenberg, F. F., Cook, T. D., Eccles, J., Elder, G. H., Jr., & Sameroff, A. (1999). *Managing to make it: Urban families and adolescent success*. Chicago, IL: University of Chicago Press.

Garbarino, J., & Kostelny, K. (1993). Neighborhood and community influences on parenting. In T. Luster (Ed.), *Parenting: An ecological perspective* (pp. 203–226). Hillsdale, NJ: Erlbaum.

Garcia, M., & Moore, C. M. T. (2012). *The cash dividend: The rise of cash transfer programs in Sub-Saharan Africa*. Washington, DC: World Bank.

Gassman-Pines, A., Gibson-Davis, C. M., & Ananat, E. O. (2015). How economic downturns affect children's development: An interdisciplinary perspective on pathways of influence. *Child Development Perspectives, 9*, 233–238.

Hailu, D., & Soares, F. V. (2008). Cash transfers in Africa and Latin America: An overview. *Poverty in Focus, 15*, 3–5.

Hart, B., & Risley, T. R. (1995). *Meaningful differences in the everyday experience of young American children*. Baltimore, MD: Paul H Brookes Publishing.

Hart, B., & Risley, T. R. (2003). The early catastrophe: The 30-million-word gap by age 3. *American Educator, Spring*, 4–9.

Henggeler, S. W., Schoenwald, S. K., Borduin, C. M., Rowland, M. D., & Cunningham, P. B. (2009). *Multisystemic therapy for antisocial behavior in children and adolescents* (2nd ed.). New York: Guilford Press.

Hill, N. E., Castellino, D. R., Lansford, J. E., Nowlin, P., Dodge, K. A., Bates, J. E., & Pettit, G. S. (2004). Parent academic involvement as related to school behavior, achievement, and aspirations: Demographic variations across adolescence. *Child Development, 75*, 1491–1509.

Hillaker, B. D., Brophy-Herb, H. E., Villarruel, F. A., & Haas, B. E. (2008). The contributions of parenting to social competencies and positive values in middle school youth: Positive family communication, maintaining standards, and supportive family relationships. *Family Relations, 57*, 591–601.

Hoff, E., Laursen, B., & Tardif, T. (2002). Socioeconomic status and parenting. In M. H. Bornstein (Ed.), *Handbook of parenting, Vol. 2: Biology and ecology of parenting* (2nd ed., pp. 231–252). Mahwah, NJ: Erlbaum.

Holleran Steiker, L. K., Castro, F. G., Kumpfer, K., Marsiglia, F. F., Coard, S., & Hopson, L. M. (2008). A dialogue regarding cultural adaptation of interventions. *Journal of Social Work Practice in the Addictions, 8*, 154–162.

Johnson, W., McGue, M., & Iacono, W. G. (2007). Socioeconomic status and school grades: Placing their association in broader context in a sample of biological and adoptive families. *Intelligence, 35*, 526–541.

Kelley, M. L., Power, T. G., & Wimbush, D. D. (1992). Determinants of disciplinary practices in low-income Black mothers. *Child Development, 63*, 573–582.

Khaleque, A., & Rohner, R. P. (2002). Perceived parental acceptance-rejection and psychological adjustment: A meta-analysis of cross-cultural and intracultural studies. *Journal of Marriage and Family, 64*, 54–64.

Kotchick, B. A., & Forehand, R. (2002). Putting parenting in perspective: A discussion of the contextual factors that shape parenting practices. *Journal of Child and Family Studies, 11*, 255–270.

Lansford, J. E., Godwin, J., Alampay, L. P., Uribe Tirado, L. M., Zelli, A., Al-Hassan, S. M. … & Tapanya, S. (2016). Mothers', fathers', and children's perceptions of parents' expectations about children's family obligations in nine countries. *International Journal of Psychology, v 51,* 366–374.

Lareau, A., & Weininger, E. B. (2003). Cultural capital in educational research: A critical assessment. *Theory and Society, 32,* 567–606.

Larson, R. W. (2000). Toward a psychology of positive youth development. *American Psychologist, 55,* 170–183.

Lee, V. E., & Burkam, D. T. (2002). *Inequality at the starting gate: Social background differences in achievement as children begin school.* Washington, DC: Economic Policy Institute.

Lerner, R. M., Almerigi, J. B., Theokas, C., & Lerner, J. V. (2005a). Positive youth development: A view of the issues. *Journal of Early Adolescence, 25,* 10–16.

Lerner, R. M., Lerner, J. V., Almerigi, J. B., Theokas, C., Phelps, E., Gestsdottir, S. ... & von Eye, A. (2005b). Positive youth development, participation in community youth development programs, and community contributions of fifth-grade adolescents: Findings from the first wave of the 4-H Study of Positive Youth Development. *Journal of Early Adolescence, 25,* 17–71.

Li, X., Fang, X., Stanton, B., Su, L., & Wu, Y. (2003). Parental monitoring among adolescents in Beijing, China. *Journal of Adolescent Health, 33,* 130–132.

Luthar, S. S., & Latendresse, S. J. (2005). Children of the affluent: Challenges to well-being. *Current Directions in Psychological Science, 14,* 49–53.

Luthar, S. S., Barkin, S. H., & Crossman, E. J. (2013). "I can, therefore I must": Fragility in the upper-middle classes. *Development and Psychopathology, 25,* 1529–1549.

McLoyd, V. C. (1998). Socioeconomic disadvantage and child development. *American Psychologist, 53,* 185–204.

Napolitano, C. M., Bowers, E. P., Gestsdottir, S., Depping, M. K., von Eye, A., & Chase, P. A. (2011). The role of parenting and goal selection in positive youth development: A person-centered approach. *Journal of Adolescence, 34,* 1137–1149.

Patel, V., Rahman, A., Jacob, K. S., & Hughes, M. (2004). Effect of maternal mental health on infant growth in low income countries: New evidence from South Asia. *British Medical Journal, 328,* 820–823.

Qin, L., Pomerantz, E. M., & Wang, Q. (2009). Are gains in decision-making autonomy during early adolescence beneficial for emotional functioning? The case of the United States and China. *Child Development, 80,* 1705–1721.

Ricketts, H., & Anderson, P. (2008). The impact of poverty and stress on the interaction of Jamaican caregivers with young children. *International Journal of Early Years Education, 16,* 61–74.

Rowe, M. L. (2012). A longitudinal investigation of the role of quantity and quality of child-directed speech in vocabulary development. *Child Development, 83,* 1762–1774.

Scaramella, L. V., Neppl, T. K., Ontai, L. L., & Conger, R. D. (2008). Consequences of socioeconomic disadvantage across three generations: Parenting behavior and child externalizing problems. *Journal of Family Psychology, 22,* 725–733.

Shek, D. T. L. (2005). Perceived parental control processes, parent-child relational qualities, and psychological well-being in Chinese adolescents with and without economic disadvantage. *Journal of Genetic Psychology, 166,* 171–188.

Tine, M. (2014). Working memory differences between children living in rural and urban poverty. *Journal of Cognition and Development, 15,* 599–613.

UNICEF (2000). *Child poverty in rich nations.* Florence, Italy: Author.

United Nations (2015). Sustainable development goals. Accessed 28/08/2016, available at www.un.org/sustainabledevelopment/sustainable-development-goals/

United Nations Development Programme (2010). *Human development report 2010*. New York: Author.

USAID (2013). *State of the field report: Holistic, cross-sectoral youth development*. Accessed 28/08/2016, available at www.usaid.gov/sites/default/files/documents/1865/USAID%20 state%20of%20the%20field%20holistic%20cross%20sectoral%20youth%20 development%20final%202_26.pdf

Wood, J. N., Medina, S. P., Feudtner, C., Luan, X., Localio, R., Fieldston, E. S., & Rubin, D. M. (2012). Local macroeconomic trends and hospital admissions for child abuse, 2000–2009. *Pediatrics, 130*, e358–e364.

World Bank (2004). *Word development indicators*. Washington, DC: Author.

World Bank (2015a). *New country classifications*. Accessed 28/08/2016, available at http:// data.worldbank.org/news/new-country-classifications-2015

World Bank (2015b). *Poverty*. Accessed 28/08/2016, available at http://data.worldbank.org/ topic/poverty

World Bank (2015c). *School enrollment, secondary (% gross)*. Accessed 28/08/2016, available at http://data.worldbank.org/indicator/SE.SEC.ENRR/countries?display=default

World Bank (2015d). *Gini index (World Bank estimate)*. Accessed 28/08/2016, available at http://data.worldbank.org/indicator/SI.POV.GINI

Zevalkink, J., & Riksen-Walraven, J. M. A. (2001). Parenting in Indonesia: Inter- and intracultural differences in mothers' interactions with their young children. *International Journal of Behavioral Development, 25*, 167–176.

## PART I

Positive Youth Development in Diverse Contexts during Economic Change

4

THE ROLE OF THE GREAT RECESSION FOR THE QUALITY OF LABOR MARKET ENTRY IN SWITZERLAND

Societal Climate, Job Opportunities, and Young People's Social Resources

Marlis Buchmann

Introduction

It is well established that young people, particularly labor market entrants, belong to those social groups that are hardest hit by economic downturns (Blossfeld, Buchholz, Bukodi & Kurz, 2008; ILO, 2013, 2015). In all Western industrialized countries, the unemployment rate of 15–24-year olds is considerably higher than that of so-called prime-age workers (25–54-year olds). This is particularly the case when the economy is weak (Breen, 2005; OECD, 2008; see Salvisberg & Sacchi, 2014 for Switzerland). Because of its world-wide spread and grave severity, the economic downturn of the Great Recession officially taking place between the end of 2007 and 2009 is unique and may thus have had particularly far-reaching consequences for labor market entrants and young workers. Of particular interest is whether the Great Recession has not only severely affected young people's objective labor market prospects but also altered their career expectations and aspirations as well as their behavior when attempting to make the transition to the labor market.

We will address this issue for Switzerland by comparing two cohorts of labor market entrants, one entering the labor market in the years before the Great Recession, the other one in the years during and immediately following the Great Recession. This comparison will be embedded in the assessment of neglected issues in research on the transition to the labor market and equally under-researched consequences of this transition for career prospects. We will first elaborate on the significance of *skill demand*, both in quantity and quality, for labor market entry. The skills and qualifications employers are looking for when attempting to fill their vacancies have been largely neglected in previous research devoted to the examination of the economic situation under which young people attempt to enter the labor market. We argue that previous research, by mostly relying on the overall unemployment rate, has insufficiently captured young people's chances of entering and/or staying in the labor market and may even have distorted the opportunities or restrictions particular groups of young people encounter. Second, failed or only marginal career entry has been studied primarily with regard to its *objective* consequences, that is, with respect to career progress (e.g., lower earning potentials, additional spells of unemployment). Much less research has been conducted on the *subjective* consequences of failed labor market integration in youth and young adulthood (e.g., aspirations, engagement, and life satisfaction). In this chapter, we develop a different line of reasoning, arguing that the overall societal climate or atmosphere – the zeitgeist of the Great Recession – may have affected young people's career expectations and aspirations and thus has eventually shaped the way in which they approach labor market entry. Third, the question of how labor market conditions, particularly the quantity and quality of skill demand, interact with young people's assets – for example, social and individual resources – to shape labor market entry has not yet been explored to its full. This is all the more important as it addresses the issue of how young people may actively cope with the labor market conditions they are encountering, thus eventually turning the odds to their favor. Here we advance the argument that in economically hard times when skill demand is weak, young people's resources will be particularly relevant to manage the transition to the labor market. The chapter will close with some reflections on how to better understand young people's capabilities to cope with cyclical economic conditions taking into account the institutional characteristics of the educational system and the labor market.

Labor Market Environments and Career Entry

To investigate the impact of the state of the economy on labor market entry, country-specific and cross-national research has mostly relied on macro-economic indicators. These include most prominently the overall or adult unemployment rates taken as proxies for the overall state of the labor market (e.g., Breen, 2005; de Lange, Gesthuizen & Wolbers, 2014). The tacit assumption is that the overall state of the economy – boom or bust – exerts a consistent effect on the opportunities encountered by labor market participants. The only notable exceptions are youth being inflicted with a higher risk of unemployment compared to adult workers and being affected more strongly by economic fluctuations (for Switzerland, see Salvisberg & Sacchi, 2014; ILO, 2015; OECD, 2008). However, cross-national evidence also shows that the *ratio* of youth to adult unemployment rates varies widely across countries, although being consistently a multiple of the adult unemployment rate (Breen, 2005). These consistent findings led researchers to the conclusion that the economic conditions impact young people's labor market opportunities differently in different countries. Obvious suspects for explaining these cross-national differences have been country-specific institutional arrangements, particularly those pertaining to the educational system and the labor market.

Countries differ in the extent to which employment is protected. Labor markets characterized by strong *employment protection legislation* reduce labor market entrants' chances of being hired as employers are prevented from dismissing workers (Breen, 2005; Breen & Buchmann, 2002). These chances are particularly dire in economically hard times when the low job turnover rate due to strong employment protection is coupled with the scarcity of job vacancies. Equally important are the institutional features of a country's educational system. Countries characterized by strong vocational education and training at the upper-secondary level tend to facilitate school-to-work transitions compared to countries whose upper-secondary educational system focuses on general education (Breen, 2005; de Lange, Gesthuizen & Wolbers, 2014; for a review article, see Raffe, 2014). In the former countries, most prominently represented by the German-speaking countries, occupation-specific skills are taught in apprenticeships that combine practical training in a firm with theoretical learning in vocational schools known as the "dual system." Not only do apprentices acquire a set of occupation-specific skills in vocational education and training; these skills are also certified in nation-wide recognized diplomas. Given the occupational specificity and high standardization of vocational education and training, these diplomas send strong signals to employers about the skills and the suitability of young job seekers for particular jobs, thus facilitating the hiring process. By contrast, in countries relying on a system of general education, most prominently represented by the USA, occupation-specific skills are not taught in school but mainly acquired in the course of "on-the-job" training. As employers are neither involved nor very familiar with what is taught in school, these school-leavers send only weak signals about their skills and competencies (compared to experienced workers), resulting in lower chances of being hired, especially in economically hard times.

Consequently, for countries characterized by a tight linkage between occupation-specific credentials and the workplace, the rate of adult unemployment, used as a proxy for the overall state of the labor market, is a poor indicator for assessing young people's chances of entering the labor market. Occupation-specific certificates send strong positive signals to employers searching for the respective occupational skills to fill vacancies and equally strong negative signals to those employers attempting to fill job openings requiring different skill sets. From the perspective of job seekers equipped with a particular occupation-specific certificate, the prospects of finding a skilled job depends therefore less on the *overall* state of the labor market and more on the availability of job vacancies requiring occupational skills for which they are trained and certified for. It is the number of these vacancies that define job seekers' *job opportunities*. The risk of failed labor market entry (or being relegated to an unskilled job) is thus strongly determined by the occupation-specific personnel needs of companies, that is, firms' skill demand (Salvisberg & Sacchi, 2014; Bell & Blanchflower, 2011). Even in times of economic recession, employers' skill demand varies greatly between occupations (Sacchi, Salvisberg & Buchmann, 2005), thus shaping the job opportunities of young people certified with a particular occupation-specific credential differently.

We put these assumptions to an empirical test for Switzerland known for its strong reliance on occupation-specific training and credentialing.[1] We examined whether the job opportunities graduates of vocational and educational training (VET) encountered when searching for the first job affected the quality of labor market entry (Bundel and Buchmann, in preparation). Quality of labor market entry was defined as *core* or *peripheral* integration into the labor market. A skill-adequate and permanent first job with a high employment level (80 percent or more) is considered as core integration whereas the absence of one of these three characteristics defines peripheral integration. Data for the labor market entrants come from two cohorts of the COCON study, last surveyed in 2006 and 2012, respectively, at the age of 21. COCON is a representative longitudinal survey of children and youth in the German- and French-speaking parts of Switzerland.[2] To assess labor market entrants' occupation-specific job opportunities, we used job advertisement data published in the press, company websites, and online job portals in Switzerland. This data was collected by the *Swiss Job Market Monitor* (SJMM) since 1950 and continues as a quarterly monitoring of the Swiss job market.[3] The aggregate number of job ads requiring particular occupation-specific skills in a given year is a sensitive and valid indicator of companies' personnel needs – and hence conversely of the job opportunities for the particular group of interest (Salvisberg & Sacchi, 2014). The annual random samples of job ads published in the three types of outlets described above for the years when VET graduates completed their training and attempted to enter the labor market allowed us to assign to each labor market entrant in a given year the precise number of occupation-specific vacancies,[4] thus measuring his or her job opportunities at the micro level and with precise timing. To our knowledge, this study is the first one to be able to do so.

We analyzed the quality of labor market entry as defined above by conducting competing risk regressions (Fine & Gray, 1999). Competing risk hazard models are designed to take multiple destinations into account. In our study, the destinations of interest are (a) first jobs providing core integration into the labor market, and (2) first jobs characterized by peripheral integration into the labor market. The results confirm indeed our assumptions that more favorable individual job opportunities facilitate finding a first job characterized by core integration into the labor market. Interesting enough, the effect of individual job opportunities on the risks of entering a job of peripheral integration into the labor market is much stronger. This amounts to saying that the more dire the individual job opportunities are at the time of transitioning to the labor market, the more likely will job searches result in a peripheral integration into the labor market. Our assumptions are further supported by the findings of several other studies of ours showing that the overall state of the labor market, proxied by the total number of advertised job vacancies per year, does not affect the quality of the first job, once individual job opportunities (i.e., the vacant positions that are potentially accessible given the occupation-specific credential) have been taken into account. These findings provide strong evidence of the fruitfulness of the conceptual approach that focuses on employers' actual skill demand and the identification of the job vacancies potentially accessible for VET-certified labor market entrants.

Subjective Assessment of Failed Labor Market Entry

Labor market entry is a milestone in young people's transition to adulthood (Buchmann & Kriesi, 2011 for Europe; Crosnoe & Johnson, 2011 for North America). From a life course perspective, unsuccessful transition to the work force may delay the adoption of other adult roles, family formation in particular (Danziger & Ratner, 2010). It may also go along with constricted opportunities for future career achievements. Research has discussed such long-term negative consequences of unemployment (or marginal employment) experiences at labor market entry, early or later in the occupational career as scarring effects (Dieckhoff, 2011; Gangl, 2006; Luijkx & Wolbers, 2009; Helbling & Sacchi, 2014). When studying these scarring effects, research has almost exclusively focused on the *objective* dimensions of labor market outcomes, such as reduced earnings potential, increased risk of further spells of unemployment, or diminished status mobility chances. Less attention has been paid to the subjective side of unsuccessful or marginal labor market entry by asking, for example, how young people assess their career prospects and whether they lower their career expectations and aspirations.

One of the few empirical studies addressing the subjective components of early unemployment consequences is Helbling and Sacchi (2014). They examined for Switzerland whether early unemployment among VET-certified young workers affected young people's assessment of their career progress. In particular, they examined whether young people with early unemployment experiences perceived their career progress as less satisfying compared to those with no experience of early unemployment. The results clearly document that the former were less satisfied. This finding is all the more remarkable as, by international comparison, the institutional settings of the Swiss educational system and the Swiss labor market do not particularly disadvantage labor market entrants and young workers compared to experienced, so-called prime-age workers. Employment protection legislation for the Swiss labor market is rather weak by international comparison, thus increasing the chances for new hires, particularly in economically hard times. The vocational specificity of VET certificates and their high standardization across the national context send strong signals to employers about the skills and suitability of job seekers for particular jobs. Despite these favorable institutional settings early unemployment does result in lower satisfaction with one's career progress. In a broader sense, this finding also underscores the importance of successful labor market entry for young people's well-being.

In our own study for Switzerland reported above, we chose to approach the question of how young people cope with adverse circumstances in their early career in a different way. We asked whether young people's perception of their labor market entry chances is influenced by the *overall* societal climate – the so-called zeitgeist – that would eventually exert an influence on their job search strategies and decisions. Of interest is whether the zeitgeist, manifested in public discourse in the media and in everyday life, shapes young people's career expectations, their aspirations, and eventually their job search behavior. The literature refers to such a homogenous impact as a *period effect*, implying that macro changes occuring at a particular time and affect all age groups and cohorts uniformly (Elder, 1996).

A case in point is the severe economic downturn brought about by the Great Recession officially taking place between the years of 2007 and 2009. We argue that the *framing* of the late noughties as the Great Recession may have led young people at the brink of labor market entry to believe that their labor market prospects are so dim that it might be wiser to accept any job than ending up with having no job at all.[5] Such subjective assessments of the labor market situation may hold irrespective of young people's *individual* labor market opportunities. One way of finding out whether such individual assessments are at work is by examining the significance of *cohort membership* for labor market entry. More specifically, we compare the quality of labor market entry as defined previously between members of a pre-recession cohort and members of a recession cohort – net of individual job opportunities. A further test pertains to the analysis of the interaction effect of cohort membership and individual job opportunities on the quality of labor market entry. In our study, the members of one of the two COCON cohorts (reported above) entered the labor market in the years 2002–2006 and constitute the *pre-recession* cohort. Members of the other COCON cohort did so in the years 2008–2012. These are the years during the time of the Great Recession and immediately following the official end of the Great Recession. These young people belong to the *recession* cohort. The results of the competing risk regression analysis revealed that cohort membership does not significantly affect the quality of labor market entry in Switzerland. Members of the recession cohort are not more likely to be in first jobs providing only peripheral labor market integration. The interaction between cohort membership and job opportunities does also not yield a significant effect. These results suggest that, for Switzerland, the zeitgeist of the Great Recession has not altered young people's approach towards entering the labor market. Although the finding is remarkable, it nonetheless does not come as a huge surprise as the Great Recession played out rather moderately in Switzerland compared to other advanced industrialized countries.

Our study did not yield a so-called period effect of the Great Recession on labor market entrants' job search behavior, thus indicating the absence of an across-the-board, global impact of this severe economic downturn on labor market entrance at least in Switzerland.[6] This does not preclude, however, that immediate changes in young people's life circumstances brought about by the Great Recession could have consequences for the way in which young people assess their labor market chances and adapt their respective expectations, aspirations, and behaviors. Along these lines, a longitudinal study by Mortimer, Zhang, Hussemann and Wu (2014) examined whether the decline in the family's economic standing between 2009 and 2011, right in the aftermath of the Great Recession, had measurable impacts on change in children's expectations and aspirations. Their findings, based on a sample of parent–child pairs in St. Paul, Minnesota last surveyed in 2009 and 2011, highlight that declining family economic resources exert no across-the-board but rather group-specific effects on shifts in offspring's economic expectations and educational aspirations. For example, young people's economic expectations – measured by shifts in chances to have a job that pays well, to have your own home, and to have a job that you enjoy – declined only among offspring of the least well-educated parents. Even more differentiated effects, particularly complex interaction effects, were reported with regard to young people's educational aspirations. This study further showed, in line with findings of other studies (Rutter, 1970; Schoon, Martin & Ross, 2007; Schoon, 2014), that young men were harder hit by the declining family economic resources than women. All in all, the authors of this study concluded that the "findings indicate that when families are more vulnerable, as a result of low parental education and prior parental unemployment experience, children's achievement orientations are more strongly threatened by the family's economic circumstances" (Mortimer, Zhang, Hussemann & Wu, 2014: 105).

Interplay of Job Opportunities and Young People's Social and Psychological Resources

It has been a long-standing truism that young people are not simply exposed to their environment. They are also actors actively coping with their environment, thus having individual, that is psychological, resources at their disposal (Vuolo, Staff & Mortimer, 2012). They also benefit from social resources available in the social contexts they are engaged in (Coleman, 1988, 1990). These context–person interactions inspired the assumption that the social and individual resources young people bring to the labor market may be helpful for finding a first job of core quality.

Starting with social resources available to young people, the significance of various components of *social background* for the quality of labor market entry has often been established in empirical research (Breen & Goldthorpe, 2001; Iannelli, 2003; Jacob, Klein & Iannelli, 2015). The *economic resources* available in the family of origin may allow young people to extend their job search period until they have found a high-quality first job. They can do so as they can count on the financial support by the family (Jacob, 2008). In our own study for Switzerland, based on longitudinal COCON data, we could show that parental economic capital (measured by residential property[7]) significantly affects the quality of first labor market integration, decreasing the likelihood of entering jobs of peripheral quality and making the transition to jobs of core quality more likely. Interestingly enough, this study further shows that in times when individual job opportunities are bleak, the economic resources accumulated in the family of origin help labor market entrants to at least find a job of peripheral quality, while their counterparts lacking economic support by the family remain in the job search process, running a much higher risk of becoming unemployed. These findings suggest that economically secured VET labor market entrants in Switzerland are somewhat protected against unemployment when their individual job opportunities are unfavorable.

With regard to labor market entry *parental education* has been associated with providing support for their sons and daughters in terms of information about job openings, best ways to apply for jobs as well as tips and hints of how to properly behave during job interviews (Bourdieu, 1986). Having been brought up in a well-educated family may give young people invaluable advantages in the job selection process as employers reward their manners, cultivated ways of speaking, and other social competences employers praise. There is reason to argue that these aspects have become increasingly important over the past decades. Labor markets increasingly dominated by service sector jobs highly value good manners, communication skills, and social competences as the ability to establish satisfactory social interactions with customers, clients or patients is crucial for these jobs. Interestingly enough, the results of our own study for Switzerland, based on longitudinal COCON data, show that neither VET graduates whose parents successfully completed upper-secondary-level schooling (i.e., mostly VET) nor those whose parents hold tertiary-level credentials are more advantaged at the transition to the labor market compared to those whose parents solely completed compulsory schooling. This is true of both observed destinations: jobs of peripheral and core quality (as defined above). However, with the decline of individual job opportunities, parental educational resources exert their effect. When competition in the labor market is stiff as many applicants rival for scarce jobs young people from well-educated families are more likely than their counterparts from low-educated families to find a first job of core quality. The former also enjoy a lower risk of transitioning to a first job of peripheral quality. These findings corroborate our assumption that higher-educated parents are able to transfer supportive resources to their sons and daughters that become particularly valuable when job opportunities are adverse and employers have therefore the freedom to raise their hiring standards. Under these particular circumstances contacts to possible employers, positively rewarded skills and manners as well as knowledge and support during the application process may qualify as protective factors against the risk of low-quality labor market integration after VET completion and as boosting factors for high-quality labor market integration.

While our COCON cohort-comparison study focused on social resources, indicating various types of family support young people could count on, another study of ours, focusing solely on the recession cohort in Switzerland, could show that labor market entrants' psychological resources, conceived as the capacity to exert individual agency, affected the speed of finding a first job of core quality (Bundel, Jaberg & Buchmann, 2014). The COCON findings show that the more developed young people's motivation to exert effort was, the faster they would find a job of core quality. While our study was able to provide evidence of a direct effect of this psychological resource, no interaction effect between this resource and individual labor market prospects, measured as occupation-specific job opportunities, was observed. This amounts to saying that, whatever the state of individual job opportunities, willingness to exert effort is equally important.

By contrast, young people's persistence and volition, which was integrated into compound construct, was particularly important when the demand for labor in the occupational segment to which a labor-market entrant's occupation-specific certificate provides access was low.[8] This provides evidence that VET graduates, endowed with persistence and volition, are particularly able to speed up labor market entry when they face unfavorable labor market conditions. To be persistent and willing despite adverse circumstances seems to be key for successful labor market entry. These psychological resources lose their significance the better the individual labor market prospects become. The observed differences in the effects of the willingness to exert effort and persistence and volition on the duration of labor market entry of core quality in relation to individual job opportunities are certainly of interest and need further examination. We regard these findings as intriguing as our study is the first one that did not rely on highly aggregate proxies for the state of the labor market but used individual-level measures indicating the pool of vacancies indeed accessible for young people taking their occupation-specific skills and credentials into account.

Conclusions

This chapter looked at the role of the Great Recession for shaping labor market entry in Switzerland. We advanced the argument that such a severe economic downturn might mold the societal climate, the *zeitgeist*, and thus exert a uniform effect on young people's labor market entry (a so-called period effect) by shaping their career expectations, aspirations, and behavior. Our findings did not show such a homogenous effect. What they showed, however, was that the job opportunities measured at the individual level and indicating the pool of vacancies accessible to a young person against his or her occupation-specific credential did indeed affect the quality of the first job. The worse these *individual* job opportunities are, the less likely are young people to find a first job of core quality and the more likely they are to be relegated to a job of peripheral quality. Significantly enough, this fate is modified by the social resources young people bring to the labor market. In times of bleak individual job opportunities young people from well-educated families are more successful in finding a first job of core quality compared to their counterparts from low-educated families. Conversely, the latter ones experience a greater likelihood of ending up in a first job of peripheral quality. These findings provide evidence that adverse job opportunities at the time of labor market entry do aggravate social inequality. However, showing strong persistence and volition under adverse circumstances seems to be an invaluable psychological resource, supporting young people in making it against the odds and find a first job of core quality. More generally, the findings of our own studies and many of those studies reported in this chapter reject a uniform impact of major social change, such as the Great Recession, and underscore that in order to understand people's responses to such change, differences at the individual level must be taken into account.

Notes

1 To this date, over 60 percent of young people in Switzerland either serve an apprenticeship in the dual system (around 83 percent) or attend a school-based vocational program (approximately 17 percent) upon completion of nine years of compulsory schooling (Salvisberg & Sacchi, 2014).

2 For more information on the COCON study, see www.cocon.uzh.ch (accessed 29/08/2016).
3 For more information on the Swiss Job Market Monitor, see www. stellenmarktmonitor.uzh.ch (accessed 29/08/2016).
4 To be more precise, we divided the number of employed in an occupation by the number of vacancies in that occupation to take the differences in the size of occupations into account. Hence, the individual job opportunities indicate the competition a labor market entrant endowed with an occupation-specific credential is facing. The more competitors per vacancy, the stiffer the competition.
5 The zeitgeist may also lead young people to not even attempt to enter the labor market but remain in education until economically better times appear on the horizon (see, for example, Tumino & Taylor, 2013 for the UK). In this regard, the notion of the "warehousing function of schools" in periods in which the labor market is tight has been coined a long time ago (see Barnhouse-Walters, 1984).
6 Crosnoe (2014), reviewing four studies on the effects of the Great Recession on youth transitions carried out in the UK, USA, and Germany, came to similar conclusions: no across-the-board effects, but severe impact on particularly disadvantaged social groups of young people (see also the comments by Heinz (2014) on the same set of studies).
7 Residential property is a good indicator for economic capital in Switzerland as the majority of people are renting apartments or houses and are not homeowners given the exceedingly high prices of property.
8 No direct effect was observed.

References

Barnhouse-Walters, Pamela. 1984. "Occupational and labor market effects on secondary and postsecondary educational expansion in the United States: 1922 to 1979." *American Sociological Review* 49: 659–671.

Bell, David N. F. and David G. Blanchflower. 2011. "Young people and the Great Recession". *Oxford Review of Economic Policy* 27(2): 241–267.

Blossfeld, Hans-Peter, Sandra Buchholz, Erzébet Bukodi, and Karin Kurz (eds). 2008. *Young workers, globalization and the labor market: Comparing early working life in eleven countries*. Cheltenham: Edward Elgar.

Bourdieu, Pierre. 1986. "The forms of capital." In John G. Richardson (ed.) *Handbook of theory and research for the sociology of education* (pp. 241–258). New York: Greenwood Press.

Breen, Richard. 2005. "Explaining cross-national variation in youth unemployment: Market and institutional factors." *European Sociological Review* 21(2): 125–134.

Breen, Richard and John H. Goldthorpe. 2001. "Class, mobility and merit: The experience of two British birth cohorts." *European Sociological Review* 17(2): 81–101.

Breen, Richard and Marlis Buchmann. 2002. "Institutional variation and the position of young people: A comparative perspective." *The Annals of the American Academy of Political and Social Science* 580(1): 288–305.

Buchmann, Marlis and Irene Kriesi. 2011. "Transition to adulthood in Europe." *Annual Review of Sociology* 37: 481–503.

Bundel, Stephanie and Marlis Buchmann. In preparation. "Labor market entry before and during the economic crisis in Switzerland: The interplay of job opportunities and young people's resources."

Bundel, Stephanie, Andrea Jaberg, and Marlis Buchmann. 2014. "Variation in job opportunities and the significance of social and personal resources for school-to-work transitions." Paper presented at the Spring Meeting of the Research Committee 28 (Social Stratification and Mobility) of the International Sociological Association. Budapest, May 8–10.

Coleman, James S. 1988. "Social capital in the creation of human capital." *American Journal of Sociology* 94: 95–120.

Coleman, James S. 1990. *Foundations of social theory*. Cambridge, MA: Harvard University Press.

Crosnoe, Robert. 2014. "Youth, economic hardship, and the worldwide Great Recession." *Longitudinal and Life Course Studies* 5(2): 199–204.

Crosnoe, Robert and Monica Kirkpatrick Johnson. 2011. "Research on adolescence in the 21st century." *Annual Review of Sociology* 37: 439–460.

Danziger, Sheldon and David Ratner. 2010. "Labor market outcomes and the transition to adulthood." *The Future of Children* 20(1): 133–158.

de Lange, Marloes, Maurice Gesthuizen and Maarten H. J. Wolbers. 2014. "Youth labour market integration across Europe." *European Societies* 16(2): 194–212.

Dieckhoff, Martina. 2011. "The effect of unemployment on subsequent job quality in Europe: A comparative study of four countries." *Acta Sociologica* 54(3): 233–249.

Elder, Glen H. 1996. "Human lives in changing societies: Life course and developmental insights." In Robert B. Cairns, Glen H. Elder, and E. Jane Costello (eds) *Developmental science* (pp. 31–62). Cambridge, UK: Cambridge University Press.

Fine, Jason P. and Robert J. Gray. 1999. "A proportional hazards model for the subdistribution of a competing risk." *Journal of the American Statistical Association* 94(446): 496–509.

Gangl, Markus. 2006. "Scar effects of unemployment: An assessment of institutional complementarities." *American Sociological Review* 71(6): 986–1013.

Heinz, Walter. 2014. "Did the Great Recession affect young people's aspirations and reinforce social inequality?" *Longitudinal and Life Course Studies* 5(2). doi: 10.14301/llcs.v5i2.288.

Helbling, Laura A. and Stefan Sachi. 2014. "Scarring effects of early unemployment among young workers with vocational credentials in Switzerland." *Empirical Research in Vocational Education and Training* 6(12): 1–22.

Iannelli, Cristina. 2003. "Parental education and young people's educational and labour market outcomes: A comparison across Europe." In Irena Kogan and Walter Müller (eds) *School-to-work transitions in Europe: Analyses of the EU LFS 2000 Ad Hoc Module* (pp. 27–53). Mannheim: Mannheimer Zentrum für Europäische Sozialforschung (MZES).

International Labour Organization (ILO). 2013. *Global employment trends for youth 2013*. Geneva, Switzerland: International Labour Office. Accessed 29/08/2016, retrieved from www.ilo.org/wcmsp5/groups/public/---dgreports/---dcomm/documents/publication/wcms_212423.pdf

International Labour Organization (ILO). 2015. *World employment social outlook: Trends 2015*. Geneva, Switzerland: International Labour Office. Accessed 29/08/2016, retrieved from www.ilo.org/wcmsp5/groups/public/---dgreports/---dcomm/---publ/documents/publication/wcms_337069.pdf

Jacob, Marita. 2008. "Unemployment benefits and parental resources: what helps the young unemployed with labour market integration?" *Journal of Youth Studies* 11(2), 147–163.

Jacob, Marita, Markus Klein, and Cristina Iannelli. 2015. "The impact of social origin on graduates' early occupational destinations: An Anglo-German comparison." *European Sociological Review* 31(4): 460–474.

Luijkx, R. and Maarten H. J. Wolbers. 2009. "The effects of non-employment in early work-life on subsequent chances of individuals in the Netherlands." *European Sociological Review* 25(6): 647–660.

Mortimer, Jeylan T., Lei Zhang, Jeanette Hussemann, and Chen-Yu Wu. 2014. "Parental economic hardship and children's achievement orientations." *Longitudinal and Life Course Studies* 5(2): 105–128.

OECD. 2008. "Off to a good start? Youth labor market transitions in OECD countries." *Employment Outlook* 26: 25–78.

Raffe, David. 2014. "Explaining national differences in education-work transitions." *European Societies* 16(2): 175–193.

Rutter, Michael. 1970. "Sex differences in children's responses to family stress." In James E. Anthony and Cyrille Koupernik (eds) *The Child in His Family*. Yearbook, vol. 1 (pp. 165–196). New York: Wiley.

Sacchi, Stefan, Alexander Salvisberg, and Marlis Buchmann. 2005. "Long-term dynamics of skill demand in Switzerland from 1950–2000." In Hanspeter Kriesi, Peter Farago, Martin Kohli, and Milad Zarin-Nejadan (eds) *Contemporary Switzerland: Revisiting the special case* (pp. 105–134). Basingstoke: Palgrave Macmillan.

Salvisberg, Alexander and Stefan Sacchi. 2014. "Labor market prospects of Swiss career entrants after completion of vocational education and training." *European Societies* 16(2): 255–274.

Schoon, Ingrid. 2014. "Parental worklessness and the experience of NEET among their offspring: Evidence from the Longitudinal Study of Young People in England (LSYPE)." *Longitudinal and Life Course Studies* 5(2): 129–150.

Schoon, Ingrid, Peter Martin, and Andy Ross. 2007. "Career transitions in times of social change: His and her story." *Journal of Vocational Behavior* 70(1): 78–96.

Tumino, Alberto and Mark Taylor. 2013. "The impact of local labour market conditions on school leaving decisions." Population Association of America Annual Meeting, New Orleans, LA.

Vuolo, Mike, Jeremy Staff, and Jeylan T. Mortimer. 2012. "Weathering the Great Recession: Psychological and behavioral trajectories in the transition from school to work." *Developmental Psychology* 48(6): 1759–1773.

5

MAKING IT AGAINST THE ODDS

A Developmental-Contextual Approach to the Study of Resilience

Ingrid Schoon

Introduction

The 2008 Great Recession, like the economic downturns before that, significantly affected education and employment opportunities, especially for young people between 16 and 24 years embarking on the transition to adult life (Bell & Blanchflower, 2011). Young people on the cusp of independent adulthood are generally entering a make-or-break period in their lives in which external shocks have the potential to create diverging destinies. Against the backdrop of a global economic decline and changing employment opportunities, there is increasing uncertainty regarding anticipated pathways into the labor market (Blossfeld, 2005; Gutman & Schoon, 2012). Moreover, young people's perception of the economic climate can impact on their aspirations and motivation regarding extended education participation, either providing an incentive to invest in the accumulation of skills if they think they need additional competencies to succeed in a competitive labor market, or discouraging them from continuing in education and pushing them into paid employment as soon as possible to avoid unnecessary expenditure on training which might not pay off (Schoon & Bynner, in press).

Yet, young people who disengage and withdraw from efforts to enhance their skills and capabilities, either through education and training or through paid work, may flounder in an ever more competitive labor market (Schoon, 2014; Vuolo, Staff, & Mortimer, 2012). The critical period of skills acquisition through education and work may then, instead of leading to a job and the foundations of independent adulthood, give way to school drop-out, labor market drift and the problematic status of inactivity, or "not in education employment or training"

(NEET), which in turn may carry with it long term "scarring" effects regarding future job prospects and progression (Dieckhoff, 2011).

The wider social context clearly plays an important role in shaping opportunities as well as young people's motivation and aspirations for the future and their subsequent behavior in the transition from school to work. The role of the context is also evident in the fact that the effects of the recession on young people's transition experiences can vary for different countries, reflecting different institutional structures and support for young people (Heinz, 2009; Schoon & Bynner, in press). For example, while countries such as Germany or Austria with strong links between the education system and employers experienced lower levels of youth unemployment in the aftermath of the 2008 recession, other countries encountered youth unemployment rates of over 35%, in particular southern European countries, such as Spain, which are characterized by a more rigid labor market and high dependency of young people on their families for support (Bell & Blanchflower, 2011). Countries with a more liberal transition regime and a highly flexible labor market, such as the UK or the US, experienced youth unemployment rates of around 20% (Schoon & Bynner, in press).

To gain a better understanding of how to support young people in their transition to independent adulthood it is thus important to conceptualize the person–context relationship. What are the specific risk factors that undermine positive youth development, how do individuals respond to and interact with these risks, and what are the resources enabling young people to beat the odds, i.e. to make it despite exposure to adversity?

The focus of this paper is on the impact of family hardship, i.e. poverty, as well as economic instability in the wider social context which can amplify the impact of family hardship on young people's lives. This chapter introduces an ecological life course approach to the study of positive youth development (PYD), examining the factors and processes enabling young people to withstand the impact of socioeconomic adversity, especially in the aftermath of the 2008 Global Recession, also drawing on lessons from previous economic downturns. A developmental-contextual systems model of resilience (Schoon, 2006, 2012) is presented that conceptualizes the developmental and contextual influences on the manifestation of individual adaptation in the face of adversity, and a selective review of studies considering preventive strategies for young people at risk is provided.

The chapter is structured in three parts. First, a definition of resilience is given, highlighting how individual behavior and adaptive capacities are shaped by contextual constraints. Second, the developmental-contextual model of resilience is introduced, conceptualizing the capacity for adaptation and self-transformation as a dynamic, socially interdependent, richly contextualized process which is circumscribed through interactions with multiple societal subsystems. Third, strategies of what can be done to foster and promote the ability to thrive in the face of adversity are discussed.

What is Resilience?

The notion of resilience generally refers to the process of avoiding adverse outcomes, to maintain effective functioning, to recover, or doing better than expected when confronted with major assaults on the developmental process (Luthar, Cicchetti, & Becker, 2000; Masten, 2014; Rutter, 2006). Pioneering studies following the lives of people thought to be at risk for unfavorable outcomes, such as children growing up with mentally ill parents (e.g. parents suffering from schizophrenia), and those who have been abused, neglected, or exposed to poverty and socioeconomic disadvantage, observed great variations in functioning, including cases of positive adaptation despite the experience of even severe adversity (Garmezy, 1974; Rutter, 1979; Werner & Smith, 1982). These observations of unexpected positive development in the face of adversity were confirmed in many subsequent studies examining exposure to poverty as well as natural disasters, institutionalization, even exposure to war and terrorism (Betancourt, McBain, Newnham, & Brennan, 2013; Masten & Narayan, 2012; Rutter, 1998).

The observation of bouncing back, despite extreme hardship, led to a paradigmatic shift in how researchers of human development began to view the causes and course of development, leading from a pathogenic to a transactional understanding, from a deficit model to models of assets and resources, and from a static to a dynamic perspective (Schoon, 2006, 2012). Historically most studies of development of at-risk individuals tried to understand adjustment problems as reflected in ill health or mental disorder, academic failure, behavioral problems, or motivational deficits. These pathogenic or deficit models failed to recognize a) the strengths and resources available to at-risk populations, b) the plasticity of human development and capacity for change, and c) the role of the larger social system in which development takes place and the dynamic interactions between individual and context. Trying to understand the processes and mechanisms that enable individuals to beat the odds led to a shift towards dynamic multi-level systems models, focusing on the possible assets and strengths within individuals and communities, and to the investigation of reciprocal person × environment transactions enabling positive adjustment despite the experience of adversity (Lerner et al., 2013; Masten, 2014).

Focusing on how to promote positive development among young people, a set of "developmental assets" has been identified, comprising characteristics of the individual (such as indicators of self-regulation, self-esteem, or school engagement) as well as characteristics of the wider social ecology, i.e. characteristics of the families, schools, and communities (such as warm and caring parent–child relationship, access to adult mentors, effective schools, support from teachers, as well as integration to the community) that can foster positive and healthy development (Benson, 2006; Theokas & Lerner, 2006). Similar "assets" have been described in terms of a "short list" (Masten, 2014), also highlighting the role of multiple influences from the individual, their families, and the wider social context.

Although these lists capture a range of factors from the wider social context, the individual has remained the focus of attention, rather than both the environment and the individual. Positive adaption is generally equated with the individual response to adversity – and how the individual has coped. Social-ecological theories of resilience, however, have argued that it is not enough to ask, for example, how the child has adjusted to a challenging situation; it is also important to know how the social context is adapting to meet the needs of the needs of the developing young person. Both halves of the person–environment equation are equally important, and resilient adaptation involves mutually beneficial individual–context relations (Lerner et al., 2013; Schoon, 2006; Ungar, 2012).

A Developmental-Contextual Systems Model of Resilience

The interplay of structural conditions and individual adjustment can be conceptualized within a developmental-contextual system approach (Schoon, 2006, 2012). The framework is informed by ecological models of human development, taking into account the multiple interacting levels of influence ranging from the micro- to the macro-context (Bronfenbrenner, 1979), the importance of timing and the wider sociohistorical context in which development takes place (Elder, 1998), assumptions of human agency (Bandura, 2006; Heckhausen, 1999), and human plasticity (Lerner, 1984). It is assumed that both individuals and their environments are potentially malleable, whereby individuals can shape their environment, which in turn influences them. The ecological perspective provides a heuristic for understanding how multiple levels of influence contribute to individual development and adjustment in a changing context, and seeks to describe, explain, and optimize individual development in context.

Interdisciplinary orientation

The developmental-contextual systems model draws on theories from across disciplines, recognizing that complex problems, such as minimizing the impact of economic hardship and poverty and improving health, well-being, and attainment for all, require the input from different fields (Schoon, 2015). In his ecological systems theory, Bronfenbrenner (1979) identified the need for the non-reductionist analysis of individual behavior requiring the simultaneous description of several spheres of influence, thereby moving beyond simple cause-and-effect explanations of behavior. His systems model is informed by the notion of self-regulating developing systems, which are open to and interact with their environment, which had been advanced by Ludwig von Bertalanffy (1968). Living systems are understood as a unified whole where most levels are interrelated and are characterized by self-activity and historicity. Development always reflects the current context as well as the history of a person's previous development, and their orientation to the future. Accordingly, resilience has to be understood as a dynamic process: individuals and their contexts are always changing, and individual development is continually produced, sustained and changed by the sociohistorical context experienced.

Social context

Human development cannot be separated from the social context. Individual and context are understood to mutually constitute each other through processes of co-regulation (Sameroff, 2010). The developing child is rooted within many inter-related systems, such as families, schools, and neighborhoods, as well as the wider sociohistorical context. Bronfenbrenner's (1979) conceptualization of context differentiates between the proximal environment, which is directly experienced by the individual (as for example lack of economic resources in the family context) and more distal cultural and social value systems that have an indirect effect on the individual, such as an economic slump, which is often mediated by experiences in the more proximal context, but can also have direct effects.

There is persistent evidence that the experience of economic hardship, i.e. lack of material resources, poverty, loss of employment or lack of employment opportunities are associated with adjustment problems (Yoshikawa, Aber, & Beardslee, 2012). For example, children born into less privileged families show, in general, lower levels of educational attainment (Engle & Black, 2008; Schoon et al., 2002), self-confidence and educational achievement motivation (Duckworth & Schoon, 2012; Mortimer, Zhang, Hussemann, & Wu, 2014; Schoon, 2014), and young people from less privileged backgrounds are leaving education earlier and are less likely to continue in higher education than their more privileged peers (Schoon & Silbereisen, 2009; Settersten, Furstenberg, & Rumbaut, 2005; Shanahan, 2000). These associations can be amplified in times of a global economic downturn.

Yet, there is also evidence that not all individuals and families are affected in the same way, and some show resilience in the face of adversity. For example, in a path-breaking study of families in the Great Depression of the 1920s Glen Elder (1974/1999) portraits the devastating impact of a global economic downturn on the capability of families to cope. Parents were confronted with poverty and lack of material resources, some fathers had to face loss of employment and of the associated status and authority, while some mothers were forced to assume domestic dominance. Nonetheless, their children showed a considerable degree of resourcefulness. Some were pushed into early employment or household responsibility, often enabling them to gain more confidence, and some developed mixed or negative images of their stressed parents. Yet they managed well on the whole, especially if they were young enough not to take on the full duties of adults (in particular regarding family formation and parenthood) and old enough to have passed through critical early stages of development to assume pre-adult awareness and responsibilities.

Similarly, a study of families in the Iowa farming crisis demonstrates how an economic crisis can impact on families, affecting their material resources as well as socioemotional relationships and interactions, which in turn influences their children's development (Conger & Elder, 1994). According to the family stress model economic hardship can trigger stress in the family system and compromise the effectiveness of parenting and family relationships, which in turn can contribute to adjustment problems in children (Conger et al., 1992). The study however also highlighted processes of resilience in the face of economic hardship that occurred in situations where the parents emotionally supported each other, demonstrated effective problem solving skills, and showed a sense of mastery and self-confidence that allowed them to persevere and reduce the level of economic stress (Conger & Conger, 2002).

A study of young people in England making the transition to adulthood during the 2008 economic recession showed that in addition to family hardship, living in a highly deprived neighborhood, characterized by high levels of unemployment and low levels of resources was a significant risk factor, undermining young people's life chances (Schoon, 2014), illustrating the effect of cumulative disadvantage. However, the study also showed that parents, even if they experienced worklessness themselves, can motivate their children to achieve despite their own precarious situation and the experience of an economic downturn (this applied in particular to parents with higher levels of education). The potential buffering effect of parental education has also been reported in a study using the US longitudinal Youth Development Study to examine whether a positive familial context of achievement, as indicated by the parents' orientations to achievement when they were adolescents and the parents' educational attainment, will reduce the effects of economic hardship experienced within the family and the wider social context (Mortimer et al., 2014). The findings suggest that parents with higher levels of education may be able to buffer the effects of economic hardship, and encourage their children in ways that are protective, irrespective of the immediate economic situation of the family and the exposure to an economic downturn in the aftermath of the 2008 Recession.

Time and Timing

Time is another essential category in conceptualizing resilience. The notion of time concerns individual aspects such as the physiological changes and processes of maturation that occur with aging, as well as aspects of the wider social context that are external to the individual. Time is often treated as synonymous with chronological age, providing a frame of reference for the study of change over time. As children get older, they may react differently to environmental risks and may be more able to determine and evaluate how that change will influence them. As shown by Elder (1974/1999) the impact of economic hardship on young people's adjustment can vary by context, age, and the timing of adverse experiences. Furthermore, factors that may confer resilience at one point in time or for one outcome may increase vulnerability at another time or another context. Thus, human development cannot be fully explained by restricting analysis to specific life stages, such as mid-childhood, adolescence or old age. It is only by following individuals over time that we can chart their developmental trajectories and pathways.

Beyond individual maturation processes, human lives are shaped by the particular social worlds and historical period encountered. For example, the birth year locates people in specific birth cohorts and accordingly to particular social changes. The short history of the twentieth century is characterized by dramatic changes including violent swings of the economic cycle, rapid technological advances, two global wars, many regional conflicts, mass migration and natural disasters. Also in the more proximal level of the family environment there have been massive changes, with an increasing number of children being born to cohabiting or single parents, or being exposed to experiences of family break-up and instability. Changes in the proximal and wider social context pose new situational demands, and bring with them changing opportunities and obstacles, influencing lives and developmental trajectories, as for example through changing expectations regarding the timing of developmental transitions.

For instance, since the 1970s the transition to adulthood has on aggregate become more prolonged due to extended education participation and delayed entry into employment and family formation (Buchmann & Kriesi, 2011; Shanahan, 2000). Extended transitions characterized by participation in higher education and subsequent employment are considered to be "optimal," while early transitions (such as early school leaving or parenthood) have been associated with problems in establishing oneself in the labor market or making the transition to independent living. The timing of transitions is thus important in determining their meaning and implications. Yet, not all young people are able to participate in higher education, and there is persistent evidence to suggest that the preparation for adulthood has been elongated especially for those who can afford to invest in their education, while young people from less privileged backgrounds are leaving education earlier and are less likely to continue in higher education than their more privileged peers (Schoon & Silbereisen, 2009; Settersten et al., 2005).

Moreover, evidence suggests that early transitions do not necessarily bring with them negative outcomes, and in certain circumstances early transitions can be beneficial for certain individuals (Booth, Rustenbach, & McHale, 2008), especially if they offer a fit to individual preferences and resources. For example, some young people succeed to make the transition to continuous employment and financial independence after leaving school early – either through learning on the job, or participating in vocational training or further (not higher) education – and they report high levels of satisfaction with their lives (Schoon & Lyons-Amos, forthcoming). Likewise the effects of early parenthood on well-being depend on marital status as well as other circumstances in life (Nomaguchi & Milkie, 2003). Indeed, a considerable number of young people are able to turn round an initially problematic transition, such as early school leaving (Schoon & Duckworth, 2010) or early parenthood (Furstenberg, 2003; Schoon & Polek, 2011), avoid financial dependence, and lead a happy and satisfied life.

Person X Environment Interactions across Time and Contexts

Change for better or worse can occur across the entire life path, and is shaped by continuous interactions between a developing individual and a changing context. Each transition can offer opportunities for change and renewal (Elder, 1998; Schoon, 2006). Individual and context mutually constitute each other through processes of co-regulation that change over time. Developmental timing also plays a key role in resilience-based theories and the effective design and implementation of interventions. Research on naturally occurring resilience suggests that there are critical windows of opportunity for change, especially when developmental processes, the context, and available opportunities converge to provide an opening for change (Masten, 2014). In particular, early childhood and the preschool years have been identified as a period of high plasticity with great importance for the development of capabilities, laying the foundations for successful development (Kautz, Heckman, Diris, Ter Weel, & Borghans, 2014; Masten, 2014). Another example is the transition to adulthood, when brain development, motivation, mentoring, training, the assumption of new social roles, and other opportunities can provide opportunities to support positive redirection of the life course (Steinberg, 2014). Life transitions into different environments can facilitate a process of readjustment, a potential turning point, allowing for new opportunities and a change in behavioral patterns. Thus what is needed is support during key transition phases, not just once during early life – but a scaffolding enabling positive development across time (Schoon, 2006).

What Can Be Done to Promote Positive Development?

This last section of the paper discusses different strategies to support young people in their transition to adulthood, comprising efforts to build competencies, to support families, to improve communities, and to eliminate or reduce risk. It is argued that efforts to promote resilience among young people have to focus both on individual and contextual resources, provide developmentally appropriate support, create supportive and sustainable relationships, adopt a holistic approach, and offer stable and dependable structures to create opportunities for positive development across time.

Support for Building Competencies

As highlighted in the "short list" of protective resources (Masten, 2014), research has identified a set of key competences that can promote positive development and effective functioning even in the face of adversity. These include problem solving, self-regulation, motivation, social skills, and metacognition. The relevance and importance of these, sometimes called "non-cognitive" or "soft" skills and their long-term benefits for developmental outcomes is now widely recognized (OECD, 2015). Indeed, they form the core of the new OECD Key Competencies framework. Individual achievement motivation and self-regulation have also been identified to support young people making the transition from school to work in times of an economic downturn (Duckworth & Schoon, 2012; Mortimer et al., 2014; Schoon, 2014).

Significant advances in developmental prevention science have generated new interventions which aim to enhance competence and coping skills by working directly with children and young people in their social contexts, i.e. families, schools, communities, and peer groups (Catalano et al., 2012; Masten, 2011; Yoshikawa et al., 2012). Here I want to emphasize in particular four types of interventions that have shown to be effective in improving the behavior, attitudes, outlook and coping strategies of children and young people. They include mentoring, experience learning, outdoor activities and social and emotional learning (Gutman & Schoon, 2015). There is consistent experimental evidence to show that these interventions can effectively promote positive behaviors and prevent problematic ones. These interventions focus on specific risk populations and specific outcomes, and the selection of an appropriate intervention strategy should be based on a thorough assessment of the needs and resources of the school/community and the specific target group and/or problems areas in question.

For example, mentoring programs (such as Big Brothers Big Sisters (BB/BS) focus on at-risk children and young people who could use extra support and guidance in their lives (Herrera, Grossman, Kauh, & McMaken, 2011), although specific subgroups may be targeted such as those belonging to racial or ethnic minority groups. Mentoring programs can be implemented in a school or community context, and provide the opportunity to establish positive relationships with non-parental adults or older peers. Through an interconnected set of processes (addressing social-emotional and cognitive needs as well as identity formation) positive developmental trajectories can be promoted, improving outcomes across behavioral, social, emotional, and academic domains (DuBois, Portillo, Rhodes, Silverthorn, & Valentine, 2011). The benefits of participation in mentoring programs are apparent from early childhood to adolescence and thus not confined to a particular stage of development, yet appear to work best for at-risk school-age children.

Service learning can be considered as a form of experiential learning, where reflection transforms experience into new and transferable understanding (see Kolb, 1984, for the Experiential Learning Model). It is an educational approach that connects formal instruction with the opportunity to engage in meaningful community activities, providing a pragmatic, progressive learning experience (Celio, Durlak, & Dymnicki, 2011). It can, for example involve a group of children or young people reading ecological literature about pollution in class and then engaging in a gardening project, or cleaning up the streets in their neighborhood, acquiring a better understanding of community needs, gaining problem solving skills, a better understanding of their own competencies and becoming socially engaged. If offered out of school, curricular approaches to service learning that emphasize reflection have better effects than non-curricular approaches.

Outdoor adventure programs, another form of experiential learning (Gass, 1993), have become increasingly popular in the past few decades. They involve direct and purposeful exposure to real life situations, such as rock climbing, orienteering or canoeing, which require problem-solving skills, dealing with the surrounding environment and the task at hand (Sheard & Golby, 2006). It represents a learning-by-challenge approach requiring participants to interpret and handle novel situations, and has been associated with an increase of feelings of self-competence. Most programs incorporate group activities. Many of the activities require communication and cooperation, which are intended to develop team work, social and interpersonal skills. Outdoor adventure programs provide a promising tool to promote the health and well-being of troubled young people, especially when they are coupled with therapeutic interventions.

Social and emotional learning (SEL) programs are characterized as the process of acquiring core competencies to recognize and manage emotions, set and achieve positive goals, appreciate the perspectives of others, establish and maintain positive relationships, make responsible decisions, and handle interpersonal situations constructively (CASEL (Collaborative for Academic, 2005). SEL is designed as a universal, school-based program with a comprehensive, coordinated approach that integrates competence promotion and youth development frameworks for reducing risk factors and fostering protective mechanisms for positive development (Durlak, Weissberg, Dymnicki, Taylor, & Schellinger, 2011; Payton et al., 2008). SEL programs typically target multiple outcomes, are multi-year in duration, coordinate school-based efforts with those in families and the larger community, and include environmental supports so that children have opportunities to practice positive behaviors and receive consistent reinforcement. They have been shown to enhance positive outcomes for a universal school-aged population and may be particularly beneficial for younger children. They are easily and effectively administered by school staff.

The evidence suggests that interventions aiming to address relational processes and competencies can be effective. The most important consideration in the implementation of any intervention program, however, is its execution (Gutman & Schoon, 2015). Well-executed programs are informed by developmental theory, are universal, aimed at the general population, provide structure and limits that are developmentally appropriate, create supportive and enduring relationships and a sense of belonging, involve parents, teachers, and the wider community, are conducted by high-quality and well-trained staff, have clear goals, rules and sanctions, are sustainable, and provide continued support over a longer time – they offer "somewhere to go to, something to do, and someone to talk to" (Schoon & Bynner, 2003).

The Parenting of Parents

The importance of parents and effective parenting has consistently been shown in resilience research, and the family constitutes the single most important contextual influence, especially during the early years (Masten & Monn, 2015). In programs to foster resilience there must always be a consideration of the family environment, and the support for effective parenting. Yet, while developmental science has produced a lot of knowledge about what parents should and should not do, there is very little attention to how parents might be helped to sustain positive parenting in difficult situations and over time, especially when they are highly stressed themselves (Luthar & Ciciolla, 2015). Parents, in particular mothers who are facing chronic poverty and lack of resources, are also experiencing major mental health problems, such as depression, anxiety, and substance abuse. Indeed, maternal or parental distress is a potential mediating process through which socioeconomic disadvantage affects parenting behavior, which in turn affects children's outcomes (Conger, Conger, & Martin, 2010). Parents facing multiple adversities need support, and access to other adults that can help them to develop effective coping strategies. More needs to be done to create dependable and mutually supportive relationships which can be sustained over time and in different contexts, i.e. in the family, the workplace, in clinics, and in neighborhoods.

Yet reaching out to those most in need is a major challenge in itself. All too often, families or individuals in greatest need receive the least support, although adequate material benefits and support would be vital to their well-being. One critical aspect of living in hardship are high levels of isolation and anxiety, and the way in which services are provided is as important as what is provided. Services need to be based on trust and respect in order to be effective (Bartley,

2006). One of the critical aspects of service provision is to offer a space where people in hard-pressed neighborhoods feel welcome and listened to, without being patronized or judged. Services must rid themselves of the perception that those in hardship and poverty are of less moral and social worth (Schoon & Bartley, 2008). Well-designed services, offering for example activities with people who share similar experiences, can provide opportunities for clients to build self-esteem and confidence, to identify skills and aptitudes, and play a key role in acknowledging and releasing often hidden capabilities.

Improve Communities

Bringing the living standards of the worst-off closer to the average will bring with it a fairer distribution of resources and opportunities. Yet, it is not just a question of commodities or goods people have, but what these enable them to do (Sen, 1993). Changes in the physical or social environment should increase the choices available, open up new possibilities, and enhance the space and enjoyment of functioning. Living in poverty not simply means not having enough money, it also means being excluded from normal social interactions in society. Poorer families are more likely to live in places where facilities and services have been stripped away and are often unable to access even essential services such as health care, child care, and education (Townsend & Gordon, 2002). Improving these services, making the regeneration of poor areas a priority, building up the local infrastructure, and preventing ghettoization would be key steps towards a fairer society (Schoon & Bartley, 2008). A stable community, where facilities such as effective schools, libraries, parks, and leisure centers provide opportunities for education, sports, hobbies, and social activities and invite participation in community life, encouraging the ability to learn, to acquire skills, and enables a neighborhood to become a community.

Eliminate or Reduce Risk

Last, but not least, there has to be a reduction of the risk factors that undermine children's development. The costs of allowing children to grow up in poverty are enormous (Yoshikawa et al., 2012). Children growing up in families experiencing poverty and adverse living conditions, such as poor housing, do less well in school, show more behavior problems, experience more mental health problems, more problems in establishing themselves in the labor market, and are less likely to be engaged in society than their more privileged peers.

In the UK in 2013–14, there were 3.7 million children living in poverty (DWP, 2015). That's 28% of children, or nine in a classroom of 30. Child poverty reduced dramatically between 1998 and 2011 when 1.1 million children were lifted out of poverty. Since 2010, child poverty figures have flat-lined. Given the persistence of poverty even in a highly developed country such as the UK, it is essential to do something about it. A basic requirement is for families to be able to live on the wages they earn, and to have a safe home. Yet wages, especially for low-skilled jobs, have declined since the 1970s – a trend that needs to be reversed. Since the 1970s, on the background of continued economic growth, the incomes of the poorest fifth have increased by just 16%, while incomes of the richest fifth have soared by 95% (Mishel & Shierholz, 2013), with wealth being concentrated in fewer and fewer hands (Piketty, 2014).

There is evidence to suggest that increases in income among poor families can have beneficial effects regarding educational and behavioral outcomes, as well as the mental health of children. For example, a quasi-experimental study in North Carolina's Great Smoky Mountains reported on experiences among Cherokee Indians who opened a casino in their reservation and decided to distribute a proportion of the profits equally among its 8,000 members (Costello, Compton, Keeler, & Angold, 2003). Before the casino opened, children living in poor families had four times more psychiatric symptoms than those who were not poor. After the opening, the level of mental health problems among those who were lifted out of poverty fell to that of those who were never poor. Follow-up studies of the same sample showed that these effects persisted into adulthood (Costello, Erkanli, Copeland, & Angold, 2010), and that an additional $4,000 per year for the poorest households increased educational attainment by one year at age 21, and reduced the chances of committing a minor crime by 22% for 16 and 17 year olds (Akee, Copeland, Keeler, Angold, & Costello, 2010). Improving the income and living conditions of poor families with children can thus go a long way in reducing the risk of adjustment problems and poor health. Moreover, the study showed that the timing and duration of the intervention mattered: children who were youngest and had the longest exposure to increased family income showed the largest effects.

Generally, the evidence suggests that programs and policies that directly reduce poverty, such as childhood allowances and tax credits, conditional cash transfer, and income supplement programs can be effective, although their effect differs by developmental period and degree of poverty-related risk highlighting the contextual dependency of individual adjustment (Yoshikawa et al., 2012).

Another leverage to reduce risks for young people in the transition to independent adulthood are national labor market and welfare policies. For example, in the UK and the USA, the dominant view is that it is the individual's responsibility to invest in their education, which will in turn influence their prospects for employment. Following a neo-classical belief in the power of the market, both countries are characterized by a very flexible labor market with minimal restrictions on how employers recruit, train, and use employees. Moreover, both countries did not develop an effective system of vocational training, and the government was not charged with providing job opportunities

(Ashton, forthcoming). Young people are expected to build up their skills and find their own jobs. When the Great Recession hit, young people in both countries suffered most, and the youth unemployment rate reached about 20%. In southern European countries, the situation of young people was arguably exacerbated by extremely low levels of welfare provision for young people in these countries.

In Germany, however, the impact of the Great Recession on young people was somehow buffered through a "social partnership" approach, where labor market issues are negotiated between strong employer associations, trade unions, and the state, and the availability of a dual education and training system preparing young people for the world of work in close collaboration between education institutions and employers (Ashton, forthcoming). In the dual education and vocational training system, the relationship between employers and labor market entrants is actively managed, both in terms of the way in which young people are matched with the requirements of firms, and in terms of the skills which they are taught. The German government responded proactively to the impact of the global economic crisis: the dual education and training system provided shelter from unemployment, and the government reduced both employee and employer unemployment insurance contributions, subsidized short-time work, increased staffing in the public employment service, and provided funding for training. As a result, Germany became one of the exceptions, and youth unemployment fell from 13.5% in 2005–7 to 11% in 2009 (Bell & Blanchflower, 2011).

There is thus nothing inevitable about labor market outcomes, and national institutions and policies play an important role in shaping young people's experience of the transition from school to work. The measures introduced by the German government are of course not beyond criticism, and even those young people on the relatively protected and advantaged pathways through higher education to the professions may confront increasing transition difficulties as career opportunities close down or are replaced by unpaid internships. Moreover, school leavers with entry requirements for university are competing with less-qualified school leavers for the most prestigious apprenticeships, making it more difficult for those with lower level qualifications to obtain an apprenticeship and to enter the dual system (Schoon & Bynner, in press).

To support the transition to independence among young people, it is thus necessary to create viable career pathways for those with and those without academic qualifications. Even in countries with high participation rates in higher education such as the USA, only about 40% obtain either an associate's or bachelor's degree by their mid-twenties (Symonds, Schwartz & Ferguson, 2011). Following the recent global recession, there are now increasing concerns regarding how to prepare young people for the transition to independence (Schoon & Bynner, in press). There are questions regarding the value of a degree, prolonged education periods without income, and rising student debt. Moreover, the fastest job growth is likely among occupations that require an associate's degree or a post-secondary vocational award (Symonds et al., 2011), and among lower-skilled occupations in caring, health, and leisure (UKCES, 2014). Interestingly, in the USA, 27% of people with post-secondary licenses or certificates – credentials short of an associate's degree – are reported to earn more than the average bachelor's degree recipient (Holzer & Lerman, 2009). Across most Western countries there is now evidence of underemployment among graduates, i.e. employed workers with a degree are in jobs that do not require higher education (Fogg & Harrington, 2011; ONS, 2013).

Leaving education relatively early with a good post-secondary qualification and engaging in continuous full-time employment might thus not necessarily be a bad strategy – if there are jobs available that pay a decent salary and provide prospects for promotion. Income earned through longer-term, full-time employment enables financial independence, the move into one's own home, and supporting one's own family at an earlier pace than among those who continue in higher education. What is required is the creation and provision of pathways to prosperity among future workers at every education level (Symonds et al., 2011). Young people have to carve their pathways to adulthood based on the resources and opportunities that are available to them. Not all young people can or want to pursue an academic career, and many young people fail to achieve their ambitious educational goals. After spending several years in higher education they leave without qualifications, are left unprepared for alternative pathways, and struggle to establish themselves in the labor market (Symonds et al., 2011). What is required is the creation of viable career pathways and the provision of effective career advice and information, aiming to create and match opportunities to the needs of the developing young person.

Conclusion

The developmental-contextual approach to the study of resilience avoids simplistic individual-focused interventions, which do not account for the wider social context in which the developing individual is embedded. It takes a holistic approach, considering the multi-dimensional forces and relationships between individuals, their families, their neighborhoods, and wider social context. It recognizes that risk factors cumulate over time, making it difficult to pinpoint one single factor or causal mechanism. It highlights the importance of timing and the design of developmentally appropriate and sustainable interventions. Change for better or worse can occur across the entire life course, suggesting that it is never too early or too late to intervene. Moreover, disadvantaged families and their children are highly diverse, rendering the quality of the implementation and service delivery a crucial issue. To be effective, interventions should be community-based and provide integrated service delivery, building up resources and sustainable relationships from inside the community, thereby strengthening the social fabric (Schoon, 2006; Schoon & Bartley, 2008; Schoon & Bynner, 2003). In addition, the recognition that developmental processes are profoundly affected by the wider social context draws the attention to the role of public policies and practices that influence the nature of the environment, and thus can have significant effects on the development of children, young people, and their families (Lerner et al., 2013; Ungar, 2012). Providing effective child care, education, and employment opportunities are basic requirements for families, children, and young people to thrive. There is not one major factor that enables individuals to cope with adversity. What is important is the combination of multiple influences that make a difference, and social policy and structures that create opportunities and resources, optimizing the life chances for all.

References

Akee, R. K. Q., Copeland, W. E., Keeler, G., Angold, A., & Costello, E. J. (2010). Parents' incomes and children's outcomes: A quasi-experiment using transfer payments from casino profits. *American Economic Journal-Applied Economics, 2*(1), 86–115.

Ashton, D. N. (forthcoming). Globalization and its impact on the political, economic and labour market aspects of transition. In I. Schoon & J. Bynner (Eds), *Young people's development and the Great Recession: Uncertain transitions and precarious futures.* Cambridge, UK: Cambridge University Press.

Bandura, A. (2006). Toward a Psychology of Human Agency. *Perspectives on Psychological Science, 1*(2): 164–180.

Bartley, M. (Ed.) (2006). *Capability and resilience: Beating the odds.* London: University College London, Department of Epidemiology and Public Health.

Bell, D. N. F., & Blanchflower, D. G. (2011). Young people and the Great Recession. *Oxford Review of Economic Policy, 27*(2), 241–267.

Benson, P. L. (2006). *All kids are our kids: What communities must do to raise caring and responsible children and adolescents.* San Francisco, CA: Jossey-Bass.

Betancourt, T. S., McBain, R., Newnham, E. A., & Brennan, R. T. (2013). Trajectories of internalizing problems in war-affected Sierra Leonean youth: Examining conflict and postconflict factors. *Child Development, 84*(2), 455–470.

Blossfeld, H. P. (2005). *Globalization, uncertainty and youth in society.* London: Routledge.

Booth, A., Rustenbach, E., & McHale, S. (2008). Early family transitions and depressive symptom changes from adolescence to early adulthood. *Journal of Marriage and Family, 70*(1), 3–14.

Bronfenbrenner, U. (1979). *The ecology of human development: Experiments by nature and design.* Cambridge, MA: Harvard University Press.

Buchmann, M. C., & Kriesi, I. (2011). Transition to adulthood in Europe. *Annual Review of Sociology, 37*, 481–503.

CASEL (Collaborative for Academic, Social and Emotional Learning). (2005). *Safe and sound: An educational leader's guide to evidence-based social and emotional learning programs,* Illinois edition. Accessed 2 September 2016, available at http://www.casel.org/library/2005/2/1/safe-and-sound-an-educational-leaders-guide-to-evidence-based-social-and-emotional-learning-programs-illinois-edition

Catalano, R., Fagan, A., Gavin, L., Greenberg, M., Irwin, C. J., Ross, D., & Shek, D. (2012). Worldwide application of prevention science in adolescent health. *The Lancet, 379*(9826), 1653–1661.

Celio, C. I., Durlak, J., & Dymnicki, A. (2011). A meta-analysis of the imapct of service-learning on students. *Journal of Experiential Education, 34*(2), 164–181.

Conger, R. D., & Conger, K. J. (2002). Resilience in Midwestern families: Selected findings from the first decade of a prospective, longitudinal study. *Journal of Marriage and the Family, 64*(2), 361–373.

Conger, R. D., & Elder, G. H. (1994). *Families in troubled times: Adapting to change in rural America.* New York: Aldine De Gruyter.

Conger, R. D., Conger, K. J., & Martin, M. J. (2010). Socioeconomic status, family processes, and individual development. *Journal of Marriage and the Family, 72*(3), 685–704.

Conger, R. D., Conger, K. J., Elder, G. H., Lorenz, F. O., Simons, R. L., & Whitbeck, L. B. (1992). A family process model of economic hardship and adjustment of early adolescent boys. *Child Development, 63*(3), 526–541.

Costello, E. J., Compton, S. N., Keeler, G., & Angold, A. (2003). Relationships between poverty and psychopathology: A natural experiment. *JAMA: Journal of the American Medical Association, 290*(15), 2023–2029.

Costello, E. J., Erkanli, A., Copeland, W., & Angold, A. (2010). Association of family income supplements in adolescence with development of psychiatric and substance use disorders in adulthood among an American Indian population. *JAMA: Journal of the American Medical Association, 303*(19), 1954–1960.

Dieckhoff, M. (2011). The effect of unemployment on subsequent job quality in Europe: A comparative study of four countries. *Acta Sociologica, 54*(3), 233–249.

DuBois, D. L., Portillo, N., Rhodes, J. E., Silverthorn, N., & Valentine, J. C. (2011). How effective are mentoring programs for youth? A systematic assessment of the evidence. *Psychological Science in the Public Interest, 12*(2), 57–91.

Duckworth, K., & Schoon, I. (2012). Beating the odds: Exploring the impact of social risk on young people's school-to-work transitions during recession in the UK. *National Institute Economic Review, 222*(October), 38–51.

Durlak, J. A., Weissberg, R. P., Dymnicki, A. B., Taylor, R. D., & Schellinger, K. B. (2011). The impact of enhancing students' social and emotional learning: A meta-analysis of school-based universal interventions. *Child Development, 82*(1), 405–432.

DWP (2015). Households below average income. London, Department for Work and Pensions. Accessed 2 September 2016, available at https://www.gov.uk/government/uploads/system/uploads/attachment_data/file/437246/households-below-average-income-1994-95-to-2013-14.pdf.

Elder, G. H. (1974/1999). *Children of the Great Depression: Social change in life experience.* Boulder, CO: Westview Press.

Elder, G. H. (1998). The life course as developmental theory. *Child Development, 69*(1), 1–12.

Engle, P. L., & Black, M. M. (2008). The effect of poverty on child development and educational outcomes. *Annals of the New York Academy of Sciences, 1136*(1), 243–256.

Fogg, N. P., & Harrington, P. E. (2011). Rising Mal-Employment and the Great Recession: The Growing Disconnect Between Recent College Graduates and the College Labor Market. *Continuing Education Review, 75*, 51–65.

Furstenberg, F. F. (2003). Teenage childbearing as a public issue and private concern. *Annual Review of Sociology, 29*, 23–29.

Garmezy, N. (1974). The study of competence in children at risk for severe psychopathology. In E. J. Anthony & C. Koupernik (Eds), *The child in his family: Children at psychiatric risk*, Vol. 3 (pp. 77–97). New York: Wiley.

Gass, M. A. (1993). *Adventure therapy*. Dubuque, IA: Kendall/Hunt Publishing Company.

Gutman, L., & Schoon, I. (2015). Preventive interventions for children and adolescents: A review of meta-analytic evidence. *The European Psychologist, 20*(4), 231–241.

Gutman, L. M., & Schoon, I. (2012). Correlates and consequences of uncertainty in career aspirations: Gender differences among adolescents in England. *Journal of Vocational Behavior, 80*(3), 608–618.

Heckhausen, J. (1999). *Developmental regulation in adulthood: age-normative and sociostructural constraints as adaptive challenges*. New York: Cambridge University Press.

Heinz, W. R. (2009). Structure and agency in transition research. *Journal of Education and Work. Special issue: Continuity and change in 40 years of school to work transitions, 22*, 391–404.

Herrera, C., Grossman, J. B., Kauh, T. J., & McMaken, J. (2011). Mentoring in schools: An impact study of Big Brothers Big Sisters school-based mentoring. *Child Development, 82*(1), 346–361.

Holzer, H., & Lerman, R. (2009). *The Future of Middle Skill Jobs*. Washington D.C.: The Brookings Institution.

Kautz, T., Heckman, J. J., Diris, R., Ter Weel, B., & Borghans, L. (2014). *Fostering and measuring skills: Improving cognitive and non-cognitive skills to promote lifetime success*. Paris: OECD Publishing

Kolb, D. A. (1984). *Experiential learning: Experience as the source of learning and development*. Englewood Cliffs, NJ: Prentice Hall.

Lerner, R. M. (1984). *On the nature of human plasticity*. New York: Cambridge University Press.

Lerner, R. M., Agans, J. P., Arbeit, M. R., Chase, P. A., Weiner, M. B., Schmid, K. L., & Warren, A. E. A. (2013). Resilience and positive youth development: A relational developmental systems model. In S. Goldstein & R. B. Brooks (Eds), *Handbook of resilience in children* (pp. 293–308). New York: Springer.

Luthar, S. S., & Ciciolla, L. (2015). Who mothers mommy? Factors that contribute to mothers' well-being. *Developmental Psychology, 51*(12), 1812–1823.

Luthar, S. S., Cicchetti, D., & Becker, B. (2000). The construct of resilience: A critical evaluation and guidelines for future work. *Child Development, 71*(3), 543–562.

Masten, A. S. (2011). Resilience in children threatened by extreme adversity: Frameworks for research, practice, and translational synergy. *Development and Psychopathology, 23*(2), 493–506.

Masten, A. S. (2014). *Ordinary magic: Resilience in development*. New York: Guilford.

Masten, A. S., & Monn, A. R. (2015). Child and Family Resilience: A Call for Intergrated Science, Practice, and Professional Training. *Family Relations, 64*(1), 5–21.

Masten, A. S., & Narayan, A. J. (2012). Child development in the context of disaster, war, and terrorism: Pathways of risk and resilience. In S. T. Fiske, D. L. Schacter, & S. E. Taylor (Eds), *Annual Review of Psychology*, Vol. 63 (pp. 227–257). Palo Alto, CA: Annual Reviews.

Mishel, L., & Shierholz, H. (2013). A lost decade, not a burst bubble: The declining living standards of middle-class households in the US and Britain. In G. Kelly &

J. Bernstein (Eds), *The squeezed middle: The pressure on ordinary workers in America and Britain* (pp. 17–30). Bristol: The Policy Press.

Mortimer, J. T., Zhang, L., Hussemann, J., & Wu, C.-Y. (2014). Parental economic hardship and children's achievement orientations. *Longitudinal and Life Course Studies, 5*(2), 105–128.

Nomaguchi, K. M., & Milkie, M. A. (2003). Costs and rewards of children: The effects of becoming a parent on adults' lives. *Journal of Marriage and Family, 65*(2), 356–374.

OECD (2015). Skills for social progress. The power of social and emotional skills., OECD Skills publishing. Accessed 2 September 2016, available at http://www.oecd-ilibrary.org/education/skills-for-social-progress_9789264226159-en

ONS (2013). Graduates in the UK Labour Market. Office for National Statistics. Available at http://www.ons.gov.uk/ons/rel/lmac/graduates-in-the-labour-market/2013/rpt---graduates-in-the-uk-labour-market-2013.html.

Payton, J., Weissberg, R. P., Durlak, J. A., Dymnicki, A. B., Taylor, R. D., & Schellinger, K. B., & Pachan, M. (2008). *The positive impact of social and emotional learning for kindergarten to eighth-grade students: Findings from three scientific reviews.* Accessed 2 September 2016, retrieved from http://files.eric.ed.gov/fulltext/ED505370.pdf

Piketty, T. (2014). *Capital in the twenty-first century.* Cambridge, MA: Belknap Press of Harvard University.

Rutter, M. (1979). Protective factors in children's responses to stress and disadvantage. In M. W. Kent & J. E. Rolf (Eds), *Primary prevention of psychopathology: Social competence in children* (pp. 49–62). Hanover, NH: University Press of New England.

Rutter, M. (1998). Developmental catch-up, and deficit, following adoption after severe global early privation. *Journal of Child Psychology and Psychiatry and Allied Disciplines, 39*(4), 465–476.

Rutter, M. (2006). Implications of resilience concepts for scientific understanding. *Annals of the New York Academy of Sciences, 1094*(1), 1–12.

Sameroff, A. J. (2010). "A Unified Theory of Development: A Dialectic Integration of Nature and Nurture." *Child Development 81*(1), 6–22.

Schoon, I. (2006). *Risk and resilience: Adaptations in changing times.* Cambridge: Cambridge University Press.

Schoon, I. (2012). Temporal and contextual dimensions to individual positive development: A developmental-contextual systems model of resilience. In M. Ungar (Ed.), *The social ecology of resilience: culture, context, resources, and meaning* (pp. 143–156). New York: Springer.

Schoon, I. (2014). Parental worklessness and the experience of NEET among their offspring. Evidence from the Longitudinal Study of Young People in England (LSYPE). *Longitudinal and Life Course Studies, 6*(6), 129–150.

Schoon, I. (2015). Let's work together: Towards interdisciplinary collaboration. *Research in Human Development, 12*(3–4), 350–355.

Schoon, I., & Bartley, M. (2008). The role of human capability and resilience. *Psychologist, 21*(1), 24–27.

Schoon, I., & Bynner, J. (2003). Risk and resilience in the life course: Implications for interventions and social policies. *Journal of Youth Studies, 6*(1), 21–31.

Schoon, I., & Bynner, J. (eds). (in press). Young People's Development and the Great Recession: Uncertain Transitions and Precarious Futures. Cambridge: Cambridge University Press.

Schoon, I., & Duckworth, K. (2010). Leaving school early – and making it! Evidence from two British birth cohorts. *European Psychologist, 15*(4), 283–292.

Schoon, I., & Lyons-Amos, M. (forthcoming). A socio-ecological model of agency. The role of psycho-social and socio-economic resources in shaping education and employment transitions in England. *Longitudinal and Life Course Studies.*

Schoon, I., & Polek, E. (2011). Pathways to economic wellbeing among teenage mothers in Great Britain. *European Psychologist, 16*(1), 11–20.

Schoon, I., & Silbereisen, K. R. (Eds) (2009). *Transitions from school to work: Globalisation, individualisation, and patterns of diversity.* New York: Cambridge University Press.

Schoon, I., Bynner, J., Joshi, H., Parsons, S., Wiggins, R. D., & Sacker, A. (2002). The influence of context, timing, and duration of risk experiences for the passage from childhood to midadulthood. *Child Development, 73*(5), 1486–1504.

Sen, A. (1993). Capability and well-being. In M. Nussbaum & A. Sen (Eds), *The quality of life* (pp. 30–53). Oxford: Clarendon Press.

Settersten, R. A., Furstenberg, F. F., & Rumbaut, R. G. (2005). *On the frontier of adulthood: Theory, research, and public policy.* Chicago, IL: University of Chicago Press.

Shanahan, M. J. (2000). Pathways to adulthood in changing societies: Variability and mechanisms in life course perspective. *Annual Review of Sociology, 26*(1), 667–692.

Sheard, M., & Golby, J. (2006). The efficacy of an outdoor adventure education curriculum on selected aspects of positive psychological development. *Journal of Experiential Education, 29*(2), 187–209.

Steinberg, L. (2014). *The age of opportunity: Lessons from the new science of adolescence.* Boston, MA: Houghton Mifflin Harcourt.

Symonds, W. C., Schwartz, R. B., & Ferguson, R. (2011). *Pathways to prosperity: Meeting the challenge of preparing young Americans for the 21st century.* Harvard, MA: Harvard Graduate School of Education.

Theokas, C., & Lerner, R. M. (2006). Observed ecological assets in families, schools, and neighborhoods: Conceptualization, measurement and relations with positive and negative developmental outcomes. *Applied Developmental Science, 10*(2), 61–74.

Townsend, P., & Gordon, D. (Eds) (2002). *World poverty: New policies to defeat an old enemy.* Bristol: Policy Press.

UKCES (2014). The labour market story: Skills for the future, UK Commission for Employment and Skills. https://www.gov.uk/government/uploads/system/uploads/attachment_data/file/344441/The_Labour_Market_Story-_Skills_for_the_Future.pdf.

Ungar, M. (2012). Annual research review: What is resilience within the social ecology of human development? *Journal of Child Psychology and Psychiatry, 54*(4), 348–366.

von Bertalanffy, L. (1968). *General system theory: foundations development applications.* New York, Braziller.

Vuolo, M., Staff, J., & Mortimer, J. T. (2012). Weathering the Great Recession: Psychological and behavioral trajectories in the transition from school to work. *Developmental Psychology, 48*(6), 1759–1773.

Werner, E. E., & Smith, R. S. (1982). *Vulnerable but invincible: A longitudinal study of resilient children.* New York: McGraw-Hill.

Yoshikawa, H., Aber, J. L., & Beardslee, W. R. (2012). The effects of poverty on the mental, emotional, and behavioral health of children and youth implications for prevention. *American Psychologist, 67*(4), 272–284.

6

CAREER ENGAGEMENT AND LIFE SATISFACTION DURING TRANSITION FROM SCHOOL TO WORK IN TIMES OF ECONOMIC DOWNTURN IN FINLAND

Katja Upadyaya and Katariina Salmela-Aro

Introduction

The recent economic downturn has hit Finland hard. Young people have been especially affected, as youth unemployment is currently over 20%. This increasing uncertainty about the future might be expected negatively to affect young people's academic engagement and motivation towards their future careers. However, in this chapter we also expected to find some degree of polarization, with some young people thriving, and others disengaging. Our results will provide new insights into the impact of the recession on ways in which young people navigate the transition to further education and employment.

The influence of macro-level events and conditions on psychological variables is of central interest within the social sciences (Fletcher, 2015). Recently there has been a growing interest on the global economic crisis on personality, mental health, and well-being (Clark & Heath, 2015). In his pioneering study, Glen Elder examined the children growing up during the Great Depression. Moreover, there is research on the impact of recession on individual level critical life events. Depending on the events, changes in well-being can rebound to original levels, rebound but never fully recover to pre-event levels or show little evidence of recovery (Lucas, 2007). Interestingly, changes tied to downturns in the economy such as unemployment tend to be less likely to recover to original levels (Lucas, 2007). However, relatively little research has examined the effect of macro-level events on positive development such as life and career satisfaction. Di Tella, MacCulloch, and Oswald (2003) revealed that a country's economic position has significant effects on well-being. They indicated that increasing unemployment that results from economic hardship has a critical effect not only on those who lose their job but also for the population as a whole (see also Gassman-Pines, Gibson-Davis, & Ananat, 2015). Thus changes in macro-level contexts, and economic conditions in particular, can have meaningful impacts on well-being and these may have an impact upon everyone, those directly and indirectly affected. In addition, the developmental stage such as adolescence and young adulthood including critical transition period might play an important role. Finally, consideration of general well-being such as life satisfaction should be supplemented by consideration of domain specific measures such as career satisfaction.

The post-high school period and transition to work life is a period in which developmental transitions are both plentiful and have considerable importance for long-term status attainment. Those making the transition from formal schooling to tertiary education or work life are particularly at risk of contextual events and influences. Such a period is defined by the convergence of developmental tasks from multiple life domains and thus it is one of the most critical developmental periods. In addition, during the transition to tertiary education or work life, the role of career engagement, life satisfaction, and career satisfaction become increasingly important in shaping young adults' future pathways. The particular danger of macroeconomic events, such as economic crisis, is the potential to drive young people out of a typical developmental track or delaying transitions and extending periods of career and educational uncertainty and related well-being. In addition, economically the unemployment is particularly high during this developmental period in Finland, making young adults more vulnerable to macro-level hardship. However, regardless of experienced difficulties, young adults are typically highly resilient (Masten et al., 2004) and experience high well-being. Consequently, this chapter aims to describe the co-development of three indicators of positive psychological well-being, taking into account general or study/work specific context (e.g., context-free life satisfaction, and study/work context-specific satisfaction and engagement) among Finnish young adults during economic downturn.

Young Adults' Career Engagement

Increasing interest in positive psychology and career development has inspired research on young adults' engagement before and after the transition to work (Li & Lerner, 2011; Salanova, Agut, & Peiro, 2005; Upadyaya & Salmela-Aro, 2013). Engagement in studies and work is often positively associated with learning (Salanova et al., 2005), self-esteem (Salmela-Aro & Upadyaya, 2012), well-being (Li & Lerner, 2011), and personal initiatives and innovativeness (Hakanen, Perhoniemi, & Toppinen-Tanner, 2008). Moreover, previous studies have shown that a continuum exists between study and work engagement, and has defined this continuum as career engagement (Upadyaya & Salmela-Aro, 2015). Similarly, career engagement is reflected in one's subsequent well-being and educational outcomes, and becomes increasingly important across educational and work transitions (Upadyaya & Salmela-Aro, 2013b; Upadyaya & Salmela-Aro, 2015).

Research drawing on the work engagement literature (Hakanen, Bakker, & Schaufeli, 2006; Salanova et al., 2005; Schaufeli, Bakker, & Salanova, 2006) has examined engagement as a phenomenon resembling flow (Csikszentmihalyi, 1990), with reference to the dimensions of energy, dedication, and absorption during studies/work (Salmela-Aro & Upadyaya, 2012; Schaufeli, Salanova, Gonzalez-Roma, & Bakker, 2002). Flow refers to an experience which itself is so enjoyable that people tend to desire it, even at great cost, purely for the sake of the experience (Csikszentmihalyi, 1990). However, the main difference between the concepts of engagement and flow is that flow refers to a short-term peak experience that is unlikely to occur in studies or work, whereas engagement is a more persistent state of mind. *Energy* refers to high mental resilience and affects while studying/working, a willingness to invest effort in one's studies/work, and a positive approach. *Dedication,* in turn, is characterized by a cognitive sense of significance, enthusiasm, pride, and inspiration regarding school/work, and perceptions of studies/work as meaningful. *Absorption* is characterized by behavioral accomplishments, fully concentrating and being happily engrossed in one's studies/work, so that time passes quickly. These three dimensions are distinct analytic constructs of career engagement, although they correlate highly with each other (Salmela-Aro & Upadyaya, 2012; Schaufeli et al., 2002), and can be used as a one-dimensional or as a three-dimensional construct, depending on the research purpose (Seppälä et al., 2009).

During secondary education, in particular, developmental changes occur in engagement (Salmela-Aro & Upadyaya, 2012), whereas engagement in work remains relatively stable, even across job changes (Seppälä et al., 2015). These changes and stability may be explained by person-environment fit (Eccles & Roeser, 2009) and by the trait-like and occasion-dependent characteristics of engagement (Seppälä et al., 2015). For example, for most young adults their higher educational institution or workplace provides a good person–environment fit, often better than the fit in their previous, secondary educational institution (Upadyaya & Salmela-Aro, 2013b). For a small proportion of young adults, the opposite is true (Upadyaya & Salmela-Aro, 2013b). Further, work engagement seems to be rather a stable state of mind, with daily fluctuation explaining a smaller amount of the variance in work engagement (Seppälä et al., 2015). Thus, in particular, when young adults enter working life and feel that their person–environment fit is good, it seems reasonable to assume that the stability of work engagement is also high.

Context-Free Well-Being: Life Satisfaction

Life satisfaction has been described as an important indicator of positive psychological well-being (Huebner, Valois, Paxton, & Drane, 2005), which reflects one's context-free happiness and cognitive assessments of life quality based on one's own standards (Erdogan, Bauer, Truxillo, & Mansfield, 2012; Lewis, Huebner, Malone, & Valois, 2011; Pavot & Diener, 1993). Increasing interest in life satisfaction in recent research reflects the increasing attention currently being paid to positive psychology, which focuses on human strengths and optimal functioning rather than on weaknesses and malfunctioning (Hakanen & Schaufeli, 2012; Seligman & Csikszentmihalyi, 2000). Life satisfaction can be described as an overall satisfaction with one's life (Upadyaya & Salmela-Aro, 2015) or as consisting of several facets reflecting different life domains (e.g., family, friends, living environment, school, self) (Huebner, Drane, & Valois, 2000; Huebner et al., 2005).

As economic downturns typically hit one's well-being (Di Tella et al., 2003), academic achievement (Stevens & Schaller, 2011), and employment status (Gassman-Pines et al., 2015), one might assume that economic downturns would show also in how general life satisfaction and study/work context-specific engagement co-develop. However, only a few studies have examined the development of life satisfaction in the academic and work environments (Chen, Morin, Parker, & Marsh, 2015; Erdogan et al., 2011; Lewis et al., 2011; Upadyaya & Salmela-Aro, 2015), even several studies have indicated the positive associations between life satisfaction and academic (e.g., academic achievement, competence, school satisfaction) (Suldo, Riley, & Shaffer, 2006) and work outcomes (e.g., job performance, commitment). According to these studies, most adolescents and young adults report positive global life satisfaction – although variation exists across domains – with middle-school and high-school students typically reporting higher dissatisfaction with their school experiences compared to other life domains (Huebner et al., 2000, 2005). Further, young adults who have received their high school diploma report higher levels of life satisfaction than their peers who obtained only general educational development tests or dropped out of school (Ou, 2008). Among adult employees, life satisfaction is often positively associated with several work-related variables, such as organizational commitment and personal growth (Erdogan et al., 2012), while it has been suggested that life satisfaction forms stronger correlations with job performance than job satisfaction (Jones, 2006).

Life satisfaction reflects one's context-free happiness and well-being (Lewis et al., 2011), whereas career engagement, similar to flow (Csikszentmihalyi, 1990), describes one's study and work context-specific well-being (Hakanen & Schaufeli, 2012; Upadyaya & Salmela-Aro, 2013). Despite these contextual differences, satisfaction in life is often associated with career engagement during different life stages. Research originating from the demands and resources model (Demerouti, Bakker, Nachreiner, & Schaufeli, 2001) has shown that high career engagement protects against ill-being and burnout symptoms, and leads to well-being and high life satisfaction (Salmela-Aro & Upadyaya, 2014). Thus, spillover exists between work context-specific well-being and ill-health, and between general well-being and ill-health (Hakanen & Schaufeli, 2012; Upadyaya & Salmela-Aro, 2015). According to the model of developmental cascades, positive development in one aspect of life (e.g., general well-being and life satisfaction) may influence adaptation in other life domains and promote context-specific well-being, reflecting developmental cascades that occur across various life stages (see Masten et al., 2010). Moreover, the broaden-and-build theory suggests that students who are satisfied with their studies and life, and experience frequent positive emotions, will exhibit adaptive coping behaviors, feel more engaged, and gain more resources which, in turn, will promote positive upward spirals of success at studies/work (see also Fredrickson, 2001). These positive cycles may become especially important during broader macro-level changes (e.g., economic downturns) and during the time when young adults face various educational and work transitions and prepare for adult work roles (Arnett, 2000). Life satisfaction, in particular, may serve as a cognitive resource built with frequent positive emotions which helps in facing a wide range of life's challenges and support positive personal growth (Cohn, Fredrickson, Brown, Mikels, & Conway, 2009). Empirical studies have shown that engagement and life satisfaction are typically highly correlated with each other (Harter, Schmidt, & Hayes, 2002), and that in particular cognitive engagement, similar to dedication (Upadyaya & Salmela-Aro, 2013), is strongly associated with life satisfaction (Lewis et al., 2011).

Various educational and work transitions as well as wider macro-level events such as economic downturns might influence the development of life satisfaction and engagement among young people. The Finnish Educational Transitions (FinEdu) Study followed adolescents and young adults ($N = 818$) through the transition to higher education or work and during the economic downturn in Finland. In this study, we used data from post-comprehensive education onwards. The first two years of measurements were carried out during each of the two post-comprehensive years: the first at half a year after the transition to post-comprehensive school (age = 17, year 2005) and the second one a year later (age = 18, year 2006). The third measurement was carried out two and a half years after the previous one (age = 21, year 2009), when most of the students had already finished their post-comprehensive education. The fourth and the fifth measurements were carried out two and four years apart (age = 23, year 2011; age = 25, year 2013).

Upadyaya and Salmela-Aro (2016b) examined the co-development of life satisfaction and career engagement by using a variable-oriented and a person-oriented approach. The aim of these two approaches was to capture the overall co-development in life satisfaction and career engagement, as well as to examine whether different homogeneous groups of young adults could be identified according to the varying levels and developmental trajectories of their life satisfaction and career engagement. The results of these analyses showed, first, that young adults' life satisfaction was quite high, however slightly decreasing over the transition to higher education or work, and continuing to decrease during the global economic downturn (Figure 6.1) (Upadyaya & Salmela-Aro, 2016b). However, at the same time young adults' career engagement increased reflecting the fact that despite the economic downturn, young adults are eager to advance in their higher education studies or work even if they might be facing some challenges which might be partly due to the recession. These challenges are mainly reflected in their life satisfaction which slightly decreased during the recession. Previous research has indicated that a country's economic position has significant effects on one's well-being (Di Tella et al., 2003) and hardly any impact on young adults' work motivation (Hagström & Gamberale, 1995). Similarly, research on the Millennial generation has shown that during recession, Millennial young adults' work motivation and expectations remain high, whereas their optimism decreases (De Hauw & De Vos, 2010). The results of the FinEdu study are in line with these previous findings and further suggest

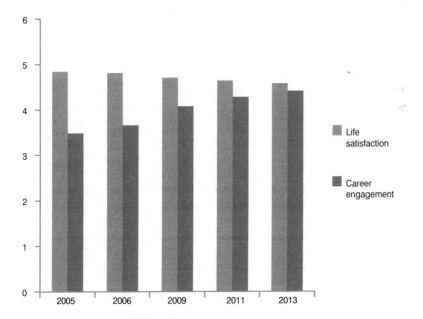

FIGURE 6.1 Co-Development of Life Satisfaction and Career Engagement among Finnish Young Adults

Based on data from Upadyaya and Salmela-Aro (2016b).

that the effects of economic downturn mainly show in general well-being (e.g., life satisfaction) rather than in career engagement.

However, it is possible that various homogeneous subgroups of young adults exist according to the initial level and developmental changes in life satisfaction and career engagement. The results of the person-oriented approach by Upadyaya and Salmela-Aro (2016b) showed that two homogeneous groups of young adults could be identified according to the initial level and developmental trajectories of their life satisfaction and career engagement. In the first "high engagement and life satisfaction" group which included 85% of the participants, young adults experienced initially high life satisfaction which slightly decreased during the economic downturn and initially high career engagement which increased across the years. The second "low engagement and life satisfaction" group which included 15% of the participants in which both initial life satisfaction and career engagement were relatively low, showed life satisfaction slightly decreasing during the economic downturn and career engagement remaining at the same lower level. These results suggested that regardless of the high/low initial level of life satisfaction and career engagement, in both groups life satisfaction decreased during the economic downturn. These results confirm the previous findings suggesting that economic downturn typically hit young adults' well-being (Di Tella et al., 2003), whereas motivation (Hagström & Gamberale, 1995), expectations (De Hauw & De Vos, 2010), and, in our study, engagement typically increase or remain at the same original level regardless of the economic downturn. Some research has also suggested that gender differences exist in life satisfaction. Although some studies have reported higher educational satisfaction among females than males, the results on global life satisfaction have been mixed, with some studies reporting similar levels of life satisfaction among females and males (Elmore & Huebner, 2010; Huebner et al., 2000), and other studies reporting higher life satisfaction among males than females (Diseth, Danielsen, & Samdal, 2012). In addition, stronger associations between job satisfaction and life satisfaction have been reported among women than among men (Babin & Boles, 1998), suggesting that females identify with their studies/work to the extent that it also manifests in their overall life satisfaction (see also Babin & Boles, 1998). However, in the FinEdu study, no gender differences were found in the co-development of career engagement and life satisfaction (Upadyaya & Salmela-Aro, 2016b). These results may reflect the higher gender equality in Nordic countries.

Context-Specific Well-Being: Career Satisfaction

Unlike context-free life satisfaction, career satisfaction reflects one's positive experiences and feelings of one's studies and work. In some studies, career satisfaction has been described as a continuum between one's satisfaction with education and later on with work (Upadyaya & Salmela-Aro, 2015), which also reflects one's subjective, cognitive appraisal of one's overall positive experiences with their career (Huebner & Gilman, 2006), and is thus an important factor describing one's study/work context-specific well-being (Upadyaya & Salmela-Aro, 2016a). Career satisfaction reflects a pleasurable emotional state at education/work contexts, fulfilled needs, and important study/job values (Wefald & Downey, 2009), and includes one's affective reactions to education/work in general or to different aspects of these (e.g., environment, peers/coworkers, teachers/supervisors) (Truxillo, Cadiz, Rineer, Zaniboni, & Fraccaroli, 2012). In addition, several context-free experiences (e.g., overall life quality, life satisfaction) and other context-specific experiences (e.g., satisfaction in family life, relationship quality) (Huebner & Gilman, 2006; Whitley, Huebner, Hills, & Valois, 2012) are positively associated with career satisfaction. Some previous studies have reported declines in one's educational satisfaction (Elmore & Huebner, 2010), whereas work satisfaction research has shown that approximately 25% of the variation in job satisfaction reflects stable characteristics, and that the remainder can be attributed to changing factors in the environment (Dormann, Fay, Zapf, & Frese, 2006).

Similar to life satisfaction, career satisfaction is also often positively associated with career engagement. Career satisfaction and engagement are two distinctive positive dimensions of study/work-related well-being (Rothmann, 2008), with varying antecedents and outcomes (Christian, Garza, & Slaughter, 2011), and are important at all stages of one's education and working life (Truxillo et al., 2012). Career satisfaction focuses on the affective aspects and engagement on the behavioral, emotional, and cognitive aspects of education/work (Schaufeli, Salanova, Gonzalez-Roma, & Bakker, 2002; Truxillo et al., 2012; Upadyaya & Salmela-Aro, 2013). According to the broaden-and-build theory (Fredrickson, 2001), students who are satisfied with their education and life, and experience frequent positive emotions, will exhibit adaptive coping behaviors, feel more engaged, and gain more resources which, in turn, will promote positive upward spirals of success at studies/work. These positive spirals become increasingly important during macro-level challenges in the society (e.g., economic downturns) promoting young adults' life course development (see also Masten et al., 2004). Similarly, the demands-resources model (Demerouti, Bakker, Nachreiner, & Schaufeli, 2001) postulates that high engagement in studies (Salmela-Aro & Upadyaya, 2014) and work protects against ill-being and burnout symptoms, and leads to well-being and higher life, educational, and work satisfaction (Upadyaya & Salmela-Aro, 2016b).

Career satisfaction has typically been investigated as an outcome of engagement (Alarcon & Edwards, 2011), with high engagement resulting in high satisfaction in education/work (Elmore & Huebner, 2010; Giallonardo, Wong, & Iwasiw, 2010). Some studies, however, have shown that frequent experiences of positive emotions and satisfaction in school (Reschly, Huebner, Appleton, & Antaramian, 2008) or at work (Simpson, 2009) lead to broadened coping strategies and career engagement. Work engagement may also mediate the associations between job satisfaction and performance (Yalabik, Popaitoon, Chowne, & Rayton, 2013). Moreover, regardless of the positive associations and changes in the development of career engagement and satisfaction different contexts of studies/work, educational and work transitions, and various macro-level events such as economic downturns, occur in their developmental trajectories. The results of the FinEdu study showed that initially high career satisfaction decreased among young adults during the transition to higher education or work and remained at the decreased level during the global economic downturn, slightly beginning to increase later on (Figure 6.2) (Upadyaya & Salmela-Aro, 2015). However, career engagement increased during the same transition and regardless of the macro-level challenges, young adults were highly engaged in their higher education studies or work. These results suggested that at the beginning of the economic downturn when the young adults were also facing a transition to higher education or work their initially high career satisfaction started to decrease, reflecting the fact that especially the affective aspect of study/work specific well-being is vulnerable to such macro-level events as economic downturn. Behavioral, emotional, and cognitive aspects of study/work specific well-being (e.g., engagement) are less vulnerable to such macro-level challenges. Alternatively, it is possible that economic downturn also increases young adults' engagement in studies/work; macro-level hardship may foster young adults' willingness to study and work and make things better in their personal life, even if they found their studies and work less satisfying than before.

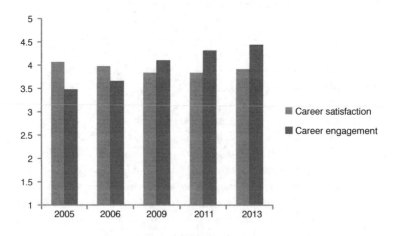

FIGURE 6.2   Co-Development of Career Satisfaction and Career Engagement among Finnish Young Adults

Based on data from Upadyaya and Salmela-Aro (2016a)

Moreover, young adults may be upset about various negative life events their peers are experiencing during economic downturn (Eckenrode & Gore, 1981) which may also boost their own desire to do well and to be more involved in their studies and work.

The decreases in career satisfaction and increases in career engagement may also reflect changes in person–environment fit (Eccles & Roeser, 2009). During educational and work transitions, simultaneous changes occur on both the individual and contextual levels such that the fit between the young adult and the educational institution/workplace is repeatedly reassessed (Eccles & Roeser, 2009). Young adults may find their new career environment more relevant and interesting, and hence a better fit with their study/job values, expectations, and goals (see also Sortheix, Dietrich, Chow, & Salmela-Aro, 2013), which manifests as an increase in their post-transition engagement. However, at the same time, study- and work-related demands and the challenges young adults face at their new study/work environments may be high, thereby decreasing young adults' career satisfaction (de Jonge et al., 2001; Karatzias, Power, Flemming, Lennan, & Swanson, 2002). It is also possible that despite being highly engaged after the transition to work, the availability of good jobs for young adults is limited (e.g., the jobs on offer may be below their expectations, present a low level of challenge, etc.) or non-existing (reflecting the 20% unemployment rate among Finnish young adults during the recession), manifesting as a decrease in job satisfaction. During recession, polarization may also occur; some young adults may face the challenge of unemployment and become cynical towards work possibilities, whereas other young adults may thrive and stay engaged. Moreover, during secondary education, support from various resources (peers, teachers, parents) shows as an increase in educational satisfaction and engagement (Rosenfeld, Richman, & Bowen, 2000). However, after the transition to a new educational institution/workplace, young adults are faced with wider social networks and may find it more difficult to establish new sources of social support, which may manifest as decreases in their career satisfaction. Young adults may also witness hardship among various members of their social networks which manifests as lower career and life satisfaction (see also Eckenrode & Gore, 1981).

The co-development of career engagement and satisfaction was also examined further with the person-oriented approach (Upadyaya & Salmela-Aro, 2015). With this approach, it was possible to examine whether various subgroups of young adults with different initial levels and developmental trajectories of career engagement and satisfaction could be identified. The results showed that two latent trajectory groups of career engagement and satisfaction could be identified, namely a 'high transitional' (87%) and a 'low increasing group' (13%). The high transitional group was described as a high initial level of career satisfaction, which slightly decreased during the economic downturn when the young adults were also facing the transition to higher education/work and then leveled off, and by a relatively high initial level of career engagement, which increased over the transition and then leveled off. The low increasing group was described by a low initial level of career engagement which increased strongly during the recession and over the transition and then leveled off, and a relatively low initial level of career satisfaction which also increased and then leveled off.

These results added to the previous literature by showing that regardless of the initial level of engagement and satisfaction, the developmental changes that occur in career engagement and satisfaction are similar across different homogeneous latent trajectory groups. These results further suggested that the transition to higher education/work promoted positive changes, as shown by the fact that their satisfaction and engagement in the low increasing group raised to the same level as that of the high transitional group (see also Upadyaya & Salmela-Aro, 2013). Thus, regardless of the high challenges presented by the economic downturn and study/work transition, all the young adults in this study were highly engaged in their subsequent higher education studies/work and experienced relatively high career satisfaction. Similarly, previous studies have shown that young adults are willing to put in extra effort and hours to help their organization to succeed during difficult times (Sturges & Guest, 2004). Thus, it is possible that young adults in the FinEdu study were also willing to put 'all in' during the macro-level hardship faced by their society.

Moreover, during secondary education (and before the economic downturn), the high transitional and low increasing groups showed greater differences in their respective levels of career satisfaction and engagement than after the transition to higher education/work, when both engagement and satisfaction became increasingly similar between the groups. These results are partially in line with previous findings that changes are more typical in study engagement (Salmela-Aro & Upadyaya, 2012) and educational satisfaction (Elmore & Huebner, 2010), whereas work engagement (Hakanen, Peeters, & Perhoniemi, 2011) and work satisfaction (Dormann et al., 2006) tend to be relatively stable characteristics of a person. These results add to these previous findings by showing that despite the initial differences in developmental trends, post-transition the latent trajectories became increasingly similar for both subgroups. These results further suggest that experiences of young adults in their new educational institutions/workplaces are similar across the different latent trajectory groups, at least with respect to career engagement and satisfaction. These results may reflect person–environment fit, adaptation (Eccles & Roeser 2009), and the increased demands of the young adults' new educational institutions/workplaces (de Jonge et al., 2001).

Conclusions

This chapter has discussed the co-development of career engagement, life satisfaction, and career satisfaction among young people during economic downturn in Finland. Life satisfaction represent one's context-free well-being, whereas career engagement and satisfaction describe study/work context-specific well-being, career engagement including an emotional, behavioral, and cognitive aspect and career satisfaction an affective aspect of well-being. All these characteristics of well-being are influenced by greater macro-level events, such as economic downturn, during which especially young adults might be vulnerable to unemployment. In the FinEdu Study which followed Finnish young adults during the economic downturn, it was found that young adults do relatively well during macro-level hardship and their career engagement even typically increases. Young adults are typically highly motivated to work and their high work expectations remain high during economic downturn (De Hauw & De Vos, 2010). However, their optimism may decrease (De Hauw & De Vos, 2010) which in the FinEdu study showed as decreases in life satisfaction and career satisfaction.

Acknowledgments

The research reported in this article has been funded by grants from the Finnish Work Environmental Fund (114417) and from the Academy of Finland (139168, 273872).

References

Alarcon, G. M., & Edwards, J. M. (2011). The relationship of engagement, job satisfaction and turnover intentions. *Stress and Health, 27*(3), 294–298. doi: 10.1002/smi.1365

Arnett, J. J. (2000). Emerging adulthood: A theory of development from the late teens through the twenties. *American Psychologist, 55*(5), 469–480.

Babin, B. J., & Boles, J. S. (1998). Employee behavior in a service environment: a model and test of potential differences between men and women. *The Journal of Marketing, 62*(2), 77–91.

Chen, X., Morin, A. J. S., Parker, P., & Marsh, H. W. (2015). Developmental investigation of the domain-specific nature of the life satisfaction construct across the post-school transition. *Developmental Psychology, 51*(8), 1074–1085. doi: 10.1037/a0039477

Christian, M. S., Garza, A. S., & Slaughter, J. E. (2011). Work engagement: A quantitative review and test of its relations with task and contextual performance. *Personnel Psychology, 64*(1), 89–136. doi: 10.1111/j.1744-6570.2010.01203.x

Clark, T., & Heath, A. (2015). *Hard times: Inequality, recession, aftermath.* London: Yale University Press.

Cohn, M. A., Fredrickson, B. L., Brown, S. L., Mikels, J. A., & Conway, A. M. (2009). Happiness unpacked: positive emotions increase life satisfaction by building resilience. *Emotion, 9*(3), 361–368. doi: 10.1037/a0015952

Csikszentmihalyi, M. (1990). *Flow: The psychology of optimal experience.* New York: Harper and Row. doi: 10.1037/0022-0663.82.4.664

De Hauw, S., & De Vos, A. (2010). Millennials' career perspective and psychological contract expectations: Does the recession lead to lowered expectations? *Journal of Business and Psychology, 25*(2), 293–302. doi: 10.1007/s10869-010-9162-9

de Jonge, J., Dormann, C., Janssen, P. P., Dollard, M. F., Landeweerd, J. A., & Nijhuis, F. J. (2001). Testing reciprocal relationships between job characteristics and psychological well being: A cross-lagged structural equation model. *Journal of Occupational and organizational Psychology, 74*(1), 29–46. doi: 10.1348/096317901167217

Demerouti, E., Bakker, A., Nachreiner, F., & Schaufeli, W. (2001). The job demands-resources model of burnout. *Journal of Applied Psychology, 86*(3), 499–512. doi: 10.1037/0021-9010.86.3.499

Diseth, Å., Danielsen, A. G., & Samdal, O. (2012). A path analysis of basic need support, self-efficacy, achievement goals, life satisfaction and academic achievement level among secondary school students. *Educational Psychology: An International Journal of Experimental Educational Psychology, 32*(3), 335–354. doi: 10.1080/01443410.2012.657159

Di Tella, R., MacCulloch, R. J., & Oswald, A. J. (2003). The macroeconomics of happiness. *Review of Economics and Statistics, 85*(4), 809–827. doi: 10.1162/003465303772815745

Dormann, C., Fay, D., Zapf, D., & Frese, M. (2006). A state trait analysis of job satisfaction: On the effect of core self evaluations. *Applied Psychology, 55*(1), 27–51. doi: 10.1111/j.1464-0597.2006.00227.x

Eccles, J. S., & Roeser, R.W. (2009). Schools, academic motivation, and stage-environment fit. In R. M. Lerner and L. Steinber (Eds), *Handbook of adolescent psychology*, 3rd ed. (pp. 404–434). Hoboken, NJ: John Wiley & Sons.

Eckenrode, J., & Gore, S. (1981). Stressful events and social supports: The significance of context. In B. H. Gottlieb (Ed.), *Social networks and social support* (pp. 43–68). Beverley Hills, CA: Sage.

Elmore, G. M., & Huebner, S. E. (2010). Adolescents' satisfaction with school experiences: Relationships with demographics, attachment relationships, and school engagement behavior. *Psychology in the Schools, 47*(6), 525–537.

Erdogan, B., Bauer, T. N., Truxillo, D. M., & Mansfield, L. R. (2012). Whistle while you work: A review of the life satisfaction literature. *Journal of Management, 38*(4), 1038–1083. doi: 10.1177/0149206311429379

Fletcher, A. J. (2015). Trading futures: Economism and gender in a changing climate. *International Social Work, 58*(3), 364–374. doi: 10.1177/0020872814556825

Fredrickson, B. L. (2001). The role of positive emotions in positive psychology: The broaden-and-build theory of positive emotions. *American Psychologist, 56*(3), 218–226. doi: 10.1037/0003-066X.56.3.218

Gassman-Pines, A., Gibson-Davis, C. M., & Ananat, E. O. (2015). How economic downturns affect children's development: An interdisciplinary perspective on pathways of influence. *Child Development Perspectives, 9*(4), 233–238. doi: 10.1111/cdep.12137

Giallonardo, L. M., Wong, C. A., & Iwasiw, C. L. (2010). Authentic leadership of preceptors: predictor of new graduate nurses› work engagement and job satisfaction. *Journal of nursing management, 18*(8), 993–1003. doi: 10.1111/j.1365-2834.2010.01126.x

Hagström, T., & Gamberale, F. (1995). Young people's work motivation and value orientation. *Journal of Adolescence, 18*(4), 475–490. doi:10.1006/jado.1995.1034

Hakanen, J. J., & Schaufeli, W. B. (2012). Do burnout and work engagement predict depressive symptoms and life satisfaction? A three-wave seven-year prospective study. *Journal of Affective Disorders, 141*(2), 415–424. doi: 10.1016/j.jad.2012.02.043

Hakanen, J. J., Bakker, A. B., & Schaufeli, W. B. (2006). Burnout and work engagement among teachers. *Journal of School Psychology*, *43*(6), 495–513. doi: 10.1016/j. jsp.2005.11.001

Hakanen, J. J., Peeters, M. C., & Perhoniemi, R. (2011). Enrichment processes and gain spirals at work and at home: A 3-year cross-lagged panel study. *Journal of Occupational and Organizational Psychology*, *84*(1), 8–30. doi: 10.1111/j.2044-8325.2010.02014.x

Hakanen, J. J., Perhoniemi, R., & Toppinen-Tanner, S. (2008). Positive gain spirals at work: From job resources to work engagement, personal initiative and work-unit innovativeness. *Journal of Vocational Behavior*, *73*(1), 78–91. doi: 10.1016/j. jvb.2008.01.003

Harter, J. K., Schmidt, F. L., & Hayes, T. L. (2002). Business-unit-level relationship between employee satisfaction, employee engagement, and business outcomes: A meta-analysis. *Journal of Applied Psychology*, *87*(2), 268–279. doi: 10.1037/0021-9010.87.2.268

Huebner, E. S., & Gilman, R. (2006). Students who like and dislike school. *Applied Research in Quality of Life*, *1*(2), 139–150. doi: 10.1007/s11482-006-9001-3

Huebner, E. S., Drane, W., & Valois, R. F. (2000). Levels and demographic correlates of adolescent life satisfaction reports. *School Psychology International*, *21*(3), 281–292. doi: 10.1177/0143034300213005

Huebner, E. S., Valois, R. F., Paxton, R., & Drane, W. (2005). Middle school students' perceptions of quality of life. *Journal of Happiness Studies*, *6*(1), 15–24. doi: 10.1007/s10902-004-1170-x

Jones, M. D. (2006). Which is a better predictor of job performance: Job satisfaction or life satisfaction. *Journal of Behavioral and Applied Management*, *8*(1), 20–42.

Karatzias, A., Power, K. G., Flemming, J., Lennan, F., & Swanson, V. (2002). The role of demographics, personality variables and school stress on predicting school satisfaction/dissatisfaction: Review of the literature and research findings. *Educational Psychology*, *22*(1), 33–50. doi: 10.1080/01443410120101233

Lewis, A. D., Huebner, E. S., Malone, P. S., & Valois, R. F. (2011). Life satisfaction and student engagement in adolescents. *Journal of Youth and Adolescence*, *40*(3), 249–262. doi: 10.1007/s10964-010-9517-6

Li, Y., & Lerner, R. M. (2011). Trajectories of school engagement during adolescence: Implications for grades, depression, delinquency, and substance use. *Developmental Psychology*, *47*(1), 233–247. doi: 10.1037/a0021307

Lucas, R. E. (2007). Adaptation and the set-point model of subjective well-being does happiness change after major life events? *Current Directions in Psychological Science*, *16*(2), 75–79. doi: 10.1111/j.1467-8721.2007.00479.x

Masten, A. S., Burt, K. B., Roisman, G. I., Obradovic, J., Long, J. D., & Tellegen, A. (2004). Resources and resilience in the transition to adulthood: Continuity and change. *Development and Psychopathology*, *16*(4), 1071–1094. doi: 10.1017/S0954579404040143

Masten, A. S., Desjardins, C. D., McCormick, C. M., Kuo, Sally I-Chun, & Long, J. D. (2010). The significance of childhood competence and problems for adult success in work: A developmental cascade analysis. *Development and Psychopathology*, *22*(3), 679–694.

Ou, S. R. (2008). Do GED recipients differ from graduates and school dropouts? Findings from an inner-city cohort. *Urban Education*, *43*(1), 83–117. doi: 10.1177/0042085907305187

Pavot, W., & Diener, E. (1993). Review of the satisfaction with life scale. *Psychological Assessment, 5*(2), 164–172. doi: 10.1037/1040-3590.5.2.164

Reschly, A. L., Huebner, E. S., Appleton, J. J., & Antaramian, S. (2008). Engagement as flourishing: The contribution of positive emotions and coping to adolescents' engagement at school and with learning. *Psychology in the Schools, 45*(5), 419–431. doi: 10.1002/pits.20306

Rosenfeld, L. B., Richman, J. M., & Bowen, G. L. (2000). Social support networks and school outcomes: The centrality of the teacher. *Child and Adolescent Social Work Journal, 17*(3), 205–226. doi: 10.1023/A:1007535930286

Rothmann, S. (2008). Job satisfaction, occupational stress, burnout and work engagement as components of work-related wellbeing: empirical research. *SA Journal of Industrial Psychology, 34*(3), 11–16.

Salanova, M., Agut, S., & Peiro, J. M. (2005). Linking organizational resources and work engagement to employee performance and customer loyalty: The mediation of service climate. *Journal of Applied Psychology, 90*(6), 1217–1227. doi: 10.1037/0021-9010.90.6.1217

Salmela-Aro, K., & Upadyaya, K. (2012). The schoolwork engagement inventory: Energy, dedication and absorption (EDA). *European Journal of Psychological Assessment, 28*(1), 60–67. doi: 10.1027/1015-5759/a000091

Salmela-Aro, K., & Upadyaya, K. (2014). School burnout and engagement in the context of the demands-resources model. *British Journal of Educational Psychology, 84*(1), 137–151. doi: 10.1111/bjep.12018

Schaufeli, W. B., Bakker, A. B., & Salanova, M. (2006). The measurement of work engagement with a short questionnaire: A cross-national study. *Educational and Psychological Measurement, 66*(4), 701–716. doi: 10.1177/0013164405282471

Schaufeli, W. B., Salanova, M., Gonzalez-Roma, V., & Bakker, A. B. (2002). The measurement of engagement and burnout: A two sample confirmatory factor analytic approach. *Journal of Happiness Studies, 3*(1), 71–92. doi: 10.1023/A:1015630930326

Seligman, M. E. P., & Csikszentmihalyi, M. (2000). Positive psychology: An introduction. *American Psychologist, 55*(1), 5–14. doi: 10.1037/0003-066X.55.1.5

Seppälä, P., Mauno, S., Feldt, T., Hakanen, J., Kinnunen, U., Tolvanen, A., & Schaufeli, W. (2009). The construct validity of the Utrecht Work Engagement Scale: Multisample and longitudinal evidence. *Journal of Happiness Studies, 10*(4), 459–481. doi: 10.1007/s10902-008-9100-y

Seppälä, P., Hakanen, J., Mauno, S., Perhoniemi, R., Tolvanen, A., & Schaufeli, W. (2015). Stability and change model of job resources and work engagement: A seven-year three-wave follow-up study. *European Journal of Work and Organizational Psychology, 24*(3), 360–375.

Simpson, M. R. (2009). Engagement at work: A review of the literature. *International Journal of Nursing Studies, 46*(7), 1012–1024. doi: 10.1016/j.ijnurstu.2008.05.003

Sortheix, F. M., Dietrich, J., Chow, A., & Salmela-Aro, K. (2013). The role of career values for work engagement during the transition to working life. *Journal of Vocational Behavior, 83*(3), 466–475. doi: 10.1016/j.jvb.2013.07.003

Stevens, A. H., & Schaller, J. (2011). Short-run effects of parental job loss on children's academic achievement. *Economics of Education Review, 30*(2), 289–299. doi: 10.1016/j.econedurev.2010.10.002

Sturges, J., & Guest, D. (2004). Working to live or living to work? Work/life balance early in the career. *Human Resource Management Journal, 14*(4), 5–20. doi: 10.1111/j.1748-8583.2004.tb00130.x

Suldo, S. M., Riley, K. N., & Shaffer, E. J. (2006). Academic correlates of children and adolescents' life satisfaction. *School Psychology International, 27*(5), 567–582. doi: 10.1177/0143034306073411

Truxillo, D. M., Cadiz, D. M., Rineer, J. R., Zaniboni, S., & Fraccaroli, F. (2012). A lifespan perspective on job design: Fitting the job and the worker to promote job satisfaction, engagement, and performance. *Organizational Psychology Review, 2*(4), 340–360. doi: 10.1080/1359432X.2013.782288

Upadyaya, K., & Salmela-Aro, K. (2013). Development of school engagement in association with academic success and well-being in varying social contexts: A review of empirical research. *European Psychologist, 18*(2), 136–147. doi: 10.1027/1016-9040/a000143

Upadyaya, K., & Salmela-Aro, K. (2015). Development of early vocational behavior: Parallel associations between career engagement and satisfaction. *Journal of Vocational Behavior, 90*, 66–74. doi:10.1016/j.jvb.2015.07.008

Upadyaya, K., & Salmela-Aro, K. (2016a). *Career satisfaction and well-being.* Manuscript in preparation.

Upadyaya, K., & Salmela-Aro, K. (2016b). *Young adults' life satisfaction and engagement: Trajectories across the transition to higher education and work.* Manuscript in preparation.

Wefald, A. J., & Downey, R. G. (2009). Construct dimensionality of engagement and its relation with satisfaction. *The Journal of Psychology, 143*(1), 91–112. doi: 10.3200/JRLP.143.1.91-112

Whitley, A. M., Huebner, E. S., Hills, K. J., & Valois, R. F. (2012). Can students be too happy in school? The optimal level of school satisfaction. *Applied Research in Quality of Life, 7*(4), 337–350. doi: 10.1007/s11482-012-9167-9

Yalabik, Z. Y., Popaitoon, P., Chowne, J. A., & Rayton, B. A. (2013). Work engagement as a mediator between employee attitudes and outcomes. *The International Journal of Human Resource Management, 24*(14), 2799–2823. doi: 10.1080/09585192.2013.7638

7

YOUTH ADAPTATION DURING THE CURRENT GREAT ECONOMIC RECESSION IN GREECE

Risk and Resilience

Frosso Motti-Stefanidi, Nancy Papathanasiou, Stefanos Mastrotheodoros, and Vassilis Pavlopoulos

During the past eight years the international community experienced one of the deepest economic recessions since the Great Depression of the 1930s. It was triggered by a financial meltdown that started in the United States but soon spread around the globe. Great economic recessions involve aggregate or systemic shocks that occur in the wider economy of countries. They differ from idiosyncratic economic shocks in that large segments of society are affected simultaneously and systematically (Lundberg & Wuermli, 2012). Individuals and families experience such shocks through job loss, a decrease in income, debt, repossession of houses, and evictions, which lead to economic pressure and uncertainty.

Many countries in the world were, and some still are, struck by the latest economic recession. However, significant diversity was observed in the degree to which the recession affected different countries (UNICEF, 2014). In Europe, southern European countries (Greece, Cyprus, Italy, Portugal, Spain), as well as Croatia and Ireland, were among the worst hit. Great variability was also observed in the way countries responded to the crisis and supported the vulnerable parts of their population (UNICEF, 2014). Some countries were better positioned to weather the economic shock. They had strong social protection measures already in place and were able to rapidly and effectively roll out safety nets. A few European countries, such as Finland and Norway, were actually able to decrease poverty for children in vulnerable households, such as for children from migrant and single-parent families, and/or from low socioeconomic status and large families.

Greece is one of the countries where child poverty increased the most (UNICEF, 2014). The number of children whose families were income-poor (income below the poverty line) increased between 2008 and 2012 from 23% to 40.5%, and those who were severely materially deprived (e.g. cannot afford to pay rent, heat their home, eat meat, or proteins regularly etc.) from 10.4% to 20.9% (see Kokkevi, Stavrou, Kanavou, & Fotiou, 2014a; Kokkevi et al., 2014b). A report commissioned by UNICEF (Kokkevi et al., 2014a) revealed that in spite of parents' best efforts to protect their children from experiencing the negative consequences of the recession, 11–15-year-old adolescents were fully aware of the economic problems troubling their families.

Economic recessions have the potential to disrupt and do permanent damage to the adaptation, mental health and development of young people (Lundberg & Wuermli, 2012). However, they are macro-level phenomena concerning the wider economy of a country. How do they come to have such a negative impact on youth? It has been argued that it is not necessarily the economic recession per se that leads to problems in the adaptation of young people (Lundberg & Wuermli, 2012). Instead, it is mainly the effect that it has on the family and other proximal contexts (such as teachers and schools) that affects their development.

Thus, the objective economic strain may result in economic pressure and insecurity in the family, which in turn may increase parental anxiety and depression, and relatedly family conflict, thus altering in a negative direction youth's developmental context (Conger et al., 1992). What is at stake in the long run is the development of healthy, productive, and effective adults.

The purpose of this chapter is to address the question: "Who among youth living in Greece during the period of the Great Recession adapt well and why?" We examine group and individual differences in youth's adaptation and mental health from a risk and resilience developmental perspective. Thus, the chapter focuses on positive adaptation during the economic crisis and revolves around two axes, one related to risk (Does the Greek economic crisis constitute a risk for youth's adaptation and well-being?) and the other to resilience (Why do some young people adapt well while others do less well?).

We address these questions based on results from the Athena Study of Resilient Adaptation (AStRA) Greek project as well as based on results from other studies conducted in Greece during the crisis. The AStRA project involved a comparison between two well-matched cohorts of adolescents living in the greater Athens area, one assessed before the crisis (see Motti-Stefanidi, 2014) and the other in the midst of the crisis (Motti-Stefanidi & Asendorpf, in press). Data were collected in both cohorts from schools in the same socially disadvantaged neighborhoods with a high proportion of immigrants. A total of more than 2,000 12-year-old adolescents, at wave 1, were followed once a year for 3 years through middle school. We assessed different domains of adaptation and well-being, as well as potential risks and resources for adaptation with repeated measures, using multiple methods and informants.

The chapter is organized in three sections. The first section examines core concepts of the resilience developmental framework. The second section examines whether the economic recession places youth adaptation and mental health at risk. The third section examines social and personal resources that promote and/or protect positive immigrant youth adaptation during this period.

The Resilience Developmental Framework

The resilience developmental framework guided the research questions addressed by the AStRA project and provided the lenses through which other Greek studies on the effect of the economic crisis on youth are examined. Resilience refers to the capacity for adaptation to challenges that threaten the function or development of a dynamic system, manifested in pathways and patterns of positive adaptation during or following exposure to significant risk or adversity (Masten, 2014). Resilience in an individual is inferred from two fundamental judgments about the individual's adaptation: First, the person must be, or have been, challenged by exposure to significant risk or adversity, and second, he/she must be "doing ok" – functioning or developing well in spite of exposures to adversity or risk.

Positive adaptation in young people often is defined based on how well they are doing with respect to age-salient developmental tasks (Masten, 2014; McCormick, Kuo, & Masten, 2011). These tasks reflect the expectations and standards for behavior and achievement that parents, teachers, and societies set for individuals over the life span in a particular context and time in history. As they grow older, children usually (though not always) come to share these criteria and evaluate their own success by these expected accomplishments. Adaptive success is multidimensional and developmental in nature.

Developmental tasks vary over the life course of the individual. Each developmental period is characterized by a group of salient developmental tasks that provide criteria for judging who is doing well. During adolescence, positive adaptation with respect to developmental tasks may be judged based on external behavior, such as success in school, having and maintaining close friendships/ being liked by peers, knowing or obeying the laws of society, civic engagement, or on internal adaptation, such as establishment of a cohesive, integrated and multifaceted sense of identity. Success in these developmental tasks does not mean that youth should exhibit "ideal" or "superb" effectiveness, but rather they should be "doing adequately well."

It should be noted here that whereas resilience investigators define positive adaptation as doing adequately well or "okay", the Positive Youth Development

(PYD) framework, which guides researchers' thinking and research in many chapters of this book, stresses indexes of optimal functioning. For PYD researchers, thriving is a key index of positive adaptation during adolescence and emerging adulthood. However, the question arises whether socialization agents across the globe consider thriving a key developmental goal and an index of youth's positive adaptation. The validity of this assumption needs to be tested in other cultures. The resilience approach to positive adaptation allows socialization agents from different cultures to define their own criteria for positive adaptation.

Why are these adaptation indices important? Families and societies value and attend to achievements in salient developmental tasks because these accomplishments are widely assumed to forecast future success (Masten & Cicchetti, 2016). Thus, how well developing individuals do with respect to developmental tasks of an earlier stage forecasts how well they will do with respect to developmental tasks of later stages. Research has shown significant continuity in main domains of adaptation, including major domains such as peer acceptance, academic achievement, externalizing (vs. rule-abiding conduct), and internalizing symptoms (see Masten, 2014). Furthermore, research has shown that over time the quality of functioning in one domain of adaptation may spread or cascade to other domains. For example, conduct problems in childhood have been shown to have negative cascading effects later in life, leading to lower academic achievement by adolescence, and indirectly, through academic achievement, to increases in symptoms of anxiety and depression in young adulthood. In contrast, positive adaptation in childhood with respect to key developmental tasks predicted success in early adulthood, through multiple possible cascade pathways (Burt, Coatsworth, & Masten, 2016).

To identify resilience, there also must be evidence of past or present threat, trauma, or negative life experiences in the life of the individual. Such hazards often co-occur or pile up in the lives of individuals or families and as risk levels rise the level of average problems or symptoms often increases as well, suggesting a cumulative risk (or dose) gradient (Obradović, Shaffer, & Masten, 2012). In the absence of risk or adversity, positive adaptation is not considered an expression of resilience but rather of competence. The resilience literature includes studies of many different kinds of risks, such as high-risk status variables (e.g. immigrant status, low SES, single-parent family), exposure to traumatic and stressful experiences (e.g. maltreatment, community violence, war), or biological risk markers (e.g. low birth weight, physical illness).

The goal of resilience research is not only to identify who is well-adapted in spite of adversity, but also to identify the processes that explain how positive adaptation was achieved. To account for group and individual differences in adaptation in the context of risk, potential predictors of positive adaptation have been examined at multiple levels of context and analysis (Masten, 2014). Two broad types of influences that counteract or mitigate the potential effects of adversity on adaptation and development have been described. The first type of influence or effects is called promotive, referring to factors that have a generally positive effect on adaptation independent of risk level. These factors reflect "main effects" in statistical terms and these effects are sometimes described as assets, resources, compensatory effects, or social and human capital. Promotive factors support positive adaptation independently of risk or adversity in the individual's life, with observable effects both in low and high adversity. The second type of influence or effect is conditional, with greater effects under more adverse conditions. These influences reflect moderating influences on risk or adversity, suggesting protective roles. Protective factors have a special function when conditions are adverse or risky, and they reflect interaction (risk × moderator) effects on adaptation.

However, risk, promotive, and protective effects are functional in nature, defined in part by the context (see Masten & Cicchetti, 2016). The same characteristic of an individual or a family can serve different functions depending on the domain of adaptation under consideration, the context, or the nature of the threat. In the context of maltreatment or war, for example, fearfulness and vigilance may well be adaptive and protective, whereas in a safe and supportive context, the same behaviors could be maladaptive. Similarly, parents who monitor their children closely in a dangerous environment may be viewed as "overprotective" in a safe context.

Is the Economic Recession a Risk for Youth's Adaptation?

In this section we will examine whether and how the Great Economic Recession in Greece has affected the adaptation and well-being of adolescents. Has the crisis placed their adaptation and well-being at high risk? The presentation will be structured around key developmental tasks and indices of mental health, which were assessed in the AStRA project (see Motti-Stefanidi & Asendorpf, in press). As was already mentioned, two cohorts of adolescents were compared, one in middle school before the economic crisis and the other during the economic crisis. Wherever results from other Greek studies are available they are also reported. These studies, which are often conducted by child psychiatrists, have mostly focused on psychological symptoms and disorders. Interestingly, the literature reveals a paradoxical mixture of risk and resilience.

First, we studied the effect of the economic recession on youth's school engagement. School engagement is an important index of adaptation as it may protect students from dropping out of school early (Fredricks, Blumenfeld, & Paris, 2004). Two economists, Ferreira and Schady (2009), reviewed on behalf of the World Bank a number of studies that examined the effects of economic shocks on children's schooling and engagement. They found that in middle-

and high-income countries, such as Greece, education outcomes during a major economic crisis are counter-cyclical; school enrolment, engagement, and attendance increase, instead of decreasing.

The AStRA project included two indices of school engagement, namely teacher-rated behavioral engagement and students' unexcused absences (Fredricks et al., 2004). The cohort comparison on these two indices produced contradictory results. Whereas crisis-cohort students' behavioral engagement did not differ from that of the pre-crisis cohort, the former had significantly more unexcused absences than the latter. However, the increase in absenteeism during the crisis seemed to be driven by a few students in particular classrooms that were often absent. These results held for Greek and immigrant students alike. Thus, students' motivation and investment in school did not diminish during the economic recession.

Second, we studied the effect of the economic recession on youth's academic achievement. For this purpose, we retrieved from school records students' GPA in core courses. In general, the extant literature shows that youth who live under conditions of socioeconomic disadvantage have lower academic achievement than their better off counterparts (McLoyd et al., 2009; Schoon et al., 2002). Even though economic loss incurred during a great recession may not necessarily push a family into poverty, it may expose its members to circumstances and stressors that usually chronically poor families experience (McLoyd et al., 2009), such as low per capita income, unmet material needs, and difficulty making ends meet (Conger & Donellan, 2007). In this line, Elder (1974) reported worse academic achievement in children of the Great Depression whose families experienced economic hardship.

Counter to expectations, results from the AStRA project revealed that crisis-cohort Greek students, compared with pre-crisis-cohort Greeks, had significant better academic achievement. Immigrant students' academic achievement was in the same direction, but did not reach significance due to a large standard error. This finding is consistent with the finding on school engagement. Youth in middle school during the crisis, compared to youth before the crisis, seem equally, and in some cases more, motivated to do well in school. Greek families have traditionally considered education as a vehicle for upward social mobility (Charalambidis, Maratou-Alipranti, & Hadjiyanni, 2004). It may be the case that in the context of the economic recession Greek families may consider education as the means for their children to overcome its impact.

Third, we studied the effect of the crisis on students' mental health. Conduct was teacher-rated and the two indices of psychological well-being examined, namely self-esteem and emotional symptoms were self-rated. The extant literature shows that family economic pressure increases the likelihood that youth will present depressed mood and externalizing behavior (e.g., Conger et al., 1992; Lempers, Clark-Lempers, & Simons, 1989; Solantaus, Leinonen, & Punamäki, 2004). However, socioeconomic disadvantage is more strongly linked with externalizing than with internalizing problems (Duncan, Magnuson, & Votruba-Drzal, 2015; Solantaus et al., 2004).

The AStRA project results show a pervasive increase of conduct problems during the economic crisis in both Greek and immigrant students. The difference between pre-crisis and crisis cohorts on conduct problems was not only significant but also large. This finding is in agreement with a number of studies (e.g. Conger et al., 1992; Lempers et al., 1989; Solantaus et al., 2004). The family stress model of economic hardship can guide the formulation of the hypothesis that economic pressure on the family may affect parenting and, thus, lead to conduct problems in children and youth (Conger & Donnellan, 2007). This point will be further discussed in the next section.

However, contrary to expectations, crisis cohort adolescents did not report worse psychological well-being (either lower self-esteem or more emotional symptoms) than pre-crisis adolescents. This finding held for both Greek and immigrant students. Kokkevi et al. (2014b), who also studied a normative Greek sample but focused on more serious mental health problems, did not find an increase in the rate of attempted suicides and running-away from home among 16-year-olds during the economic crisis. Actually, they report that the prevalence of both behaviors was very close to the averages in other European countries. One hypothesis is that parents and extended family might play a protective role for youth's mental health during these trying times (Georgas, 2006). Greek grandparents play a key role in children's lives providing emotional and financial support, often from their very low pensions, to their children and grandchildren.

Two more studies based on nationwide data, which included young people, focused on emotional disorders and found contradictory results. Fountoulakis et al. (2013), based on official data concerning completed suicides, accidental falls, and poisoning retrieved from the Hellenic Statistical Authority, found no increase in suicidality during the economic crisis in Greece and no relationship between suicidal rates with socioeconomic indices either. In contrast to these findings, Economou, Madianos, Peppou, Patelakis, and Stefanis (2012), who conducted two nationwide cross-sectional telephone surveys, one before and one during the crisis, found that, among others, young people were at increased risk during the crisis, compared to before the crisis (prevalence rates 8.2% vs. 3.3%, respectively), for developing major depression.

At first glance, some of the findings presented in this section seem contradictory. On the one hand, we found first, that students exhibited more conduct problems during the crisis compared to students before the crisis, and, second, that they continued to be motivated to do well in school, and, actually, received better grades. On the other hand, some of the other studies focusing on youth psychopathology during the crisis found a significant increase particularly in the prevalence of major depression. How could we explain these seemingly contradictory findings?

In what concerns the AStRA project results, they seem to be inconsistent with the within-cohort positive correlation between positive conduct with engagement and achievement. However, the different correlations of conduct with engagement and achievement *within* versus *between* cohorts suggest different causal mechanisms for the *within* versus *between* effects. Thus, some antisocial students may determine the increase in conduct problems during the crisis, whereas other students may invest more in learning and doing well in school in order to cope with the crisis. These hypotheses refer to two different crisis-specific mechanisms. In what concerns the suggested increase in serious internalizing problems during the crisis, we could argue that this finding strengthens the argument that there are significant individual differences in the way young people react to, and deal with, the economic hardship afflicted by the Great Economic Recession.

Why Do Some Young People Adapt Well during the Crisis While Others Do Less Well?

In the previous section, we examined whether and how the Great Economic Recession in Greece affects youth's adaptation and well-being. Evidence indicates a mixture of risk and resilience. Some youth show resilient adaptation during the crisis whereas others are not as successful. These findings suggest that certain resources contribute to youth's positive adaptation despite the adversity in their lives. What makes the difference for youth who do well in spite of the social challenges that they face?

Resources, just as risks, may stem from youth's social context and/or from their own individual attributes (Masten, 2014). As was previously discussed, the crisis is not expected to directly affect youth's adaptation and well-being. Instead its influence is filtered through, and transmitted by, youth's proximal contexts, mainly the family but also schools, teachers, peers etc. Contexts where the young person is in direct interaction with others are the drivers of their adaptation and development. They may render young people vulnerable to the impact of the economic hardship but have also the power to buffer them from its effect.

The role of the family in youth's adaptation during times of economic hardship has received the lion's share of attention from scientists. Parents' psychological reaction to the crisis, potential marital conflict, and their parenting have been shown to mediate the relation between economic hardship and youth's adaptation and mental health (Conger & Donnellan, 2007; Conger et al., 1992; Lempers et al., 1989; Solantaus et al., 2004). The family's inability to make ends meet (e.g. pay bills, provide for children), and the pressure to cut back on everyday expenses in order to live within available means may result in their feeling inadequate and hopeless, as well as in a loss of status. These may lead to increases in parental anxiety and depression, and in some cases in substance abuse, which in turn may lead to severe family conflict, domestic violence, and family abandonment. As a result, parents may withdraw from their children, even become hostile towards them. There may be a decrease in learning and cognitive stimulation within the home, and in enforcement of rules and routines.

There is a lack of empirical evidence on the role of the family, or any other proximal context, on youth's adaptation during this period of economic recession. We examined based on the crisis-cohort longitudinal data of the Greek AStRA project whether different dimensions of parenting longitudinally mediated the relation between, on the one hand, family economic problems and hardship and, on the other, different domains of youth's adaptation (Motti-Stefanidi, Pavlopoulos, & Asendorpf, 2016). We found that the effects of family variation in economic problems on student self-efficacy and conduct are fully mediated by parenting for both boys and girls, and similarly for Greeks and immigrants. These results, which are based on longitudinal, rather than cross-sectional, mediations, corroborate previous findings.

Thus, depending on the way the family navigates through, and copes during, these difficult times will either place their children at risk for adaptation difficulties or may, in contrast, function as a resource for their adaptation and mental health. Some families have personal and social resources that support them during times of adversity. The argument presented earlier, that the extended Greek family, and particularly grandparents, often provide emotional and financial support to their children and grandchildren, is a case in point. However, this is a hypothesis which needs to be tested. In our own AStRA study it would require to test for a moderated mediation on the findings previously presented.

Even though contexts play a preponderant role for youth's adaptation, they are clearly not its sole determinant. Young people are active agents in their development. Their personal attributes are expected to contribute, both independently and in interaction with contextual factors, to their adaptation during times of high adversity, such as this. We tested this hypothesis based on our two matched (pre-crisis and during the crisis) cohorts of adolescents (Asendorpf & Motti-Stefanidi, 2016). We examined whether the Big Five personality factors moderated the relation between cohorts (historical effect) and different domains of youth's adaptation.

We found that youth's personality characteristics played a special role during the crisis. For example, before the crisis, low emotional stability predicted lower self-esteem than high emotional stability. However, during the crisis youth rated high on emotional stability did not differ from their counterparts before the crisis, whereas youth rated low on emotional stability had significantly lower, and with a large difference, self-esteem. Thus, emotional stability played a protective role for youth's adaptation during the economic crisis.

Conclusions

The Great Economic recession has had, and actually continues to have, a significant impact on people in Greece. It has brought great economic hardship to families, which often had to drastically change their style of living in order to make ends meet. The AStRA project data as well as other studies conducted in Greece during the crisis reveal that youth's adaptation with respect to core developmental tasks, as well as their mental health show signs both of risk and resilience. Sometimes in agreement with the international literature and other times contrary to expectations, significant individual differences emerge in the way young people living in Greece cope and adapt in the context of this adversity. Some young people seem more motivated, try harder, and invest more in their learning, others show heightened conduct problems, and still others exhibit serious psychological disorders. An examination of factors and processes that either place at risk or protect youth's adaptation shows that both context and youth's characteristics contribute to their adaptation and mental health. More research focusing on positive adaptation, instead of on psychopathology, and on younger ages, as well as on the role of other proximal contexts, such as the school, for adaptation during this period is needed. Findings will help us understand how to support youth to better cope with the situation and how to promote and protect their positive adaptation and development in these challenging conditions.

Acknowledgments

Preparation of this chapter was supported by an Excellence grant to Frosso Motti-Stefanidi co-funded by the European Social Fund and Greek National Resources (ESPA-Excellence II).

References

Asendorpf, J. B., & Motti-Stefanidi, F. (2016). Personality effects on adaptation and well-being moderated by environmental risk: A study of the Greek crisis. Manuscript in preparation.

Burt, K. B., Coatsworth, J. D., & Masten, A. S. (2016). Competence and psychopathology in development. In D. Cicchetti (Ed.), *Developmental Psychopathology* (3rd ed., Vol. IV, pp. 435–484). New York: Wiley.

Charalambidis, D., Maratou-Alipranti, L., & Hadjiyanni, A. (2004). *Recent Social Trends in Greece 1960–2000*. Montreal: McGill-Queen's University Press.

Conger, R. D., & Donnellan, M. B. (2007). An interactionist perspective on the socioeconomic context of human development. *Annual Review of Psychology, 58*, 175–199. doi: 10.1146/annurev.psych.58.110405.085551

Conger, R. D., Conger, K. J., Elder, G. H., Lorenz, F. O., Simons, R. L., & Whitbeck, L. B. (1992). A family process model of economic hardship and adjustment of early adolescent boys. *Child development*, *63*(3), 526–541. doi: 10.1111/j.1467-8624.1992. tb01644.x

Duncan, G. J., Magnuson, K., & Votruba-Drzal, E. (2015). Children and socioeconomic status. In M. E. Lamb & R. M. Lerner (Eds), *Handbook of Child Psychology and Developmental Science: Vol. 4. Ecological Settings and Processes* (7th ed., pp. 534–573). Hoboken, NJ: Wiley & Sons.

Economou, M., Madianos, M., Peppou, L.E., Patelakis, A., & Stefanis, C.N. (2012). Major depression in the era of economic crisis: A replication of a cross-sectional study across Greece. *Journal of Affective Disorders*, *145*(3), 308–314. doi: http://dx.doi.org/10.1016/j.jad.2012.08.008

Elder, G. H. (1974). *Children of the Great Depression: Social change in Life Experience*. Chicago, IL: University of Chicago Press.

Ferreira, F. H., & Schady, N. (2009). Aggregate economic shocks, child schooling, and child health. *The World Bank Research Observer*, *24*(2), 147–181. doi: 10.1093/wbro/lkp006

Fountoulakis, K. N., Savopoulos, C., Siamouli, M., Zaggelidou, E., Mageiria, S., Iacovides, A., & Hatzitolios, A. I. (2013). Trends in suicidality amid the economic crisis in Greece. *European Archives of Psychiatry and Clinical Neuroscience*, *263*(5), 441–444. doi: 10.1007/s00406-012-0385-9

Fredricks, J. A., Blumenfeld, P. C., & Paris, A. H. (2004). School engagement: Potential of the concept, state of the evidence. *Review of Educational Research*, 74(1), 59–109. doi: 10.3102/00346543074001059

Georgas, J. (2006). Families and family change. In J. Georgas, J. W. Berry, F. J. R. van de Vijver, C. Kagitcibasi, & Y. H. Poortinga (Eds), *Families across Cultures: A 30-Nation Psychological Study* (pp. 3–50). Cambridge: Cambridge University Press.

Kokkevi, A., Stavrou, M., Kanavou E., & Fotiou A. (2014a). *The Repercussions of the Economic Recession in Greece on Adolescents and their Families*. Innocenti Working Paper No. 2014-07. Florence: UNICEF Office of Research.

Kokkevi, A., Rotsika, V., Botsis, A., Kanavou, E., Malliori, M., & Richardson, C. (2014b). Adolescents' self-reported running away from home and suicide attempts during a period of economic recession in Greece. *Child and Youth Care Forum*, *43*(6), 691–704. doi: 10.1007/s10566-014-9260-3

Lempers, J., Clark-Lempers, D., & Simons, R. (1989). Economic hardship, parenting, and adolescent distress. *Child Development*, *60*(1), 25–39. doi: 10.2307/1131068

Lundberg, M., & Wuermli, A. (2012). *Children and Youth in Crisis: Protecting and Promoting Human Development in Times of Economic Shocks*. Washington, DC: World Bank.

Masten, A. S. (2014). *Ordinary Magic: Resilience in Development*. New York: Guilford Press.

Masten, A. S., & Cicchetti, D. (2016). Resilience in development: Progress and transformation. In D. Cicchetti (Ed.), *Developmental Psychopathology* (3rd ed., Vol. 4, pp. 271–333). New York: Wiley.

McCormick, C.M., Kuo, S.I., & Masten, A.S. (2011). Developmental tasks across the lifespan. In K. L. Fingerman, C. Berg, J. Smith, & T. C. Antonucci (Eds). *The Handbook of Lifespan Development* (pp. 117–140). New York: Springer.

McLoyd, V. C., Kaplan, R., Purtell, K. M., Bagley, E., Hardaway, C. R., & Smalls, C. (2009). Poverty and socioeconomic disadvantage in adolescence. In R. M. Lerner & L. Steinberg (Eds), *Handbook of Adolescent Psychology: Vol. 2. Contextual Influences on Adolescent Development* (3rd ed., pp. 444–491). Hoboken, NJ: Wiley & Sons.

Motti-Stefanidi, F. (2014). Immigrant youth adaptation in the Greek school context: A risk and resilience perspective. *Child Development Perspectives, 8*(3), 180–185. doi: 10.1111/cdep.12081

Motti-Stefanidi, F., & Asendorpf, J.B. (in press). Adaptation during a great economic recession: A cohort study of Greek and immigrant youth. *Child Development.*

Motti-Stefanidi, F., Pavlopoulos, V., & Asendorpf, J.B. (2016). Economic problems, parenting, and adaptation during the great recession: a longitudinal mediation study of immigrant and Greek youth. Manuscript in preparation.

Obradović, J., Shaffer, A., & Masten, A. S. (2012) Risk in developmental psychopathology: Progress and future directions. In L. C. Mayes & M. Lewis (Eds), *The Cambridge Handbook of Environment of Human Development: A Handbook of Theory and Measurement* (pp. 35–57). New York: Cambridge University Press.

Schoon, I., Bynner, J., Joshi, H., Parsons, S., Wiggins, R. D., & Sacker, A. (2002). The influence of context, timing, and duration of risk experiences for the passage from childhood to midadulthood. *Child Development, 73*(5), 1486–1504. doi: 10.1111/1467-8624.00485

Solantaus, T., Leinonen, J., & Punamäki, R. L. (2004). Children's mental health in times of economic recession: replication and extension of the family economic stress model in Finland. *Developmental Psychology, 40*(3), 412–429. doi:10.1037/0012-1649.40.3.412

UNICEF (2014). *Children of the Recession: The Impact of the Economic Crisis on Child Well-Being in Rich Countries: Innocenti Report Card 12.* Florence: UNICEF Office of Research.

8

A NEW PERSPECTIVE ON THREE OLD METHODOLOGICAL ISSUES

The Role of Time, Missing Values, and Cohorts in Longitudinal Models of Youth Development

Manuel C. Voelkle

The study of positive youth development is inextricably tied to the analysis of longitudinal data. Most researchers working in this field have probably been exposed to methodological questions regarding the design, analysis, and/or adequate interpretation of longitudinal studies. Unfortunately, longitudinal statistical analysis can be full of pitfalls and, as apparent from the history of longitudinal statistical analysis in the social sciences, the literature is peppered with questionable recommendations and myths, resulting in inadequate conclusions, confusion about which methods to use, or even resignation by avoiding longitudinal data altogether (Cronbach & Furby, 1970; Harris, 1963; Rogosa, 1995; Voelkle & Adolf, 2015). Three particularly fundamental issues regard (a) the conception and statistical treatment of *time* in longitudinal models, (b) the treatment of *missing values,* such as missing measurement occasions, and (c) the presence of multiple *cohorts* in longitudinal models of youth development.

At first glance, the issue of time may seem trivial – "Absolute, true and mathematical time, of itself, and from its own nature flows equably without regard to anything external" (Newton, 1687) – so it is "just there" and there is nothing we can do about it. However, as already apparent from Newton's reflections on "relative time" and Leibniz's conception of time as something purely relative "an order of successions" (tempus est ordo existendi eorum quae non sunt simul), there are different ways to use time as a "general order of change" (as cited in Reichenbach, 1979, p. 422). Are we interested in change over measurement occasions or change over chronological time? In the case of the latter, are we interested in change over time that is relative to the individual (e.g., years from the date of birth of this individual) or relative to a universally accepted reference point (e.g., the birth of Jesus Christ or the beginning of the school year)? Furthermore, can we use time to explain development or is time just the "theatrical stage upon which the processes of development are played out" (Baltes, Reese, & Nesselroade, 1988, p. 108)? Building upon these considerations, we will distinguish between static and dynamic models for the analysis of change in the first part of the chapter. We will argue that dynamic models are particularly useful when it comes to understanding the mechanisms underlying developmental processes, and will quickly discuss cross-lagged panel models as a prototypical representative of dynamic models. However, we will also point to shortcomings in the present literature on how time is typically handled in these models and will introduce continuous time modeling as a better alternative that overcomes these problems. The latter will be illustrated with a little example from the literature.

In contrast to problems related to the handling of time in longitudinal models – which may not always be immediately apparent – the problem of missing values seems obvious. This is particularly true if missing values appear as "holes" in the dataset that need to be taken into account when analyzing the data. Most researchers will be well aware of the fact that traditional approaches like listwise or pairwise deletion are almost always suboptimal and that better ways to handle missing values exist (Enders, 2010; Graham, 2009; Rubin & Little, 2002; Schafer & Graham, 2002). This applies equally to the analysis of longitudinal data. However, what is a missing value in a longitudinal study? If measurements would have been obtained on April 1, May 1, July 1, and August 1, are the measurements on June 1 missing? Should I handle them via any of the proposed missing value techniques such as (multiple) imputation? What if I never intended to obtain a measurement on June 1? Do I still need to account for this "hole" in the time series? What about May 15 or July 28; are these measurement occasions missing as well and should be treated accordingly? In the second part of the chapter, we will show how "thinking continuous time" offers a new perspective on missing values in longitudinal data analysis. From this perspective, a missing measurement occasion simply translates into an unequally spaced time interval and may be handled via the method described in the first section. It will be shown that this approach is particularly useful for dynamic models with a large number of missing values (i.e., unequally spaced measurement occasions). Based on previous research, we will show that such a situation may even improve model estimation as compared to a balanced design and we will reflect upon how this insight may help to improve the design of longitudinal studies on positive youth development. Along the way we will demonstrate how oscillating processes may be easily fit by *ctsem*, an R-package for estimating continuous time models by means of structural equation modeling.

Studies on youth development often involve multiple cohorts. Broadly speaking, there are four common reasons (and many combinations thereof) for working with multiple cohorts in longitudinal studies: First, because they cannot be avoided but are irrelevant to the primary research question. For example, one may be interested in the effects of a new school meal program in a developing country on cognitive abilities in 1st to 4th graders. By comparing to a control group, this question could be addressed by repeatedly observing 1st to 4th graders even though the composition of the sample may change because new 1st graders may be admitted to the sample, while 4th graders may leave the sample if the observation period is long enough. In such a so-called time-sequential design, differences between cohorts are only of interest to the degree that the new meal program may be differentially effective and may thus bias the overall effect. Second, a possible cohort-differential *development* of cognitive abilities may also be of primary research interest. In this case, one would need to repeatedly observe the same group of 1st to 4th graders in order to assess their change and cohort-related differences in change. This requires a true longitudinal design. Third, one may also be interested in whether the program itself improves over time and may therefore be better accepted by children who enter the program at a later point in time. In order to test this hypothesis, one would have to observe different cohorts longitudinally, for example by opening up the meal program for a new group of 1st to 4th graders at the beginning of each year. This is called a cohort-sequential design (Little, 2013; Schaie, 1965, 1994). Finally, different cohorts may be used to approximate a true longitudinal study if the latter is not feasible. For example, one may be interested in cognitive development during the first seven years of schooling, but only has funding for a three-year long study. The solution could be a so-called cross-sequential design, that is, to observe different cohorts at multiple time points (Little, 2013; Schaie, 1965, 1994). For example, if one assesses 1st, 3rd, and 5th graders at the first measurement occasion and follows the three cohorts across three years, one obtains the full span of seven grades. Obviously this only works if one is willing to accept certain assumptions. What are these assumptions and how can we test them? In the last part of the chapter we will provide a continuous time perspective on these more complex designs. We will particularly focus on the cross-sequential design and show how to implement and test it by means of *ctsem*.

Problems related to the best treatment of time, missing values, and multiple cohorts have long plagued longitudinal studies on positive youth development – and continue to do so. All three problems have also been covered extensively in the methodological literature. In this regard the present chapter adds little to the list that has not been said or written before. However, by combining these three seemingly unrelated problems, reducing them to a common core, and proposing a single solution, this chapter attempts to offer a new perspective on three old issues. It is hoped that this will encourage more researchers to think continuous time and to apply continuous time models in their own research.

The Role of Time in Longitudinal Models of Youth Development

The left part of Figure 8.1 illustrates one of the most basic statistical models with a single outcome variable y_i measured across different individuals $i = 1, ..., N$, and a single predictor x_i observed for the same individuals. The model postulates an effect a of x on y. As illustrated by the first equation in Figure 8.1, this could be a simple linear regression analysis where the criterion y is regressed on x, with w_i representing the error term. The parameter a in this model can be interpreted in two different ways. We may either conceive of it as a simple description of the strength of the relationship between x and y, or we may interpret it as the causal effect of x on y. Whether the latter interpretation is justified, of course, depends on the underlying research design. For instance, if x is a dummy variable representing an intervention and control group with random assignment of a

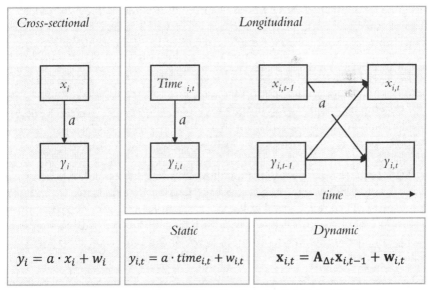

FIGURE 8.1 Illustrating the Role of Time in Longitudinal Models. In contrast to certain (e.g., randomized control trials) cross-sectional models (left) and dynamic models of change (right), the parameter a cannot represent a causal effect in static models of change (middle). It may describe, but cannot explain, the causal mechanisms underlying a change in y.

large number of individuals to either group, the interpretation of a as the causal treatment effect seems warranted. If x and y are just two arbitrarily measured variables, however, there is little reason to believe that a actually represents a causal effect. The distinction of these two interpretations is often of primary concern in the sciences and it is up to us as the researchers to find out via clever research designs, which of the two interpretations is correct.

Static Versus Dynamic Models of Change

What happens if we adopt the same research design for the analysis of longitudinal data as illustrated in the middle part of Figure 8.1? Here the predictor x has been replaced by *time*, for example, the exact date where an individual i has been observed in a series of measurement occasions $t = 1,\ldots, T$. As illustrated by the second equation in Figure 8.1, this could be a simple linear mixed model analysis where the criterion y is regressed on x, with time points nested in individuals and $w_{i,t}$ representing the prediction error of individual i at time point t. In contrast to the previous cross-sectional model, in this case we no longer have two different options to interpret the parameter a. The parameter a will never represent a causal effect, because by the very definition of a causal effect, the cause has to precede the effect in time (c.f., Cook & Campbell, 1979; Mill, 1848). With time itself being the alleged cause, however, this is clearly impossible. It is important to note that a may still serve as a useful proxy for the true causal effect. This, for example, would be the case if *time* is perfectly related to the actual causal variable (e.g., an intervention with time coding the difference between pre- and post-test). The parameter a may also serve as a proxy to *describe* the effects of more general developmental processes (e.g., improvements in cognition due to the developing brain); however, time itself may only *describe* but not *explain* the underlying causal mechanisms. For this reason, we speak of descriptive or *static models*. Put more eloquently in the words of Baltes, Reese, and Nesselroade:

> ...although time is inextricably linked to the concept of development, in itself it cannot explain any aspect of developmental change. [...] Time, rather like the theatrical stage upon which the processes of development are played out, provides a necessary base upon which the description, explanation, and modification of development proceed.
>
> (Baltes et al., 1988, p. 108)

In contrast to static models, in dynamic models (right part of Figure 8.1), *time* is not used explicitly as an explanatory variable but only implicitly by providing an order of change, much like in the sense of Gottfried Wilhelm Leibniz. For example, in vector-autoregressive cross-lagged panel models, a common representative of dynamic models illustrated by the third equation in

Figure 8.1, the process and relationship between variables is modeled across the dimension of time, illustrated by the time arrow at the bottom.[1] Other than in static models, the parameter *a* may now capture the actual causal mechanisms of change processes – provided certain assumptions are met. Thus, dynamic models are particularly suited when we are not only interested in describing change, but rather in identifying the causal mechanisms underlying the change processes. For this reason, we want to focus on dynamic models for the analysis of change during the remainder of this chapter.

Cross-Lagged Panel Models

The probably most commonly used class of dynamic models in the social sciences are cross-lagged panel models. Cross-lagged panel models have been used to study a variety of different topics in research on youth development, such as the bidirectional relationship between parenting and delinquency (Gault-Sherman, 2012), the relation between perceived social support and academic achievement in students (Mackinnon, 2012), or the causal influence of teachers' expectations on children's academic performance (Crano & Mellon, 1978). The basic model has already been introduced in Figure 8.1 and is repeated in Equation 8.1, augmented by a *p*-dimensional intercept vector **b**.

$$\mathbf{x}_{i,t} = \mathbf{A}(\Delta t)\, \mathbf{x}_{i,t-1} + \mathbf{b} + \mathbf{w}_{i,t} \tag{8.1}$$

The *p*-dimensional vector **x** contains the number of (possibly latent) variables observed for individual *i* at time point *t*. Accordingly the $p \times p$ dimensional matrix $\mathbf{A}(\Delta t)$ contains the autoregressive parameters in the main diagonal and cross-lagged parameters in the off-diagonals. The former show how the values of each variable are affected by the values at the previous time point $t - 1$, the latter how two or more variables affect each other over time (e.g., the parameter *a* in the right part of Figure 8.1). By writing $\mathbf{A}(\Delta t)$ as a function of $\Delta t = t - (t-1)$, it is made explicit that $\mathbf{A}(\Delta t)$ depends on the time intervals between measurement occasion, an important point as will be discussed in the following. Finally, $\mathbf{w}_{i,t}$ is a *p*-dimensional error vector.

As discussed before, cross-lagged panel models as defined in Equation 8.1 (and their various extensions) are not only powerful when it comes to analyzing causal mechanisms of change processes, but are also commonly used in the social sciences. Unfortunately, however, the way they are used often rests on unrealistic assumptions which may result in biased parameter estimates and wrong conclusions. Ultimately, current practice hampers the production of cumulative scientific knowledge. To illustrate this drastic statement, consider the example in Figure 8.2, which shows two different cross-lagged panel designs to study the relationship between *x* and *y*. The only difference between the two designs is the length of the sampling interval between measurement occasions.

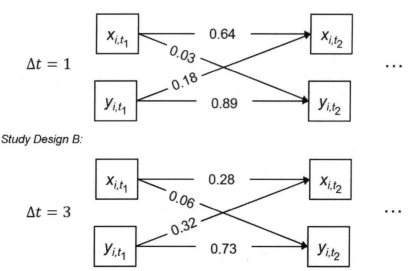

Study Design A:

Study Design B:

FIGURE 8.2 Two Different Cross-Lagged Panel Designs to Study the Relationship between x and y across T Measurement Occasions. The dots to the right of the figure indicate that the time series continues, assuming time-invariant population parameters.

In Study A, an interval length of $\Delta t=1$ (e.g., 1 week) is used, in Study B an interval of $\Delta t=3$ (e.g., 3 weeks). Obviously, the results differ. For example, while in Study A, the autoregressive effect of x is 0.64, it is only about half the size in Study B (0.28). In contrast, the cross effect of y on x is almost twice as high in Study B (0.32) as compared to Study A (0.18). Given such divergent results, one can easily imagine the debate in the scientific community about which study is closer to the truth. However, given the difference in time intervals, is it legitimate to compare the parameter estimates in the first place? If not, should all researchers be enforced to use the same time intervals in order to make their results comparable? Obviously, the example in Figure 8.2 is also greatly simplified. In reality, time intervals may not only differ between studies but also within one and the same study. Even worse, time intervals may also differ across individuals within one and the same study. For example, in a study with $N = 100$ individuals and $T = 10$ time points, we may end up with a maximum of 900 different time intervals. These time intervals have a complex non-linear effect on the parameter estimates in a cross-lagged panel model. It should be easily apparent that current practice of simply ignoring the length of the time intervals is not only suboptimal but may yield completely meaningless results. Fortunately, continuous time models offer a solution.

Continuous Time Models

By bringing information on the exact timing back into cross-lagged panel models, continuous time models resolve the problem of unequal time intervals in discrete time models. Although continuous time models can be mathematically challenging, their basic idea is quite simple. Instead of predicting $x_{i,t}$ by $x_{i,t-1}$ as in Equation 8.1, we predict the so-called difference quotient, that is the difference $\Delta x(t)$ between $x(t)$ and $x(t-\Delta t)$ divided by the length of the time interval Δt. This is shown in Equation 8.2:

$$\frac{\Delta \mathbf{x}(t)}{\Delta t} = \mathbf{A}_{\star}\mathbf{x}(t - \Delta t) \tag{8.2}$$

Note, that by changing the notation from $x_{i,t}$ to $x(t)$ it is now made explicit that the values of $\mathbf{x}$ are a function of time, with time t being continuous.[2] Note also, that by standardizing $\Delta \mathbf{x}(t)$ by Δt on the left-hand side of Equation 8.2, $\mathbf{A}_{\star}$ becomes independent of Δt. If we now – hypothetically – let the time intervals between measurement occasions approach zero, we can rewrite Equation 8.1 as a differential equation:

$$\frac{\mathrm{d}\mathbf{x}(t)}{\mathrm{d}t} = \mathbf{A}\mathbf{x}(t) + \mathbf{b} + \mathbf{G}\frac{\mathrm{d}\mathbf{W}(t)}{\mathrm{d}t} \tag{8.3}$$

The differential equation describes the *change* in $\mathbf{x}$ as a function of $\mathbf{x}$ (plus $\mathbf{b}$ and an error term) in continuous time. Solving the differential equation for any initial value and observed time interval puts us into the position of relating the continuous time coefficients (e.g., the so-called drift matrix $\mathbf{A}$, which contains the auto- and cross-effects in continuous time) to their discrete time realizations for any actually observed time interval. It can be shown that in case of the drift matrix $\mathbf{A}$, this relationship corresponds to the matrix exponential function:

$$\mathbf{A}(\Delta t) = e^{\mathbf{A}\cdot\Delta t} \tag{8.4}$$

Having determined the relationship between discrete time (e.g., $\mathbf{A}(\Delta t)$) and continuous time parameters (e.g., $\mathbf{A}$), it becomes possible to constrain the discrete time parameters to the underlying continuous time parameters during the estimation process. Given the actually realized, discrete, measurement occasions, this enables us to infer the underlying continuous time parameters. Based on the continuous time parameters, one may now reconstruct the discrete time parameters for any arbitrary time interval and/or compare parameter estimates across studies and/or individuals with different measurement occasions. The same logic applies to all other parameters of a given model.

Although the basic idea may be simple, obviously this paragraph cannot replace a solid introduction to continuous time modeling. For this we refer the reader to Voelkle, Oud, Davidov, & Schmidt (2012) and Oud and Jansen (2000).

In this chapter we want to stay at a somewhat more abstract level and focus on a couple of simple examples that highlight the importance of continuous time models, how they are implemented and interpreted, and how thinking continuous time may ultimately advance research on youth development. For this we will make use of a new R-package *ctsem*, which provides an easy way to implement a broad range of continuous time models, thus making the technique available to a wide audience. For a more comprehensive introduction to *ctsem*, the reader is referred to Driver, Oud, and Voelkle (in press) and the help files of the package.

Putting Theory into Practice: ctsem for Panel Data

The package *ctsem* is available on CRAN and can be downloaded and installed by typing *install.packages("ctsem")* into the R-console (Driver et al., in press; R Core Team, 2015). For this chapter, R version 3.2.2 and ctsem version 1.1.5 were used. As for all R-packages, it is loaded by the command *library(ctsem)*. Core of the package are the two functions *ctModel()* and *ctFit()*. The first is used to specify the model of interest, the second to fit the model to a given dataset. Additional information on the functions, including a comprehensive description of all arguments, can be obtained by typing *?ctModel()*, *?ctFit()* respectively, into the R-console. The package comes along with a number of example datasets and input codes, including the empirical example used by Voelkle et al. (2012), which is concerned with the relationship between two variables (authoritarianism and anomia) in a sample of 2,722 participants observed across five measurement occasions in 2002, 2003, 2004, 2006, and 2008 (Heitmeyer, 2012, 2004). Because of the unequal time intervals of 1, 1, 2, and 2 years, the situation resembles that in Figure 8.2, with the only difference that time intervals vary within one and the same study rather than between different studies. The problem, however, remains the same: Parameter estimates in a discrete time model, as given in Equation 8.1, depend on the length of the time interval. If parameters are freely estimated and differ across measurement occasions, we do not know whether they differ because the process differs or because the time intervals differ (in addition to the problem that we would not be able to make any predictions). In contrast, if we constrain parameter estimates to equality across time, this will result in biased parameter estimates, because the length of the time interval is not adequately taken into account. By constraining the discrete time parameters to the underlying continuous time parameters, *ctsem* resolves this predicament. The data used by Voelkle et al. (2012) are included in *ctsem* and can be accessed via **data(AnomAuth)**. The continuous time version of a bivariate autoregressive crossed-lagged panel model on the relationship between authoritarianism and anomia may then be simply specified via:

```
AnomAuthmodel <- ctModel(LAMBDA = matrix(c(1, 0, 0, 1), nrow
= 2, ncol = 2), Tpoints = 5, n.latent = 2, n.manifest = 2,
MANIFESTVAR=diag(0, 2), TRAITVAR = NULL)
```

Given the dataset **AnomAuth**, the resulting model **AnomAuthmodel** may be estimated by:

```
AnomAuthfit <- ctFit(AnomAuth, AnomAuthmodel)
```

As for most R-packages, a summary of the most important results is obtained via the summary() and plot() functions, in our example **summary(AnomAuthfit)** and **plot(AnomAuthfit)**. For a comprehensive discussion of the input specification and the entire output, the interested reader is referred to Driver et al. (in press). Most importantly for our purposes, the first element of the output shows the continuous time drift matrix $\mathbf{A} = \begin{pmatrix} -0.447 & 0.234 \\ 0.043 & -0.117 \end{pmatrix}$.

Knowing the drift matrix, we can now go ahead and compute the discrete time parameters for any arbitrary discrete time interval via Equation 8.3. For example, for $\Delta t = 1$, $\mathbf{A}(\ddot{A}t = 1) = e^{\begin{pmatrix} -0.447 & 0.234 \\ 0.043 & -0.117 \end{pmatrix} \cdot 1} = \begin{pmatrix} 0.643 & 0.176 \\ 0.033 & 0.893 \end{pmatrix}$ or for

$\Delta t = 3$, $\mathbf{A}(\Delta t = 3) = e^{\begin{pmatrix} -0.447 & 0.234 \\ 0.043 & -0.117 \end{pmatrix} \cdot 3} = \begin{pmatrix} 0.278 & 0.316 \\ 0.059 & 0.727 \end{pmatrix}$. Figure 8.3 shows the

cross-lagged parameters for all other time intervals $0 < t \leq 6$. From the figure it is easily apparent that the effects of x_1 on x_2, and vice versa, change dramatically as a function of the time interval. While for some intervals the difference is negligible, for others it is quite large. It may also happen that the signs of the effects change as a function of the time interval and under certain conditions even the relative sizes of the effects may reverse. By comparing Figure 8.2 and Figure 8.3 it becomes apparent how continuous time modeling resolves the issue of different time intervals. The fact that the cross-lagged effects lie on the same trajectories in Figure 8.3 suggests that the true underlying continuous time model is the same and that the only reason for different discrete time parameter estimates is the use of different time intervals (the same holds true for all other parameters). Thus the discussion in the scientific community whether to trust the parameters in Study Design A or Study Design B in Figure 8.2 is resolved by showing that they can be equally trusted, because any differences are just due to the study design but not due to different processes. In a meta-analysis, for instance, the two effect sizes should also be treated as equivalent.

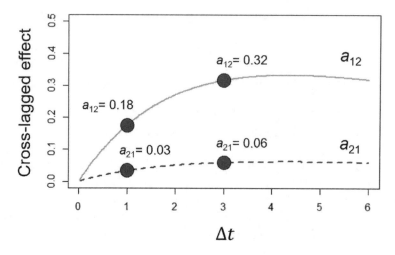

FIGURE 8.3 Cross-Lagged Parameters a_{12} of x_2 (Authoritarianism) on x_1 (Anomia) and Vice Versa (a_{21}) as a Function of the Length of the Time Interval between Measurement Occasions (Δt). Selected parameter estimates are shown for $\delta t=1$ and $\delta t=3$.

Missing Values in Longitudinal Models of Youth Development

In the previous paragraph we have seen how continuous time models may resolve the problem of different measurement intervals in dynamic models of change. However, apart from being a statistical tool that resolves a well-defined problem in parameter estimation, "thinking continuous time" may also help to gain a new perspective on developmental processes. In this section I want to illustrate the advantages of thinking continuous time by reflecting upon our conceptualization of missing values in longitudinal studies.

The "Traditional" Perspective on Missing Values

Panel A in Figure 8.4 shows the traditional discrete time perspective on missing values. According to this perspective, there should have been eight measurement occasions (illustrated by the eight circles) of which only five could be realized, resulting in three missing measurement occasions (illustrated by the crossed-out circles). So a missing value is a value that should have been obtained but was not, and whether it should have been obtained is dictated by the design of the study. Note that with exactly the same five measurement occasions, the percentage of missing values would have been 95%, instead of 3/8 = 37.5%, if we would have planned to have 100 measurement occasions, instead of eight.

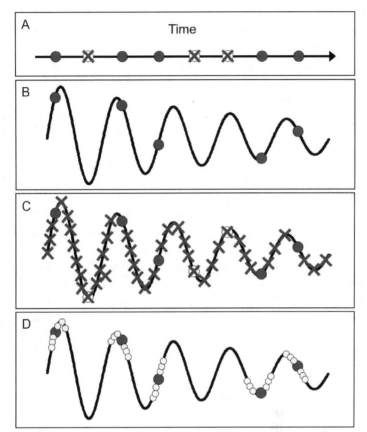

FIGURE 8.4 Different Ways To Conceptualize Missing Values in Longitudinal Studies. The discrete time perspective of missing values as missing measurement occasions (A). The continuous time perspective (B). The discrete time perspective applied to a continuous time process (C). The continuous time perspective with individually varying time intervals (D). See text for details.

The Continuous Time Perspective on Missing Values

Instead of the study design, the continuous time perspective starts with the process of interest, by assuming that it changes continuously over time. The process, for example, could be mood swings in adolescents as illustrated by a damped linear oscillator in Panel B. However, since it is impossible to *observe* mood swings continuously over time, the actual continuous time process needs to be inferred from few (here: five) discrete measurement occasions. From this perspective the notion of a missing value does not exist. Rather, the question must be raised, whether the research design (i.e., the five measurement occasions) is sufficient to recover the true underlying process.

The difference between the two perspectives becomes most obvious when applying the traditional notion of missings to a continuous time process (Panel C). In this case, we are faced with an infinite number of missing values, because apart from the few existing measurement occasions, there could have been an infinite number of additional measurements that were never realized (illustrated by the crosses in Panel C).

The goal of finding a research design that is optimally suited to detect an underlying process – rather than to minimize missing values in a longitudinal study – lies at the heart of signal detection theory (Swets, 1964). In this regard, a particularly important theorem is the so-called Nyquist Shannon sampling theorem (Lüke, 1999), which states that a signal with a frequency of no higher than H hertz is determined if the sampling rate (i.e., the number of measurement occasions per time interval) is higher than $2H$. For example, ignoring the dampening, the oscillation shown in Figure 8.4 has a frequency of 1 hertz, so more than two measurements per cycle would be needed in order to recover the underlying oscillating process. With only few equally spaced measurement occasions with a measurement interval $\Delta t > 0.5$, this would not be possible. However, in a simulation study (Voelkle & Oud, 2013) we could show that even though in practice it may be impossible to increase the overall number of measurement occasions, it may already help to have individuals observed at irregular time intervals. If every individual is observed just a little bit before or after the average measurement occasion, this may suffice to create a situation where the Nyquist Shannon criterion may be met for some (combinations) of cases, even though it is not met at the average level. This is illustrated in Panel D of Figure 8.4, in which the little dots around the average measurement occasions represent individuals. Even by pure visual inspection it is much easier to detect that the dots are indicative of an oscillating process, rather than, say, a linear decline with some measurement error.

In other words, what this example shows is that what may be considered an optimally designed and carried out study from a traditional perspective on missing values (i.e., a study with T equally spaced measurement occasions with one and the same Δt and no missing values) may actually be suboptimal to detect certain processes (e.g., an oscillating process with a period length $\leq 2 \Delta t$). Maybe counterintuitively from this perspective, *introducing missing* values by creating unequally spaced measurement occasions where only some individuals have been observed may help to recover the true generating process. This is readily apparent from a continuous time perspective on missing values.

Unfortunately, however, there is no free lunch. Just because adopting a different perspective on missing values may help to reconsider the way we design and analyze longitudinal studies, does not mean that a change in perspective makes all problems go away. As pointed out by Rubin (1976) and others (cf., Rubin & Little, 2002; Schafer & Graham, 2002), it is crucial to consider the missing data mechanisms: *Why* did some people drop out or not respond? From a continuous time perspective these questions translate into questions regarding the mechanisms of the (time) sampling process: Is there a systematic pattern behind the choice of measurement occasions and if yes, is the pattern planned (e.g., because the researcher designed the study that way), is it known and can be controlled for (e.g., we would like to have measurement occasions every hour of the day for 24 hours, but know that it is much more difficult to obtain measurement at night), or are there unknown patterns (e.g., some people may only respond to questions in an experience sampling study when they are in a good mood, but the mood is not known to the researcher)? These considerations are closely tied to whether missing values are missing completely at random (MCAR), missing at random (MAR), or missing not at random (MNAR). If the choice of measurement occasions is driven by systematic, but unknown, factors, parameter estimates will be biased, no matter whether a discrete or continuous time perspective on missing values is adopted.

Likewise, even though the use of individually varying measurement occasions may help to identify the true generating process, the approach rests on the assumption that the process is the same for all individuals. This is particularly important because in this case we are using between person differences (in measurement occasions) to make within person inferences (about the average within person-generating process). If the assumption of a general underlying process is not justified, parameter estimates will be biased.

Putting Theory into Practice: ctsem for Modeling Oscillation

The syntax below gives an example of how *ctsem* can be used to fit oscillating processes. Although the model can be easily extended to multivariate (coupled and/ or damped) oscillating processes with unequally spaced time intervals, we constrain ourselves to a simple univariate damped linear oscillator. The data are taken from Voelkle and Oud (2013) and can be obtained via the command **data(Oscillating)**.

```
inits <- c(-38,-.5,1,10,10)
names(inits) <- c('cross','auto','diffusion22','T0var11','T0var22')
oscillatingmodel <- ctModel(n.latent = 2, n.manifest=1, Tpoints=11,
MANIFESTVAR=matrix(c(0), nrow=1, ncol=1), LAMBDA=matrix(c(1,
0), nrow=1, ncol=2), DRIFT=matrix(c(0, "cross", 1, "auto"),
nrow=2, ncol=2), CINT=matrix(c(0,0), ncol=1, nrow=2, ),
DIFFUSION=matrix(c(0, 0, 0, "diffusion22"), nrow=2, ncol=2),
startValues = inits)
oscillatingfit <- ctFit(Oscillating, oscillatingmodel)
```

As before, the model is fit via the **ctFit()** function:

```
oscillatingfit <-ctFit(Oscillating, oscillatingmodel)
```

and parameter estimates and obtained via **summary()**, plots via **plot()**, respectively. The only differences to the previous example are the use of user-defined initial values via the **inits** argument. Because oscillating processes are somewhat more challenging to fit, providing reasonable starting values is recommended (if possible). This is done via the **inits** command. For details on the *ctsem* specification, the reader is referred to Driver et al. (in press); for details on the mathematical background of continuous time oscillating models with individually varying time intervals, the reader is referred to Voelkle and Oud (2013).

Cohorts in Longitudinal Models of Youth Development

After considering the role of time and missing values in the analysis of longitudinal data, in this last section I want to focus on the third problem: The use of multiple cohorts in longitudinal studies. As already discussed in the introduction, there are different reasons why researchers use multiple cohorts in longitudinal studies. Accordingly, different data analytic strategies have been proposed (Schaie, 1994). From a continuous time perspective, however, the use of different cohorts is just a special case of the missing data situation discussed in the previous part, with the only difference that one is now dealing with *groups* of individuals (i.e., cohorts) rather than individual subjects (cf. Oud & Voelkle, 2014).

Single Cohort Versus Cross-Sequential Designs

To illustrate this point, consider Panel A in Figure 8.5, which shows a standard longitudinal design according to which a single group of individuals was repeatedly observed across seven measurement occasions. As discussed in the previous parts of this chapter, the measurement intervals may be equal or unequal. For example, we may conduct an annual interview with children at the age of 10, 11, ..., 16 years. The lower arrow in Figure 8.5 indicates the timeline, while the upper line shows the schematic development over time. In this example, this would be a simple linear increase, but of course the approach generalizes to more complicated trajectories.

In contrast to Panel A, multiple cohorts are present in the cross-sequential design depicted in Panel B. Here three different cohorts are observed across three measurement occasions each. For example, instead of following the same group of individuals across six years (from 10 to 16), three different cohorts may have been observed at the ages of 10, 11, 12 (Cohort A), 12, 13, 14 (Cohort B), and 14, 15, 16 (Cohort C). In other words, measurements at the

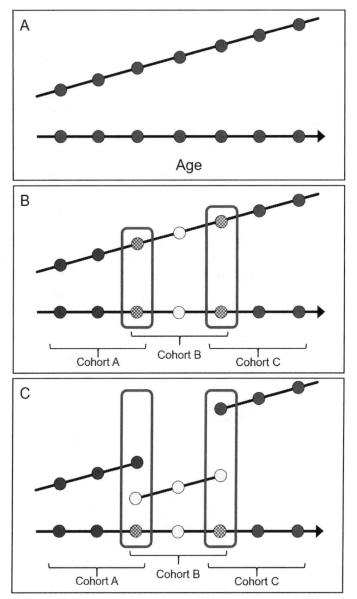

FIGURE 8.5 Three Different Examples of Longitudinal Studies. Panel A: A standard longitudinal design consisting of a single cohort and seven measurement occasions. Panel B: A longitudinal design with three equivalent cohorts observed at measurement occasions 1, 2, 3 (Cohort A), 3, 4, 5 (Cohort B), and 5, 6, 7 (Cohort C). Note that Cohort A and B overlap at the third measurement occasion, while Cohort B and C overlap at the fifth measurement occasion. Panel C: The same design as in panel B, but with non-equivalent cohorts.

age of 13 to 16 are missing in Cohort A, measurements at the age of 10, 11, 15, and 16 are missing in Cohort B, and measurements at the age of 10 to 13 are missing in Cohort C. Obviously, a cross-sequential design thus translates into a missing value problem, which may be solved by means of continuous time modeling as discussed in the previous sections. Since the exact time points of measurement are taken into account in a continuous time framework, model specification and estimation (e.g., via *ctsem*) proceeds in exactly the same way as discussed before.

However, as also discussed before, the validity of this procedure rests on the assumption that the same model applies to all individuals, cohorts, respectively (i.e., there exists no systematic, but unknown, missing data mechanism or sampling mechanism). In case of multiple cohorts, however, this may be an unrealistic assumption because the cohorts were deliberately chosen to differ in age. Whether they also differ in terms of the underlying model, is an empirical question. If there is no temporal overlap between cohorts, there is no (scientific-statistical) way to find out. However, if cohorts overlap like in Figure 8.5, where Cohorts A and B were both observed at the age of 12, while Cohorts B and C were both observed at the age of 14, we may reject – but cannot confirm – the assumption of model equivalence across cohorts.

To this end, we compare a model that assumes equivalence across cohorts against a number of alternative models that relax the assumption of cohort equivalence for selected (or all) parameters. The procedure will be illustrated by means of a little example in the following.

Putting Theory into Practice: ctsem for Cross-Sequential Designs

As before, *ctsem* is used for setting up and estimating continuous time cross-sequential models. Although individually varying time intervals may also be used in cross-sequential designs, we constrain ourselves to an example with equal measurement intervals of $\Delta t=1$. Furthermore, for didactic reasons we work with simulated data making use of the Monte Carlo functionality in *ctsem*. The *R*-code for the complete example is provided in Appendix A and may be easily adopted by researchers to their specific needs. Because not all of the code in Appendix A is of relevance for gaining a basic understanding of the approach, we discuss only selected parts within the main text of this paragraph.

In a first step, a true model with known population parameters is specified. This is also done via the **ctModel()** command with the only difference that the chosen numbers represent population parameters.

```
complete_model <-ctModel(Tpoints=7, n.latent=1, n.manifest=1,
LAMBDA=matrix(c(1),ncol=1), DRIFT=matrix(c(-0.1), nrow=1),
MANIFESTVAR=diag(1),DIFFUSION=matrix(c(.5),1,1),
```

```
CINT=matrix(c(2),ncol=1), T0MEANS=matrix(c(5),ncol=1,nrow=1),
T0VAR=matrix(c(2),nrow=1))
```

Here we chose a univariate autoregressive panel model with $T = 7$ measurement occasions, a population mean (**T0MEANS**) of 5, and a standard deviation[3] (**T0VAR**) of 2 at the first measurement occasion. By choosing a drift parameter close to zero (–0.1) and a positive continuous time intercept (2), the resulting mean trajectory is almost linear, resembling the one depicted in Figure 8.5. Data for $N = 600$ individuals are generated via the **ctGenerate** function given below:

```
complete_data <-ctGenerate(complete_model,n subjects=600,burnin=0)
```

The descriptive means of the total sample and individual trajectories of $N = 100$ randomly selected individuals are shown in Figure 8.6 (Panel A). If we estimate a standard continuous time model as discussed before and as illustrated in Step 2 in Appendix A, we obtain parameter estimates close to the population parameters, suggesting that data simulation and model estimation worked correctly. Population parameter and parameter estimates (Model 1) are shown in Table 8.1. What happens, however, if we create three artificial cohorts, as shown in Figure 8.5, by dropping the last four measurement occasions from Cohort 1, the first and last two measurement occasions form Cohort 2, and the first four occasions from Cohort 3 (Step 3 in Appendix A)? Because the dataset changes by dropping 57% of all observations, the parameter estimates will change as well. However, because the three cohorts were created from the same population and do not differ apart from the different measurement occasions, parameter estimates are still close to the population parameters (Table 8.1; Model 2). For example, by dropping the equality constraint on the initial mean of the three cohorts, the model fit reduces only slightly, resulting in a non-significant likelihood ratio test $(2\log(L_{M2}) - 2\log(L_{M3}) = 6565.024 - 6562.819 = 2.205;$ $df(M_2) - df(M_2); p = 0.332)$. In addition, the additional parameter estimates remain close to the constrained estimate of 4.838 as apparent from Model 3. Using the same approach, one could easily explore cohort equivalence for all other parameters in the same fashion. If there are cohort differences, this should be reflected in a significant reduction in model fit. To illustrate this point, let us generate a new dataset in which the population parameters of the initial mean of the three cohorts differ by subtracting 1 in Cohort 1 and adding 2 in Cohort 3 (resulting in population parameters of 5, 4, and 7 for the initial means). In this situation, a model which incorrectly assumes cohort equivalence (Model 4) would fit the data significantly worse than a model without such constraints on the initial means (Model 5; $2\log(L_{M4}) - 2\log(L_{M5}) = 6713.039 - 6540.7212 = 172.319;$ $p < 0.001$). Allowing additional parameters to vary across cohorts, however, does not significantly improve model fit as apparent from comparing Model 5 to Model 6, in which the drift coefficients were also

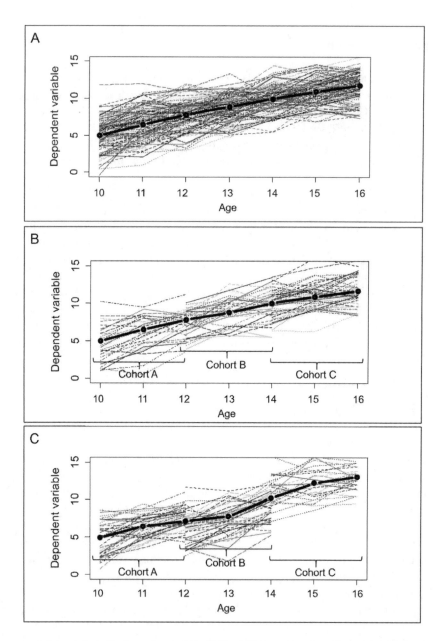

FIGURE 8.6 Mean Trajectories and Individual Trajectories for $N = 100$ Randomly Chosen Individuals (Per Group) under Three Different Conditions Panel A: Longitudinal design. Panel B: Cross-sequential design with three equivalent cohorts. Panel C: Cross-sequential design with three (non-equivalent) cohorts differing in the level of the dependent variable.

TABLE 8.1 Different Continuous Time Cross-Sequential Analyses. The analyses are based on three different datasets: A full longitudinal dataset (Model 1), a cross-sequential dataset with identical population parameters across cohorts (Model 2 and 3), and a cross-sequential dataset with different initial means across cohorts (Model 4, 5, 6)

Parameter Name	Population Parameter	Model 1	Model 2	Model 3	Model 4	Model 5	Model 6
Drift (a) Cohort 1	-0.1	-0.101	-0.123	-0.127	-0.075	-0.1	-0.124
Drift (a) Cohort 2							-0.124
Drift (a) Cohort 3							-0.111
Initial Mean Cohort 1	5	4.985	4.838	4.96	4.813	4.942	4.93
Initial Mean Cohort 2	(4)★			4.629		3.543	3.485
Initial Mean Cohort 3	(7)★			4.578		7.169	6.891
Initial Variance	4	3.915	4.035	4.049	4.309	3.678	3.874
Measurement Error	1	0.974	0.904	0.896	0.939	0.945	0.905
Diffusion (g)	0.25	0.28	0.372	0.386	0.317	0.278	0.345
Intercept (b)	2	2.009	2.233	2.286	1.9	2.007	2.167
−2logLikelihood		14538.47	6565.024	6562.819	6713.039	6540.721	6539.526

Note: Population Parameter = True parameters chosen for the single cohort longitudinal sample with $N = 600$ at $T = 7$ measurement occasions. Population parameters marked with ()★ apply to the final dataset (Model 4, 5, 6) only. Model 1 = Parameter estimates for the single cohort longitudinal sample with all $N = 600$ individuals observed at all $T = 7$ measurement occasions. Model 2: Cross-sequential model with all parameters constrained to equality across 3 cohorts ($N = 200$ per cohort), with each cohort being observed at three consecutive measurement occasions as described in the text. Model 3: Identical to Model 2, but with initial mean estimates allowed to differ across the three cohorts. Model 4: Identical to Model 2, but based on a dataset with three different initial population means across cohorts. Model 5: Identical to Model 3, but based on a dataset with three different initial population means across cohorts. Model 6: Identical to Model 5, but with estimated drift coefficients allowed to vary across cohorts.

allowed to vary across groups, despite their equivalence in the population $2\log(L_{M5}) - 2\log(L_{M6}) = 6540.721 - 6539.526 = 1.194$; $df(M_5) - df(M_6) = 2$; $p = 0.550$). See Table 8.1 for details.

General Discussion

We live in a constantly changing world. Not only are individuals developing over time, but the context in which such development takes place is changing as well. The global situation in which young people grow up today is significantly different from the world a few decades ago, and the pace at which the social and economic context is changing seems to be ever increasing. When the wind of change blows, some people build walls, others build windmills, as the old saying goes. What applies to the object of our research applies equally to the researchers who try to understand the determinants, consequences, and possibilities to achieve positive youth development. Using three old methodological problems in longitudinal data analysis as an example, the purpose of this chapter was to illustrate how continuous time modeling may serve as a "windmill" that capitalizes on the nature of continuously changing processes to gain a better understanding of their underlying mechanisms. This was contrasted to "building walls" by casting a continuous time world in discrete snapshots of the world, just because this fits conventional statistical models.

The first part of the chapter dealt with the role of time in longitudinal models. The advantages of dynamic over static models of change were spelled out and I pointed to problems in commonly used discrete time analyses – such as the cross-lagged panel model – that can be overcome by continuous time modelling. Most importantly, while continuous time models try to infer underlying continuous time processes from discrete measurement occasions, discrete time models assume such processes to develop in exactly the same steps that were used for their assessment. As a result, discrete time parameter estimates are always bound to the research design that was used for their estimation. The R-package *ctsem* was introduced and an empirical example was used to illustrate how to specify and interpret continuous time models. In the second part of the chapter, it was shown how missing values in longitudinal studies may be conceived of as unequally spaced measurement occasions. Using an oscillating process as an example, it was argued that this perspective may offer new ways to think about the design of longitudinal studies by maximizing the amount of information about an underlying continuous time process, rather than minimizing the amount of missing values. In the last part, it was shown how cohorts may be used to gain a better understanding of developmental processes. Using simulated data, it was shown how *ctsem* may be used to estimate continuous time cross-sequential designs and how we can test different assumptions of cohort (non-)equivalence.

Obviously, this chapter cannot provide a comprehensive introduction to continuous time modeling and the reader is referred to the existing literature for more detailed information (e.g., Oud & Jansen, 2000; Voelkle et al., 2012). In particular, I did not discuss the separation of between-person and within-person information in order to better capture the actual mechanisms of change processes (e.g., see the recent critique of crossed-lagged panel models by Hamaker, Kuiper, & Grasman, 2015). I also did not discuss the inclusion of time dependent and/or time independent predictors, which may often be of interest to researchers on positive youth development, in order to better capture the context in which such development takes place. The R-package *ctsem* introduced in this chapter allows not only for the separation of between and within-person variance but also offers different options for the inclusion of predictors and I encourage the reader to learn more by consulting the relevant literature (Driver et al., in press). Although at times the discussion of technical details may have been a bit superficial, I hope that by reconsidering the role of *time, missing values*, and *cohorts* as three pertinent methodological issues from a continuous time perspective, this chapter will encourage more researchers to "think continuous time" when studying (youth) development.

Acknowledgments

I thank Han Oud and Charles Driver for always interesting and insightful discussions about continuous time modeling.

Notes

1 In this example the 2-dimensional vector $\mathbf{x}^{T}$ represents the transposed vector $[x, y]^{T}$. In contrast to static models of change, dynamic models also allow reciprocal effects among variables. For example, as illustrated by the dashed arrow, y may not only be affected by x, but may in turn also affect x.
2 A more precise notation would be $\mathbf{x}_i(t_i)$ instead of $\mathbf{x}(t)$, highlighting that $\mathbf{x}$ not only takes on different values for different individuals ($\mathbf{x}_i$), but that time points may also differ across individuals (t_i). To improve readability, we use the simpler, but somewhat less precise, notation in this chapter.
3 Technically speaking, T0VAR specifies the lower triangular Cholesky matrix of the covariance matrix of latent variables at the initial time point. In case of a univariate process, this reduces to the standard deviation of the initial latent variable.

References

Baltes, P. B., Reese, H. W., & Nesselroade, J. R. (1988). *Life-Span Developmental Psychology: Introduction to research methods* (2nd ed.). Hillsdale, NJ: Erlbaum.
Cook, T. D., & Campbell, D. T. (1979). *Quasi-Experimentation: Design and analysis issues for field settings*. Chicago, IL: Rand McNally.

Crano, W. D., & Mellon, P. M. (1978). Causal influence of teachers' expectations on children's academic performance: A cross-lagged panel analysis. *Journal of Educational Psychology, 70*(1), 39–49. doi:10.1037/0022-0663.70.1.39

Cronbach, L. J., & Furby, L. (1970). How we should measure "change" – or should we? *Psychological Bulletin, 74*(1), 68–80. doi:10.1037/h0029382

Driver, C. C., Oud, J. H. L., & Voelkle, M. C. (in press). Continuous time structural equation modeling with R package ctsem. *Journal of Statistical Software.*

Enders, C. K. (2010). *Applied Missing Data Analysis.* New York: Guilford Press.

Gault-Sherman, M. (2012). It's a two-way street: The bidirectional relationship between parenting and delinquency. *Journal of Youth and Adolescence, 41*(2), 121–145. doi:10.1007/s10964-011-9656-4

Graham, J. W. (2009). Missing data analysis: Making it work in the real world. *Annual Review of Psychology, 60*, 549–576. doi: 10.1146/annurev.psych.58.110405.085530

Hamaker, E. L., Kuiper, R. M., & Grasman, R. P. P. P. (2015). A critique of the cross-lagged panel model. *Psychological Methods, 20*(1), 102–116. doi:10.1037/a0038889

Harris, C. W. (Ed.) (1963). *Problems in Measuring Change.* Madison, WI: The University of Wisconsin Press.

Heitmeyer, W. (Ed.) (2004). *Deutsche Zustände: Folge 3 [Current state in Germany: Series 3].* Frankfurt: Suhrkamp.

Heitmeyer, W. (2012). *Group-Oriented Animosity Against People (GMF-Survey 2007).* GESIS Data Archive, Cologne. ZA5572 Data file Version 1.0.0.

Little, T. D. (2013). *Longitudinal Structural Equation Modeling.* New York: The Guilford Press.

Lüke, H. D. (1999). The origins of the sampling theorem. *IEEE Communications Magazine, 37*(4), 106–108. doi: 10.1109/35.755459

Mackinnon, S. P. (2012). Perceived social support and academic achievement: Cross-lagged panel and bivariate growth curve analyses. *Journal of Youth and Adolescence, 41*(4), 474–485. doi:10.1007/s10964-011-9691-1

Mill, J. S. (1848). *A System of Logic.* London: Parker.

Newton, I. (1687). *Philosophiæ Naturalis Principia Mathematica.*

Oud, J. H. L., & Jansen, R. A. R. G. (2000). Continuous time state space modeling of panel data by means of SEM. *Psychometrika, 65*(2), 199–215. doi:10.1007/BF02294374

Oud, J. H. L., & Voelkle, M. C. (2014). Do missing values exist? Incomplete data handling in cross-national longitudinal studies by means of continuous time modeling. *Quality & Quantity, 48*(6), 3271–3288. doi:10.1007/s11135-013-9955-9

R Core Team (2015). *R: A Language and Environment for Statistical Computing.* Vienna, Austria: R Foundation for Statistical Computing. Retrieved from www.R-project.org/

Reichenbach, H. (1979). *Die philosophische Bedeutung der Relativitätstheorie [The Philosophical Meaning of Relativity Theory]* (Vol. 3). Wiesbaden: Vieweg.

Rogosa, D. R. (1995). Myths and methods: "Myths about longitudinal research" plus supplemental questions. In J. Gottman (Ed.), *The Analysis of Change* (pp. 3–66). Mahwah, NJ: Lawrence Erlbaum Associates.

Rubin, D. B. (1976). Inference and missing data. *Biometrika, 63*(3), 581–592.

Rubin, D. B., & Little, R. J. A. (2002). *Statistical Analysis with Missing Data* (2nd ed.). New York: Wiley.

Schafer, J. L., & Graham, J. M. (2002). Missing data: Our view of the state of the art. *Psychological Methods, 7*(2), 147–177. doi:10.1037/1082-989x.7.2.147

Schaie, K. W. (1965). A general model for the study of developmental problems. *Psychological Bulletin, 64*(2), 92–107. doi:10.1037/h0022371

Schaie, K. W. (1994). Developmental designs revisited. In S. H. Cohen & H. W. Reese (Eds), *Life-Span Developmental Psychology: Theoretical issues revisited* (pp. 45–64). Hillsdale, NJ: Erlbaum.

Swets, J. A. (Ed.) (1964). *Signal Detection and Recognition by Human Observers.* New York: Wiley.

Voelkle, M. C., & Adolf, J. (2015). History of longitudinal statistical analysis. In N. A. Pachana (Ed.), *Encyclopedia of Geropsychology* (pp. 1–10). New York: Springer.

Voelkle, M. C., & Oud, J. H. L. (2013). Continuous time modelling with individually varying time intervals for oscillating and non-oscillating processes. *British Journal of Mathematical and Statistical Psychology, 66*(1), 103–126. doi:10.1111/j.2044-8317.2012.02043.x

Voelkle, M. C., Oud, J. H. L., Davidov, E., & Schmidt, P. (2012). An SEM approach to continuous time modeling of panel data: Relating authoritarianism and anomia. *Psychological Methods, 17*(2), 176–192. doi: 10.1037/a0027543

Appendix A

```
###########################################################
### Generating and fitting data of a cross-sequential design under two different conditions of ###
### cohort equivalence and cohort non-equivalence.                                             ###
###########################################################

library(ctsem)
set.seed(8181)

### Step 1. Generate data of single group model-------------------------
complete_model <-ctModel(Tpoints=7, n.latent=1, n.manifest=1, LAMBDA=matrix(c(1),ncol=1),
                         DRIFT=matrix(c(-0.1),nrow=1),MANIFESTVAR=diag(1),DIFFUSION=matrix(c(.5);1,1),
                         CINT=matrix(c(2),ncol=1),nrow=1),TOMEANS=matrix(c(.5),ncol=1,nrow=1), TOVAR=matrix(c(2),nrow=1))

N <- 600 #select total N
complete_data  <-ctGenerate(complete_model,n.subjects=N,burnin=0)
complete_data  <-data.frame(complete_data)

### Step 2. Estimate full (single group) model------------------------
inits     <- c(-0.1, 5, 2, 0.5, 2, 1.1) #set starting values (not necessary, but speeds up the
estimation)
names(inits) <-c("a", "TOmeans", "TOvar", "Q", "cint", "vare")
complete_model_specification <-ctModel(Tpoints=7, n.latent=1, n.manifest=1, LAMBDA=matrix(c(1),ncol=1),
                         DRIFT=matrix(c("a"),nrow=1),
                         MANIFESTVAR=matrix(c("vare"),nrow=1),
DIFFUSION=matrix(c("Q"),1,1),CINT=matrix(c("cint"),ncol=1),TOMEANS=matrix(c("TOmeans"),ncol=1,nrow=1),
                         TOVAR=matrix(c("TOvar"),nrow=1),
                         startValues = inits)

complete_model_out <- ctFit(datawide=complete_data, ctmodelobj=complete_model_specification, showInits
=TRUE, stationary=NULL)
summary(complete_model_out)

### Step 3. Split sample in three cohorts------------------------
mg_data     <- complete_data
mg_data$group <- c(rep("g1",(N/3)), rep("g2",(N/3)), rep("g3",(N/3)))

mg_data[mg_data$group == "g1",][,4:7] <- NA        #delete data group 1
mg_data[mg_data$group == "g2",][,c(1:2,6:7)] <- NA #delete data group 2
mg_data[mg_data$group == "g3",][,c(1:4)] <- NA     #delete data group 3
```

```r
### Step 4. Estimate model under the assumption of cohort equivalence-----------------------------------------
mg_model1_out <- ctFit(datawide=mg_data[,-14], ctmodelobj=complete_model_specification, stationary=NULL,
  showInits =TRUE)
summary(mg_model1_out)

### Step 5. Estimate model under the assumption of cohort equivalence using multiple group sem (equivalent
to Step 4).
mg_constrained <- complete_model_specification
mg_constrained$DRIFT          <- "groupfixed"   # constrain all parameter to equality across cohorts
mg_constrained$MANIFESTVAR    <- "groupfixed"
mg_constrained$DIFFUSION      <- "groupfixed"
mg_constrained$T0VAR          <- "groupfixed"
mg_constrained$T0MEANS        <- "groupfixed"
mg_constrained$CINT           <- "groupfixed"
mg_constrained_out <-   ctMultigroupFit(datawide=mg_data[,-14], groupings=mg_data$group,
                          ctmodelobj=complete_model_specification,
                          fixedmodel=mg_constrained)

summary(mg_constrained_out)

### Step 6. Test hypothesis of differing T0MEANS across cohorts----------------------------------------------
mg_T0MEANSfree              <- mg_constrained
mg_T0MEANSfree$T0MEANS      <- "groupfree"
mg_T0MEANSfree_out          <- ctMultigroupFit(datawide=mg_data[,-14], groupings=mg_data$group,
                                 ctmodelobj=complete_model_specification,
                                 fixedmodel=mg_T0MEANSfree)

summary(mg_T0MEANSfree_out)
mxCompare(mg_T0MEANSfree_out$mxobj, mg_constrained_out$mxobj) # Likelihood ratio test (n.s.)

### Step 7 Generate three cohorts that differ in T0MEANS (g2:-1; g3:+2)--------------------------------------
g1_model <-ctModel(Tpoints=7, n.latent=1, n.manifest=1, LAMBDA=matrix(c(1),ncol=1),
                    DRIFT=matrix(c(-0.1),nrow=1),MANIFESTVAR=diag(1),DIFFUSION=matrix(c(.5),1,1),
                    CINT=matrix(c(2),ncol=1),T0MEANS=matrix(c(5),ncol=1,nrow=1), T0VAR=matrix(c(.5),1,1))
g2_model <-ctModel(Tpoints=7, n.latent=1, n.manifest=1, LAMBDA=matrix(c(1),ncol=1),
                    DRIFT=matrix(c(-0.1),nrow=1),MANIFESTVAR=diag(1),DIFFUSION=matrix(c(.5),1,1),
                    CINT=matrix(c(2),ncol=1),T0MEANS=matrix(c(4),nrow=1,ncol=1), T0VAR=matrix(c(.5),1,1))
g3_model <-ctModel(Tpoints=7, n.latent=1, n.manifest=1, LAMBDA=matrix(c(1),ncol=1),
                    DRIFT=matrix(c(-0.1),nrow=1),MANIFESTVAR=diag(1),DIFFUSION=matrix(c(.5),1,1),
                    CINT=matrix(c(2),ncol=1),T0MEANS=matrix(c(7),ncol=1,nrow=1), T0VAR=matrix(c(.5),1,1))
g1_data  <-ctGenerate(g1_model,n.subjects=(N/3),burnin=0)
g2_data  <-ctGenerate(g2_model,n.subjects=(N/3),burnin=0)
g3_data  <-ctGenerate(g3_model,n.subjects=(N/3),burnin=0)
```

```r
row.names(g1_data) <- NULL
row.names(g2_data) <- NULL
row.names(g3_data) <- NULL
mg_data_leveldifferences <- data.frame(rbind(g1_data,g2_data,g3_data))
mg_data_leveldifferences$group <- c(rep("g1",(N/3)), rep("g2",(N/3)), rep("g3",(N/3)))
mg_data_leveldifferences[mg_data_leveldifferences$group == "g1",][,4:7] <- NA      #delete data group 1
mg_data_leveldifferences[mg_data_leveldifferences$group == "g2",][,c(1:2,6:7)] <- NA   #delete data group 2
mg_data_leveldifferences[mg_data_leveldifferences$group == "g3",][,c(1:4)] <- NA   #delete data group 3

### Step 8. Test hypothesis of differing TOMEANS across cohorts------------------
mg_TOMEANSfixed            <- mg_constrained
mg_TOMEANSfixed_out        <- ctMultigroupFit(datawide= mg_data_leveldifferences[, -14],
groupings=mg_data_leveldifferences$group,
                            ctmodelobj=complete_model_specification,
                            fixedmodel=mg_TOMEANSfixed)

summary(mg_TOMEAN Sfixed_out)
mg_TOMEANSfree         <- mg_TOMEANSfixed
mg_TOMEANSfree$TOMEANS  <- "groupfree"
mg_TOMEANSfree_out2     <- ctMultigroupFit(datawide=mg_data_leveldifferences[,  -14],
                            ctmodelobj=complete_model_specification,
                            fixedmodel=mg_TOMEANSfree, showInits=TRUE)
groupings=mg_data_leveldifferences$group,

summary(mg_TOMEANSfree_out2)
mxCompare(mg_TOMEANSfree_out2$mxobj, mg_TOMEANSfixed_out$mxobj) # Lik elihood ratio test (significant)   ------------------

### Step 9. Test hypothesis of differing TOMEANS and differing DRIFT across cohorts   ------------------
mg_TOMEANS_DRIFT_free       <- mg_TOMEANSfree
mg_TOMEANS_DRIFT_free$DRIFT  <- "groupfree"
mginitslog <- c(5, log(0.1), 1, lo g(0.5), log(4), 2, 4, log(0.1), 7, log(0.1))
names(mginitslog) <- c("g1_TOmeans", "g1_a", "vare", "Q", "TOvar", "cint", "g2_TOmeans", "g2_a",
"g3_TOmeans", "g3_a")
mg_TOMEANS_DRIFT_free_out <- ctMultigroupFit(datawide=mg_data_leveldifferences[,  -14],
groupings=mg_data_leveldifferences$group,
                            ctmodelobj=complete_model_specification,
                            fixedmodel=mg_TOMEANS_DRIFT_free,
                            showInits=TRUE, retryattempts = 10,

omxStartValues=mginitslog)
summary(mg_TOMEANS_DRIFT_free_out)

mxCompare(mg_TOMEANS_DRIFT_free_out$mxobj, mg_TOMEANSfree_out2$mxobj) # Likelihood ratio test (n.s.)
```

9

FAMILY CONNECTEDNESS AND ITS ASSOCIATION WITH PSYCHOLOGICAL WELL-BEING AMONG EMERGING ADULTS ACROSS FOUR CULTURAL CONTEXTS

Amina Abubakar, Maja Schachner,
Arzu Aydinli Karakulak, Itziar Alonso-Arbiol,
Virginia Martinez-Fernandez, Moses Kachama
Nyongesa, and Halimu Shauri

Background

When a person is actively involved with another person, object, group, or environment, then the person is said to be socially connected (Hagerty, Lynch-Sauer, Patusky, & Bouwsema, 1993). Karcher, Holcomb, and Zambrano posit that connectedness reflects a youth's volitional involvement in relationships, contexts and activities that they find worthwhile and important, and that provides positive experiences (Karcher, Holcomb, & Zambrano, 2008). Connectedness is ecological in nature and it involves all-important micro-, macro- and meso-systems that the adolescent experiences (Karcher & Santos, 2011). The micro-system here includes important relationships such as parents, siblings, teachers, and peers. The macro-system is made up of institutions in the youth's life that he or she experiences on a day-to-day basis such as family, school, religious, and ethnic/cultural groups. Additionally, connectedness is assumed to be developmental in nature and may develop as a result of: (a) attachment to caregivers, (b) interpersonal support, and (c) group level experiences (Karcher et al., 2008).

The study of connectedness has become more popular as there is growing empirical evidence indicating that connectedness acts as a protector against negative developmental outcomes such as depression, suicide, and suicidal ideation among others (Mcgraw, Moore, Fuller, & Bates, 2008; Millings, Buck, Montgomery, Spears, & Stallard, 2012; Shochet, Homel, Cockshaw, & Montgomery, 2008; Whitlock, Wyman, & Moore, 2014). Connectedness has been associated to various positive developmental outcomes such as enhanced psychological well-being, life satisfaction, and school completion among others (Abubakar, van de Vijver, Mazrui, Murugami, & Arasa, 2014; Crespo, Jose, Kielpikowski, & Pryor, 2013; Jose, Ryan, & Pryor, 2012). Moreover, connectedness has been observed to be especially amenable to intervention; this implies that studying this area and understanding moderating factors has implications for practitioners interested in initiating programs for positive youth development.

Family connectedness refers to the extent to which children feel that closeness, warmth, support, and responsiveness is important for their psychological well-being. The influence of family connectedness on the behavior of children has been widely documented. For instance, a recent study in the US indicated that family connectedness acts as a protective factor against depression (Houltberg, Henry, Merten, & Robinson, 2011). In this study, 248 students from a public high school were administered a set of measures including those of family connectedness and depressed mood (Houltberg et al., 2011), then various models were tested. In all the tested models, it was observed that family connectedness was negatively associated with depressed mood. Few studies have analyzed the comparative strength of different domains of connectedness (e.g., family, peers, and school) to determine where limited resources might best be focused when planning an intervention. A study involving 4,131 7th–12th graders in the US reported that family connectedness was a stronger predictor than connectedness to peers, school, or adults at school for non-suicidal self-harm, suicidal ideation, suicide plans, and non-fatal suicidal behavior (Kaminski et al., 2010). These results suggest that although all aspects of connectedness are important, family connectedness is especially salient for the well-being of a person. However, there are important gaps in the literature including the extent to which the same patterns can be observed among emerging adults, the cross cultural invariance of the reported relationships, and a strong focus on negative aspects of functioning such as problem behavior and mental health issues.

Emerging Adulthood

Chronologically, emerging adulthood was initially defined as a time between 18–25 years (Arnett, 2000) although the upper limit has now been revised to 29 years (Arnett, 2011). During this life stage, people are no longer adolescents yet they may not have fully assumed adulthood roles. This period in many countries usually coincides with undergraduate studies, for those who go ahead and pursue higher education.

From adolescence to young adulthood, within the family context, there is usually a renegotiation of the parent–child relationship. During this time, there is a movement toward autonomy although lots of effort is put into ensuring that the connectedness between family members is not totally disrupted. In line with theoretical assertions that the transition to adulthood does not imply a disruption of family bonds but a transformation in the direction of a greater interdependence, it would generally be assumed that even at emerging adulthood, family connectedness would still remain important. However, few studies such as those by Lee and Robbins (2000) have investigated connectedness among undergraduate students. Even fewer studies have looked at the associations between family connectedness and functioning among university students. It was therefore important to evaluate the extent to which the patterns observed at adolescence can still be observed at this age.

Moderators of the Association between Family Connectedness and Well-Being: Culture and Gender

In terms of interpersonal relationships, cultures differ in the manner in which they emphasize the relative contribution of autonomy and relatedness (Greenfield, Keller, Fuligni, & Maynard, 2003; Kağitçibaşi, 2013; Keller, 2012). Some cultures place relatively more importance on autonomy, personal achievement, and self-directedness while other cultural groups place more emphasis on group harmony, cohesion, and common goals. Kağitçibaşi (2006) notes that there are societal changes taking place in many countries with a strong tradition of relatedness and interdependency. Due to these changes, a significant proportion of their population is becoming more modern, urbanized, and educated. In such countries, a value pattern in which both economic independence and emotional interdependence are valued can emerge. These patterns of cultural values may imply that the significance or saliency of family connectedness to psychological well-being may be moderated by culture. These assertions are further supported in conclusions reached by Townsend and McWhirter (2005) in their review more than a decade ago. In this review, the authors reported that the health benefits of connectedness were moderated by culture and gender. They noted that there was empirical evidence to indicate that there may be key differences in the way connectedness is expressed and experienced in Western versus non-Western settings. Based on both theoretical and empirical evidence, we would expect that in cultural contexts such as Germany where autonomy is emphasized, connectedness would be important but not as important as in cultural contexts where interdependence is emphasized, such as, for example, Turkey and Kenya. Therefore, we expected that culture would moderate the relationship between family connectedness and psychological well-being.

Gender has been observed to shape the experiences of emerging adults. Both gender-based similarities and differences are noted in the literature (for details, see Norona, Preddy, & Welsh, 2015). Some of the key areas that have been observed to be gender influenced include family relationships and identity formation. Norona and colleagues when discussing the influence of gender on interpersonal relationships note that although there are differences, there are a lot more similarities with males and females working towards building emotional and financial independence from their parents during this developmental period (Norona et al., 2015). The literature on connectedness and gender presents inconsistent findings, with some studies reporting a gender difference while others do not observe this difference (Bekker & van Assen, 2008). Karcher and Lee (2002), in a study involving high school students from Taiwan, noted that girls reported consistently higher scores than boys in almost all the subscales examined. In another study carried out in the USA, using photographic depictions, it was reported that women were more likely to define themselves in a more socially connected manner than men (Clancy & Dollinger, 1993). However, other studies such as those by Lee and Robbins (1995, 2000) do not report clear-cut gender differences. For instance, Lee and Robbins (2000) observed that connectedness was important for both genders, although the domains and relationships emphasized varied as a result of the gender. Although the empirical evidence on gender is still quite mixed, the overwhelming amount of evidence seems to indicate that gender does not moderate the relationship between family connectedness and psychological outcomes.

According to the family capital theory (Waithaka, 2014), families with more resources will invest relatively more resources into both tangible and non-tangible activities and items aimed at enhancing the well-being of their children. Empirical evidence supports these assertions. For instance, earlier studies indicate that children from higher socioeconomic status (SES) will present with higher social connectedness scores, higher life satisfaction scores, and lower scores in mental health problems. Based on both empirical and theoretical evidence we would expect that high SES in our sample will be associated with better family connectedness and high life satisfaction scores and lower scores on mental health problems.

Current Study

The purpose of the study was to investigate relationships between family connectedness and psychological well-being across cultural contexts and gender. The sampling was carried out to enhance diversity both in economic standards, i.e., Germany (high income), Spain (middle/high income), Turkey (middle/low income), and Kenya (low income). Also, the sampling was carried out to enhance variability in core cultural dimension (relatedness vs. autonomy). We look at this as a continuum and we expect variations from highly autonomous (Germany) then Spain, Turkey, and Kenya being at the highest level of interdependency. In this section, we will start by providing details of the contexts in which we sample from before discussing the research questions and specific hypothesis.

Germany is located in central Europe. It has a total population of 80.89 million people as per the 2014 demographics. The GDP as at 2014 was estimated at 3.868 trillion US dollars. Gross national income (GNI) per capita as of 2014 was estimated at 47,640 US dollars (World Bank, 2016). It is estimated that about 15% of Germans are now living below the poverty line. Sixty-eight percent of the population is Christian while a minority of 3.7% practice Islamic religion, 28.3% of the German population has no religious affiliation, or belong to other religious groups (CIA, 2016). On Hofstede cultural value, Germany is a highly individualistic society (Hofstede, 2016) where autonomy is valued and socialized early; Germans value secularism over traditionalism. There is a strong pressure towards raising independent children and this has been observed to manifest itself early including through encouraging infants to sleep alone (Valentin, 2005).

Spain is a country with a current population of more than 45 million inhabitants, mostly nationals (only 10% immigrants), and of Catholic faith. Social indicators point to a significant reduction in poverty levels (20.9% of unemployment in 2015) and economic inequality levels, and a narrower coverage of the social welfare system as compared to the 1990s (Instituto Nacional de Estadística, 2015). According to Hofstede's (2016) cultural values, Spain may be considered as a collectivist country when compared with the rest of the European countries (with the exception of Portugal), although in a more global context may be seen as individualist. Hence, the autonomy of young Spaniards as compared to other European cultures is not a priority, still valuing the maintenance of family bonds and social cohesion (Oliva & Parra, 2001), although to a lesser extent than Portugal and Latin American countries, such as Colombia (Musitu, 2000).

Turkey is a country with a total population of 80 million, with the majority of residents (almost 99%) self-identifying as Muslim (Pew Research Center, 2014). Over the last decades, Turkey underwent a process of modernization and globalization, having moved from a predominantly rural and agricultural society in the 1950s towards an economically more developed and more urban and industrialized society (Rasuly-Paleczek, 1996). Even through Turkey is currently ranked on an intermediate position between individualism and collectivism (Hofstede, Hofstede, & Minkov, 2010), its strong focus on collectivistic values (Göregenli, 1997), conservatism, hierarchy, and harmony values (Schwartz, 1999) cannot be neglected. Contrary to predictions of modernization theories (e.g., Inkeles & Smith, 1974), Turkey did *not* give up its traditional values. In spite of economic development, Turkish culture places huge emphasis on familial ties and bonds and on religious and spiritual values (Carkoglu & Kalaycioglu, 2009; Kağitçibaşi, 2005, 2007) which is supported by contemporary surveys. For instance, 72% of the Turkish population reports that family solidarity represents their *most important value* when bringing up their children (Anna Lindh Foundation, 2014), and 85% of the Turkish population (and 73% of those with a university degree) consider themselves as religious (World Values Survey, 2011). By that, Turkey seems to represent neither a typically Western nor a typically Eastern culture: Even though economic development lessened financial dependencies between family members and relatives, emotional dependencies, expressing themselves in an emphasis on maintaining close relationships and strong emotional ties with family members, exist (Kağitçibaşi, 2007). Turkish culture therefore describes a cultural context that is both high in autonomy and relatedness, both modern and religious, and both individualistic and collectivistic.

Kenya is a country on the East African Coast. It is home to an estimated 44.86 million people. The country is made up of diverse ethnic groups (estimated 42 different ethnic groups). Kenya is categorized as low–middle income with an estimated GDP per capita of 1,358 US dollars. It is estimated that 45.9% of Kenyans live below the poverty line. In terms of religion, the largest population in Kenya is Christian (80%). The other religions include Islam, traditional religions, Judaism among others. On Hofstede's cultural dimension, Kenya is very low on individualism and high on collectivism (Hofstede, 2016). This is evidenced by a culture of long term commitment to social groups, e.g., extended families. In Kenya, family ties are generally very strong with the practice of communitarianism being extremely common. Communitarianism is the practice of familism and collectivism over individualism in resource generation and distribution and is still widely practiced (Njue, Rombo, & Ngige, 2007). Familism ensures that the family members allocate their resources to helping other less fortunate members of the family. For instance, it is common to find more educated family members contributing to meeting the education costs of younger siblings and relatives as a means of reciprocating with their parents for their own upbringing (Njue et al., 2007). These characteristics have been observed to provide the family with resilience even in the case of many challenges. Traditionally, Kenyan families lived in extended homesteads. However, social changes have contributed to more and more families living in nuclear units especially when they are in urban settings.

Based on state-of-the-art recommendations to first test the validity and measurement invariance of a measure before application in studies across nations (van de Vijver & Leung, 1997), we first carried out tests of measurement invariance across cultural groups. We followed multiple hierarchical steps (Byrne & van de Vijver, 2010; van de Schoot, Lugtig, & Hox, 2012) by testing configural invariance (the same number of factors and pattern of fixed and freely estimated parameters hold across groups) and metric invariance (equivalence of factor loadings indicating that respondents from multiple groups attribute the same meaning to the latent construct of interest). Next, we addressed the main research goal by testing a model of relationships between family connectedness and psychological well-being. In this study, the term psychological well-being is used to encompass both positive psychological functioning (assessed by life satisfaction) and negative psychological functioning (assessed by poor mental health). A partial mediated model, where parental education was associated with family connected and psychological well-being, was hypothesized. Figure 9.1 presents the hypothesized model. Specifically, we hypothesized that:

1   A high level of parental education would be positively associated with family connectedness.
2   High scores on family connectedness and high levels of parental education would be associated with enhanced psychological well-being across cultural contexts.
3   Relationships between family connectedness and psychological well-being would be moderated by cultural context.
4   Relationships between family connectedness and psychological well-being will not be moderated by gender.

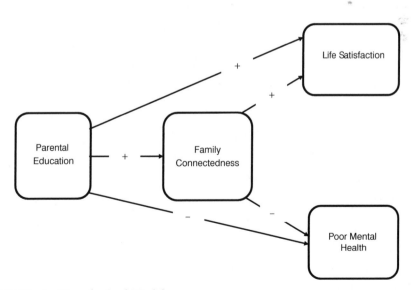

FIGURE 9.1   Hypothesized Model

Method

Study Sites and Sample

The study was carried out in four countries, namely Kenya, Spain, Germany, and Turkey. The sample was made up of undergraduate students from various countries. A total of 498 students (females: 66.3%) were sampled for this study. From Germany (n = 91), Kenya (n = 192), Spain (n = 98), and Turkey (n = 112) participants were sampled. The mean age was 21.27 years (SD = 2.30). Table 9.1 below presents more details on the basic characteristics of the sample. Most of the data was collected in the classroom during lecture hours with the exception of Turkey where data were collected using an online survey.

TABLE 9.1 Demographics

	Germany	*Kenya*	*Spain*	*Turkey*
N	91	193	98	116
Age in Years				
Range (Min–Max)	17–29	18–28	17–28	18–28
Mean (SD)	21.37 (2.74)	21.53 (1.95)	20.30 (2.60)	21.63 (2.11)
Gender				
Frequency (%)				
Females	77 (84.6)	81 (42.0)	74 (75.5)	98 (84.5)
Highest Level of Education (Father)				
Frequency (%)				
Unschooled	0 (0.0)	13 (6.7)	1 (1.0)	1 (0.9)
Primary Education	1 (1.1)	23 (11.9)	19 (19.4)	10 (8.6)
Secondary Education	44 (48.4)	44 (22.8)	58 (59.2)	45 (38.8)
Tertiary/University	44 (48.4)	106 (54.9)	19 (19.4)	60 (51.7)
Missing	2 (2.2)	7 (3.6)	1 (1.0)	0 (0.0)
Highest Level of Education (Mother)				
Frequency (%)				
Unschooled	0 (0.0)	19 (9.8)	1 (1.0)	3 (2.6)
Primary Education	2 (2.2)	45 (23.3)	18 (18.4)	14 (12.1)
Secondary Education	39 (42.9)	52 (26.9)	50 (51.0)	50 (43.1)
Tertiary/University	50 (54.9)	75 (38.9)	27 (27.6)	49 (42.2)
Missing	0 (0.0)	2 (1.0)	2 (2.0)	0 (0.0)

TABLE 9.2 Means, Standard Deviations, and Alphas of Each Scale per Country

	Germany	Kenya	Spain	Turkey
Family Connectedness				
Mean (SD)	44.37 (7.7)	42.35 (8.3)	41.93 (7.1)	44.22 (8.6)
Cronbach's alpha	0.89	0.90	0.88	0.93
General Health Questionnaire				
Mean (SD)	11.62 (4.6)	10.83 (6.9)	11.30 (4.4)	14.04 (6.1)
Cronbach's alpha	0.80	0.84	0.74	0.87
Life Satisfaction				
Mean (SD)	33.05 (4.5)	31.04 (6.1)	35.57 (3.8)	30.62 (5.3)
Cronbach's alpha	0.76	0.82	0.80	0.75

Measures

The scales used in this study were translated from English into each country's language using recommended guidelines for ensuring linguistic equivalence (van de Vijver & Leung, 1997). Using Cronbach's coefficient alpha, we investigated the internal consistency of the connectedness and measures of psychological well-being scales per country. All coefficients were above the recommended cut-off of .70 indicating good internal consistency (Cicchetti, 1994). The results of the alphas are shown in Table 9.2.

Social Demographics

Students provided data on their age, gender, and parental education. The mother's and father's level of education was coded on a four-point scale (1 = *no education*, 2 = *primary education*, 3 = *secondary education*, and 4 = *tertiary education*). In our analysis, we summed up maternal and paternal education to get a composite parental education score.

Family Connectedness

We used a previously published scale to *measure* family connectedness (Jose et al., 2012). The measure has 11 items measuring various components of family connectedness including cohesion and mutual activities. Sample items include "For my family, spending time together is very important" and "We are proud to be members of our family." The measure is scored on a five-point Likert scale from 1 "Strongly disagree" to 5 "Strongly agree."

Poor Mental Health

The 12-item General Health Questionnaire (GHQ-12) was administered to evaluate mental health (Goldberg, 1992). The GHQ-12 was developed as a screening tool for detecting minor psychiatric disturbance or strain. The measure assesses changes in affective and somatic symptoms. In the current study, a Likert response scale was used, with scoring options of 0-1-2-3. A sample item includes "Have you recently felt that you couldn't overcome your difficulties, 0 = not at all, 1 = no more than usual, 2 = rather more than usual, 3 = much more than usual." Cross-cultural validity of GHQ-12 has previously been reported (Abubakar & Fischer, 2012; Abubakar et al., 2014). Table 9.2 presents the alphas of the GHQ-12 per country.

Life Satisfaction

The Brief Multidimensional Students' Life Satisfaction Scales (BMSLSS) was administered (Huebner, Suldo, Valois, & Drane, 2006). This scale has six items inquiring on satisfaction with different domains (e.g., school and family) and a global question. A sample item includes "I would describe my satisfaction with my school experiences as…" It is scored on a seven-point Likert scale ranging from 1 (*terrible*) to 7 (*delighted*). Cross-cultural validity of BMSLSS has previously been reported (Abubakar et al., 2016). Table 9.2 presents the alphas of the BMSLSS per country.

Analytic Procedures

Three steps were carried out in analyzing the data. First, to investigate factorial structure of the measures to be used, a confirmatory factor analytic approach was used. We assessed the goodness of fit for each model using various parameters. The general guideline is that a non-significant Chi-square reflects an acceptable fit to the data. However, given the sensitivity of the Chi-square statistic to sample size, we did not consider this in the current study. Instead, values greater than .95 for the Tucker-Lewis index (TLI) and Comparative Fit Index (CFI) are considered to reflect an excellent fit (Hu & Bentler, 1999), while values between .95 and .90 are considered indicative of an acceptable fit. In a multi-group analysis, the change in CFI is an important indicator for evaluating the suitability of hierarchically nested models; a CFI change of less than .010 is taken to be supportive of the more restrictive model (Milfont & Fischer, 2015). The Root Mean Squares Error of Approximation (RMSEA) are also reported since they have been shown to be sensitive to model misspecification; values of less than .06 are considered indicative of a good fit while those between .06 and .08 are considered indicative of an acceptable model. Second, bivariate correlational analysis between key variables was carried out to investigate the relationship between the variables of interest. Since we were not interested in looking at the effects of age, we corrected for age. To age standardize our scores, we used regression methods where age was an independent variable and each of the other variables (family connectedness, life satisfaction, and poor mental health) were dependent variables. We saved the standardized residuals from each of this analysis and use these standardized residuals in our path analytic model. Third, path analytic procedures were used to investigate the relationship between connectedness, life satisfaction, and mental health.

Results

Confirmatory Factor Analyses and Measurement Invariance

We implemented a set of measurement models to establish whether the factor structure of the family connectedness showed invariance across groups. We tested a single latent variable and the results indicated a good fit of the one factor model to the data and an acceptable metric invariance [$(\chi^2$ (194, $N = 498)$ $= 437.54, p < .001, \chi^2/$ df $= 2.25$, TLI $= .910$, CFI $= .920$, Δ CFI$= .008$ and RMSEA $= .050$]; although several of the error variances had to be correlated.

Associations between Connectedness and Psychological Well-being

Table 9.3 presents the correlation matrix for the variables in the study by country. The table indicates that in all the four countries, family connectedness is positively and significantly associated with life satisfaction. Family connectedness was also negatively and significantly associated with mental health problems; these patterns were similar in all four countries.

Invariance of the Associations between Family Connectedness and Psychological Well-Being across Cultures

We tested the associations between parental education, family connectedness, life satisfaction, and mental health using a multi-group path analytic model. Having evaluated the correlational patterns between parental education and the outcome variables, we did not fix the factor loadings since we expected that the associations between the factor loadings and the outcome variables will vary by national context. The structural weights model indicated a very good fit of the data to the proposed model [$(\chi^2$ (6, $N = 498) = 6.98, p = .327, \chi^2/$ df $= 1.156$, TLI $= .965$, CFI $= .995$, Δ CFI$= .005$ and RMSEA $= .018$]) implying a partial invariance in the relationship between these variables across countries. See Figure 9.2 for the standardized coefficients from this path analytic model.

TABLE 9.3 Correlation between Key Variables

		1	2	3	4	5
	Germany					
1	Life Satisfaction	1				
2	Mental Health	−.428★★	1			
3	Family Connectedness	.330★★	−.122	1		
4	Age	−.208★	.193	−.254★	1	
5	Gender	−.089	.202	.174	−.065	1
6	Parental Education	.083	−.079	.193	.100	.076
	Kenya					
1	Life Satisfaction	1				
2	Mental Health	−.286★★	1			
3	Family Connectedness	.543★★	−.238★★	1		
4	Age	.067	−.115	−.032	1	
5	Gender	−.125	.009	−.074	−.252★★	1
6	Parental Education	.126	−.146★	.198★★	−.153★	.280★★
	Spain					
1	Life Satisfaction	1				
2	Mental Health	−.340★★	1			
3	Family Connectedness	.547★★	−.249★	1		
4	Age	−.267★★	.140	−.338★★	1	
5	Gender	−.044	.083	−.067	.056	1
6	Parental Education	.123	.030	.124	−.157	.010
	Turkey					
1	Life Satisfaction	1				
2	Mental Health	−.374★★	1			
3	Family Connectedness	.440★★	−.300★★	1		
4	Age	.028	.092	.046	1	
5	Gender	.074	.075	.056	.063	1
6	Parental Education	.039	−.253★★	−.072	.072	−.001

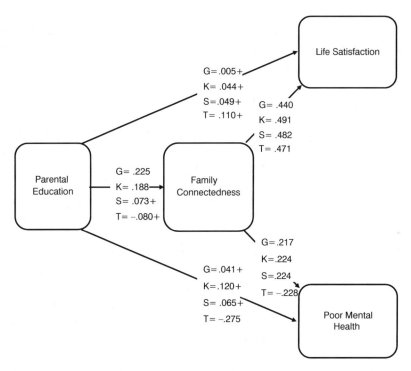

FIGURE 9.2 Standardized Regressions Weight from the Path Analysis

NB: G= Germany, K= Kenya, S= Spain, and T= Turkey

+ represents non-significant coefficients

Noteworthy is the fact that the amount of variance explained for life satisfaction and mental health across countries was largely small or moderate, although the variance explained for life satisfaction is consistently higher than that of mental health. For life satisfaction, the variance explained ranged from 8.7% in Germany to 30% in Kenya, while for mental health it ranged from 1.2% in Germany to 16.4% in Turkey.

Invariance of the Associations between Family Connectedness and Psychological Well-Being by Gender

We also examined whether or not the association between parental education, family connectedness, and psychological well-being was invariant by gender. The results indicated a good fit of the data to the proposed model as seen by the structural weight model results [(χ^2 (6, N = 498) = 6.65, p = .354, χ^2/ df = 1.109, TLI = .988, CFI = .996, Δ CFI= .004 and RMSEA = .015], implying an invariance in the relationship between these variables across gender. Again here, the variance explained for life satisfaction was consistently higher than that of mental health. For life satisfaction, the variance explained was 19.7% for females and 18.4% for males, while for mental health it was 3.4% for females and 8.1% for males.

Discussion

We set out to evaluate the extent to which family connectedness is potentially associated with psychological well-being among emerging adults across cultural contexts. Our results indicate that the relationship between family connectedness and psychological well-being is invariant across cultural contexts and across gender. Consistent with our first hypothesis, we observed that connectedness was positively associated with life satisfaction and negatively associated with mental health problems. These results are concurrent with what has been earlier reported (Abubakar et al., 2014; Crespo, Kielpikowski, Jose, & Pryor, 2010; Jose & Crespo, 2011). Moreover, the results are in line with theory; as noted by scholars such as Baumeister and Leary (1995), the need to belong is universal and connectedness does serve this need.

The role of the family across cultural contexts has been discussed extensively in the literature with both empirical and theoretical evidence indicating that different cultural groups put different levels of emphasis on relatedness and autonomy (Greenfield et al., 2003; Keller, 2012). Based on these theoretical suppositions, one would have expected that the associations between connectedness and psychological well-being to be moderated by culture; with some cultures which are high on interrelatedness (e.g., Kenya and Turkey) having stronger associations between family connectedness and well-being. Contrary to our second hypothesis, we did not see any moderation by culture. There are two potential explanations for the lack of cultural differences in our study. One explanation is that family connectedness played an equally important role in fostering well-being. This would be in line with theoretical suppositions from fields such as evolutionary psychology where next of kins are equally important regardless of the cultural contexts. Another potential line of explanation is the sample we have. One of the key things we wanted to vary in our study was the economic standing of the different groups. While we clearly achieved this at the country level, at the individual level it is not very clear if this was achieved. Noteworthy here is the fact that both the Kenyan and Turkish sample report having highly educated parents; a rate much higher than expected national average. Therefore, parental SES may have influenced the patterns we observed. As we do not have similar studies to compare our patterns of results, it is best to see these as preliminary findings worth replicating with more cultural groups involved.

In line with our third hypothesis, gender did not moderate the association between family connectedness and psychological well-being. The debate on whether or not gender is an important moderator on levels of connectedness and its association with different outcomes has been ongoing for some time; however, there was sufficient data to indicate that in the association between family connectedness and psychological well-being, gender is not a moderator. For instance, a study by Abubakar et al. (2014) indicated the association between social connectedness (encompassing more than family connectedness) and psychological well-being was invariant by gender, although contradicts other studies such as those by our findings on gender invariance need to be interpreted with caution. First, there is a need for further replication in different cross-cultural groups, which would allow for more firm conclusions. Additionally, due to sample size constraints, we did not get an opportunity to evaluate the potential role of gender-culture interactions.

Psychological well-being has been vastly defined. An important discussion here has always been that the absence of mental health problems does not necessarily imply that someone is doing well mentally (Huppert & Whittington, 2003). Moreover, pathways to poor negative psychological outcomes and positive psychological outcomes may vary. Therefore, it has been suggested that in measuring well-being, it is important to look at both positive and negative aspects of well-being. Previous research shows that sometimes the associations between positive and negative aspects of well-being and psychological with antecedent variables may differ considerably. For instance, a meta-analysis on associations between ethnic identity and psychological well-being observed:

> Studies correlating ethnic identity with self-esteem and positive well-being yielded average effect sizes twice as large as those from studies correlating ethnic identity with personal distress or mental health symptoms. Thus ethnic identity was more strongly related to positive well-being than to compromised well-being.
>
> (Smith & Silva, 2011, p. 42)

We were therefore keen to examine the associations between connectedness and both negative and positive well-being. Our results are similar to what was reported in the meta-analysis on ethnic identity (Smith & Silva, 2011). It seems that for positive youth development, connectedness explains more variance for positive well-being consistently as compared to negative well-being. Based on our results, one could conclude that, while family connectedness has important protective effects both for positive and negative aspects of well-being, it is more salient for the positive well-being. These results may imply that connectedness needs to be a stronger target for interventions on positive youth development.

Implications for Practice to Promote Positive Youth Development

Intervention strategies that aim at enhancing the level of connectedness that emerging adults feel towards their families of origin need to be developed as this is likely to enhance their well-being. In brief, a few practical implications are outlined here.

- Research indicates that poor psychological functioning and mental health problems are common among emerging adults at the universities (Bayram & Bilgel, 2008; Eisenberg, Gollust, Golberstein, & Hefner, 2007; Ovuga, Boardman, & Wasserman, 2006). These factors interfere with their optimal functioning. Our findings imply that one way to address this problem is to implement intervention strategies aimed at fostering connectedness between the emerging adults and their families. Most of the interventions so far aimed at fostering connectedness have been largely focused on adolescents (Karcher, 2005; Karcher & Santos, 2011). There is, therefore, a necessity for concerted efforts to develop intervention programs aimed at addressing the need of emerging adults.
- Cross-cultural and gender invariance observed in our study implies that the interventions developed may potentially be useful across a large population. This potential makes the work more efficient and easy to implement. Formal evaluations of programs need to be undertaken before more firm conclusions can be reached.
- As alluded to by the theoretical suppositions by Karcher et al. (2008), family connectedness has developmental roots in levels of attachment. So it is expected that emerging adults reporting higher levels of connectedness will have experienced high levels of attachment security even when they were young. The cross-sectional nature of our study implies that we cannot make very strong conclusions on this. However, the implication of this is that there may be a need to implement interventions on connectedness early in life to optimize on the positive impact of these interventions on positive youth development.

Limitations

Our findings add some interesting insights on how to optimize the outcomes of emerging adults at university. However, the study has three important limitations. First, it is all based on self-report which may increase self-report bias. Data arising from multi-informants and multi-method may increase the validity of the findings. Second, connectedness has different ecological bases including family, school, and community. We only evaluate a single setting. The extent to which the other settings are important would add important information on the diversity of interventions needed to optimize outcomes. Last, our study is cross-sectional in nature. This implies that we can only look at associations and not causations.

Conclusions

Concurrent with earlier observations, we observed that family connectedness plays an important role in shaping psychological outcomes of emerging adults across very different cultural settings. Programs and interventions aimed at enhancing family connectedness are likely to contribute to positive youth development on a global scale.

Funding

Amina Abubakar is supported by a Marie Curie Individual European Fellowships [grant number PIEF-GA-2013-629874]. Data collection of the Spanish sample was made possible thanks to a grant from the Spanish Ministry of Economy and Competitivity (PSi2012-35471).

References

Abubakar, A., & Fischer, R. (2012). The factor structure of the 12-item General Health Questionnaire in a literate Kenyan population. *Stress and Health, 28*(3), 248–254. http://dx.doi.org/10.1002/smi.1420

Abubakar, A., van de Vijver, F. J., Mazrui, L., Murugami, M., & Arasa, J. (2014). Connectedness and psychological well-being among adolescents of immigrant background in Kenya. In Dimitrova, R., Bender, M., & van de Vijver, F. J. R. (Eds), *Global perspectives on well-being in immigrant families* (pp. 95–111). New York: Springer.

Abubakar, A., van de Vijver, F., Alonso-Arbiol, I., He, J., Adams, B., Aldhafri, S., ... & Dimitrova, R. (2016). Measurement Invariance of the Brief Multidimensional Student's Life Satisfaction Scale Among Adolescents and Emerging Adults Across 23 Cultural Contexts. *Journal of Psychoeducational Assessment, 34*(1), 28–38.

Anna Lindh Foundation (2014). *The Anna Lindh Report 2014: Intercultural trends and social change in the Euro-Mediterranean region.* Retrieved from www.annalindhfoundation. org/sites/annalindh.org/files/documents/page/anna_lindh_report14.pdf, accessed on March 17, 2016.

Arnett, J. J. (2000). Emerging adulthood: A theory of development from the late teens through the twenties. *American Psychologist, 55*, 469–480.

Arnett, J. J. (2011). Emerging adulthood(s): The cultural psychology of a new life stage. In Arnett, L. A. Jensen (Ed.), *Bridging cultural and developmental approaches to psychology: New syntheses in theory, research, and policy* (pp. 255–275). New York: Oxford University Press.

Baumeister, R. F., & Leary, M. R. (1995). The need to belong: Desire for interpersonal attachments as a fundamental human motivation. *Psychological Bulletin, 117*(3), 497–529.

Bayram, N., & Bilgel, N. (2008). The prevalence and socio-demographic correlations of depression, anxiety and stress among a group of university students. *Social Psychiatry and Psychiatric Epidemiology, 43*(8), 667–672.

Bekker, M. H., & van Assen, M. A. (2008). Autonomy-connectedness and gender. *Sex Roles, 59*(7–8), 532–544.

Byrne, B. M., & van de Vijver, F. J. R. (2010). Testing for measurement and structural equivalence in large-scale cross-cultural studies: Addressing the issue of nonequivalence. *International Journal of Testing, 10*(2), 107–132.

Carkoglu, A., & Kalaycioglu, E. (2009). *Religiosity in Turkey: A cross-national investigation.* Istanbul: Sabanci University, Istanbul Policy Center.

CIA (2016) The world factbook. Accessed on 19 March, 2016, retrieved from https://www.cia.gov/library/publications/resources/the-world-factbook/geos/ke.html

Cicchetti, D. V. (1994). Guidelines, criteria, and rules of thumb for evaluating normed and standardized assessment instruments in psychology. *Psychological Assessment, 6*(4), 284–290.

Clancy, S., M., & Dollinger, S. J. (1993). Photographic depictions of the self: Gender and age differences in social connectedness. *Sex Roles, 29*, 477–495.

Crespo, C., Jose, P. E., Kielpikowski, M., & Pryor, J. (2013). "On solid ground": Family and school connectedness promotes adolescents' future orientation. *Journal of Adolescence, 36*(5), 993–1002.

Crespo, C., Kielpikowski, M., Jose, P. E., & Pryor, J. (2010). Relationships between family connectedness and body satisfaction: A longitudinal study of adolescent girls and boys. *Journal of Youth and Adolescence, 39*(12), 1392–1401.

Eisenberg, D., Gollust, S. E., Golberstein, E., & Hefner, J. L. (2007). Prevalence and correlates of depression, anxiety, and suicidality among university students. *American Journal of Orthopsychiatry, 77*(4), 534–542.

Goldberg, D. (1992). *General Health Questionnaire (GHQ-12).* Windsor, UK: NFER-Nelson.

Göregenli, M. (1997). Individualistic-collectivistic tendencies in a Turkish sample. *Journal of Cross-Cultural Psychology, 28*(6), 787–794.

Greenfield, P. M., Keller, H., Fuligni, A., & Maynard, A. (2003). Cultural pathways through universal development. *Annual Review of Psychology, 54*(1), 461–490.

Hagerty, B. M., Lynch-Sauer, J., Patusky, K. L., & Bouwsema, M. (1993). An emerging theory of human relatedness. *Journal of Nursing Scholarship, 25*(4), 291–296.

Hofstede, G. (2016). *The Hofstede Centre.* Retrieved from http://geert-hofstede.com/spain.html, accessed on March 17, 2016.

Hofstede, G., Hofstede, G. J., & Minkov, M. (2010). *Cultures and organizations: Software of the mind.* New York: McGraw-Hill.

Houltberg, B. J., Henry, C. S., Merten, M. J., & Robinson, L. C. (2011). Adolescents' perceptions of family connectedness, intrinsic religiosity, and depressed mood. *Journal of Child and Family Studies, 20*(1), 111–119.

Hu, L. T., & Bentler, P. M. (1999). Cutoff criteria for fit indexes in covariance structure analysis: Conventional criteria versus new alternatives. *Structural Equation Modeling: A Multidisciplinary Journal, 6*(1), 1–55.

Huebner, E. S., Suldo, S. M., Valois, R. F., & Drane, J. W. (2006). The Brief Multidimensional Students' Life Satisfaction Scale: Sex, race, and grade effects for applications with middle school students. *Applied Research in Quality of Life, 1*(2), 211–216.

Huppert, F. A., & Whittington, J. E. (2003). Evidence for the independence of positive and negative well-being: Implications for quality of life assessment. *British Journal of Health Psychology, 8*(1), 107–122.

Inkeles, A., & Smith, D. H. (1974). *Becoming modern: Individual changes in six developing countries.* Cambridge, MA: Harvard University Press.

Instituto Nacional de Estadística (2015). Indicadores sociales [Social indicators]. Madrid, Spain: Instituto Nacional de Estadística. Accessed on March 17, 2016, retrieved from: http://www.ine.es/daco/daco42/sociales11/sociales.htm

Jose, P. E., & Crespo, C. (2011). Social connectedness. In *Encyclopedia of Adolescence* (pp. 2759–2768). New York: Springer.

Jose, P. E., Ryan, N., & Pryor, J. (2012). Does social connectedness promote a greater sense of well-being in adolescence over time? *Journal of Research on Adolescence, 22*(2), 235–251.

Kağıtçıbaşi, C. (2005). Autonomy and relatedness in cultural context: Implications for self and family. *Journal of Cross-Cultural Psychology, 36*(4), 403–422.

Kağıtçıbaşi, C. (2006). Theoretical perspectives on family change. In Georgas, J., Berry, J. W., van de Vijver, F. J. R., Kağıtçıbaşi, C., & Poortinga, Y. H. (Eds), *Families across cultures: A 30-nation psychological study* (pp. 72–89). New York: Cambridge University Press.

Kağıtçıbaşi, C. (2007). *Family, self, and human development across cultures: Theory and applications* (2nd ed.). Mahwah, NJ: Lawrence Erlbaum.

Kağıtçıbaşi, C. (2013). *Family, self, and human development across cultures: Theory and applications.* (2nd ed.) New York: Routledge.

Kaminski, J. W., Puddy, R. W., Hall, D. M., Cashman, S. Y., Crosby, A. E., & Ortega, L. A. (2010). The relative influence of different domains of social connectedness on self-directed violence in adolescence. *Journal of Youth and Adolescence, 39*(5), 460–473.

Karcher, M. J. (2005). The effects of developmental mentoring and high school mentors' attendance on their younger mentees' self esteem, social skills, and connectedness. *Psychology in the Schools, 42*(1), 65–77.

Karcher, M. J., & Lee, Y. (2002). Connectedness among Taiwanese middle school students: A validation study of the Hemingway Measure of Adolescent Connectedness. *Asia Pacific Education Review, 3*(1), 95–114.

Karcher, M. J., & Santos, K. (2011). Promoting connectedness through developmental interventions: Adapting the Cross-Age Mentoring Program (CAMP) for youth in Asia. *Asian Journal of Counselling, 18*(1), 125–147.

Karcher, M. J., Holcomb, M., & Zambrano, E. (2008). Measuring adolescent connectedness: A guide for school-based assessment and program evaluation. In Coleman, H. L. K. & Yeh, C. (Eds), *Handbook of school counseling* (pp. 649–669). Mahwah, NJ: Lawrence Erlbaum.

Keller, H. (2012). Autonomy and relatedness revisited: Cultural manifestations of universal human needs. *Child Development Perspectives, 6*(1), 12–18.

Lee, R. M., & Robbins, S. B. (1995). Measuring belongingness: The Social Connectedness and the Social Assurance scales. *Journal of Counseling Psychology, 42*(2), 232–241.

Lee, R. M., & Robbins, S. B. (2000). Understanding social connectedness in college women and men. *Journal of Counseling and Development, 78*(4), 484–491.

Mcgraw, K., Moore, S., Fuller, A., & Bates, G. (2008). Family, peer and school connectedness in final year secondary school students. *Australian Psychologist, 43*(1), 27–37.

Milfont, T. L., & Fischer, R. (2015). Testing measurement invariance across groups: Applications in cross-cultural research. *International Journal of Psychological Research, 3*(1), 111–130.

Millings, A., Buck, R., Montgomery, A., Spears, M., & Stallard, P. (2012). School connectedness, peer attachment, and self-esteem as predictors of adolescent depression. *Journal of Adolescence, 35*(4), 1061–1067.

Musitu, G. (2000). Socialización familiar y valores en el adolescente: Un análisis intercultural. *Anuario de Psicología, 31*(2), 15–32.

Njue, J. R. M., Rombo, D. O., & Ngige, L. W. (2007). Family strengths and challenges in Kenya. *Marriage & Family Review, 41*(1–2), 47–70.

Norona, J. C., Preddy, T. M., & Welsh, D. P. (2015). How gender shapes emerging adulthood. In Arnett, J. J. (Ed), *The Oxford Handbook of Emerging Adulthood,* (pp. 62–69). Oxford: Oxford University Press.

Oliva, A., & Parra, A. (2001). Autonomía emocional durante la adolescencia. *Infancia y Aprendizaje, 24*(2), 181–196.

Ovuga, E., Boardman, J., & Wasserman, D. (2006). Undergraduate student mental health at Makerere University, Uganda. *World Psychiatry, 5*(1), 51–52.

Pew Research Center. (2014). *Worldwide, many see belief in god as essential to morality.* Retrieved from www.pewglobal.org/files/2014/05/Pew-Research-Center-Global-Attitudes-Project-Belief-in-God-Report-REVISED-MAY-27-2014.pdf, accessed on March 17, 2016.

Rasuly-Paleczek, G. (1996). Some remarks on the study of household composition and intrafamily relations in rural and urban Turkey. In Rasuly-Paleczek, G. (Ed.), *Turkish families in transition* (pp. 1–44). Frankfurt: Peter Lang.

Schwartz, S. H. (1999). Cultural value differences: Some implications for work. *Applied Psychology: An International Review, 48*(1), 23–47.

Shochet, I. M., Homel, R., Cockshaw, W. D., & Montgomery, D. T. (2008). How do school connectedness and attachment to parents interrelate in predicting adolescent depressive symptoms? *Journal of Clinical Child & Adolescent Psychology, 37*(3), 676–681.

Smith, T. B., & Silva, L. (2011). Ethnic identity and personal well-being of people of color: a meta-analysis. *Journal of Counseling Psychology, 58*(1), 42–60.

Townsend, K. C., & McWhirter, B. T. (2005). Connectedness: A review of the literature with implications for counseling, assessment, and research. *Journal of Counseling and Development, 83*(2), 191–201.

Valentin, S. R. (2005). Commentary: Sleep in German infants – the "cult" of independence. *Pediatrics, 115*(Supplement 1), 269–271.

van de Schoot, R., Lugtig, P., & Hox, J. (2012). A checklist for testing measurement invariance. *European Journal of Developmental Psychology, 9*(4), 486–492.

van de Vijver, F. J. R., & Leung, K. (1997). *Methods and data analysis for cross-cultural research.* Thousand Oaks, CA: SAGE.

Waithaka, E. N. (2014). Family capital: Conceptual model to unpack the intergenerational transfer of advantage in transitions to adulthood. *Journal of Research on Adolescence, 24*(3), 471–484.

Whitlock, J., Wyman, P. A., & Moore, S. R. (2014). Connectedness and suicide prevention in adolescents: Pathways and implications. *Suicide and Life-Threatening Behavior, 44*(3), 246–272.

World Bank (2016). *Germany country profile.* Retrieved from: http://data.worldbank.org/country/germany, accessed on March 18, 2016.

World Values Survey (2011). *World Values Survey Wave 6 Turkey Data.* Retrieved from www.worldvaluessurvey.org/WVSDocumentationWV6.jsp, accessed on March 17, 2016.

10

YOUTH–ADULT RELATIONSHIPS AS ASSETS FOR YOUTH

Promoting Positive Development in Stressful Times

Stephen F. Hamilton, Mary Agnes Hamilton, David L. DuBois , M. Loreto Martínez, Patricio Cumsille, Bernadine Brady, Pat Dolan, Susana Núñez Rodriguez, and Deborah E. Sellers

In this chapter we examine relationships between youth and adults outside their families as sources of strength that can help young people thrive even in the face of stressful economic and social change. Such relationships are counted among the assets that promote positive youth development (Eccles & Gootman, 2002). Our treatment of the topic will emphasize the needs of low-income and otherwise marginalized youth. While acknowledging the primacy of family relationships for nearly all youth, we focus primarily on relationships with adults who are not family members, addressing the value of these relationships, what forms they take, which adults are most likely to be involved, and finally how such relationships can be fostered so that more of the youth who need them have access to, and benefit from, them.

The metaphor, social capital, is useful for our purpose. In a seminal article, Coleman (1988) wrote about "social capital in the creation of human capital," calling attention to the link between people's capacity to earn a living and the nature of their social networks. Lin (2001, p. 29) defined social capital as, "resources embedded in a social structure that are accessed and/or mobilized in purposive actions." In simpler language, social capital inheres in a person's ability to achieve her or his goals with the aid of people she or he knows. A person whose family, friends, neighbors, and other acquaintances can be called upon to help out has more social capital than one who is either more isolated – having a sparser social network – or whose acquaintances are less able to help.

A classic example is finding a job through "contacts," acquaintances who know about openings and perhaps can offer a recommendation. Three refinements of social capital theory are especially useful in the present context. The first is from Granovetter (1983), whose phrase, "the strength of weak ties," captures his discovery that the best sources for job prospects are people the job-seeker knows only slightly, such as a friend of a friend. The reason is that people with whom a person is closely associated tend to have the same sources of information and access. As a result, they add little to the job-seeker's search. People on the periphery of the job-seeker's network are most likely to know about new prospects and to be acquainted with people the job-seeker does not know. Hence it is through "weak ties" that a job search is most likely to succeed. More generally, this example illustrates how expanding one's network beyond close acquaintances can provide access to new resources that can prove important in achieving a goal.

The strong vs. weak tie distinction is related to a second refinement, the distinction Putnam (2000) made between "bonding" and "bridging" social capital. Bonding social capital exists among people who share many characteristics. Families, for example, share a common culture, traditions, language, often religion, and political preferences as well. Neighbors, members of religious congregations, and voluntary associations are also high in bonding social capital, which gives them a sense of identity with the group, of belonging, of being part of something larger than themselves. Bridging social capital, as the metaphor suggests, reaches across these kinds of group boundaries, making connections between people who belong to different groups. These connections enable people to encounter others who are different and to make connections and be stimulated in ways that may not happen within their more closely bonded communities. A low-income youth of color who attends an elite university not only gains a good education but builds bridging social capital as well.

The third refinement to social capital theory, related to bridging social capital, is the designation of some social network members as "institutional agents" (Stanton-Salazar, 2001, 2011), that is, as representatives of important social institutions who by virtue of their position and knowledge are able to aid outsiders, young people among them, in gaining entrée to those institutions and access to their resources.[1] College admissions officers are exemplars of institutional agents, as are people with authority to make or influence hiring decisions.

This conceptual orientation strongly suggests that family connections (i.e., bonding) are necessary but not sufficient as sources of social capital for youth from families and communities with limited resources. The job recommendation from such a family member might help a youth find a position in a beauty parlor or a corner grocery store but not a business office or large factory. That person might accurately urge the youth to study hard to get into college but have no knowledge of financial aid or of the difference between enrolling in a nearby college that is a local institution and another whose alumni move on to top graduate and professional schools.

The studies cited and reported in this chapter further elaborate evidence of the social class-based differentiation of young people's opportunities to form relationships with adults. Young people from low-income families whose parents have little education need assistance in building bridging social capital, in the form of relationships with people who have more resources, to aid their acquisition of greater human capital. A second topic is the contribution of youth organizations and schools to young people's opportunities to form development-enhancing relationships with adults. While these relationships arise in the course of youth program activities as a kind of second-order effect (Hirsch, Deutsch, & DuBois, 2011), growing appreciation of the importance of young people's relationships with adults outside their families has contributed to a movement to make mentors available to vulnerable youth (Rhodes, 2002), not only in the US, but in other countries as well. Data from a study of the Irish version of Big Brothers Big Sisters illuminates the different kinds of support mentors can provide. However, there are never enough volunteers and program staff to meet the needs of youth who could benefit from a mentor (Stukas, Clary, & Snyder, 2014). Moreover, most mentoring-type relationships occur naturally or informally, outside of mentoring programs. Hence, it is useful to examine how mentoring occurs naturally, both to deepen our understanding of who mentors are and what they do, and to gain leverage to foster such relationships intentionally, among other ways by designing programs in which mentoring occurs without formal one-to-one matching of youth with mentors.

The four studies reported in this chapter, from Brazil, Chile, Ireland, and the US, will be described serially. Themes tying the studies together will be identified as well and discussed in the conclusion section.

The Importance of Social Class: Differences in Brazilian Youths' Perceived Autonomy

In times of economic distress, those who are already in distress inevitably suffer the most. A dramatic illustration of this fact of life is found in a study of "informal mentors" in US high schools by Erickson, McDonald, and Elder (2009). Drawing on the National Longitudinal Study of Adolescent Health, the investigators found that students from families with lower parent education and family income who nonetheless had someone at school they could talk to – a teacher mentor – were nearly twice as likely to enroll in college as comparable students without such an adult relationship (65% compared to 35%), and nearly as likely to enroll as students whose parents had more education and more money but no teacher mentor (67%). Those students with more family resources, who had a teacher mentor as well were even more likely to enroll in college (75%) but the difference attributable to having a teacher mentor was not nearly so great. This study, employing a representative sample of the US student population and controls for other likely influences on the dependent variable such as grades and test scores, indicates that youth whose families have the least resources benefit the most from relationships with adults outside the family.

Susana Núñez Rodriguez studied autonomy and relatedness in Brazilian youth. At the time of this study, Brazil was experiencing strong economic growth combined with modest declines in income inequality and dramatically rising secondary school completion rates. Autonomy, competence, and relatedness are the three basic psychological needs identified in self-determination theory (Deci & Ryan, 1985, 2000). According to this theory, human behavior is driven by the quest for their fulfillment. The need for autonomy refers to the individual's will and desire to organize experiences and carry out activities coherently within an integrated sense of self (Deci & Ryan, 2000). According to Chirkov (2007), individuals may choose experiences that allow them to fulfill their need for autonomy within a collectivist environment as well as an individualistic one. The need for relatedness is met when a person has satisfying relations with friends and family, feels accepted by and is accepting of others for who they truly are, and is able to establish and maintain close and committed intimate relationships (Kasser, Cohn, Kanner, & Ryan, 2007).

Brazilian Study Design

Núñez's study included 970 participants, ages 18–30 years ($M = 22.8$; $SD = 3.4$) recruited from universities and schools in different regions of the country. In addition to a sociodemographic questionnaire, participants filled out, online or on paper, a Portuguese version of the Basic Psychological Needs Scale (BPNS, Gagné, 2003) and the Satisfaction with Life Scale (SWLS, Diener, Emmons, Larsen, & Griffin, 1985). Exploratory and confirmatory factor analyses were performed on the BPNS results. Multidimensional scaling was used to test for differences in autonomy related to participants' socioeconomic status (SES). Being predominately university and graduate students (90%), most participants were classified as coming from middle (54%) or high (32%) income families.

Brazilian Study Findings

Two findings are of particular interest for this chapter. One is that social class conditioned the association between relatedness and autonomy. For participants classified as lower SES, a stronger association was evident between autonomy and relatedness than those classified as higher SES. There was a statistically significant difference in need for autonomy according to SES (H(3, 970) = 10.274, p = .001), with high SES showing an average level of 516.58 and lower SES showing an average of 416.25. The investigators linked this finding to other research in Brazil indicating differences in the appraisal of autonomy and its association with SES (Vieira et al., 2010; Seidl-de-Moura et al., 2008; Barbosa & Wagner, 2013). These results suggest that, at least for lower-class Brazilian youth, autonomy is not necessarily a matter of gaining independence by leaving behind close ties but is a need that also can be fulfilled on the foundation of relationships.

The second finding is that the three-factor solution to the model of basic psychological needs that has been validated in the US and several other countries did not fit the Brazilian data, another indication of cultural differences in the meaning of autonomy to Brazilian youth. Rather than forming three distinct factors representing autonomy, relatedness, and competence, the responses of the Brazilian sample loaded on two factors that were best understood as representing competence and relatedness (see Table 10.1). While some items from the autonomy sub-scale could be joined with one of the other sub-scales, the most satisfactory solution dropped autonomy completely, in recognition that the BPNS did not adequately capture the meaning of autonomy for Brazilian youth. The resulting two-factor version demonstrated good internal consistency (alphas of .76 and .73 for relatedness and competence, respectively) and the subscales correlated well (.45, .54, p < .01) with the Satisfaction with Life Scale, demonstrating evidence of construct validity.

TABLE 10.1   Fit Indexes of the 3 and 2 Factor Models obtained in the Factorial Analysis

Factor Analysis	X^2	df	WRMR/ SRMR[1]	RMSEA[2]	CFI[3]	TLI[4]
CFA[5] (3 factors) (N = 294)	1558.797*	186	2.057	.112	.799	.773
EFA[6] (2 factors**) (N = 294)	905.771*	169	.060	.086	.892	.866
CFA (2 factors) (N = 301)	126.375*	43	.081	.087	.938	.921

(* p < .001; **Common shared variance = 64.96%)

1 Weighted Root Mean Square Residual/Standardized Root Mean Square Residual
2 Root Mean Square Error of Approximation
3 Comparative Fit Index
4 Tucker Lewis Index
5 Confirmatory Factor Analysis
6 Exploratory Factor Analysis

Brazilian Study Implications

The findings of this study suggest that relatedness and autonomy, even if they are fundamental human needs, along with competence, have different meanings depending on young people's social class and on their cultural background. Perceptions of relatedness and competence were differentiated among Brazilian youth, as captured in the factorial model. However, the items did not capture the perception of autonomy for Brazilian youth from different social class backgrounds, as they did in other countries, despite a very careful translation process. In Brazil, especially among lower-SES youth, the sense of self is associated with their relationships with others (e.g., family) and associations with their environment (e.g., school). In addition to pursuing the measurement issues raised by these findings, it would be intriguing to explore the behavioral implications, especially to learn what relatedness and autonomy mean for lower-class Brazilian youth and how both can be enhanced. (See also comparable findings from Chile by Martínez, Pérez, & Cumsille, 2014.)

Contexts for Adult Relationships: Youth Organizations in Chile

Participation in youth organizations can cultivate values (e.g., tolerance, social responsibility; Flanagan & Faison, 2001) and promote skills (Kirshner, 2008) that advance youth civic development when they provide opportunities for interaction and learning that match youths' developmental needs, abilities, and interests (Zeldin, 2004). Young people are most likely to benefit when organizations foster their active participation and when the quality of relationships that adults establish with young participants is high. Adult partners in youth programs and organizations can promote positive outcomes by encouraging participation, by mentoring (Rhodes, Reddy, Roffman, & Grossman, 2005), by employing good teaching skills, and by linking youth with community resources and leaders (Camino & Zeldin, 2002; Zeldin, Petrokubi, & MacNeil, 2008). The benefits of participation in youth organizations can be expected to occur when youth hold meaningful roles, have opportunities for collaboration in decision making (Finn & Checkoway, 1998; Zeldin, Camino, & Calvert, 2003), and share power with adults (Watts, Williams, & Jaegers, 2003). One such benefit that is especially important because it has implications for a healthy civil society is a growing sense of sociopolitical control, which includes leadership competence and political efficacy (Zimmerman & Zahniser, 1991).

Chilean Study Design

M. Loreto Martínez and Patricio Cumsille examined Chilean youth organizations as contexts for youth–adult relationships, focusing specifically on how those relationships build a sense of sociopolitical control. In addition to calling attention to the importance of the quality of youth–adult relationships and the distinctive characteristics of youth organizations in their country, they explored the function of identity as a mediator.

Growing up in a country that is still recovering its democratic institutions, Chilean youth are skeptical about government and the efficacy of participation in politics. Only 34% of 18–29-year-olds [INJUV, 2012] endorsed compliance with government as essential for democracy and 40% reported that they did not think it was possible to influence political matters. On the other hand, half were favorable toward participation in civil society and 45% said they participated in social organizations; 61% said social networks are more effective channels for expressing demands than voting (INJUV, 2012).

Participants in Martínez and Cumsille's study were recruited through youth organizations, assuring a higher than average level of membership. The sample included 370 older adolescents and young adults ($M = 21.18$, $SD = 2.37$, range = 17–26 years; 50.9% males), from Santiago and the Maule region. Most were students (89.7%); the majority came from middle-SES families (56%), indexed by parental education; low- and high-SES were equally represented among the remainder (i.e., about 22% each). Participants filled out a questionnaire on their perceptions of their *relationships with adults* in the organizations in which they were involved, including *caring/support* (6 items, $\alpha = .89$), *opportunities for reflection/ processing* (4 items, $\alpha = .81$), and for *active participation in decision-making* within the organization (8 items, $\alpha = .87$). Identity measures included questions about *future orientation goals* (6 items, $\alpha = .82$) and *sense of personal coherence* (3 items, $\alpha = .80$). Finally, two indicators of sense of sociopolitical control were included as dependent variables, namely *leadership* (5 items, $\alpha = .76$) and *political efficacy* (4 items, $\alpha = .76$).

Chilean Study Results

These measures allowed for a test of a hypothesized model proposing that youth gain sociopolitical control when adults provide emotional support, opportunities for reflecting on experience, and opportunities to have a voice and role and when those characteristics of youth–adult relationships positively relate to youth identity. As Figure 10.1 shows, all measured indicators loaded high on their corresponding latent variables, thus providing evidence of the measurement properties of the model. Overall, the hypothesized model had an excellent fit to the data [χ^2 (11, n = 370) = 11.11, $p = .43$, CFI = 1, TLI = 1, RMSEA = .005]. As hypothesized, the quality of youth–adult relationships within organizations had a positive association with identity ($\beta = .36$, $p < .001$), which in turn had a positive association with sense of sociopolitical control ($\beta = .57$, $p < .001$). More important, the hypothesized mediational role of identity was supported by the data (.20, $p = <.001$, 95% CI [.13:31]). Unlike the bivariate association between relational context and sociopolitical control, the regression coefficient

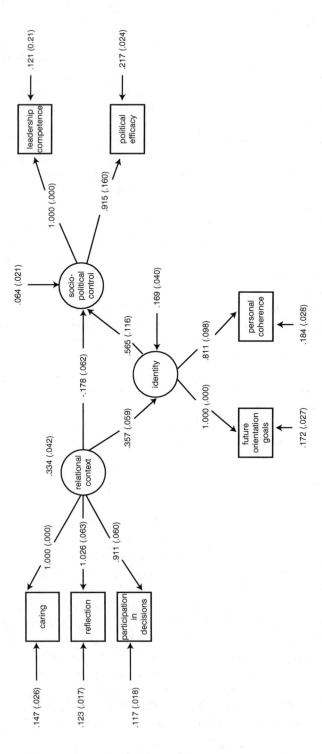

FIGURE 10.1 Hypothesized Model

linking relational context to sociopolitical control, even while controlling for the effect of identity, was significant. However, the association was, unexpectedly, negative ($\beta = -0.18$, $p < .01$), suggesting that identity acts as a suppressor in the relation between relational context and sociopolitical control.

Chilean Study Implications

This study offers support for the idea that the interpersonal context provided by supportive and caring adults in youth organizations allows adolescents and young adults to explore and consolidate their identity (Eccles, 2005; Kirshner, 2009; Larson, 2006; Larson & Angus, 2011). In turn, identity consolidation is reflected in youths' beliefs about their capacity to exert influence on sociopolitical issues. The findings also suggest that the quality of the relationships that youth establish with adults are relevant to identity across a range of organizational contexts. However, the unexpected negative direct association between relational context and sociopolitical control, after accounting for contributions of identity, suggests that whatever positive effects the relational context has on sociopolitical control goes through identity and, further, that the remaining variability in sociopolitical control that is not associated with identity is negatively associated to relational context. This latter possible process remains obscure, requiring further research. Perhaps when the relational context does not promote an autonomous self (identity), it is not conducive to an enhanced sense of sociopolitical efficacy but may be useful in other ways, such as for mental health or personal well-being. Both replication and triangulation using observational methods would help illuminate this issue. However, the capacity of youth organizations to give youth access to close relationships with adults who matter to them is clearly supported.

Forms of Support Adults Give to Youth: Findings from an Irish Mentoring Program

The creation of mentoring programs is the most direct response to the perception that youth benefit from close, caring, and enduring relationships with adults who are not family members. Resilience (Rutter, 1985; Werner & Smith, 1982) is one of multiple strands of theory and research that has contributed to the rationale for and design of mentoring programs. Previous research has revealed much about how youth mentoring programs work, including the contexts in which they are most likely to be successful, and their limitations (see DuBois & Karcher, 2013 for a comprehensive treatment of mentoring programs). Positive outcomes have been demonstrated in an array of areas, including emotional well-being, educational achievement, risky behavior, and relationships with parents and peers (Blinn-Pike 2007; DuBois, Portillo, Rhodes, Silverthorn, & Valentine,

2011; Tierney, Grossman, & Resch, 1995). Qualitative studies have explored some of the processes underpinning mentoring relationships. For example, studies by Spencer illustrated relational processes of authenticity, empathy, collaboration, and companionship in mentoring relationships (Spencer, 2006), reasons behind the termination of relationships (Spencer et al., 2014), and ways families are involved in mentoring programs (Spencer & Basualdo-Delmonico, 2014).

One of the primary purposes of mentoring programs is to strengthen the social support that young people receive (Barrera & Bonds, 2005). We know that the presence of at least one caring adult in a young person's life can help reduce stress and improve mental well-being (Dooley & Fitzgerald, 2012). However, the mentoring literature provides little guidance on the nature of the support provided by adults in youth mentoring relationships. By drawing on an in-depth study of nine successful mentoring pairs in the Irish Big Brothers Big Sisters (BBBS) program, Bernadine Brady and Patrick Dolan sought to identify distinctive types of support and highlight perceived improvements in the young person's welfare, particularly in terms of their emotional and behavioral well-being, that may have occurred as a result of this support.

Irish Study Design

The qualitative data reported here were collected as part of a larger mixed methods investigation that include a longitudinal quantitative study using a randomized controlled design ($n = 164$) (see Dolan et al., 2011a & b). At the time of recruitment to the qualitative strand, approximately 50 young people had been matched with mentors as part of the longitudinal quantitative strand of the study. BBBS project staff asked these participants (young people and parents) if they would also be willing to participate in a series of interviews with the research team. Twenty-one youth–parent pairs agreed and a purposive sample of 10 was selected to represent a balance across age, gender, location, family situation, and reason for referral. Two interviews were conducted with the mentor and youth as well as with the parent and caseworker on two occasions – at the early stages of the relationship and approximately six months later. One youth declined to participate after the first interview, leaving a sample of nine. At both the first and second round, five interviews could not be conducted (yielding 35 interviews in round one and 31 in round two).

After reading interview notes and transcripts several times to get a sense of the development of each match, and to note whether and how outcomes were reported in each case, the researcher identified themes and coded the data according to them, using NVivo software. Initial themes were then grouped into higher order categories. After coding all interviews, the researcher re-read transcripts and interview notes in full and made some revisions to the codes. Having four perspectives (mentee, mentor, parent, and caseworker) on each mentoring relationship enabled triangulation among different viewpoints regarding outcomes and processes.

Five male and four female mentees took part in the study. Their average age at the time of referral was 12 years. Only three of the youth lived with both parents at the time of the study intake. All the young people were Irish and all lived in rural areas or towns in the West of Ireland. The young people were dealing with a range of family and personal issues, including break-up of their parents' relationship, bereavement, incarceration of family members, behavioral problems, and low literacy. The average age of the mentor was 33 years on recruitment to the program; most mentors were single and had some higher education. Mentors and youth were matched by gender.

Irish Study Findings

Previous studies of social support in interpersonal relationships (Cutrona & Russell, 1990; Wills, 1991) have identified five types of social support: concrete (also called tangible, instrumental, or practical), companionship, emotional, esteem, and advice. These categories served well to group the kinds of support described in the interviews.

Concrete support is defined as the provision of practical acts of assistance (Cutrona, 2000; Dolan & Brady, 2012), whereas *companionship support* is defined as giving people a sense of social belonging (Wills, 1991). It enhances the pleasure of everyday life and contributes to emotional well-being (Rook & Underwood, 2000; Spencer, 2006). In mentoring relationships these two types of support are often intertwined. Many parents commented that their child "did not get out much," mostly because they as parents did not have time, money, or resources to make that possible and, in some cases, because the young person was shy and unwilling to engage in social events with peers. One of the most obvious forms of support offered by mentors was the companionship support of taking the young person out of the house to do something different for a few hours every week. The weekly activities involved companionship, including one-to-one activities such as going to cafes, cinema, and cooking, but also group events such as sports or youth clubs.[2] Parents and mentors who described this type of support also tied it to desirable outcomes, including increased confidence and new relationships with others in the community.

Concrete and companionship support was evident at initial interviews. Based on the analysis of interview data, it can be argued that this support can be provided before a close bond has been formed, helping to create a context and structure from which a friendship and discovery of shared interests can emerge, and from which emotional, esteem, and advice support can more readily be offered and accepted (see Keller, 2005, for a related discussion of the interplay of more relational and instrumental forms of activity, including the potential for instrumental activities to serve as important contexts for relationship development in a reciprocal manner).

Cobb (1976) defined *emotional support* as actions that lead a person to believe he or she is cared for. Emotional support took many forms in the mentoring relationships studied, including the mentor listening to and empathizing with the young person and acting as a "sounding board," and listening to accounts of daily events and challenges. Theoretically, emotional support can and should be provided in different ways to match the needs and coping styles of the youth. Illustrations in line with this idea were found in the interviews, for example, of girls who appreciated having someone to talk to about the stresses they were feeling. In comparison, the mentors' emotional support for boys was often less direct. One boy, for example, did not confide to his mentor for several months that his parents had broken up, yet seemed to gain emotional strength from the consistency of his relationship with the mentor.

> Myself and his father broke up in the last year, so there has been an awful lot of changes for Brendan. But I just think that Alan gives him that stability whereas I didn't, and his father didn't, you know? He still has a continuum with Alan; Alan was still here on the dot every week, once a week, sometimes twice a week. So it's certainly helped … He's had consistency as far as Brendan goes.
>
> (parent)

Esteem support results from one person expressing love and concern for another (Cutrona, 2000). Youth inferred their mentors' concern for them from the time they spent with them, while mentors' encouragement and praise for their mentees added to this feeling. There were also examples in the research of a mentee showing a mentor how to play or improve their skills in particular activities (such as music, swimming, or handball) and enjoying the positive feedback or esteem of the mentor for doing so.

Advice support is the fourth type identified. Mentors offered information and guidance. The feedback from research participants is that the ability to offer advice was something that came more easily when the relationship was better established, and where advice could be given in the course of a normal conversation, rather than more didactically. For example, one mentor, Liam, described how his mentee, Dylan, asked his advice regarding school and education.

> With regard to school I suppose he has not been asking me advice but we have kind of ended up talking about school and what he was going to do … so yes, I suppose he would have asked me advice on that or I'd have given my advice, I'm not sure which.
>
> (Liam, mentor)

Irish Study Implications

Inferences about the effects of these types of social support are all based on the testimony of those interviewed, not on formal measures. Yet, that testimony tended to converge around some of the same changes in emotional well-being and behavior control. Mentees were described as happier and calmer, more involved with other people, and more confident. Among their conclusions, the researchers found that their data and interpretation support the findings of other studies that if they are to flourish, mentoring relationships need frequent, consistent, and enduring meetings – and space – openness, and responsiveness to the needs of the youth.

Functional Roles of Natural Mentors in the US

Mentoring programs exist because, as Erickson et al. (2009) reported, those who most need mentors are least likely to have them. Most adult mentors of youth are not part of mentoring programs, and those programs face a chronic shortage of appropriate volunteers (MENTOR, 2005). Another concern is that mentoring programs can have iatrogenic effects (i.e., harm resulting from treatment). A young person whose assigned mentor does not work out for some reason can suffer from that failure, looking worse than a control group participant who never had a match (Grossman & Rhodes, 2002). The magnitude of the estimated effect found by Erickson et al. of having a natural mentor is noteworthy. The near doubling of college enrollment among low-resource students with a school-related natural mentor is far greater than effect sizes reported from mentoring program evaluations (DuBois et al., 2011). Although they applied multiple controls, Erickson and his colleagues reported a correlational finding, meaning that other factors may be at play. Still, their findings are certainly notable enough to warrant further research.

Natural mentors are non-parental adults who act as mentors without being assigned to do so through a program designed for that purpose (Hamilton & Hamilton, 2004; Zimmerman, Bingenheimer, & Behrendt, 2005). Young people find natural mentors in schools (Greenberger, Chen & Beam, 1998), workplaces (Mortimer, 2003), youth development organizations (Hirsch, Deutsch, & DuBois, 2011), other organizations, and in their communities. In addition to looking at natural mentors, this study asked youth about more than the provision of social support by mentors. While Brady and Dolan's focus on social support is prominent and appropriate in studies of mentoring, especially for younger youth, developmental theory and research tell us that older youth also need a goal orientation (Clausen, 1993; Schneider & Stevenson, 1999). Karcher and Nakkula (2010; see also Nakkula & Harris, 2014) helpfully treat the goal orientation (or instrumental) and socioemotional emphases of mentoring relationships as compatible.

US Study Design

These considerations motivated Mary Agnes Hamilton, Stephen F. Hamilton, David L. DuBois, and Deborah E. Sellers to investigate natural (or informal) mentors. The study employed the concept of functional roles (Darling, Hamilton, Toyokawa, & Matsuda, 2002; Hamilton & Darling, 1989), which adds depth and detail to the broad distinction between socioemotional and instrumental mentoring. The research drew both on the research just cited, which was done with middle school students and college students, and on retrospective interviews with two groups of young adults from low-income and minority communities on promising paths (Hamilton & Hamilton, 2012). Interview respondents talked about adults who taught them useful lessons and supported or encouraged them, who inspired and challenged them, who linked them with other people and resources, and who helped them acquire a sense of direction or purpose. We designated these functional roles: *Teacher, Supporter, Role Model, Challenger, Connector,* and *Compass.*

The study was conducted in two small southern California high schools that are part of a charter school organization. Students are accepted by lottery, to represent the income and ethnicity/racial diversity of their district. The mean age of students in both schools was 15.7 years ($SD = 1.2$). Young women were slightly over-represented in each school. A majority (70%) of Site 1 students self-identified as Hispanic/Latino(a), whereas this was true of 38% of students at Site 2. These percentages are close to the overall percent Hispanic/Latino(a) reported by each school. The response rate at Site 1 was 59% ($n = 355$ of 598); at Site 2 it was 54% ($n = 313$ of 583).

Following basic demographic questions, the survey asked students to identify their primary caregivers (i.e., parents or up to two other adults who were most responsible for raising them), then up to one additional important relative, and, finally, up to three important adults outside their family. For each of these adults, youth were asked to respond to the same set of 21 functional role items on a five-point response scale: not at all, a little, some, quite a bit, a lot. Students accessed the web-based survey on a computer, tablet, or smartphone. Exploratory factor analysis was used to investigate the factor structure of the items as rated for students' relationships with important non-familial adults. If a youth reported more than one such adult, ratings from the first (most important) adult were used. Additional analyses examined whether a similar factor structure was evident in ratings of students' experiences in their relationships with their parent/guardians and other important related adults (see Hamilton, Hamilton, DuBois, & Sellers, 2016).

US Study Findings

Surprisingly, only 22% of the students who took the survey ($n = 148$) reported having an important non-related adult in their lives; of those who did, 44% (n

= 66) identified just one such adult, 34% (*n* = 50) identified two, and 22% (*n* = 32) identified three. Students reported that they knew most of these adults (66%) in their school, either as teachers or in another role such as an advisor, administrator, or coach; 18% of the adults were reported to be known through involvement in other organizations (e.g., faith-based, sports, arts); the remaining 16% were described as having informal social roles in the youth's life such as an older friend, neighbor, or family friend.

Factor analyses of the functional role items for important non-related adults were conducted using an iterative process. The final solution was based on 14 of the 21 items and included four factors that accounted for 72.1% of the variance in the items. This factor solution is shown in Table 10.2.

Three of the factors consisted entirely of items intended for the *Supporter*, *Challenger*, and *Connector* roles, respectively, whereas the remaining factor included a mix of items intended for either the *Model* or *Compass* roles (the items intended for each functional role are indicated in Table 10.2). Scales based on the items that loaded most strongly on each of the factors demonstrated satisfactory internal reliability (coefficient alphas ranging from .77 to .87).

US Study Implications

This research sought to empirically differentiate the functions of mentors for youth with a higher level of detail and theoretical grounding than has been typical of prior work. Initial findings are consistent with the value of a functional roles framework for understanding natural mentoring among youth and, as such, could ultimately prove useful in the design and evaluation of initiatives to foster youth access to mentoring as one strategy to reduce inequalities (Putnam, 2015).

The survey measure that resulted from this research clearly should be regarded as preliminary and in need of further investigation, which should include examining support for the salience of the associated functional roles within larger and more demographically diverse samples of youth. Also meriting study are the associations of functional roles of familial and non-familial important adults as assessed on the instrument with expected influences on youth access to mentoring (e.g., neighborhood resources, school environment) as well as anticipated outcomes of mentoring (e.g., academic achievement, health, delinquent activity). Such research would serve the dual purposes of clarifying issues of construct validity and advancing theory (Smith, 2005).

These needs for further research notwithstanding, the four functional roles identified offer promising characterizations of the ways in which youth see their mentors. Combining the Compass and Model roles makes some sense insofar as youth may tend to look to mentors they want to emulate as sources for values. Distinguishing among mentors' functional roles opens the door to more refined studies in which the independent variable is not simply the presence

TABLE 10.2 Factor Loadings and Intercorrelations for Mentoring Functional Role Items

Item[a]	Supporter	Model/ Compass	Challenger	Connector
	Rotated Factor Pattern Loadings[b]			
This person stands up for me.	.79			
This person is there when I need him/her.	.73			
This person cares about me.	.72			
This person helps me understand things about life.		.84		
This person helps me reflect on my purpose in life.[c]		.66		
I want to be like this person in some ways.[d]		.90		
I want to do things as well as this person.[d]		.65		
This person pushes me to do my best.			−.91	
This person gets me to work harder.			−.79	
This person holds me to high standards.			−.76	
This person points out where I need to improve.			−.75	
This person connected me to someone to learn what I want to know.				.86
This person connected me to someone to help me meet my goals.				.82
This person takes me to new places.				.42

Factor	Factor Intercorrelations			
Supporter	–			
Model/Compass	.45	–		
Challenger	−.33	−.46	–	
Connector	.25	.37	.38	–

Note. The following seven items were not included in the final factor solutions (intended functional roles are indicated in parentheses): "This person supports me in what I do" (Supporter), "This person teaches me how to do things" (Model), "I respect what this person has achieved" (Model), "I get values from this person" (Compass), "Ideas I have about right/wrong come from this person" (Compass), "This person helps me see the impact of my behavior on others" (Compass), and "I do things with this person I haven't done before" (Connector).

a For each item, the youth rated how much the statement described their relationship with this adult: Not at all, A little, Some, Quite a bit, A lot.

b Factor loadings <.35 are not included in the table.

c Item intended to assess the Compass functional role.

d Item intended to assess the Model functional role.

of a mentor but the profile of mentoring functions a youth is receiving. It also makes possible examination of different functions that might be performed by multiple mentors for one youth, simultaneously or sequentially, thus informing a social network perspective on mentoring that to date is largely lacking in the literature (Keller & Blakeslee, 2014).

A concern raised by this study is that only a minority of survey respondents reported an important unrelated adult: 21% of those at Site 1, 23% at Site 2. This aspect of our findings was discordant with previous research (e.g., Bruce & Bridgeland, 2014; DuBois & Silverthorn, 2005). In an effort to better understand what might have happened, we conducted brief focus groups and interviews with students in both schools. Seven focus groups were conducted with a total of 77 students and individual interviews were conducted with 27 additional students, five of whom had not taken the survey. These were convenience samples; they included approximately equal numbers of male and female students from all racial and ethnic groups. In stark contrast to the survey, nearly every student we asked face-to-face told us about at least one important non-family adult in his or her life. Only two of the students interviewed said they could not identify such an adult.

Although average completion time for the survey was only 12 minutes, our conversations with students revealed that several of them found the survey too long and too repetitive. They simply stopped responding before getting to the questions about non-family adults. We believe improving the survey design and recruitment would increase participation. We had both higher response rates and far more reports of important adults outside the family on a simpler paper-and-pencil survey in a pre-test. In the focus groups, students told us they would have been more likely to complete the survey if they had been asked to do it in class-time. Some suggested using Instagram or Facebook, technology more appealing than web surveys. Students also told us that talking face-to-face and hearing our explanation of why we were asking the questions and what we planned to do with the data made them more interested in participating. They also said incentives for participation were appealing. Finally, several students strongly endorsed the idea of engaging students in designing and conducting a survey.

Implications and Conclusions from the Four Studies

The four studies presented in this chapter from three continents all sound variations on the theme of young people's relationships with adults outside their families as resources in times of stressful economic and social change. The importance of those relationships is well-grounded in the research literature; these studies illuminate some of the intricacies inherent in them.

By showing that relatedness and autonomy are positively associated among low-SES Brazilian youth and that the factor structure of the widely used Basic Psychological Needs Scale works best without autonomy for their Brazilian sample (with only relatedness and competence), Nuñéz's work reminds us that neither relationships nor their impact should be expected to be uniform across social classes and cultures. This poses a warning to researchers planning to measure these constructs that instruments developed in one culture may not be valid in another and to policy makers and practitioners that mentoring and other interventions designed to meet young people's basic psychological needs are not necessarily transferable. What works for some youth in some contexts may well not work for others.

Martínez and Cumsille's study of Chilean youth is encouraging. Despite considerable skepticism among youth about conventional political engagement, Chilean youth organizations offer a space for participation, leadership, and the development and enactment of caring and supportive relationships with adults, decision making, leadership, political efficacy, and opportunities for reflection, all desirable and productive. Unexpectedly, the predicted association of the quality of youths' relationships with adults in these settings with sociopolitical control proved to be negative, raising questions to be answered in the future. But two conclusions seem warranted. One is that youth organizations can provide many constructive experiences for young people, including the chance to build relationships with adults outside the family. The other is that simply being there is not enough. Quality counts. The programs and the relationships have to be good. The adults need to be skilled. Most of all they need to be willing and able to share power with young people, to give them real responsibility, making them part of the decision-making process. Adults must create partnerships with youth (Zeldin, Camino, & Mook, 2005) and make multiple careful judgments in the moment about what young people can manage, when to push, and when to stand back (Larson, Walker, & Pearce, 2005).

Brady and Dolan help to open up the nature of high-quality youth–adult relationships, differentiating the core concept of social support into five types: concrete, companionship, emotional, esteem, and advice. This typology helps to explicate what a high-quality relationship looks like between an adult mentor and a young person, especially one whose family has limited capacity. The observation that a mentor can provide concrete and companionship support without a close and strong relationship but that such support can become a platform for the more personal types of support (emotional and esteem) offers a suggestion about the possible developmental trajectory of a close and enduring mentoring relationship that should be useful to mentors and those who work with them.

Hamilton, Hamilton, DuBois, and Sellers (2016) offer a related but somewhat different typology in which support(er) is an important function of mentoring but is joined by three more functions: challenger, connector, and model/compass, all having a more instrumental or goal-directed orientation, possibly because they studied older youth. When mentoring programs, youth organizations, schools, and communities are all considered potential sources of adult relationships for youth, the opportunities appear broader. These findings also point to different facets of mentoring relationships, both natural and program-supported, that merit further examination both in terms of processes involved and developmental outcomes to examine. We need to learn more about the nature of support exchanges and roles in mentoring, the quality of youth–adult relationships in youth programs and their association with different developmental outcomes. The Brazilian study reminds us that the influences of culture and social class should be examined in relation to all of these issues.

Social Inventions to Increase Access to Natural Mentors

If we accept the premise of this chapter that such relationships are beneficial and that they are especially important for youth facing stressful times with few resources, then the question becomes how to create more opportunities for those youth. Mentoring programs have demonstrated their value in giving youth greater access to adults. While advocating their greater use we also propose the modification of existing organizations and institutions creating social inventions (Hamilton & Hamilton, 2015) to enhance natural mentoring without necessarily matching mentors and mentees one-to-one. Some illustrations follow, drawn from or suggested by the reports above.

Advisory Groups

The small high schools studied by Hamilton et al. (2015) are examples of what Freedman (1993) called "mentor-rich environments," places where mentoring is likely to happen without formal intervention. One social invention (Whyte, 1982) in those schools, but not unique to them, is the advisory group, in which a stable cross-age set of students meets regularly with a teacher or staff member to do things together and talk about issues of mutual interest. This group is an example of the kind of invention that is needed to take full advantage of making any school experientially smaller for students even if the school's total size remains large.

Civic Engagement Projects

Martínez and Cumsille's study of Chilean youth organizations demonstrates that political attitudes and the skills needed for community involvement are formed not only in explicitly political contexts but also in civil society more broadly. Participation in decision making as well as experiences in leadership and planning in contexts such as youth organizations and school can build a sense of competence and commitment that carries over to political and non-political organizations in the larger community and nation. As they and others pointed out, adults need to make it possible for youth to take real responsibilities, wield genuine power, and have a chance to think and talk or reflect on their experiences. Service-learning is an especially powerful form of civic engagement for youth in which action to improve the community is central, but opportunities for youth learning are equally important. The convergence between mentoring and service-learning is illustrated by the Irish Big Brothers Big Sisters program's sponsorship of citizenship projects by participants (www.foroige.ie/citizenship/inspiration-your-citizenship-project).

Jobs and Internships

Work and work-like experiences can be used for career exploration, job training, or more general education. They give young people paid or unpaid work-based learning experiences in which they can engage with adults in goal-directed activity. As with civic engagement projects done in partnership with adults, these experiences are conducive to the formation of close relationships (Hamilton & Hamilton, 2004). Despite the fact that many youth jobs offer only limited contact with adults, a surprising number of young workers report that their adult supervisors are important people in their lives (Mortimer, 2003). We can hypothesize that the process of joint engagement in instrumentally meaningful activities can foster close ties, or, in functional role terms, that instrumental roles may evolve into more personal, emotional roles. This would appear to be a complementary trajectory to concrete and companionship support serving as a foundation for deeper and more personal mentoring relationships observed in the Irish study.

Community Activation

When citizens and leaders, including youth, come together and agree that it is important for youth to be incorporated into the life of their community, they can find many ways to change organizations, in addition to creating new programs, for this purpose.[3] Consider, for example, taking greater advantage of the cross-age membership of faith-based organizations. Although families may participate in some services, other activities are age-graded when young people might be intentionally integrated with adults as a way of sharing the responsibilities of nurturing children beyond the immediate family and enabling the youth to get to know a wider range of caring adults. This kind of change, like adding youth members to local government committees, takes a consensus within the community or organization that youth belong in such places, that they should have a voice, and that adults who are not their parents and teachers bear some responsibility for promoting their development. In view of the sad reality that some adults are capable of doing harm to young people, that consensus should extend to the creation of new norms, expectations, and procedures around youth–adult relationships. Youth can learn how to invite adults to become their mentors and then how to make the most of the opportunity. Adults can be encouraged to welcome such invitations, to initiate them, and be coached in how to be an effective mentor. Parents should be involved appropriately in those relationships in recognition that they retain primary responsibility for their child's welfare and that one of the benefits of having a mentor is that it can improve relations with parents (Rhodes, Grossman, & Resch, 2000).

Cultural Norms and Youth Voice

We should also acknowledge that our recommendations presume an appreciation of youth empowerment that is not universal. Some societies and certainly some segments of all societies emphasize subordination to elders and view the idea of youth–adult partnership as improper. This may mean that the relationships look different in different locations and cultures, as suggested by Núñez's study, perhaps more hierarchical than we have envisioned. Research on this topic would be welcome.

That young people facing economic and social change need education and jobs is indisputable. Far too many need food, shelter, and protection from violence and diseases as well. Their parents and other family members should remain their primary sources of support whenever possible. But as we seek to promote the positive development of all youth we need to attend to their opportunities to watch, talk with, learn from, pattern themselves after, and interact on a progressively more equal way with adults who are not family members. Access to these opportunities comes with the privilege of attending a well-resourced institution of higher education, indenture in a high-quality apprenticeship, or membership in a high-functioning community. For the vast majority of young people who do not enjoy these privileges we must be more intentional and invest more resources to make these opportunities available. The studies reported and cited in this chapter provide some guidance toward that aim.

Acknowledgments

S. F. Hamilton organized the symposium at which the studies reported in this chapter were presented and was the principal author of the chapter. M. A. Hamilton collaborated in shaping and editing the chapter. D. L. DuBois, M. L. Martínez, and P. Cumsille also contributed to improving the entire chapter. The other co-authors are listed alphabetically.

Notes

1   This construct is related to "linking social capital," which is used in public health. See, for example, Szreter and Woolcock, 2004.

2 Unlike in the USA, the Irish BBBS programme is integrated into a "parent" youth service, which gives mentors and mentees access to groups and facilities if desired.
3 The Search Institute has methods and capacity to help communities coalesce around youth development goals.

References

Barbosa, P. V., & Wagner, A. (2013). A autonomia na adolescência: Revisando conceitos, modelos e variáveis. *Estudos de Psicologia (Natal), 18*(4), 649–658. doi:10.1590/S1413- -294X2013000400013

Barrera, M., & Bonds, D. D. (2005). Mentoring relationships and social support. In D. L. DuBois & M. J. Karcher (Eds), *The handbook of youth mentoring* (pp. 133–142). Thousand Oaks, CA: Sage.

Blinn-Pike, L. (2007). The benefits associated with youth mentoring relationships. In T. D. All, & L. T. Eby (Eds), *The Blackwell handbook of mentoring: A multiple perspectives approach* (pp. 165–188). Malden, MA: Blackwell Publishing.

Bruce, M., & Bridgeland, J. (2014). *The mentoring effect: Young people's perspectives on the outcomes and availability of mentoring.* Washington, DC: Civic Enterprises in association with Hart Research Associates for MENTOR, the National Mentoring Partnership. Retrieved from www.mentoring.org/images/uploads/Report_TheMentoringEffect.pdf (accessed 15/03/2015).

Camino, L., & Zeldin, S. (2002). From periphery to center: Pathways for youth civic engagement in the day-to-day life of communities. *Applied Developmental Science, 6*(4), 213–220.

Chirkov, V. I. (2007). Culture, personal autonomy, and individualism: Their relationships and implications for personal growth and well-being. In G. Zheng, K. Leung, & J. G. Adair (Eds), *Perspectives and progress in contemporary cross-cultural psychology* (pp. 247–263). Beijing, China: China Light Industry Press.

Clausen, J. S. (1993). *American lives: Looking back at the children of the Great Depression.* New York: Free Press.

Cobb, S. (1976). Social support as a moderator of life stress. *Psychosomatic Medicine, Vol. 38* (No. 5 September–October 1976), 300–313.

Coleman, J. S. (1988). Social capital in the creation of human capital. *American Journal of Sociology, 94* (Suppl.), S95–S120.

Cutrona, C. E. (2000). Social support principles for strengthening families. In J. Canavan, P. Dolan, & J. Pinkerton (Eds), *Family support: Direction from diversity* (pp. 103–122). London: Jessica Kingsley.

Cutrona, C. E., & Russell, D. W. (1990). Type of social support and specific stress: Toward a theory of optimal matching. In B. R. Sarason, I. G. Sarason, & G. R. Pierce (Eds), *Social support: An interactional view* (pp. 319–366). New York: John Wiley & Sons.

Darling, N., Hamilton, S. F., Toyokawa, T., & Matsuda, S. (2002). Naturally occurring mentoring in Japan and the United States: Social roles and correlates. *American Journal of Community Psychology, 30*(2), 245–270.

Deci, E. L., & Ryan, R. M. (1985). The general causality orientation scale: Self-determination in personality. *Journal of Research in Personality, 19*(2), 109–134.

Deci, E. L., & Ryan, R. M. (2000). The "what" and "why" of goal pursuits: Human needs and the self-determination of behavior. *Psychological Inquiry, 11*(4), 227–268.

Diener, E., Emmons, R. A., Larsen, R. J., & Griffin, S. (1985). The Satisfaction with Life Scale. *Journal of Personality Assessment, 49*(1), 71–75.

Dolan P., & Brady B. (2012). *A guide to youth mentoring. Providing effective social support.* London: Jessica Kingsley Publishers.

Dolan, P., Brady, B., O'Regan, C., Russell, D., Canavan, J., & Forkan, C. (2011a). Big Brothers Big Sisters of Ireland: Evaluation study. Report one: Randomised controlled trial and implementation report. Galway: Child and Family Research Centre.

Dolan, P., Brady, B., O'Regan, C., Russell, D., Canavan, J., & Forkan, C., (2011b). *Big Brothers Big Sisters of Ireland: Evaluation study. Report two: Qualitative evidence.* Galway: Child and Family Research Centre.

Dooley, B., & Fitzgerald, A. (2012). *My World survey: National study of youth mental health.* Dublin: Headstrong & UCD School of Psychology.

DuBois, D. L., & Karcher, M. J. (Eds) (2013) *Handbook of youth mentoring* (2nd ed.). Thousand Oaks, CA: Sage.

DuBois, D. L., & Silverthorn, N. (2005). Characteristics of natural mentoring relationships and adolescent adjustment: Evidence from a national study. *Journal of Primary Prevention, 26*(2), 69–92.

DuBois, D. L., Portillo, N., Rhodes, J. E., Silverthorn, N., & Valentine, J. C. (2011). How effective are mentoring programs for youth? A systematic assessment of the evidence. *Psychological Science in the Public Interest, 12*(2), 57–91.

Eccles, J. (2005). The present and future of research on activity settings. In J. Mahoney, R. Larson,, & J. Eccles (Eds) *Organized activities as contexts of development* (pp. 353–371). Mahwah, NJ: Lawrence Erlbaum Associates.

Eccles, J., & Gootman, J. A. (Eds) (2002). *Community programs to promote youth development.* Washington, DC: National Academy Press.

Erickson L. D., McDonald S., & Elder, Jr., G. H. (2009). Informal mentors and education: Complementary or compensatory resources? *Sociology of Education, 82*(4), 344–367.

Finn, J. L., & Checkoway, B. (1998). Young people as competent community builders: A challenge to social work. *Social Work, 43*(4), 335–345.

Flanagan, C., & Faison, N. (2001). Youth civic development: Implications of research for social policy and programs. *Social Policy Report, 15*(1), 3–14.

Freedman, M. (1993). *The kindness of strangers: Reflections on the mentoring movement.* San Francisco, CA: Jossey-Bass.

Gagné, M. (2003). The role of autonomy support and autonomy orientation in prosocial behavior engagement. *Motivation and Emotion, 27*(3), 199–223.

Granovetter, M. (1983). The strength of weak ties: A network theory revisited. *Sociological Theory, 1*, 201–233.

Greenberger, E., Chen, C., & Beam, M. (1998). The role of "very important" nonparental adults in adolescent development. *Journal of Youth and Adolescence, 27*(3), 321–343.

Grossman, J. B., & Rhodes, J. E. (2002). The test of time: Predictors and effects of duration in youth mentoring relationships. *American Journal of Community Psychology, 30*(2), 199–218.

Hamilton, S. F., & Darling, N. (1989). Mentors in adolescents' lives. In K. Hurrelmann & U. Engel (Eds), *The social world of adolescents: International perspectives* (pp. 121–139). Berlin: Walter deGruyter.

Hamilton, S. F., & Hamilton, M. A. (2004). Contexts for mentoring: Adolescent-adult relationships in workplaces and communities. In R. M. Lerner & L. Steinberg (Eds), *Handbook of adolescent psychology* (pp. 492–526). New York: Wiley.

Hamilton, M. A., & Hamilton, S. F. (2012, October). *Mentoring in retrospect.* Presentation at the Society for Research on Child Development Themed Conference on Transition to Adulthood. Tampa, FL.

Hamilton, M.A., & Hamilton, S.F. (2015). Seeking social inventions to improve the transition to adulthood. *Applied Developmental Science, 19*(2), 87–107.

Hamilton, M. A., Hamilton, S. F., DuBois, D. A., & Sellers, D. E. (2016). Functional roles of important nonfamily adults for youth. *Journal of Community Psychology 44*(6), 799–806. doi: 10.1002/jcop.21792

Hirsch, B. J., Deutsch, N. J., & DuBois, D. L. (2011). *After-school centers and youth development: Case studies of success and failure.* New York: Cambridge University Press.

INJUV (2012). *7a Encuesta Nacional de Juventud 2012* [7th National Survey of Youth 2012]. Retrieved from: http://www.injuv.gob.cl/portal/wp-content/files_mf/septimaencuesta nacionainjuvcorr2.pdf (accessed 31/08/2016).

Karcher, M. J., & Nakkula, M. J. (2010). Youth mentoring with a balanced focus, shared purpose, and collaborative interactions. In M. J. Karcher & M. J. Nakkula (Eds), *Play, talk, learn: Promising practices in youth mentoring. New Directions in Youth Development* (No. 126, pp. 13–32). San Francisco: Jossey-Bass.

Kasser, T., Cohn, S., Kanner, A. D., & Ryan, R. M. (2007). Some costs of American corporate capitalism: A psychological exploration of value and goal conflicts. *Psychological Inquiry, 18*(1), 1–22.

Keller, T. E. (2005). The stages of development of mentoring relationships. In D. L. DuBois & M. J. Karcher (Eds), *Handbook of youth mentoring* (pp. 82–99). Thousand Oaks, CA: Sage.

Keller, T. E., & Blakeslee, J. E. (2014). Social networks and mentoring. In D. L. DuBois & M. J. Karcher (Eds), *Handbook of youth mentoring* (2nd ed., pp. 129–142). Thousand Oaks, CA: Sage.

Kirshner, B. (2008). Guided participation in three youth activism organizations: Facilitation, apprenticeship, and joint work. *Journal of Learning Sciences, 17*(1), 60–101.

Kirshner, B. (2009). "Power in numbers": Youth organizing as a context for exploring civic identity. *Journal of Research on Adolescence, 19*(3), 414–440.

Larson, R. (2006). Positive youth development, willful adolescents, and mentoring. *Journal of Community Psychology, 34*(6), 677–689.

Larson, R. W., & Angus, R. M. (2011). Adolescents' development of skills for agency in youth programs: Learning to think strategically. *Child Development, 82*(1), 277–294.

Larson, R., Walker, K., & Pearce, N. (2005). A comparison of youth-driven and adult-driven youth programs: Balancing inputs from youth and adults. *Journal of Community Psychology, 33*(1), 57–74.

Lin, N. (2001). *Social capital: A theory of social structure and action.* Cambridge, UK: Cambridge University Press.

Martínez, M. L., Pérez, J. C., & Cumsille, P. (2014). Chilean adolescents' and parents' views on autonomy development. *Youth and Society, 46*(2), 176–200.

MENTOR (2005). *Mentoring in America 2005: A snapshot of the current state of mentoring.* Washington, DC: Author. Retrieved from www.mentoring.org/downloads/mentoring_523.pdf (accessed 03/10/2015).

Mortimer, J. T. (2003). *Working and growing up in America.* Cambridge, MA: Harvard University Press.

Nakkula, M. J., & Harris, J. T. (2014). Assessing mentoring relationships. In D. L. DuBois & M. J. Karcher (Eds), *Handbook of youth mentoring* (2nd ed., pp. 45–62). Thousand Oaks, CA: Sage.

Putnam, R. D. (2000). *Bowling alone: The collapse and revival of American community*. New York: Simon & Schuster.

Putnam, R. D. (2015). *Our kids: The American dream in crisis*. New York: Simon & Schuster.

Rhodes, J. E. (2002). *Stand by me: The risks and rewards of mentoring today's youth*. Cambridge, MA: Harvard University Press.

Rhodes, J. E., Grossman, J. B., & Resch, N. L. (2000). Agents of change: Pathways through which mentoring relationships influence adolescents' academic adjustment. *Child Development, 71*(6), 1662–1671.

Rhodes, J., Reddy, R., Roffman, J., & Grossman, J. (2005). Promoting successful youth mentoring relationships: A preliminary screening questionnaire. *Journal of Primary Prevention, 26*(2), 147–167.

Rook, K. S., & Underwood, L. G. (2000). Social support measurement and interventions: Comments and future directions. In S. Cohen, L. Underwood & B. Gottlieb (Eds), *Social support measurement and intervention: A guide for health and social scientists* (pp. 311–334). Oxford: Oxford University Press.

Rutter, M. (1985). Resilience in the face of adversity: Protective factors and resistance to psychiatric disorders. *British Journal of Psychiatry, 147*(6), 589–611.

Schneider, B., & Stevenson, D. (1999). *The ambitious generation: America's teenagers, motivated but directionless*. New Haven, CT: Yale University Press.

Seidl-de-Moura, M. L., Lordelo, E., Vieira, M. L., Piccinini, C. A., Siqueira, J. O., Magalhaes, C. M. C., Pontes, F. A. R., Salomao, N. M., & Rimoli, A. (2008). Brazilian mothers' socialization goals: Intracultural differences in seven Brazilian cities. *International Journal of Behavioral Development, 32*(6), 465–472.

Smith, G. T. (2005). On construct validity: Issues of method and measurement. *Psychological Assessment, 17*(4), 396–408.

Spencer, R. (2006) Understanding the mentoring process between adolescents and adults. *Youth & Society, 37*(3), 287–315.

Spencer, R., & Basualdo-Delmonico, A. (2014) Family involvement in the youth mentoring process: A focus group study with program staff. *Children and Youth Services Review, 41*, 75–82.

Spencer, R., Basualdo-Delmonico, A., Walsh, J., & Drew, A.L. (2014) Breaking up is hard to do: A qualitative interview study of how and why youth mentoring relationships end. *Youth & Society*, 1–23. doi: 10.1177/0044118X14535416

Stanton-Salazar, R. D. (2001). *Manufacturing hope and despair: The school and kin support networks of U.S.–Mexican youth*. New York: Teachers College Press.

Stanton-Salazar, R. D. (2011). A social capital framework for the study of institutional agents and their role in the empowerment of low-status students and youth. *Youth and Society, 43*(3), 1066–1109.

Stukas, A. A., Clary, E. G., & Snyder, G. (2014). Mentor recruitment and retention. In D. L. DuBois & M. J. Karcher (Eds), *Handbook of youth mentoring* (2nd ed., pp. 397–409). Thousand Oaks, CA: Sage.

Szreter, S., & Woolcock, M. (2004). Health by association? Social capital, social theory, and the political economy of public health. *International Journal of Epidemiology, 33*(4), 650–667.

Tierney, J., Grossman, J., & Resch, N. (1995) *Making a difference: An impact study of Big Brothers Big Sisters of America.* Philadelphia, PA: Public Private Ventures.

Vieira, M. L., Seidl-de-Moura, M. L., Macarini, S. M., Martins, G. D. F., Lordelo, E. R., Tokumaru, R. S., & Oliva, A. D. (2010). Autonomy and interdependence: Beliefs of Brazilian mothers from state capitals and small towns. *The Spanish Journal of Psychology, 13*(2), 818–826.

Watts, R.J., Williams, N. C., & Jaegers, R. J. (2003). Sociopolitical development. *American Journal of Community Psychology, 31*(1–2), 185–194.

Werner, E. E., & Smith, R. S. (1982). *Vulnerable but invincible: A study of resilient children.* New York: McGraw-Hill.

Whyte, W. F. (1982). Social inventions for solving human problems. *American Sociological Review, 47*(1), 1–13.

Wills, T. A. (1991). Social support and interpersonal relationships. In C. Margaret (Ed.), *Pro-social behavior, review of personality and social psychology* (pp. 265–289). Thousand Oaks, CA: Sage.

Zeldin, S. (2004). Youth as agents of adult and community development: Mapping the processes and outcomes of youth engaged in organizational governance. *Applied Developmental Science, 8*(2), 75–90.

Zeldin, S., Camino, L., & Calvert, M. (2003). Toward an understanding of youth in community governance: Policy priorities and research directions. *Social Policy Report, 23*(3), 3–20.

Zeldin, S., Camino, L., & Mook, C. (2005). The adoption of innovation in youth organizations. *American Journal of Community Psychology, 33*(1), 121–135.

Zeldin, S., Petrokubi, J., & MacNeil, C. (2008). Youth–adult partnerships in decision making: disseminating and implementing an innovative idea into established organizations and communities. *American Journal of Community Psychology, 41*(3–4), 262–277.

Zimmerman, M. A., & Zahniser, J. H. (1991). Refinements of sphere-specific measures of perceived control: Development of a sociopolitical scale. *Journal of Community Psychology, 19(2)*, 189–204.

Zimmerman, M. A., Bingenheimer, J. B., & Behrendt, D. E. (2005). Natural mentoring relationships. In D. L. DuBois, & M. J. Karcher (Eds), *Handbook of youth mentoring* (pp. 143–157). Thousand Oaks, CA: Sage.

11

IDENTITY RESOURCES FOR POSITIVE ADAPTATION OF ROMA ETHNIC MINORITY YOUTH IN ALBANIA, BULGARIA, THE CZECH REPUBLIC, ITALY, KOSOVO, AND ROMANIA

*Radosveta Dimitrova, Pasquale Musso,
Amina Abubakar, Iva Polackova Solcova,
Delia Stefenel, Fitim Uka, Skerdi Zahaj,
Peter Tavel, and Venzislav Jordanov*

Roma are Europe's largest and most vulnerable minority, currently making up nearly 12 million people, a figure that is projected to grow in the coming years because of their relatively high birth rates (Council of Europe, 2010). Despite their relevance in size and demographic increase, Roma have traditionally been subjected to severe marginalization and therefore represent the most oppressed ethnic minority in Europe (European Commission, 2013). The detrimental life conditions and chances of Roma youth in this part of the world are rooted in historic ethnic tensions and a policy of assimilation during the communist rule (major Roma settlement is in countries of the former communist bloc such as Romania, the Czech Republic, and Bulgaria). With this context in mind, we examine Roma youth through a strengths-based, positive youth development (PYD) perspective of adolescence. In so doing, we investigate ethnic and national identity resources underlying positive adaptation in Roma youth in Albania, Bulgaria, the Czech Republic, Kosovo, Italy, and Romania. In all countries, Roma represent a large national minority group, traditionally marginalized, and repeatedly recognized to be those most in need of support.

In fact, improving life conditions of Roma communities across Europe is one of the foremost policy issues in the European Union Framework for National Roma Integration Strategies up to 2020 (European Commission, 2011). We address this urgent issue by targeting positive adaptation among Roma and ways to derive optimal well-being for youth in contrast to a deficit-oriented approach that focuses on how they are problematic and lag behind their peers from the majority populations. As explained further in more detail, policies toward Roma differ among these countries, with the Czech Republic and Romania being most effective in implementing integration strategies followed by Albania, Italy, Kosovo, and Bulgaria. We are interested in differences in the current contextual conditions across all countries under investigation and in the ramifications of these differences for identity and well-being of Roma youth. We also extend a prior line of research (Dimitrova, Chasiotis, Bender, & van de Vijver, 2013, 2014) by examining multiple identity resources of Roma to outline mechanisms to enhance well-being in these youth.

Traditional Frameworks on Ethnic and National Identity

Developmental theory and research has shown that establishing a coherent sense of identity is a core developmental task with achievement (firm commitment after identity exploration) and diffusion (neither engagement in exploration nor commitment) proposed as polar points of this development (Erikson, 1968; Marcia, 1980). Ethnic minority youth have to navigate and achieve multiple social identities (e.g., ethnic, national) as they live in a multicultural environment with the ability to identify with different social reference groups (Crocetti, Fermani, Pojaghi, & Meeus, 2011). In fact, both social identity (Tajfel & Turner, 1986) and self-categorization theories (Turner, Hogg, Oakes, Reicher, & Wetherell, 1987) acknowledge the importance of societal context for identity formation, particularly for ethnic minority groups. By building on these theoretical premises, we set out to investigate two specific types of social identity referring to heritage ethnic and national host culture. Ethnic identity is the process of maintaining positive attitudes toward specific ethnic groups (Erikson, 1968; Phinney, 1989; Phinney & Ong, 2007) and has been consistently shown to relate positively to psychological well-being of youth (Rivas-Drake et al., 2014; Schwartz, Zamboanga, Wiesskirch, & Rodriguez, 2009). National identity concerns the degree of identification with the (host) culture of settlement, including feelings of belonging and commitment to the host society where an ethnic minority group lives (Phinney & Devich-Navarro, 1997).

The most widely applied model of acculturation, referring to a two-dimensional process in which ethnic heritage culture maintenance and national host culture adoption are negotiated, has conceptualized interactions among ethnic and national identities. Therefore, the combination of both preserving one's ethnic heritage culture and adopting the national culture (labeled integration) is the most beneficial for minority groups in terms of positive adaptation (Berry, 1997). Additional models have provided useful tools to interpret the complexity of relations between ethnic and national identity. The Rejection-Identification Model suggests that people who belong to ethnic minority groups perceive that others will reject them on the basis of their group membership, and therefore identify more strongly with their own group to derive psychological well-being (Branscombe, Schmitt, & Harvey, 1999). The Rejection Dis-identification Model states that members of ethnic minority groups distance themselves from people who reject them on the basis of their group memberships (Jasinskaja-Lahti, Liebkind, & Solheim, 2009). The latter model also suggests that people who are rejected are less likely to identify with their host country. Based on these theoretical premises, we set out to assess both ethnic and national identity as potential resources of optimal psychological outcomes among understudied Roma groups in six European countries. Brief descriptions of Roma groups in these countries are presented below.

The Roma Minority

The Roma population across Europe ranges from 7 to 12 million people (European Union Agency for Fundamental Rights, 2010). They are Europe's largest and fastest growing ethnic minority, settled mainly in Central and Eastern Europe (Vermeersch & Ram, 2009). Yet, alongside these similarities, differences in Roma populations and their integration exist among all six countries investigated here.

Albania

Roma estimates in Albania range from 1,300 up to 120,000 out of the 3.4 million national population (Koinova, 2000). Roma in Albania are officially recognized as an ethnic-linguistic minority that has a judicial status. Yet, their situation is difficult with high rate of unemployment and poor living conditions. Roma have weak political representation and do not receive education in their mother tongue. In 2006, the Ministry of Tourism, Culture, Youth and Sports adopted an action plan for Roma in the fields of culture, youth, and sports to raise awareness of Romani traditions and create equal opportunities for the integration of Roma youth in the society (Council of Europe, 2007).

Bulgaria

Roma estimates in Bulgaria range between 325,000 and 800,000 people out of the national population of nearly 7 million (National Statistics Institute,

2011). Bulgaria has a historical record of ethnic tensions with its national ethnic minorities that experienced severe assimilation campaigns during the communist rule. In contrast to other countries, Bulgaria adopted a policy of strict repression of ethnic identity of Roma and banned the use of their Roma language (Csepeli & Simon, 2004). Today, official policies targeting the improvement of Roma conditions are scarce and a political will is lacking to factually improve their situation (Civil Society Monitoring Report Bulgaria, 2013).

The Czech Republic

Census data report estimates between 150,000 and 400,000 Roma in the Czech Republic (European Commission, 2013; Romea, 2013). They are a nationally recognized minority and their needs are addressed by social policy measures supporting the Roma language, culture, and identity (Civil Society Monitoring Report Czech Republic, 2013). The development of these measures is the responsibility of the Department for Human Rights and Minorities Protection, especially the Council for Roma Community Affairs, being composed of 15 Roma delegates who contribute to formulate new policies for Roma.

Italy

There are between 120,000 and 180,000 Roma out of the total 65 million Italian population mostly living in central and southern Italy (Council of Europe, 2013). About half of them are Italian citizens and belong to groups that have lived in Italy for centuries. Around 35,000 Roma migrated to Italy from the Balkans, with recent arrivals of immigrants estimated to number about 50,000 people (European Commission against Racism and Intolerance, 2012). Italy is the European country with the higher anti-Roma sentiments. As reported by the Pew Research Center (2014), the majority of Italians (85%) have unfavorable opinions of Roma who live in their country. This is the result of specific policies toward Roma communities that have generated tremendous controversy in recent years, as well as a general uncertain climate towards immigration and diversity.

Kosovo

Roma estimates are approximately 40,000 people out of the 2 million national population (Tcherenkov & Laderich, 2004). Roma are the most vulnerable group that after the war in Kosovo either remained marginalized or emigrated. Currently, there is a government institutional plan for Roma integration in areas of education, employment, health, and social affairs. Yet, the lack or non-provision of financial resources and the devastating postwar reality had weakened the efficacy of these actions (European Roma Rights Centre, 2011).

Romania

According to data provided by the latest Census, Roma living in Romania are 622,000 people out of 20,122,000 total population (National Institute of Statistics Romania, 2011). Roma are a national minority with representation in public and political life but are still socially and economically the most disadvantaged group in the country. Yet, Romania was among the first to sign the Decade of Roma Inclusion (2005–2015) in line with the political commitment by European governments to eliminate discrimination against Roma and promote the Strategy of Inclusion of the Roma Minority for the period 2012–2020. In fact, the National Agency for Roma (NAR) has been established to monitor and implement measures for the improvement of Roma conditions. Yet, no action plan of the Decade has been adopted by the Romanian government (Civil Society Monitoring on the Implementation of the National Roma Integration Strategy and Decade Action Plan in 2012 in Romania, 2013).

In summary, policies toward Roma differ among the countries investigated here, with the Czech Republic and Romania being slightly more active in Roma integration policy, followed by Albania, Italy, Kosovo, and Bulgaria. Although it is not easy to directly assess implications of such contextual diversity for youth, we investigated whether there might be differences in Roma youth's identity and well-being across countries.

Aims and Hypotheses

This study investigated ethnic and national identity and well-being in terms of self-esteem in Roma adolescents across six European countries by testing the following hypotheses. First, we expected mean level differences in ethnic and national identity within the Roma samples, such that Roma ethnic identity would be more endorsed by Roma youth in countries with more explicit integration policies (e.g., The Czech Republic and Romania) (Hypothesis 1a), and that national identity would be more endorsed by Roma youth in countries with more assimilation policies and/or lack of effective policies toward Roma integration (e.g., Bulgaria, Albania, Italy, and Kosovo) (Hypothesis 1b). Second, in concordance with previous findings (Dimitrova, Buzea, Jordanov, & Ljujic, 2015), we expected specific associations among Roma ethnic and national identities and self-esteem across countries. We hypothesized a positive effect of Roma ethnic identity on self-esteem for Roma youth in countries with more pronounced integration policies (Hypothesis 2a). National identity on the other hand was expected to be positively related to self-esteem in countries with more assimilation pressure and anti-Roma sentiments (e.g., Bulgaria, Albania, Kosovo, and Italy) (Hypothesis 2b).

TABLE 11.1 Means and Standard Deviations for Roma Adolescents across Countries

	Albania	Bulgaria	Czech Republic	Italy	Kosovo	Romania
	n = 90	n = 91	n = 99	n = 98	n = 78	n = 57
Age, Mean (SD)	14.21 (1.08)	15.98 (1.28)	14.59 (.89)	15.27 (1.89)	15.10 (1.59)	16.72 (1.45)
			Gender, %			
Female	51	42	63	40	53	49
Male	49	58	37	60	47	51
			Variables, Mean (SD)			
Self-Esteem	3.04 (.69)	3.07 (.52)	3.89 (.71)	2.88 (.28)	3.30 (.61)	3.33 (.52)
			Identity			
Roma	2.61 (1.41)	3.02 (1.16)	3.74 (.95)	4.31 (.42)	3.26 (1.40)	1.20 (.88)
National	4.21 (.90)	3.37 (1.06)	2.85 (.94)	2.58 (1.00)	2.77 (1.35)	4.12 (.56)
Cohen's d	0.95	0.19	−0.70	−1.55	−0.25	2.83

Note. Cohen's d effect size refers to comparisons between national and Roma identity within each country group.

Method

Participants and Procedure

Data for this study were drawn from a larger study designed to examine contextual predictors of well-being and positive adaptation among adolescents with Roma background in six European countries. Participants were 513 adolescents with Roma background (age: $M = 15.21$ years, $SD = 1.59$) of whom 90 were in Albania, 91 in Bulgaria, 99 in the Czech Republic, 98 in Italy, 78 in Kosovo, and 57 in Romania (see Table 11.1). Participants were recruited from public schools in major towns with a large number of Roma in Albania (Tirana, Durrës, and Elbasan), Bulgaria (Simeonovgrad, Harmanli, and Haskovo), the Czech Republic (Ostrava and Brno), Kosovo (Pristina), Italy (Palermo), and Romania (Sibiu, Hunedoara, and Prahova). Prior to data collection, local school authorities were contacted and informed about the purpose and methods of the study to acquire their consent. Upon agreement by the schools to take part in the study, parental and student consent was obtained. Students filled out the questionnaire during regular school hours.

Measures

Sociodemographics

Participants in all countries provided information on their ethnicity, age, socioeconomic status (SES; based on participants' parental education), and gender.

Identity

Identity measures for this study have been previously used in work with Roma youth to comprehensively assess ethnic and national identity (Dimitrova et al., 2013, 2014). Respondents were asked to indicate their answers using a five-point Likert scale ranging from *completely disagree* to *completely agree*. Items were scored so that higher scores indicated greater levels of ethnic and national identity endorsement, respectively. The *Roma Ethnic Identity Scale* contained items such as "I see myself as Roma," "I feel strongly connected to Roma people," "I am proud to be a member of the Roma community." The scale had excellent internal consistencies with values between .83 and .97 across Roma samples. The *National Identity Scale* included items like "I see myself as Bulgarian/Czech/Albanian/Italian/Romanian," "I feel strongly connected to Bulgarian/Czech/Albanian/Italian/Romanian people," and "I am proud to be a member of the Bulgarian/Czech/Albanian/Italian/Romanian community." The internal consistencies ranged from .74 to .96 across Roma samples.

Well-Being

We used Rosenberg's Self-Esteem Scale (Rosenberg, 1989) to measure youth self-esteem or how participants value themselves on a four-point Likert scale from *completely disagree* to *completely agree*. Sample items were "On the whole, I am satisfied with myself," "I feel that I have a number of good qualities," and "I am able to do things as well as most other people." Items were scored so that higher scores indicated greater levels of self-esteem. The internal consistencies ranged from .70 to .81 across Roma samples.

Results

Preliminary analyses tested for cross-cultural equivalence across groups. Structural equivalence was evaluated with Tucker's phi (above .90 as acceptable and above .95 excellent) (van de Vijver & Leung, 1997) and checked through comparing each group factor solution. The values of Tucker's phi across Roma groups ranged from .99 to 1.00 for Roma identity, from .98 to 1.00 for national identity, and from .99 to 1.00 for self-esteem. We can conclude that all groups showed very good structural equivalence and therefore can be compared.

The first set of hypotheses refers to mean level difference between ethnic and national identities across samples. We applied paired samples t-test for each Roma group that showed results partially in agreement with expectations. As expected, Roma identity was stronger than national identity for adolescents in the Czech Republic, $t(98) = 6.89, p < .001$. The same pattern was found for youth in Kosovo, $t(77) = 2.18, p < .05$, and Italy, $t(97) = 14.50, p < .001$. Results also showed that national compared to Roma ethnic identity was stronger for youth in Romania, $t(56) = 20.63, p < .001$, and Albania, $t(89) = 8.82, p < .001$. No significant difference emerged in the Bulgarian group, $t(90) = 1.56$, $p = .12$. In addition, we report Cohen's d values as effect sizes for comparisons among identity domains (Roma and national identity) in each group (Sánchez-Meca & Marín-Martínez, 2010). The interpretation of Cohen's d was as follows: 0.20 considered a small effect, 0.50 a medium effect, and 0.80 a large effect (Cohen, 1988; DeCoster, 2004). As can be seen in Table 11.1, effects of identity comparisons were mostly medium or large in size.

According to the second set of hypotheses, we expected specific associations among all identities and self-esteem across groups. Table 11.2 presents bivariate Pearson correlations among all study variables for Roma youth in each country. As can be seen there, results are partially in line with expectations and this was mostly the case for the association between ethnic identity and well-being for Roma youth in the Czech Republic (in line with Hypothesis 2a), $r(99) = .35$, $p < .001$. Roma ethnic identity showed no significant correlations with self-esteem in Albania, Bulgaria, Italy, Kosovo, and Romania. On the other hand,

TABLE 11.2 Correlations among All Study Variables for Roma Adolescents across Countries

	Albania			Bulgaria			Czech Republic			Italy			Kosovo			Romania		
	1.	2.	3.	1.	2.	3.	1.	2.	3.	1.	2.	3.	1.	2.	3.	1.	2.	3.
1. ROI	—			—			—			—			—			—		
2. NI	-.06	—		-.37**	—		.09	—		-.24**	—		-.03	—		-.03	—	
3. SE	.04	.61**	—	-.01	.42**	—	.35**	.12	—	.01	-.09	—	-.05	-.13	—	-.05	.47**	—

Note: ROI = Roma Identity; NI = National Identity; SE = Self-Esteem. **p < .001.

national identity was significantly and positively related to self-esteem for youth in Albania, $r(90) = .61$, $p < .001$, Bulgaria, $r(91) = .42$, $p < .001$, and Romania, $r(57) = .47$, $p < .001$, whereas no such relations emerged for the Czech Republic, Kosovo, and Italy.

Finally, the effects of identity variables on well-being outcomes were examined in a series of linear regression models with Roma and national identity as independent factors, self-esteem as outcome variable, and SES, age, and gender as the covariate variables. The results showed significant positive effects of Roma identity on self-esteem for youth in the Czech Republic only ($\beta = .30$, $p < .001$). National identity was positively related to self-esteem in Albania ($\beta = .42$, $p < .001$), Bulgaria ($\beta = .28$, $p < .001$), and Romania, ($\beta = .47$, $p < .001$).

Discussion

The objective of this chapter was to compare how ethnic and national identities are related to well-being in Roma adolescents living in Albania, Bulgaria, the Czech Republic, Italy, Kosovo, and Romania. Policies and support available to Roma communities to improve their conditions vary across these countries, with the Czech Republic and Romania being slightly more active in Roma integration policy. Our study suggests that differences in identity endorsement reflect differences in these national policies, combined with other potential contextual factors.

With regard to our first prediction, we expected mean level differences in ethnic and national identity within samples such that Roma ethnic identity is stronger than national identity in countries with more effective integration policies toward Roma, and the latter is stronger than ethnic identity in countries with more assimilation policies and/or lack of effective integration policies. We could detect significant within-group effects among these two identity domains, confirming only partially our expectations. As predicted, in the case of Roma group in the Czech Republic, Roma identity had high endorsement levels. However, this pattern can also be observed in Kosovo and Italy. Yet, the interpretation for these results may change depending on the specific country context.

The Czech Republic is the country with more explicit integration policy promoting the Roma language, culture, and identity (Civil Society Monitoring Report Czech Republic, 2013). So, ethnic background may provide a stronger source of identification than national one for Roma youth. In a different way, Kosovo and Italy are countries where Roma continued to remain generally marginalized with high negative anti-Roma sentiments especially in Italy (Pew Research Center, 2014). In such a context, our findings on the Roma suggest the Rejection-Identification Model (Branscombe et al., 1999) that perceived discrimination encourages hostility towards the national out-group and increases ethnic identification. Moreover, recently the Rejection Dis-identification Model

(Jasinskaja-Lahti et al., 2009) has also suggested that rejection prevents minority groups from developing a sense of belonging to the national dominant group. Although our study did not directly measure perceived rejection, we found that Roma youth in Kosovo and Italy tend to identify with the national culture at a much lower level than with their Roma culture and identity.

Also contrary to expectations, Roma ethnic identity was found to be the lowest for Roma youth in Romania compared to their peers in other countries. Despite the fact that Romania has developed relatively fine integration policies, the underlying strategy seems to not adequately recognize Roma background and identity, as it is in the Czech Republic. This ambiguous situation between formal tolerance and lack of identification (Giurca, 2012; Preoteasa, Şerban, & Tarnovschi, 2011) may prompt youth to consider the Romanian dimension as the best positive source of identification (Preoteasa et al., 2011; Zamfir, 2014), suggesting a sort of paradox that increases the national identification at the expense of the ethnic one. The same trend of relationship, but in line with our expectations, was evident for Roma youth in Albania, a context with undeveloped integration policies although without significant forms of rejection, and tangentially also in Bulgaria, the country with the severe assimilation policies.

In summary, the salience of ethnic and national identities for Roma is moderated by contextual factors of the specific countries in which they live. In countries with active integration policies, such as the Czech Republic, or with factual marginalization or rejection, such as Kosovo and especially Italy, Roma youth show a higher endorsement of ethnic identity than national identity. On the contrary, in countries with ambiguous integration strategies, such as in Romania, or with undeveloped integration policies and low rejection, such as in Albania, or with assimilation policies, such as in Bulgaria, the dynamic is inversed, with a higher endorsement of national identity than ethnic identity.

With regard to our second prediction, we expected to observe specific associations among Roma ethnic and national identities and self-esteem across countries. We expected to find a positive effect of ethnic identity on self-esteem in countries with more pronounced integration policies and a positive effect of national identity on self-esteem in countries with more anti-Roma sentiments and assimilation pressure. Our findings partly confirmed this hypothesis. We observed a significant and moderately-sized association between ethnic identity and self-esteem in the Czech Republic. We also found that, on the one hand, ethnic identity was not substantially associated with self-esteem for youth in Albania, Bulgaria, Italy, Kosovo, and Romania, whereas, on the other hand, national identity was positively related to self-esteem in Albania, Bulgaria, and Romania. These findings seem to reflect the contextual characteristics mentioned previously.

Thus, in the Czech Republic, ethnic identity may serve as a positive source of optimal adaptation for Roma youth given the active and clear integration policies. On the contrary, this is not the case for the other countries (including

Romania), where the integration policies vary from ambiguous to lacking, and where there may be assimilation or marginalization and rejection phenomena. In brief, Roma ethnic identity seems to be predictive of well-being only when there are effective integration policies, possibly signifying concrete opportunities for positive development of youth.

Relatedly, national identity may be a positive resource of well-being in countries with assimilation policies, such as in Bulgaria, and with ambiguous or underdeveloped integration policies and lower rejection, such as in Romania and Albania. In both cases, possibly Roma youth perceive the chance of tangible benefits of identifying with the dominant culture. This confirms past research showing that national identity is quite salient identity for Roma in Bulgaria (Dimitrova et al., 2013, 2014) and this study shows the same to be true for Roma in Romania and Albania, whereas a different pattern seems to characterize Kosovo and Italy. Kosovo and especially Italy are countries where Roma marginalization or rejection prevail, suggesting certain constraints for positive well-being. Furthermore, Kosovo is a very recent state with still a low degree of national identity development, and Italy is the only country among the others here represented without a communist heritage and with a long historical debate on the weak national identity. In such contextual conditions, national identity has plausibly no impact on well-being.

In conclusion, these findings support the notion that ethnic and national identities can be regarded as a psychological resource to face challenges for youth, particularly those with Roma background. However, their effects depend on the contextual circumstances. In a context clearly active in terms of integration policies, ethnic identity may be the best psychological resource for optimal adaptation, whereas in contexts with ambiguous, undeveloped, or assimilation policies, national identity may serve as the best source for enhanced well-being.

Limitations and Conclusions

Although novel in its unique sample representativeness, our study is not without limitations. First, we lacked qualitative information on identity among Roma communities, which could be critical in further understanding their multiple identities. Future studies can gather qualitative data through interviews and focus groups. A second important limitation concerns the sample selection. By necessity, we focused on Roma youth who attended public schools and were available to participate in the survey. As school dropout is very common among Roma students (Ringold, 2000), we cannot generalize our findings to students who drop out of school and are clearly at risk for poor well-being. Another shortcoming was our inability to directly assess specific public policies toward improvement of life conditions and integration of Roma in various countries. Linking external country-level indicators of successful local policy implementation and positive identity and adaptation of Roma might be particularly valuable. We also lacked examining self-perceptions of our participants regarding the rejection they experience by the dominant society they live in. For example, growing nationalism and Romaphobia have been documented as being important sources of mistrust, perceived threat, and negative evaluation of the Roma (Dimitrova et al., 2015; Ljujic, Vedder, Dekker, & Geel, 2012). Despite these limitations, this chapter stresses the relevance of contextual conditions to advance our knowledge about how ethnic and national identities are related to enhanced well-being of Roma youth. These findings and implications of this study are relevant both to understand Roma adolescents' multiple identity dynamics and provide new insights of these dynamics related to optimal adaptation of such relevant ethnic minority groups across Europe.

Acknowledgments

The authors would like to acknowledge the support by a COFAS FORTE (Swedish Research Council for Health, Working Life and Welfare) Marie Curie Grant (Forte Projekt 2013–2669) to the first author, and Lily Konowitz for her thoughtful language revision of the paper. We are also extremely grateful to the following organizations and people for their help in carrying out the study in Bulgaria (Eva Jecheva and the National Agency for Child Protection, all schools, students, and teachers and particularly Neli Filipova, Ivanina Noncheva, Radka Kostandinova, Albena Damianova, Stoyka Jekova, Svetla Atanasova, Neli Kiuchukova, Ani Angelova, Lilia Stoyanova, Tianka Kardjilova, Zvetan Terziev, Elena Ianeva, Venizslav Chobanov, Kamelia Mateva, and Petko Petkov), Italy (Michele Mannoia for his pertinent remarks and useful suggestions, Manuela Casamento for her role of cultural mediator, all the schools, and adolescents), the Czech Republic (the Olomouc University Social Health Institute (OUSHI), in particular Zuzana Puzova, Katerina Hamplova, and Helena Pipova, all schools and institutions across the country, and the support by the Czech Academy of Sciences RVO 6808174 created as part of Strategy AV21), Romania (all teachers, colleagues, and especially to Simona Steluta Marti, Iuliana Ilie, Ionut Cojan, Alina Manescu, and Luiza Bratu), and Kosovo (Genc Rexhepi, Argjend Abazi, Kastriot Hasaj, Enteela Kamberi, Erduana Dermaku, Miran Xhelili, Alma Sherifi, Hillari Alidema, Elina Morina and Blerton Jakupi).

References

Berry, J. W. (1997). Immigration, acculturation, and adaptation. *Applied Psychology, 46,* 5–34. doi:10.1111/j.1464-0597.1997.tb01087.x

Branscombe, N. R., Schmitt, M. T., & Harvey, R. D. (1999). Perceiving pervasive discrimination among African Americans: Implications for group identification and well-being. *Journal of Personality and Social Psychology, 77*, 135–149. doi:10.1037/0022-3514.77.1.135

Civil Society Monitoring on the Implementation of the National Roma Integration Strategy and Decade Action Plan in 2012 in Romania (2013). *Civil society monitoring report on the implementation of the national Roma integration strategy and decade action plan in 2012 in Romania.* Accessed September 12, 2015 at www.romadecade.org/cms/upload/file/9270_file24_ro_civil-society-monitoring-report_en.pdf

Civil Society Monitoring Report Bulgaria (2013). *Implementation of the national Roma integration strategy and decade action plan in 2012.* Accessed October 11, 2015 at www.romadecade.org/cms/upload/file/9270_file4_bg_civil-society-monitoring-report_en.pdf

Civil Society Monitoring Report Czech Republic (2013). *Implementation of the national Roma integration strategy and decade action plan in 2012.* Accessed October 11, 2015 at www.romadecade.org/cms/upload/file/9270_file6_cr_civil-society-monitoring-report_en.pdf

Cohen, J. (1988). *Statistical power analysis for the behavioral sciences* (2nd ed.). Hillsdale, NJ: Lawrence Erlbaum Associates.

Council of Europe (2007). *Second report submitted by Albania pursuant to Article 25, paragraph 1 of the Framework Convention for the Protection of National Minorities.* Accessed October 15, 2015 at www.coe.int/t/dghl/monitoring/minorities/3_FCNMdocs/PDF_2nd_SR_Albania_Annexes_en.pdf

Council of Europe (2010). *Statistics.* Accessed October 15, 2015 at www.coe.int/t/dg3/romatravellers/default_en.asp

Council of Europe (2013). *Thematic report on combating anti-Gypsyism hate speech and hate crime against Roma.* Retrieved from www.coe.int/it/web/portal/cahrom

Crocetti, E., Fermani, A., Pojaghi, B., & Meeus, W. (2011). Identity formation in adolescents from Italian, mixed, and migrant families. *Child & Youth Care Forum, 40*, 7–23. doi:10.1007/s10566-010-9112-8

Csepeli, G., & Simon, D. (2004). Construction of Roma identity in Eastern and Central Europe: Perception and self-identification. *Journal of Ethnic and Migration Studies, 30*, 129–150. doi:10.1080/1369183032000170204

DeCoster, J. (2004). Meta-analysis. In K. Kempf-Leonard (Ed.), *The encyclopedia of social measurement* (pp. 683–688). San Diego, CA: Academic Press.

Dimitrova, R., Buzea, C., Jordanov, V., & Ljujic, V. (2015). Nationalistic attitudes and perceived threat determine Romaphobia among Bulgarian and Romanian youth. *Social Work Review, 3*, 33–47.

Dimitrova, R., Chasiotis, A., Bender, M., & van de Vijver, F. J. R. (2013). Collective identity and well-being of Roma adolescents in Bulgaria. *International Journal of Psychology, 48*, 502–513. doi:10.1080/00207594.2012.682064

Dimitrova, R., Chasiotis, A., Bender, M., & van de Vijver, F. J. R. (2014). Collective identity of Roma youth and their mothers. *Journal for Youth and Adolescence: Special Issue on Challenges and Resilience of Indigenous Adolescents for Positive Youth Development, 43*, 375–386. doi:10.1007/s10964-013-0043-1

Erikson, E. (1968). *Identity: Youth and crisis.* New York: Norton.

European Commission (2011). *An EU framework for national Roma integration strategies up to 2020.* Accessed October 20, 2015 at http://ec.europa.eu/justice/policies/discrimination/docs/com_2011_173_en.pdf

European Commission (2013). *Roma integration concept for 2010–2013*. Accessed October 20, 2015 at http://ec.europa.eu/justice/discrimination/files/roma_czech_republic_strategy_ en.pdf

European Commission against Racism and Intolerance (2012). *ECRI report on Italy (fourth monitoring cycle)*. Strasbourg: Council of Europe. Retrieved from www.coe.int/t/dghl/ monitoring/ecri/Country-by-country/Italy/ITA-CbC-IV-2012-002-ENG.pdf

European Roma Rights Centre (2011). *Abandoned minority: Roma rights history in Kosovo.* Retrieved from www.errc.org/cms/upload/file/abandoned-minority-roma-rights-history-in-kosovo-dec-2011.pdf

European Union Agency for Fundamental Rights (2010). *Addressing the Roma issue in the EU*. Accessed May 12, 2015 at http://fra.europa.eu/fraWebsite/roma/roma_en.htm

Giurca, D. (2012). *Roma inclusion in Romania: Policies, institutions and examples.* Constanța, Romania: Dobrogea. Retrieved from www.fundatia.ro/sites/default/files/ro_123_ studiu_ro.pdf

Jasinskaja-Lahti, I., Liebkind, K., & Solheim, E. (2009). To identify or not to identify? National disidentification as an alternative reaction to perceived ethnic discrimination. *Applied Psychology: An International Review, 58*, 105–128. doi:10.1111/ j.1464-0597.2008.00384.x

Koinova, M. (2000). *Roma of Albania: Albanian Helsinki Committee (CEDIME-SE).* Retrieved from www.greekhelsinki.gr/pdf/cedime-se-albania-roma.doc

Ljujic, V., Vedder, P. H., Dekker, H., & Geel, M. (2012). Serbian adolescents' Romaphobia and their acculturation orientations towards the Roma minority. *International Journal of Intercultural Relations, 36*, 53–61. doi:10.1016/j.ijintrel.2010.11.015

Marcia, J. E. (1980). Identity in adolescence. In J. Adelson (Ed.), *Handbook of adolescent psychology* (pp. 159–187). New York: Wiley.

National Institute of Statistics Romania (2011). *The 2011 population and housing census. Results.* Retrieved from www.recensamantromania.ro/noutati/volumul-ii-populatia-stabila-rezidenta-structura-etnica-si-confesionala/

National Statistics Institute (NSI) (2011). *Census 2011*. Sofia, Bulgaria: NSI Press.

Pew Research Center (2014). *A fragile rebound for EU Image on eve of European parliament elections*. Retrieved from www.pewglobal.org/files/2014/05/2014-05-12_Pew-Global-Attitudes-European-Union.pdf

Phinney, J. S. (1989). Stages of ethnic identity development in minority group adolescents. *Journal of Early Adolescence, 9*, 34–49. doi:10 .1177/0272431689091004

Phinney, J. S., & Devich-Navarro, S. M. (1997). Variations in bicultural identification among African American and Mexican American adolescents. *Journal of Research on Adolescence, 7* (1), 3–32.

Phinney, J. S., & Ong, A. D. (2007). Conceptualization and measurement of ethnic identity: Current status and future directions. *Journal of Counseling Psychology, 54*, 271–281. doi:10.1037/0022-0167.54.3.271

Preoteasa, A. M., Şerban, M., & Tarnovschi, D. (2011). *EU inclusive data transfer and exchange of good practices regarding the inclusion of Roma population between Romania, Bulgaria, Italy and Spain: Roma situation in Romania, 2011. Between social inclusion and migration: Country report.* Bucharest, Romania: Soros Foundation. Retrieved from www.fundatia.ro/sites/ default/files/en_122_Roma%20situation%20in%20Romania.pdf

Ringold, D. (2000). *Roma and the transition in Central and Eastern Europe: Trends and challenges*. Washington, DC: The World Bank.

Rivas-Drake, D., Syed, M., Umaña-Taylor, A. J., Markstrom, C., French, S., Schwartz, S. J., Lee, R. M., & Ethnic and Racial Identity Study Group (2014). Feeling good, happy, and proud: A meta-analysis of positive ethnic-racial affect and adjustment. *Child Development, 85*, 77–102. doi:10.1111/cdev.12175

Romea, O. S. (2013). *Report on the Roma minority in the Czech Republic in 2010.* Retrieved from www.romea.cz/dokumenty/zprava-romove-CR-2010.pdf

Rosenberg, M. (1989). *Society and the adolescent self-image*, revised edition. Middletown, CT: Wesleyan University Press.

Sánchez-Meca, J., & Marín-Martínez, F. (2010). Meta-analysis in psychological research. *International Journal of Psychological Research, 3*, 150–162.

Schwartz, S. J., Zamboanga, B. L., Weisskirch, R. S., & Rodriguez, L. (2009). The relationships of personal and ethnic identity exploration to indices of adaptive and maladaptive psychosocial functioning. *International Journal of Behavioral Development, 33*, 131–144. doi:10.1177/0165025408098018

Tajfel, H., & Turner, J. C. (1986). The social identity theory of intergroup behavior. In S. Worchel, & W. G. Austin (Eds.), *The social psychology of intergroup relations* (pp. 7–24). Chicago, IL: Nelson- Hall.

Tcherenkov, L., & Laderich, S. (2004). *The Roma.* Basel, Switzerland: Schwabe Verlag.

Turner, J. C., Hogg, M. A., Oakes, P. J., Reicher, S. D., & Wetherell, M. S. (1987). *Rediscovering the social group: A self-categorization theory.* Oxford, UK: Blackwell.

van de Vijver, F. J. R., & Leung, K. (1997). *Methods and data analysis for cross-cultural research.* Thousand Oaks, CA: Sage.

Vermeersch, P., & Ram M. H. (2009). The Roma. In B. Rechel (Ed.), *Minority rights in Central and Eastern Europe* (pp. 61–73). London: Routledge

Zamfir, C. (2014). Social report: 2014. Evaluating the institutional capacity of the National Agency for Roma. *Social Innovation Online Journal, 6.* Retrieved from www.inovatiasociala.ro/articol/125/

## PART II

Interventions to Support and Promote Positive Adaptation and Development

12

INNOVATIVE APPROACHES TO PROMOTING POSITIVE YOUTH DEVELOPMENT IN DIVERSE CONTEXTS

Novel Applications of Participatory Research and New Technologies

Emily J. Ozer, Amber Akemi Piatt, Ingrid Holsen, Torill Larsen, James Lester, and Elizabeth M. Ozer

Introduction: Why Focus on Positive Youth Development (PYD) among Adolescents?

In recent decades, there has been much important international attention to promoting the healthy development of young children and investing resources in human capital development programs focused on early childhood education and nutrition, especially among those families experiencing intergenerational poverty (Daelmans et al., 2015). While the gains of these global efforts have yielded increased survival of children into adolescence, critical questions about what happens to developmental trajectories during adolescence have yet to be addressed. Adolescents are now about 20% of the global population, with the highest concentration of adolescents in the poorest regions such as sub-Saharan Africa (UNICEF, 2012). We are now seeing a demographic "youth bulge" in many low-income countries, with a higher proportion of their population comprising adolescents. Globally, we see major health and educational disparities within and across countries, disproportionately affecting adolescent girls and low-income adolescents who have already entered the labor market (UNICEF, 2012).

Widespread concern about the latest global financial crisis prompted the Director-General of the World Health Organization (WHO) to convene a high-level consultation to investigate how the global economic downturn has affected global health. Among other findings, the report highlighted that although the impacts on health vary by country and context, the poor are the hardest hit as their risk management options are the most limited and they are often squeezed out of public health care systems (WHO, 2009). The World Bank similarly reported that food and fuel crises in the wake of the recent global economic downturn put an additional 100 million people in poverty, hurting the health and education of millions of youth due to reduced quality and/or quantity of food, school, and basic services (World Bank, 2008).

The relative neglect of adolescents – at our peril – has sparked several recent major reports from highly influential sources – such as *The Lancet*, UNICEF, and the WHO – that all emphasize the need to transform how we frame and promote adolescent health (UNICEF, 2012, 2015; Viner et al., 2012). The longstanding approach to adolescent health and medicine tends to be organized around discrete problems, such as violence, pregnancy, and sexually-transmitted infections, without sufficient focus on positive developmental processes or on strengthening the "social determinants" of health and well-being, such as family, school, and neighborhood microsystems, as well as broader political and economic conditions (Ozer & Russo, in press).

One major response to this need is the formation of *The Lancet* Commission on Adolescent Health and Well-being, an international inter-disciplinary collaboration charged with establishing a research and policy agenda for adolescent health globally (Patton et al., 2014). The commission is organized around six main themes: (1) adolescence within the life course, (2) promoting health equity and justice for young people, (3) increasing global visibility, monitoring, and accountability related to young people, (4) strengthening protective environments for young people, (5) scaling up sustainable and effective actions among young people, and (6) engaging and empowering young people (*The Lancet Youth*, 2014). Overall, the Commission explicitly calls for a greater focus on cross-disciplinary and cross-sector work to promote the health of young people rather on specific problem areas (Sawyer et al., 2012). In response to current calls for integrative approaches, developmentally-informed scientists across disciplines are working to establish a research agenda for adolescent and young adult health (for example, in the U.S., Maternal Child Health Bureau-funded Adolescent & Young Adult Health Research Network) and identify innovative approaches to promoting PYD that are potentially scale-able to exert population-level impacts (Center on the Developing Adolescent, 2015).

As noted above, youth engagement and empowerment is a key theme of *The Lancet* Commission; its importance was also emphasized by the United Nations' declaration of youth participation and empowerment as a "moral right" (UNCRC, 1989). While there may be broad political support for the concept of youth engagement and empowerment, this is an area with relatively little systematic research and evaluation to guide such efforts. There is a great need for innovative models that link youth engagement with PYD, especially with potentially scalable diffusion in diverse country and community contexts.

Focus and Organization of Chapter

Our symposium at the 2014 Society for Research on Child Development Special Topics Meeting on Positive Youth Development considered innovative models to promote PYD implemented by four interdisciplinary teams from three countries (Portugal, Norway, U.S.), with a focus on expanding the meaningful participation of young people in health and educational systems and interventions. In this chapter, we provide an overview of these models, reflecting on their innovative qualities, systems targeted, use of new technologies, and relevance in the context of economic recession. We also consider next steps for research and potential scaling efforts.

The Portuguese project (Margarida Gaspar de Matos, presenter and principal investigator [PI]), *Dream Teens,* engages diverse young people nationally in youth-led participatory action research projects focused on issues of their choosing to inform public policy (see brief description below). The Norwegian study (Ingrid Holsen, presenter and PI) presents a model for Norwegian teens participating in the *Dream School* program to promote a positive psychosocial learning climate, youth well-being, and achievement through participatory activities in the class and school environment (see detailed description below). One of the U.S. projects (Emily J. Ozer, presenter and PI), discusses a mixed-methods program of research on youth-led participatory research (YPAR) in urban schools for promoting PYD, with consideration of the opportunity for using web-based technology to "scale" YPAR internationally and embed YPAR in broader policy efforts (see detailed description below). The other U.S. research (Elizabeth M. Ozer, presenter and PI), informed by social cognitive theory, uses cutting-edge, personally-adaptable technology to develop, and eventually disseminate, narrative-centered, game-based interventions to promote adolescent health.

Portugal: Dream Teens Model

The *Dream Teens* model in Portugal was developed to promote PYD and empower young people on a national level by fostering youth-led participatory action research projects to inform public policies. In *Dream Teens,* the project's researchers and staff use social media and in-person meetings to support the research of youth from across the country in key domains of youth health and well-being. The youth were selected for the project via a national application process, with the engagement of sports figures and entertainers to advertise the effort. After the research projects developed their findings and recommendations, the project works to strengthen civic participation and systems change by bringing diverse Portuguese youth, decision makers, and media to a national conference in which youth researchers present their recommendations to key national ministries, such as health and education. The recommendations generated by the first cohort of youth researchers at their November 2014 youth conference were positively received and were posted on the Ministry of Health's website (*Dream Teens*, 2014). The project is continuing with subsequent cohorts and is conducting evaluations on the program's effects on the youth participants and the health and educational systems. To our knowledge, *Dream Teens* is the first national model of its kind, innovatively engaging youth expertise in research and public policy through both online and in-person meetings. Furthermore, the project has thrived in the context of Portugal's economic recession and without strong historical precedent for meaningful youth–adult partnerships with government officials. Please see www.dreamteens-en.aventurasocial.com/ for detailed information regarding the *Dream Teens* project (Frasquilho et al., 2016).

Norway: The Dream School

The *Dream School* program in Norway engages young people as both the users and facilitators of health promotion and education programming in schools. The *Dream School* sets out to facilitate and nurture the development of competence, caring, confidence, character, and connection through peer support and a focus on participatory learning activities (Cornwall & Jewkes, 1995). It was developed in accordance with the priorities of the Public Health Act (2012) in Norway, which examines the implementation and effects of health promotion programs aiming to promote positive psychosocial development, mental health and well-being, and academic achievement among young people. This act specifically emphasizes creating engaging, safe, socially competent, and connected school environments.

By way of context, it is important to note the structure of secondary schools in Norway. First, education in Norway is mandatory for all children aged 6 to 16. The ten-year school track separates primary school (first through seventh grade) from lower secondary school (eighth through tenth grade). Once students finish tenth grade, they can opt to attend a three-year upper secondary public school that focuses either on vocational education programs or a general studies program. The *Dream School* is an intervention in Norwegian lower and upper secondary schools that aims to create positive psychosocial learning environments, including mental health promotion, to bolster students' motivation to stay in school. The program was developed and delivered by a non-governmental organization called Adults for Children (*Voksne for Barn*) and has been implemented in 19 Norwegian schools to date. Foundationally, the program weaves together a health promotion perspective, participatory learning activities, peer-support initiatives, and a focus on solutions, motivation, and opportunities. The program achieves its goals through four main actors: the Dream Class, the Peer Leaders, the Resource Group, and the Teachers. The program has its own Facebook page where the respective actors post and share activities implemented at their schools.

The central activity and key element of the *Dream School* is the Dream Class. The Dream Class consists of two three-hour sessions facilitated by the Resource Group and the Peer Leaders. The first three-hour session takes place in all new classes in the first or second week of the school year, and the second session occurs the following January during the spring semester. The students and teachers are all active participants. The two main aims of the Dream Class are: (1) to provide the teacher and class with tools to establish a good psychosocial environment, characterized by safety, belonging, healthy communication, and positive relationships between the students and the teacher, and (2) to develop an action plan for the class to use throughout the school year. The students and their teacher discuss their ideal class environment, and they mutually identify specific actions the class can take to become that dream class. Examples of specific actions they initiated included everyone warmly greeting each other in the morning, treating each other with respect, being quiet and paying attention during classes, and leading activities during breaks where everyone is included. The teachers in particular are accountable for keeping the group on track with the action plan.

The Peer Leaders are students in the ninth and tenth grades at the lower secondary school (ages 13–15) or in the second and third grades at the upper secondary school (ages 16–19). Students are invited to apply for the Peer Leader jobs via posters, school newspapers, and school webpages with special attention focused on recruiting students who are motivated, well-liked, and credible among their peers. The students are then interviewed and selected by the Resource Group to represent a heterogeneous student group along gender and academic performance lines. The selected students receive two days of training off campus from Adults for Children on how to be a good peer leader and how to implement activities in classes and at the school. The Resource Groups supervise the Peer Leaders throughout the year, and Adults for Children later gathers the Peer Leaders and the Resource Groups to share experiences. Along with taking part in the Dream Class, teams of two or three Peer Leaders are together responsible for following up with their assigned class ("mentor class") during the school year and for creating activities on the school's campus that are open to all students.

The Resource Groups include representatives from the school management, staff, and student council, and thus broadly anchor the program in the whole school. The Resource Groups are trained together with the Peer Leaders by Adults for Children. They are charged with facilitating the Dream Class sessions together with the Peer Leaders and with providing structural support to the Peer Leaders.

The Teachers receive half-day training from Adults for Children where they are introduced to the Teachers' role in the program. Teachers must both participate together with the students during the Dream Class session and be responsible for tracking the action plan's implementation and adherence throughout the school year. Moreover, the Teachers serve as important collaboration partners for the Peer Leaders in their work with the classes in that they invite the Peer Leaders to take part in sessions where the class discusses the action plan.

As a whole, the project aims to generate new knowledge that supports the thematic priorities outlined in a recent Norwegian government white paper on youth development, coping, and opportunities (Det Kongelige Helse- og Omsorgsdepartement, 2015). The project is also rooted in research that draws a strong link between social inequality and mental health (Herrman, Saxena, Moodie, & Walker, 2005). The Dream School Program has been strategically applied within a whole school context in an attempt to intervene on issues of social inequality. The complementary focus on involvement and participation is especially important for students low in socioeconomic status (SES) (Finn & Rock, 1997), as this represents a unique opportunity not necessarily provided at home to the same extent as for students from families with high SES (Hoover-Dempsey, Bassler, & Brissie, 1987).

To date, preliminary results suggest that Norwegian schools that implemented the *Dream School* have reduced dropout rates and improved academic performance, which has been highlighted in several recent newspaper articles. Additionally, one of the schools received the Queen Sonja's School Award for their learning environment and their focus on youth participation through the use of peers as leaders and facilitators. This prize is given each year to a school that works systematically with their learning environment to promote equity and inclusion while fostering an environment characterized by participation, safety, and a strong sense of community.

Findings from a pilot study of the *Dream School* program in 2012 suggest that the involvement of peers as leaders and facilitators in the program was successful when they had strong, consistent adult support (Holsen, Larsen, Tjomsland, & Servan, 2014). Under these conditions, there was a positive impact on new students, and the peer leaders themselves gained a lot as well. The main challenge during the implementation of the program was the involvement of teachers and their collaboration with the peer leaders. In a revised version of the program, steps have been taken to address these challenges. The teachers and peer leaders now participate in modules of the training together, and they meet regularly during the school year. Further results from the pilot study of the program, using an age cohort design where schools serve as their own control, are forthcoming. In collaboration with education authorities at the county level in Norway, a grant application for a more extensive evaluation of the program has been submitted to the Ministry of Education.

United States: Youth-Led Participatory Action Research Study

Youth-led participatory action research is an approach to youth development that trains young people to identify concerns, conduct research to understand the nature of the problems, and take leadership in influencing policies and decisions that affect them.[1] YPAR is a form of community-based participatory research (CBPR), in which research is conducted in partnership with community members directly affected by the problem under study, not just by academically-trained researchers (Minkler & Wallerstein, 2008). CBPR seeks to democratize research by involving those who can generate evidence and by using research to address inequalities and enhance the empowerment of marginalized communities. The YPAR field has grown substantially; a literature search using the terms "CBPR" and "youth" in the English-based database *PsycINFO* generated nearly 600 citations. YPAR projects in diverse fields concerned with PYD such as education, public health, and community psychology have focused on a range of areas such as addressing inequalities in educational systems, improving healthy food access in low-income communities, cyber-bullying, and racial profiling by police (Cammarota & Fine, 2008; Dill, 2015; Garcia, Minkler, Cardenas, Grills, & Porter, 2014; Vaughan, 2014).

Like many approaches in communities and schools intended to promote PYD, systematic evaluation of the effects of YPAR on the young people who participate and the settings targeted for improvement has lagged behind the growth in practice. To help address these gaps, Emily J. Ozer and her UC-Berkeley student team launched a study to assess the processes and outcomes of YPAR in an urban school district. The five-year study used a multi-method cluster-randomized design in school sites that served diverse students and was conducted in partnership with Peer Resources, a community-based organization that offers elective youth development classes in public high schools (Ozer et al., 2008). Below, we provide an overview of the YPAR model developed and tested in the "UCB-PEERS" project, as well as the published findings (please see Ozer & Wright [2012] and Ozer & Douglas [2013] for further detail regarding sample, design, analytic methods, and results) (Ozer & Douglas, 2013; Ozer & Wright, 2012).

UCB-PEERS Overview

Five schools in total participated in the study over the course of five years; these schools varied with respect to size, student demographics and socioeconomic status, and aggregate achievement. Schools were selected for inclusion in the study on the basis of having an existing Peer Resources program with a teacher willing to engage in the training to implement YPAR and take the time to work with the research team; all qualifying schools were invited to participate. Each school site had several existing Peer Resources elective classes, taught by a certified teacher, in which all students received training in communication skills, team-building, and social justice/equity frameworks before receiving direct services skills training. In the existing Peer Resources model, students then served as a peer conflict mediator or peer educator. As part of the study design for the UCB-PEERS study, at least one class within each school site was randomized to participate in the YPAR (experimental) condition; the comparison classes were trained in the regular Peer Resources class with the direct service model of peer education. The YPAR curriculum used in the UCB-PEERS study was adapted from existing curricula and is available for reference at yparhub.berkeley.edu (London, 2001; Sydlo, 2000; UC Regents, 2015).

Those randomized to the YPAR class moved through research and action phases, starting with identifying issues that mattered to them that they wanted to study and change. The topics focused on by students ranged widely, including student dropout/push out, academic stress, improving the quality of school lunches, cyber-bullying, and strengthening the quality and cultural responsiveness of the teaching. Through guided activities that analyze the "root" of problems in their schools and communities, the YPAR process seeks to promote inquiry into factors that underlie complex social problems and inequalities and youth's sense of critical consciousness–critical reflection, motivation, and action to address these problems (Diemer, McWhirter, Ozer, & Rapa, under review). After the issue identification process, students received training in research methods (e.g., surveys, interviews, observations) to help understand the issue. After gathering and analyzing data, they made presentations in which they shared their findings and recommendations to stakeholders such as principals and teachers.

How YPAR can Promote PYD

YPAR is an innovative and promising model for promoting PYD in several key respects. First, because YPAR facilitates young people to use insider expertise to work directly on conditions that influence their health, there can be direct effects on "upstream" conditions that affect PYD, such as educational inequalities affecting health disparities. Second, YPAR is relevant to the identity-related developmental "tasks" of adolescence, especially individual and collective sense of "mattering," positive ethnic identity, and purpose (Damon, 2003). Challenges in developing a positive sense of identity – resisting the internalization of negative stereotypes held by others – are particularly notable for youth from marginalized groups.

Because YPAR could potentially exert effects on multiple levels – student, classroom, and school – we hypothesized theories of change at all three. The intended processes and effects map directly on to the characteristics of settings that promote PYD: promoting developmentally-appropriate spaces to foster a sense of efficacy, mattering, and belonging that provide skill-building opportunities, caring and supportive relationships, high expectations for behavior, and positive social norms (Eccles & Gootman, 2002). At the classroom level, we hypothesized that well-implemented YPAR would generate (a) a learning climate of inquiry and analysis of evidence, (b) teachers' sharing of power with students, (c) students engaging in productive group work, and (d) opportunities to develop skills in research and advocacy. Students worked together on issues that they cared about, using interactive activities guided by their teacher to solve disagreements and move forward with research and action. The primary student outcomes were skills and self-efficacy in research and advocacy as well as psychological empowerment, operationalized in terms of participatory engagement, motivation to influence their schools and communities, perceived control, and sociopolitical skills (Eccles & Gootman, 2002).

The innovative classrooms in which students worked together then functioned as a home base and launching pad for broader engagement with the rest of the school community (and in some cases, outside of the school into networks of community leaders). At the school level, we hypothesized that YPAR could create more meaningful roles for students in influencing school policies and practices, opportunities for student-teacher inquiry and co-learning, and also strengthen collective efficacy for students to improve their schools and communities.

Effects of YPAR on Students and Schools

We used quantitative and qualitative methods to examine research questions regarding the effects of YPAR on participating students and their schools. At the student level, survey data using a cluster-randomized design (classes randomized within school) demonstrated that students in the YPAR classes, as compared with the direct service classes, showed higher levels of psychological empowerment in the domains of participatory behavior, strategic thinking, and motivation to improve their schools (Ozer & Douglas, 2013). This was the first quantitative study to our knowledge to generate experimental evidence for psychological empowerment effects for YPAR or any youth empowerment approach using a school-based sample. The design used to test student-level effects was highly conservative, since both YPAR and direct service classes participated in a youth development program with the same teacher; this design, however, provided a highly rigorous test of the YPAR approach.

Extensive interview and observation data aided the team in the interpretation of the quantitative findings. Although we found experimental effects for psychological empowerment, we did not find that YPAR students showed increases in self-esteem or perceived control relative to students in the comparison classes. The lack of an experimental contrast effect for self-esteem was not surprising given the conservative design discussed above. Our interpretation of the lack of effect for perceived control at school was informed by qualitative data in which students discussed that working on change in their role as youth researchers taught them key skills – and increased their motivation to do make change – but also showed how hard it is to make change.

To examine the effects of YPAR on the school environment, we utilized a qualitative approach that included extensive classroom observations and interviews with school stakeholders (administrators, teachers not involved with the YPAR project, teachers involved in the YPAR project, and students). In Ozer and Wright (2012), we analyzed how YPAR projects at different schools participating in the study were effective in: a) creating or strengthening opportunities for students to provide input on decisions, policies, and practices within these school settings; and b) expanding the students' social networks and engaging adults as allies in their research and change efforts (Ozer & Wright, 2012). Further, we found that YPAR expanded the domains of student influence, beyond the planning of extracurricular "spirit" activities to providing input on core academic issues. We found that, despite differences across sites, there was evidence that YPAR generated processes of student "professionalization" that helped students and adults to see student researchers as "experts" who could make collegial contributions to solving school problems. This was a novel framing of youth roles, particularly in schools with generally low achievement in which there were lower expectations for what students could do. Interviews with students underscored these identity themes strongly, with students discussing how they and others now see themselves as people who could make a difference in their community, not in terms of the stereotypes like "gangbanger" attributed to them as youth of color in urban U.S. communities.

Next Steps: Efforts to Embed and "Scale" YPAR for Greater Impact

Based on our and others' work, we have initial evidence that YPAR and other related youth empowerment and organizing approaches can make a difference for young people and schools (e.g., Mitra, 2004; Berg, Coman, & Schensul, 2009; Cammarota & Fine, 2008; Kirshner, 2015), but many questions remain. For example, how do we move from small projects to working to integrate YPAR and other youth voice efforts into broader policy and programmatic efforts? How do we deal with the problem of scale with this kind of flexible and intensive intervention approach? How can YPAR diffuse beyond specific sites to grow into a practice that can benefit youth more broadly? In-person consultation to guide YPAR is time-intensive. Web-based platforms and "apps" can potentially build the capacity of youth and adult facilitators to do high-quality implementation of YPAR and aid its integration into the decision making of schools, districts, and government. We developed the YPAR Hub (yparhub.berkeley.edu), a web-based platform, to support skill development, data gathering, and analysis, as well as communication among youth researchers and adult stakeholders who hold power over settings and systems that affect PYD. The YPAR Hub was launched in English in 2016 and is intended to connect YPAR projects globally via video and other media, with forthcoming translation into other languages. Through international collaboration, the goal is to promote and test the impact of YPAR on systems that affect PYD in a range of contexts, particularly those who must confront economic shocks and poverty as part of their development.

United States: Interactive Technology and Health

Adolescence is a time for developing competencies, emerging independence, and beginning to assume responsibility for one's own behavior and health (Ozer & Irwin, 2009). As noted earlier, behaviors initiated during adolescence, such as substance use and abuse, early sexual behavior, and risky driving, are responsible for the majority of deaths and disabling conditions in adolescence and through the fourth decade of life (Viner et al., 2012). Navigating difficult social situations and enhancing self-regulatory skills are critical to adolescent (and adult) success in school, college, and the workplace.

The research projects described below reflect an innovative approach to enhancing adolescent health and well-being that utilizes social cognitive theory to contribute to understanding how adolescents learn through technology. The first project (Ozer, PI, National Science Foundation [NSF]) envisions young people learning problem-solving skills through an interactive graphic novel that can be easily accessed online or as an application on mobile devices including smart phones and tablets. Graphic novels are extraordinarily popular with youth. While traditional graphic novels (non-interactive) have recently been utilized in health education, creating interactive graphic novels that leverage both well-established theories of behavior change and advanced technology creates significant opportunity. The second project (Ozer and Lester, joint-PIs, NSF) focuses on designing, implementing, and investigating INSPIRE, a narrative-centered, self-adaptive personalized behavior change system for adolescent preventive health. The system integrates artificial intelligence planning techniques and game technologies to generate narratives with character interactions and virtual worlds to help adolescents develop an understanding of the dynamics and consequences of substance use decisions. This project investigates the impact of the system on adolescent behavior change in an integrated clinic/home intervention, thus anchoring the interactive narrative environment's activities with linkages to the primary care provider that foster reflection and provide reinforcement.

Narrative-centered learning environments are game-based environments that prominently feature stories, which provide a compelling causal structure. Narrative-centered learning environments provide adaptive, effective, story-centered pedagogy that is both meaningful and motivating (Rowe, Shores, Mott, & Lester, 2011), and learning activities occur in the context of engaging dynamically generated interactive narratives (Lee, Rowe, Mott, & Lester, 2013). The trans-disciplinary team developed the projects through an iterative development and refinement process that links the research with ongoing feedback from youth. Reflecting the focus on increasing the relevance of interventions and thus likelihood for success (National Institutes of Health, 2008), as well as approaches focused on strengthening the participation and influence of young people (London, Zimmerman, & Erbstein, 2003; Ozer, Wanis, & Bazell, 2010), adolescents participate in all phases of the development and piloting process. Through multi-platform deployments (e.g., laptop, mobile computing devices), these interactive narratives may serve as empowering tools for adolescents, making them participants in their own well-being.

Social Cognitive Theory and Advanced Learning Technologies

Social cognitive theory (Bandura, 1986) provides a conceptual framework to guide this research. Personal efficacy – beliefs in one's capability to organize and execute specific courses of action – plays a central role in determining behavior across diverse domains (Bandura, 1982; Ozer et al., 2004; Ozer & Bandura, 1990). Perceived self-efficacy is a strong predictor of behavior, as people tend to avoid activities that they believe they cannot carry out and engage in activities they judge themselves capable to handle. Mastery experiences are a key way of developing a strong sense of efficacy; self-efficacy can also be instilled and strengthened by vicarious experiences, such as modeling.

The globalization of technological modes of influence has expanded modeling influences beyond the social practices and behaviors of one's community. In observational learning, a single model can transmit new ways of thinking and behaving simultaneously to a great number of people in different places. For example, social cognitive principles have been successfully applied internationally to creating radio and television dramatic series with story lines focused on modeling family planning, women's equality, preserving the environment, and developing effective life skills (Bandura, 2002, 2004). New technology enables targeting and tailoring messages to factors causally related to behavior, such as efficacy beliefs, outcome expectations, and perceived impediments. On the behavioral adoption side, interactive technologies provide a way to individualize the type and level of guidance needed to bring about change. They provide a promising solution to increasing behavioral interventions for adolescents as advanced technology can be designed to assess an adolescent's risk or skill level, and provide a convenient, individualized means for informing, enabling, motivating, and guiding adolescents to make changes in their lives (Bandura, 2004). For example, interactive narratives contribute participant agency (Riedl, Saretto, & Young, 2003) and participant-tailored experiences with customized plot elements and character behaviors (Lee, Mott, & Lester, 2012).

Advanced learning technologies have tremendous potential to promote learning and behavior change in adolescents as they can be designed to help build the knowledge, personal efficacy, and self-regulatory skills necessary to enable teenagers to engage in healthy behavior and to enhance their well-being. Yet, the application and generalizability of social cognitive theory, as it relates to technological learning and behavior change interventions, is an area that deserves attention. More needs to be done to translate the knowledge of social cognitive theory and established cognitive interventions to easily accessible and scalable settings.

Interactive Online Graphic Novel

In this project, the interactive graphic novel emphasized the development of general strategies for thinking about and coping with a broad range of social problems that adolescents age 14 to 16 years are likely to experience as they transition into the high school years. The goal was to create engaging narrative experiences that utilize a compelling storyline along with characters with whom adolescents can easily identify. In "The Secret Yearbook," the main character describes a different kind of high school "yearbook," one that tells the secrets passed down through the ages of how to handle the tougher situations life throws at students. He shares his experience of being rejected by a good friend as they began high school and how he drew on the book's "secrets" to begin to help him handle his emotions, clarify his problem, set a goal, and determine what strategies work for him in reaching his goal. Figure 12.1 is an example of an option that the adolescent might choose to try. Ongoing feedback from youth through focus groups and pilot testing suggested that graphic novels have strong resonance with the target adolescent audience and that the initial narrative framework (the voice, the characters, the branching narrative structure) created an appealing experience for them. In the future interactive technology version, adolescents will be able to control how long to continue within a specific scenario, engage in interactive dialog choices, or try a different type of coping strategy to apply to stressful events that might happen with peers, parents, or teachers in their day-to-day lives.

INSPIRE: Self-Adaptive Personalized Behavior Change for Adolescent Preventive Health

Most adolescents in upper-middle-income and high-income countries visit a healthcare provider once a year, providing an ideal opportunity to integrate

FIGURE 12.1   Illustration from Interactive Graphic Novel, Jacob Glaser, Artist, 2013 (Monsef, Keys, Lester, & Ozer, 2014)

behavioral health screening into clinical care. Health information technology, linked to developing computationally-enabled models of health behavior change, has tremendous potential to improve healthcare quality and subsequent behavioral health outcomes for adolescents (Osheroff et al., 2007); however, few health information technology interventions have been integrated into adolescent care. The objective of INSPIRE is to design, implement, and investigate a self-adaptive personalized behavior change system for adolescent health focused on: 1) increasing adolescents' self-efficacy with respect to making healthy decisions about health behaviors; and 2) reducing alcohol use.

Extending prior funded research using interactive health technology (Ozer, Martin, Jasik, Adams, & Gonzales, 2013), adolescents who endorse alcohol use on an iPad behavioral health screen during a primary care clinic visit are invited to interact with INSPIRE's health behavior change environment over the course of four weeks at home on their platform of choice (e.g., laptop, desktop, tablet, or smartphone). Featuring a rich cast of characters with whom they interact in a series of narrative episodes, INSPIRE dynamically orchestrates the events in the storyworld to pose situational dilemmas, enabling learners to take control of a virtual character, explore alternate approaches to decision making, and experience the virtual consequences of their decisions.

Based on social cognitive theory, machine learning, and user modeling, characters' personae and avatars, virtual environments, and narratives for INSPIRE were developed and initially tested for navigation with input from 76 ethnically diverse high school students participating in focus groups in the San Francisco, California area. The narrative comprises four serialized episodes, focused on a teenaged boy re-living the events of a high school party that spun out of control and the mystery of a younger sister who has gone missing. See Figure 12.2 for the virtual agent characters and Figure 12.3 for the virtual environment. Next, INSPIRE will be pilot tested within adolescent primary care; integrated into the clinical workflow; and through patient portal systems, linked to communication with the primary care provider.

These research projects provide examples of how technological advances, coupled with behavior change theories, have tremendous potential to promote learning and behavior change through developing health behavior interventions that enable adolescents to increase competence and engage in healthy behavior. One next step for INSPIRE entails partnership with international organizations with established websites and social media spaces to facilitate direct access to adolescents, such as ReachOut.com and The Young and Well Cooperative Research Centre in Melbourne, Australia; these collaborations provide the potential to reach millions of adolescents.

FIGURE 12.2   INSPIRE Cast of Characters (Ozer et al., 2016)

FIGURE 12.3   INSPIRE Narrative Setting (Ozer et al., 2016)

Cross-Project Discussion

The innovative models reviewed in this chapter worked on strengthening the participation and influence of youth in different systems – all of which are important for the promotion of PYD. The U.S. YPAR study focused on schools and local community agencies; the Norwegian *Dream School* focused on schools and broader educational systems; the Portuguese *Dream Teens* model worked on a national level to affect larger systems with target audiences of the Ministries of Health and Education; and the U.S. technology and health project focused on tailoring health care for the needs and resources of youth. All enhanced the participatory roles of youth in ways expected to strengthen PYD, such as creating roles of youth as researchers and advisors to powerful adult stakeholders like administrators, teachers, and policy makers; training youth as Peer Leaders to create an action plan for the school site; and creating the technology for youth to be authors of their own storylines in theory-based health interventions in medical settings.

A strong theme across these innovative models was the use of new digital and cellular technologies to connect networks of young people working to promote PYD as well as to develop adaptable, youth-centered interventions. The intersection of PYD and technology presents a major opportunity for synergy – especially in the context of economic recession – given the dramatic rise in the use of smartphones, computers, and tablets among adolescents in high-income countries, and in the use of cellphones among youth in low- and middle-income countries (World Bank, 2012). There is a growing body of evidence showing that technologies, including text message reminders or mobile-based conditional cash transfers, can promote positive behavior change (Fjeldsoe, Marshall, & Miller, 2009; Labrique, Vasudevan, Kochi, Fabricant, & Mehl, 2013). We note that the innovative uses of technology presented here are theoretically and developmentally grounded and seek to strengthen the bridge between practice and research. Each project has taken steps to appropriately respond to and evolve with the changing landscape in ways that do not simply employ technology for novelty's sake but rather that fit the interventions' theories of change.

There are key questions facing the field regarding when and how to integrate new technologies to promote PYD, especially in economically challenged contexts. Although technology has the potential to produce cost effective and widely accessible solutions, the initial costs, knowledge, and infrastructure required for large-scale mobile health implementation can present insurmountable barriers in low-income settings, such as some African countries (WHO, 2011). Given the inability to shoulder upfront costs, even for the sake of long-term cost saving, health systems in poorer regions may decide to rely on pre-existing systems (WHO, 2011). Thus, while technology may be a good fit for cost-effective interventions in the context of economic shocks and downturns in middle- and high-income countries, more assistance is needed to promote technological interventions globally. New technologies can provide important opportunities for flexible interventions, as opposed to the manualized approaches typical in evidence-based interventions for youth; such flexibility is important for considering how to scale and adapt projects across highly diverse contexts.

Acknowledgments

Emily J. Ozer's research on youth-led participatory research was supported by a William T. Grant Scholars Award; the YPAR Hub project and travel to the SRCD Prague meeting were supported by the UC-Berkeley Peder Sather Fund.

Emily J. Ozer expresses appreciation to the UC-Berkeley-PEERS research team and to San Francisco Peer Resources and the students and school staff who participated in the studies, and to Dr. Margarida Gaspar de Matos for participating in the SRCD Prague symposium.

The research of Elizabeth M. Ozer has been supported by the following: National Science Foundation (NSF) EAGER planning grant (Elizabeth M.Ozer, PI; grant #: 1255695); National Science Foundation (NSF) Smart and Connected Health Award (James Lester & Elizabeth M.Ozer, Joint-PIs; grant #: IIS- 1344670); and Agency for Healthcare Research & Quality (Elizabeth M.Ozer, PI; grant #: R21 HS020997). Additional support was provided by the Maternal and Child Health Bureau's (MCHB) Adolescent and Young Adult Health Research Network (Elizabeth M. Ozer, PI; grant #: UA6MC27378).

Note

1 Please see yparhub.berkeley.edu for curricular resource and illustrative case examples from projects in the U.S. and other countries.

References

Bandura, A. (1982). Self-efficacy mechanism in human agency. *American Psychologist, 37*(2), 122–147.

Bandura, A. (1986). *Social foundations of thought and action: A social cognitive theory*. Upper Saddle River, NJ: Prentice Hall.

Bandura, A. (2002). Growing primacy of human agency in adaptation and change in the electronic era. *European Psychologist, 7*(1), 2–16.

Bandura, A. (2004). Social cognitive theory for personal and social change by enabling media. In A. Singhal, M. J. Cody, E. M. Rogers, & Sabida, M. (Eds), *Entertainment-education and social change: History, research, and practice* (pp. 75–96). Mahwah, NJ: Lawrence Erlbaum.

Berg, M., Coman, E., & Schensul, J. J. (2009). Youth action research for prevention: A multi-level intervention designed to increase efficacy and empowerment among urban youth. *American Journal of Community Psychology, 43*(3–4), 345–359.

Cammarota, J., & Fine, M. (Eds). (2008). *Revolutionizing education: Youth participatory action research*. New York: Routledge.

Center on the Developing Adolescent. (2015). I4Y UC Berkeley School of Public Health. Accessed 11 November, 2015, retrieved from http://developingadolescent. berkeley.edu/i4y-uc-berkeley-school-of-public-health.html

Cornwall, A., & Jewkes, R. (1995). What is participatory research? *Social Science & Medicine, 41*(12), 1667–1676. Accessed 11 November, 2015, retrieved from www.ncbi. nlm.nih.gov/pubmed/8746866

Daelmans, B., Black, M. M., Lombardi, J., Lucas, J., Richter, L., Silver, K., ... & Rao, N. (2015). Effective interventions and strategies for improving early child development. *British Medical Journal, 351*, h4029.

Damon, W. (2003). The development of purpose during adolescence. *Applied Developmental Science, 7*(3), 119–128.

Det Kongelige Helse- og Omsorgsdepartement (2015). *Governmental white paper nr 19: Public health – coping and opportunities*. Oslo, Norway.

Diemer, M. A., McWhirter, E., Ozer, E. J., & Rapa, L. J. (under review). Advances in the conceptualization and measurement of critical consciousness. *Urban Review*.

Dill, L. J. (2015). Poetic justice: Engaging in participatory narrative analysis to find solace in the "killer corridor". *American Journal of Community Psychology, 55*(1–2), 128–135.

Dream Teens (2014). *Dream Teens* recommendations for Portugal. Accessed 11 November, 2015, retrieved from Portuguese Ministry of Health website: www.portaldasaude.pt/ NR/rdonlyres/23D1EF38-AA48-457F-B9EC-2F5A0F1936DB/0/Recomendacoes_ DreamTeens2014.pdf

Eccles, J. S., & Gootman, J. A. (Eds). (2002). *Community programs to promote youth development*. Washington, DC: National Academy Press.

Finn, J. D., & Rock, D. A. (1997). Academic success among students at risk for school failure. *Journal of Applied Psychology, 82*(2), 221–234. Accessed 11 November, 2015, retrieved from www.ncbi.nlm.nih.gov/pubmed/9109280

Fjeldsoe, B. S., Marshall, A. L., & Miller, Y. D. (2009). Behavior change interventions delivered by mobile telephone short-message service. *American Journal of Preventive Medicine, 36*(2), 165–173.

Frasquilho, D., Ozer, E. J., Ozer, E. M., Branquinho, C., Camacho, I., Reis, M., & Gaspar de Matos, M. (2016). Dream Teens: Adolescents-led participatory project in Portugal in the context of the economic recession. *Health Promotion Practice*. Retrieved from http://hpp.sagepub.com/content/early/2016/07/27/1524839916660679.abstract

Garcia, A. P., Minkler, M., Cardenas, Z., Grills, C., & Porter, C. (2014). Engaging homeless youth in community-based participatory research: a case study from Skid Row, Los Angeles. *Health Promotion Practice, 15*(1), 18–27.

Herrman, H., Saxena, S., Moodie, R., & Walker, L. (2005). Promoting mental health as a public health priority promoting mental health: Concepts, emerging evidence, practice. Report of the World Health Organization, Department of Mental Health and Substance Abuse in collaboration with the Victorian Health Promotion Foundation and the University of Melbourne.

Holsen, I., Larsen, T., Tjomsland, H. E., & Servan, A. K. (2014). Exploring the importance of peers as leaders in the Dream School program: From the perspectives of peer leaders, teachers and principals. *Advances in School Mental Health Promotion, 8*(1), 4–16.

Hoover-Dempsey, K. V., Bassler, O. C., & Brissie, J. S. (1987). Parent involvement: Contributions of teacher efficacy, school socioeconomic status, and other school characteristics. *American Educational Research Journal, 24*(3), 417–435.

Kirshner, B. (2015). *Youth activism in an era of education inequality*. New York: NYU Press.

Labrique, A. B., Vasudevan, L., Kochi, E., Fabricant, R., & Mehl, G. (2013). Health innovations as health system strengthening tools: 12 common applications and a visual framework. *Global Health: Science and Practice, 1*(2), 160–171.

Lee, S., Mott, B., & Lester, J. (2012). *Real-time narrative-centered tutorial planning for story-based Learning*. Paper presented at the Eleventh International Conference on Intelligent Tutoring Systems, Crete, Greece.

Lee, S., Rowe, J., Mott, B., & Lester, J. (2013). A supervised learning framework for modeling director agent strategies in educational interactive narrative. *Transactions on Computational Intelligence and AI in Games – Special Issue on Computational Narrative and Games, 6*(2), 1–13.

London, J. (2001). *Youth rep: Step by step – An introduction to youth-led evaluation and research*. Oakland, CA: Youth in Focus.

London, J., Zimmerman, K., & Erbstein, N. (2003). Youth-led research and evaluation: Tools for youth, organizational, and community development. *New Directions in Evaluation, 98*, 33–45.

Minkler, M., & Wallerstein, N. (2008). *Community-based participatory research for health: From process to outcomes.* San Francisco, CA: Jossey-Bass.

Mitra, D. L. (2004). The significance of students: Can increasing student voice in schools lead to gains in youth development? *Teachers College Record, 106*(4), 651–688.

Monsef, K., Keys, S., Lester, J., & Ozer, E. M, concept art presented in E. M. Ozer, S. Keys, & J. Lester (2014) *Using Interactive Technology in Preventive Interventions to Promote Competence and Healthy Behaviors in Adolescents.* Paper presented at the Society for Research in Child Development (SRCD) Special Topic Meeting: Positive Youth Development (PYD) in the Context of the Global Recession, Prague, Czech Republic, October 2014.

National Institutes of Health (2008). *Community participation in research: NIH guide to grants.* Retrieved from http://grants.nih.gov/grants//guide/pa-files/PA-08-074.html

Osheroff, J. A., Teich, J. M., Middleton, B., Steen, E. B., Wright, A., & Detmer, D. E. (2007). A roadmap for national action on clinical decision support. *Journal of the American Medical Informatics Association, 14*(2), 141–145.

Ozer, E. M., & Bandura, A. (1990). Mechanisms governing empowerment effects: a self-efficacy analysis. *Journal of Personality and Social Psychology, 58*(3), 472–486. Accessed 11 November, 2015, retrievedfrom www.ncbi.nlm.nih.gov/entrez/query.fcgi?cmd=Retr ieve&db=PubMed&dopt=Citation&list_uids=2324938

Ozer, E. J., & Douglas, L. (2013). The impact of participatory research on urban teens: an experimental evaluation. *American Journal of Community Psychology, 51*(1–2), 66–75.

Ozer, E. M., & Irwin, C. E., Jr. (2009). Adolescent and young adult health: From basic health status to clinical interventions. In R. Lerner & R. Steinberg (Eds), *Individual basis of adolescent development. Volume 1: Handbook of adolescent psychology*, 3rd edition (pp. 618–641). Hoboken, NJ: Wiley.

Ozer, E. J., & Russo, I. (in press). Development and context. In M.A. Bond, C.B. Keys, I. Serrano-Garcia, & M. Shinn (Eds), *Handbook of community psychology.* Washington, DC: American Psychological Association.

Ozer, E. J., & Wright, D. (2012). Beyond school spirit: The effects of youth-led participatory action research in two urban high schools. *Journal of Research on Adolescence, 22*(2), 267–283.

Ozer, E. M., Adams, S. H., Gardner, L. R., Mailloux, D. E., Wibbelsman, C. J., & Irwin, C. E., Jr. (2004). Provider self-efficacy and the screening of adolescents for risky health behaviors. *Journal of Adolescent Health, 35*(2), 101–107. Accessed 11 November, 2015, retrieved from www.ncbi.nlm.nih.gov/entrez/query.fcgi?cmd=Retrieve&db= PubMed&dopt=Citation&list_uids=15261638

Ozer, E. J., Cantor, J. P., Cruz, G. W., Fox, B., Hubbard, E., & Moret, L. (2008). The diffusion of youth-led participatory research in urban schools: the role of the prevention support system in implementation and sustainability. *American Journal of Community Psychology, 41*(3–4), 278–289.

Ozer, E. J., Wanis, M. G., & Bazell, N. (2010). Diffusion of school-based prevention programs in two urban districts: adaptations, rationales, and suggestions for change. *Prevention Science, 11*(1), 42–55.

Ozer, E. M., Martin, M., Jasik, C., Adams, S., & Gonzales, R. (2013). *The development of a clinic-based interactive behavioral health screening module for adolescents.* Paper presented at the 2013 International Congress on Adolescent Health, Istanbul, Turkey.

Ozer, E. M., Jasik, C. B., Tebb, K. P., Erenrich, R., Berna, M., Rowe, J. P., Mott, B., & Lester, J. C. (2016). Development of a self-adaptive personalized behavior change system for adolescent preventive healthcare. *Journal of Adolescent Health, 58*(2), S70.

Patton, G. C., Ross, D. A., Santelli, J. S., Sawyer, S. M., Viner, R. M., & Kleinert, S. (2014). Next steps for adolescent health: A Lancet Commission. *The Lancet, 383*(9915), 385–386.

Riedl, M., Saretto, C., & Young, M. (2003). *Managing interactions between users and agents in a multiagent storytelling environment.* Paper presented at the Second International Joint Conference on Autonomous Agents and Multi-Agent Systems, Melbourne.

Rowe, J. P., Shores, L. R., Mott, B. W., & Lester, J. C. (2011). Integrating learning, problem solving, and engagement in narrative-centered learning environments. *International Journal of Artificial Intelligence in Education, 11*(1–2), 115–133.

Sawyer, S. M., Afifi, R. A., Bearinger, L. H., Blakemore, S. J., Dick, B., Ezeh, A. C., & Patton, G. C. (2012). Adolescence: A foundation for future health. *The Lancet, 379*(9826), 1630–1640.

Sydlo, S. J. (2000). *Participatory action research: Curriculum for empowering youth.* Hartford, CN: National Teen Action Research Center, Institute for Community Research.

The Lancet Youth (2014). About the commission. Accessed 11 November, 2015, retrieved from http://thelancetyouth.com/about-the-commission/

UC Regents (2015). YPAR Hub. Accessed 11 November, 2015, retrievedfrom yparhub.berkeley.edu

UNCRC (1989). United Nations convention on the rights of the child. Accessed 11 November, 2015, retrievedfrom www.unhchr.ch/tbs/doc.nsf/898586b1dc7b4043c1256a450044f331/4c6c8d9ee8b9c104c12569ce0054e917/$FILE/G0045810.pdf

UNICEF (2012). Progress for children: A report card for adolescents. Accessed 11 November, 2015, retrieved from: www.unicef.org/publications/files/Progress_for_Children_-_No._10_EN_04272012.pdf

UNICEF (2015). Progress for children: Beyond averages – learning from the MDGs. Accessed 11 November, 2015, retrievedfrom: www.unicef.org/publications/files/Progress_for_Children_No._11_22June15.pdf

Vaughan, C. (2014). Participatory research with youth: Idealising safe social spaces or building transformative links in difficult environments? *Journal of Health Psychology, 19*(1), 184–192.

Viner, R. M., Ozer, E. M., Denny, S., Marmot, M., Resnick, M., Fatusi, A., & Currie, C. (2012). Adolescence and the social determinants of health. *The Lancet, 379*(9826), 1641–1652.

WHO (2009). The financial crisis and global health: Report of a high-level consultation. Accessed 11 November, 2015, retrieved from www.who.int/topics/financial_crisis/financialcrisis_report_200902.pdf?ua=1

WHO (2011). mHealth: New horizons for health through mobile technologies. Accessed 11 November, 2015, retrieved from www.who.int/goe/publications/goe_mhealth_web.pdf

World Bank (2008). Global financial crisis and implications for developing countries. Accessed 11 November, 2015, retrieved from www.worldbank.org/financialcrisis/pdf/G20FinBackgroundpaper.pdf

World Bank (2012). Information and communications for development 2012: Maximizing mobile. Accessed 11 November, 2015, retrieved from http://siteresources.worldbank.org/EXTINFORMATIONANDCOMMUNICATIONANDTECHNOLOGIES/Resources/IC4D-2012-Report.pdf

13

DUAL-GENERATION APPROACHES TO ADDRESS ADOLESCENT MOTHERHOOD AND HUMAN DEVELOPMENT IN THE CONTEXT OF ECONOMIC DOWNTURNS AND POVERTY IN LOW- AND MIDDLE-INCOME COUNTRIES

Alice J. Wuermli and Hirokazu Yoshikawa

Introduction

This chapter presents an argument for dual-generation intervention approaches to protect and promote the development of adolescent mothers and their children, especially during times of economic crises in low- and middle-income countries (LAMICs). The issue of early childbearing in LAMICs is not a new one. There has been a substantial amount of research and policy discussions around questions of reducing adolescent fertility (McQueston, Silverman, & Glassman, 2012). Yet there is a remarkable dearth of recent research around how to best support adolescent mothers and mothers-to-be in ways that would improve their own development and that of their children in an effort to break the intergenerational transmission of poverty and disadvantage. This is not entirely surprising; the political economy around adolescent pregnancy and motherhood has a strong preference for preventative efforts. While prevention of adolescent pregnancy may be the first best solution, we risk losing the productive potential of multiple generations to come, as reductions in adolescent fertility are happening very slowly in some parts of the world.

We first provide an overview of the problems associated with adolescent childbearing globally. We then outline likely mechanisms that are leading to worse developmental outcomes in adolescent mothers and their children, and how poverty and economic crises may exacerbate the risks to human development of adolescent mothers and their children. Based on our argument that economic crises may shake up existing systems and may allow for substantial social and political change, we present a framework for thinking about dual-generation programs tailored to the specific needs of adolescent mothers and their children in LAMICs.

Adolescent Motherhood – A Global Concern

Adolescent pregnancies are highly prevalent in many parts of this world, in particular low-income populations in LAMICs. Approximately 17 million girls of 19 years or younger give birth every year globally (WHO, 2014). Adolescent motherhood may interrupt and jeopardize the development of the adolescent girl, resulting in low educational attainment, restricted economic opportunities, and often unstable relationships with the child's father (Coley & Chase-Lansdale, 1998; Geronimus & Korenman, 1993; Lee & Gramotnev, 2006; Paranjothy, Broughton, Adappa, & Fone, 2009; Taylor, 2009). In addition, adolescent motherhood has also been associated with poorer outcomes in their children. The WHO reports higher perinatal complications and maternal mortality, and a 50% higher risk of stillbirths and infant deaths within the first weeks of life for adolescents and their babies compared to older women (WHO, 2014).

Some of this increased risk to adolescent mothers and their infants can be attributed to confounding factors, such as poverty, poorer prenatal care, or more births outside of adequately equipped health clinics (Elster, 1984; WHO, 2008). Yet studies that control for some of these potential confounders still find significantly increased risks for adolescent mothers of adverse pregnancy and birth related outcomes (Fraser, Brockert, & Ward, 1995). While many of these studies come from the US, studies from low- and middle-income countries find similar results. Conde-Agudelo, Belizan, and Lammers (2005) use data from the Perinatal Information System database which recorded details on pregnancies from 1985 through 2003 from 18 Latin American Countries. They compared over 300,000 adolescents to over 500,000 non-adolescents, controlling for 16 confounding factors including gestational age at first antenatal visit and total number of visits, and found significant differences between adolescent mothers and older mothers, including higher rates of maternal and neonatal death, anemia, postpartum hemorrhage, low birth weight, preterm delivery, and small-for-gestational age infants, while probabilities for cesarean delivery, third-trimester bleeding, and gestational diabetes are lower. These results strongly suggest that adolescents and their infants face substantially higher risks for adverse pregnancy and birth related outcomes compared to children born to non-adolescent mothers.

Understanding Mechanisms and Processes Underlying Heightened Risk of Adolescent Motherhood to Their own and Their Children's Health and Development

An informed policy response requires adequate knowledge about the underlying risk factors, mechanisms, and processes that lead to heightened risk associated with adolescent motherhood. For example, adolescent mothers may be less responsive and involved with their infants, and use punishment more often than their non-adolescent comparisons (Garcia Coll, Vohr, Hoffman, & Oh, 1986). These factors in return predicted their infant's cognitive and socioemotional development.

However, most of the studies of children born to adolescent mothers linking child outcomes to postnatal factors, such as parenting practices and the like, come from the United States (Brooks-Gunn & Furstenberg Jr, 1986; Jaffee, Caspi, Moffitt, Belsky, & Silva, 2001; Moore & Brooks-Gunn, 2002). Methodological problems of these studies make interpretation and generalizability of these findings difficult (Brooks-Gunn & Furstenberg Jr, 1986; Moore & Brooks-Gunn, 2002). For one, in the US and elsewhere, socioeconomic disadvantage and teen parenting tend to go hand in hand, making it hard to separate out the independent effects. Common confounders in the population from US studies (race/ethnicity, urban residence, poverty status, and unmarried status) make generalizations difficult (Brooks-Gunn & Furstenberg Jr, 1986). For example, in contrast to the US context where by 1999 79% of adolescent births were to non-married teens (Ventura & Bachrach, 2000), about 90% of adolescent births in low-income countries occur within marriages (WHO, 2008). Based on Demographic and Health Survey (DHS) data from 51 LAMIC countries from the late 1990s through mid-2000s, rates of adolescent births within marriage range from approximately 64% in eastern/southern Africa to 99% in western Asia/northern Africa (WHO, 2008).

Nonetheless, the experience of stress associated with early marriage and motherhood may be close to universal, involving multiple simultaneous major life transitions (including motherhood), and in some cases, fewer resources, less control over resources, or a smaller social and child care support network. This is especially true in the case of unplanned pregnancies to unwed adolescent girls. Thus there seem to be mechanisms pertaining specifically to adolescent mothers' experiences of stressful life circumstances, how stress affects their socioemotional health and well-being, and their capacity to effectively self-regulate. Moreover, the particulars of adolescent brain development, including heightened sensitivity to reward and suboptimal prefrontal control (Casey, Jones, & Hare, 2008), may render adolescent mothers more sensitive to and less able to cope with simultaneous major transitions and life events (i.e., navigating adolescence and the transition to motherhood) (Ge, Conger, & Elder, 2001), and the realities of looming parenthood, the stress associated with caring for an infant, as well as social stress that often comes with adolescent pregnancy (e.g., stigma and peer victimization) (Leerlooijer et al., 2013). This additional stress can put children born to adolescents at particular risk of prenatal and postnatal exposure to stress, prenatally through neuroendocrine processes associated with the physiological stress response, and postnatally through potentially inconsistent, withdrawn, or harsh caregiving with little stimulating interaction. These processes perpetuate the intergenerational transmission of poverty, poor health, and development.

There is a growing body of evidence linking prenatal and early life stress to later life outcomes. Disparities in health and well-being at the societal level have been attributed to early exposure to severe levels of stress (Shonkoff, 2012; Shonkoff & Phillips, 2000). Early life stress increases the risk for an array of later life physical and mental health outcomes, and may account for a significant proportion of the non-communicable disease burden globally. In addition, early life exposure to stress has been linked to impaired cognitive performance, impulsivity, aggression, and reduced self-regulatory capacity, the ability to flexibly regulate emotions, thoughts, and behaviors according to the demands of a particular context (Baumeister & Vohs, 2007; Bell & Deater-Deckard, 2007; Juster, McEwen, & Lupien, 2010; Karatoreos & McEwen, 2013; Lupien, McEwen, Gunnar, & Heim, 2009; Mead, Baumeister, Gino, Schweitzer, & Ariely, 2009; Posner & Rothbart, 2000; Vohs et al., 2008). There is convincing evidence linking early self-regulatory capacity, to school readiness (Raver, Garner, & Smith-Donald, 2007), educational success and achievement (Best, Miller, & Naglieri, 2011), as well as a range of other life outcomes including but not limited to social relationships and labor market outcomes (Heckman & Rubinstein, 2001; Heckman, Stixrud, & Urzua, 2006; Raver et al., 2007).

Higher levels of physiological stress in the adolescent mother also affect her own development. The parts of the brain shown to be affected by persistently high levels of certain stress hormones are also the ones prominently involved in self-regulatory processes of psychosocial stressors. The pubertal transition has been identified as a period of increased likelihood of internalizing and externalizing symptoms (Brooks-Gunn & Petersen, 1991; Ge, Brody, Conger, & Simons, 2006; Petersen et al., 1993), and this relationship seems to be amplified if puberty coincides with stressful life events and multiple simultaneous life transitions (Ge et al., 2001). Early pregnancy is likely to trigger additional major events and transitions, including early school leaving, and transitioning into adult roles and responsibilities as a home keeper and spouse.

In many parts of the world, pregnancy requires school leaving, cutting education short, and curtailing future educational and livelihoods opportunities and aspirations with few options of making up for it later. Pregnancy during adolescence is also in many parts of the world associated with a great deal of stigma and a source of bullying and ostracism, especially in unmarried adolescent girls. As areas of the brain involved in social cognitive processing are undergoing drastic changes during adolescence, peer rejection may have severe consequences. In fact, research indicates that adolescent girls showed greater affective responses to experimentally manipulated peer rejection than female adults possibly pointing toward substantial developmental changes in the ability to self-regulate emotions related to social stress (Sebastian, Viding, Williams, & Blakemore, 2010). In short, the specifics of adolescent neurobiological development influence their ability to self-regulate and manage stressful situations, which in turn affects their ability to effectively parent a child.

The Stress of Adolescent Motherhood in Low-Income Countries

The first pregnancy and transition to motherhood is more or less fraught with anxiety (Miller & Sollie, 1986; Rossi, 1968). And of course there are a myriad of factors that affect the level of anxiety and stress related to this transition. There are several reasons why the transition to motherhood may be more stressful for adolescent girls. More than not, pregnancy during adolescence, especially early adolescence, is not intended. This in and of itself is a major source of stress and often related to emotional challenges. In low-income countries, access to birth control is often not readily available to adolescent girls. The reasons for this vary by culture and context and can be of infrastructural and/ or cultural nature.

Importantly, adolescent girls are less likely than older women to have access to and power over resources (financial, social) to call on for support. There is a substantial body of research investigating intra-household bargaining within the context of gender relations (Agarwal, 1997; Kabeer, 1997; Lundberg & Pollak, 1996). A woman's age, education, and income-earning opportunities influence her bargaining power (Adato, de la Brière, Mindek, & Quisumbing, 2000; Kabeer, 1997), and more bargaining power, or control over resources, has been linked to reductions in domestic violence (Aizer, 2010), increased use of reproductive health services (Beegle, Frankenberg, & Thomas, 2001), and an increase in the likelihood of investments in their children (Benería & Roldan, 1987; Haddad, Hoddinott, & Alderman, 1997; Hoddinott & Haddad, 1995; Quisumbing & de La Brière, 2000; Richards et al., 2013). The inherent younger age, lower education, and thus fewer income-earning opportunities of adolescent wives and mothers therefore puts them and their children at a substantial disadvantage, and increases their vulnerability to unhealthy and potentially abusive relationships (Jensen & Thornton, 2003). In addition, studies indicate that mother's education has a significantly larger effect on children's health and education than that of fathers (Adato et al., 2000; Behrman, Foster, Rosenzweig, & Vashishtha, 1999; Paul Schultz, 2002), further highlighting the additional risks to children born to adolescent mothers. Effective programs and policies to support adolescent mothers and their children are thus of great importance to prevent an intergenerational transmission of poverty.

Adolescent Motherhood in the Face of Economic Crises

Economic crises and poverty are likely to exacerbate the risks to adolescent mothers and their young children, especially in low-income populations in LAMICs. Societies are concerned about the potential consequences of deep and prolonged economic crises on the development of children, and thus the health and prosperity of future generations, and nations as a whole (Lundberg & Wuermli, 2012). The effects of poverty on children's development have been documented in high- as well as low- and middle-income countries (Walker et al., 2011; Walker et al., 2007; Yoshikawa, Aber, & Beardslee, 2012). There is reason to believe that adolescent mothers and their young children bear even greater risks in low-resource contexts.

It is unclear how economic crises affect adolescent girls' development. The evidence on how economic crises affect children's development more generally is mixed (Elder Jr, 1999; Elder Jr, Van Nguyen, & Caspi, 1985; Gassman-Pines, Gibson-Davis, & Ananat, 2015; Lundberg & Wuermli, 2012; Weiland & Yoshikawa, 2012). The mechanisms through which recessions affect children and youth are diverse and complex, and differ depending on the gender, age, and stage of the child's development (Kalil, 2013; Lundberg & Wuermli, 2012).

In many LAMICs, girls are generally at greater risk for early school-leaving and marriage (Alderman & King, 1998; Glick & Sahn, 2000; Mensch & Lloyd, 1998). These risks might be exacerbated during economic crises. For example, a study from Mexico shows that there was a significant added worker effect regarding spouses during the Mexican crisis in 1995 (but no impact on labor force participation of children and youth age 12–24) (Skoufias & Parker, 2006). In fact, they find that secondary school enrollment increased for teenage boys. However, there seemed to be a statistically significant fall in enrollment rates for teenage girls in households where mothers started to work, indicating that girls were substituting for their mothers in domestic chores (Skoufias & Parker, 2006).

Furthermore, in some contexts, increased economic hardship may also put pressure on women in general, but especially young unmarried women, to engage in transactional sex, and/or marriage, increasing the likelihood of early and unplanned pregnancy. However, the evidence on causal effects of economic crises on transactional sex and early marriage is mixed (Chatterji, Murray, London, & Anglewicz, 2005). An experimental evaluation of a conditional cash transfer program in Malawi aimed at increasing educational attainment and reducing early marriage and risky sexual behavior in adolescent girls found significant declines in early marriage and adolescent pregnancy in the treatment group compared to the control group (Baird, Chirwa, McIntosh, & Ozler, 2010).

While a first best strategy might be to encourage girls to stay in school, and support them in an attempt to prevent transactional sex and early marriage, this may fail to reach the most vulnerable girls who are already at risk for low educational attainment and early childbearing with potential consequences for multiple generations down the line. In addition, in so far as economic crises pose a stressful experience for pregnant women and new mothers, crises could have substantial long-term impacts on cognitive, social-emotional, and behavioral development of the adolescent mother as well as her child with long-term consequences for health and well-being.

Potential Opportunities for Social Change during Crises

The existing evidence suggests that large-scale shocks may trigger substantial restructuring of economic, political, and social systems and dynamics, requiring a range of psychological and social adaptations (Pinquart & Silbereisen, 2004; Tomasik & Silbereisen, 2009). Combined with the right policies and programs, these shifts may bring unexpected opportunities for social change in ways that could have long-term benefits for previously underrepresented or disenfranchised groups, including women. Studies from the United States indicate that the Great Depression contributed substantially to the dramatic increase in high school graduation rates for young women and men (Goldin, 1998, 1999), and played an important role in female labor market participation (Goldin, 1994).

As mentioned earlier, households may draw on female labor power to supplement household income during dire times. In response to the collapse of the financial system in Argentina in 2001–2002, women flooded the informal sector labor market in order to counter the loss in income due to their partner's job loss. Esquivel (2006) concludes that women constituted a buffer stock of labor during the Argentinean crisis. Conversely, in the US during the Great Recession, there seemed to be a reduction in market work for both women and men (Aguiar, Hurst, & Karabarbounis, 2013).

Where market work increases for women, this is not always met by an equal shift in time spent in domestic chores and child care activities between male and female members of a household. In the United States, women's reduced time in the labor market during the Great Recession resulted in increases in home production work and sleep, while men's time use shifted to TV watching and education (Aguiar et al., 2013). Similarly, in Argentina, men had cultivated strong identities with their previous jobs, were often too proud to engage in informal activities, and were not willing to take on domestic chores (Esquivel, 2006). However, these studies do not distinguish between parents and other adults. Kalil and Ziol-Guest (2011) specifically look at changes in time use in married couples with children during the Great Recession in the United States. They find that the likelihood for fathers to participate in child care and housework increases, whereas the likelihood stayed the same for mothers. However, time spent in such activities decreased for fathers who had previously participated, and women also spent less time in household chores and child care.

While taking on additional work outside of the home may add to the overall workload and burden women carry in many and most parts of the world, this may also provide unique opportunities for women to gain exposure, access skills training, and increase monetary resources in their control. As mentioned earlier, these are assets that are associated with increased household bargaining power, increasing women's decision-making power on how resources should be spent (Kabeer, 1997). It is thus in the interest of society at large to implement appropriate policies and programs to support such shifts and ensure that these changes yield sustainable improvements in livelihoods for future generations while avoiding "lost generations".

Dual-Generation Programs and Policies to Foster Healthy Development in Adolescent Mothers and Their Children

While economic crises may pose additional risks to adolescent mothers and their children, there are opportunities nested in dual-generation intervention approaches tailored to the particular developmental needs of adolescent girls. However, most interventions with rigorous experimental evaluations have either focused on children (parenting, child care/preschool), or on improving labor market outcomes of un- and underemployed workers. In both cases, the evidence is mixed on the effectiveness of these programs at improving child learning and development (Pianta Barnett, Burchinal, & Thornburg, 2009) and employment (Card, Luve, & Weber, 2009), respectively. In addition, there are questions around what type of skills are needed to succeed in leading a productive and healthy life, and how to best foster such skills in disadvantaged and troubled youth (Cunha & Heckman, 2008; Heckman & Rubinstein, 2001).

The previously outlined specifics of neuroendocrine development during adolescence have implications for programs and policies. Programmatic approaches need to consider adolescents' potentially limited capacity to self-regulate, and specifically target the strengthening and development of this competence. In other words, a program working with adolescent mothers may need to more specifically target the self-regulatory capacity needed to deal with psychosocial stress associated with their situation, and implement effective and positive parenting practices. It is important to keep in mind that prefrontal cortical development accelerates during adolescence and concludes in the mid- to late twenties, indicating this period of development as a huge opportunity to "reverse" vestiges of early life stress, and/or redirect the developmental trajectory for the better.

There have been a number of interesting approaches to improving youth's labor market outcomes. For example, programs such as *Year Up* in the US indicate great success. *Year Up* targets urban youth (age 18–24) and provides a one-year intensive program combining technical and professional skills training with a six-month internship in the IT sector while earning college credits (Roder & Elliott, 2014). However, eligibility criteria, and the program not providing child care support, make it unlikely for the most disadvantaged youth to be able to benefit from *Year Up*, in particular when balancing work and parenthood.

In LAMICs, studies indicate that comprehensive youth training and employment programs, such as the *Jovenes* programs launched in many Latin American and Caribbean countries, seem to be most effective at producing improved labor market outcomes (Ibarrarán & Rosas Shady, 2009). While these programs seem to benefit women and socioeconomically disadvantaged participants more than others, they also rely on a network of private training centers, a healthy private sector willing to absorb young trainees, and generally a strong macro-economic context indicative of a growing labor market. In countries that face problems meeting one or several of these criteria, focus has shifted to self-employment programs, programs that provide micro-finance assistance and/or business skills training.

Many micro-finance and business skills training programs have found at least some positive results from impact evaluations (Adoho, Chakravarty, Korkoyah, Lundberg, & Tasneem, 2014; Karlan & Valdivia, 2011), with some indication that such programs are more effective for women (Khandker, 2005). However, if not specifically targeted at and designed to cater to specific needs and constraints of female workers, it can be difficult to recruit women into such programs, in particular the most vulnerable (Adoho et al., 2014). The *Adolescent Girls Initiative* (AGI) livelihoods and skills training programs have been tested in a number of countries (Liberia, Uganda, Jordan, Nepal, Afghanistan, South Sudan, Rwanda, Haiti, and Lao PDR (Adoho et al., 2014). The results from impact evaluations are promising in showing improved employment and earnings. For example, in Liberia the program showed a 47% increase in employment (both self- and wage employment); an 80% increase in income (earnings more than doubled for those who received business skills training); and increased savings and loans in the treatment group. However, the effects were larger for the more educated and younger (15–19) participants. In addition, recruiting adolescent girls into these AGI programs proved challenging across countries for a myriad of reasons, and there is reason to believe that these programs, for the most part, did not reach the most vulnerable adolescent girls.

It may be imperative to specifically target and encourage women, especially adolescent mothers, to participate in such programs, and adapt the particulars of the program to meet young women's needs (Katz, 2008). This may entail providing preparatory training (e.g., literacy and numeracy) to enable learning of more sophisticated skills, providing safe spaces and transportation to and from the training or work place (Erulkar, Ferede, Girma, & Ambelu, 2013;

Gillibrand, Robinson, Brawn, & Osborn, 1999; Levitt-Dayal, Motihar, Kanani, & Mishra, 2003), or adjustments to women's time-use constraints and child care needs (Benería, 2003). However, such programs catering to young mothers from disadvantaged backgrounds in low-income countries are as of yet few and far between, as is the evidence on their impact on participants' young children.

Experimental studies of the effects of livelihood programs on child outcomes come predominantly from the US trials of welfare-to-work programs (Morris, Duncan, & Clark-Kauffman, 2005). For example, *New Hope*, a comprehensive antipoverty experiment in the 1990s, provided extensive support services (earnings supplement, health and child care subsidies, career counseling, temporary community service jobs) to low-income, un-/underemployed adults conditional on a minimum of 30 hours of work per week (Duncan, Bos, Gennetian, & Hill, 2009). The study showed improvements in child outcomes (9–19 years) at eight-year follow-up: higher participation in extra-curricular activities, future orientation, and employment experiences for boys. Few if any rigorous studies exist in LAMICs. Two of the AGI evaluations collected data on child outcomes (Liberia and South Sudan), though neither of these so far have been analyzed for child outcomes.

Meanwhile, there is a considerable evidence base on the effectiveness of comprehensive early childhood development (ECD) programs from LAMICs (Grantham-McGregor, Fernald, Kagawa, & Walker, 2014). In fact, an evaluation of a large-scale program providing a range of services to foster ECD in India found positive effects for children from adolescent mothers (Kapil, 2002). While very few programs targeting ECD have measured maternal outcomes, a couple of studies have found positive effects on maternal employment in evaluations of preschool programs in Argentina and Mozambique (Berlinski & Galiani, 2007; Berlinski, Galiani, & McEwan, 2009; Martinez, Naudeau, & Pereira, 2012). A study in Pakistan in fact incorporated a short cognitive-behavioral intervention into a home-visiting program providing nutrition, health, and parenting support explicitly aimed at improving mother's psychosocial well-being (Zafar et al., 2014). While not technically a dual-generation program as defined in this chapter, this is a good example of a program that has recognized the importance of catering to the mother's personal needs to improve child development and family well-being.

Being Explicit about a Dual-Generation Focus of Programs Targeted at Adolescent Mothers

Dual-generation programs combine attention to parental employment support and high-quality early childhood care and education (Chase-Lansdale & Brooks-Gunn, 2014). Several are being evaluated currently in the United States. For example, Career*Advance*®, in Tulsa, adds intensive and sector-specific high-quality training in select occupations (identified through an industry sector analysis as having a shortage of skilled labor for employment that met pay and benefit requirements) for parents to a quality 0–5 early childhood care and education program, including income support, benefits, and career opportunities and advancement (Sommer et al., 2012). While the program initially only offered postsecondary education and training in healthcare careers, Career*Advance*® now offers training in manufacturing, and opportunities for secondary education, GED preparation, and English as a second language (Gomez, 2016). It was implemented following the Great Recession (however, the Tulsa area had relatively low levels of economic hardship compared to other regions of the country). Initial results show higher levels of retention and advancement than is typical in job training-only programs (Sabol et al., 2015). However, some of the eligibility requirements preclude some of the most vulnerable young parents from participating, including minimum age of 18 years, passing a criminal background check, and 4th grade academic skills or above. Furthermore, some youth may encounter difficulties passing selection criteria such as dress and language, financial stability, and access to transportation.

Project Redirection, the *Yale Child Welfare Program,* and *New Chance* may provide initial guidance from the US context regarding what a dual-generation program tailored to the specific developmental needs of adolescent mothers could look like. *Project Redirection,* a project implemented in the early 1980s, targeted socioeconomically disadvantaged teen mothers, pregnant or parenting, age 17 or younger, who did not have a high school degree or GED, and were on or eligible for welfare benefits. The program duration was one year throughout which they received individual counseling, training in life management, parenting, and employment skills, referrals to health, education, and employment services, stipends, and child care if needed. The program was innovative in that it supported individual participant plans, participation in peer group sessions, and provided mentoring by older women in their community.

The evaluation was based on a quasi-experimental design and showed mixed results at five-year follow-up. While participating mothers showed some improvement in employment history and average earnings, the overall improvements in employment and welfare dependence were underwhelming. However, participants who scored higher on parenting skills, were more likely to have breastfed, and had a higher rate of enrolling their children in Head Start preschool programs. Children of project participants (at age 5) showed improvements in cognitive, social, and emotional development compared to the comparison children (Polit, 1988, 1989).

One of the most well-known US dual-generation programs targeting adolescent mothers to date is the *Yale Child Welfare Program,* which was implemented in the 1970s and evaluated using an experimental design. Participating adolescent mothers of 0–3-year-olds received educational and workforce development services, and high-quality center-based care was offered to their children. A 10-year follow-up showed longer subsequent childbirth spacing; higher earnings and lower welfare grant use among the mothers; and higher achievement and lower behavior problems among the children (Seitz, Rosenbaum, & Apfel, 1985). A diffusion analysis subsequently showed positive effects on the developmental outcomes of later-born siblings (not program focal children) (Seitz & Apfel, 1994). The program addressed both the developmental needs specific to adolescence and young adulthood, while assisting them in their role as a caregiver and provider. For example, the adolescent mothers were provided a home-like environment for the program with attention to both adult mentorship and peer support.

One of the only larger, multi-site evaluations of dual-generation programs for adolescent mothers is the *New Chance* demonstration (Quint, Bos, & Polit, 1997). This experimental study evaluated a community-based organization model of comprehensive services (child care support; job training support; educational and human capital development activities for parents), for adolescent mothers of 0–3-year-olds. An experimental evaluation showed positive effects on attainment of high school equivalency degrees, and some improvements in parenting practices, but no effects on young children's cognitive or behavioral outcomes at a 3.5-year follow-up. However, focusing on the high-service-use families and applying a causal Heckman selection model, further analysis showed positive effects for these families that utilized the full range of dual-generation services (Yoshikawa, Rosman, & Hsueh, 2001).

Of course such dual-generation programs from the US have limited applicability in LAMICs without undergoing substantial adaptation. The cultural, political, institutional, and economic context provides the parameters to which a program needs to be adapted to. Nevertheless, combinations of evidence-based programming for ECD and adolescent girls' livelihoods can inform a truly dual-generation approach serving adolescent mothers and their young children in LAMICs.

Figure 13.1 adapts a diagram by Chase-Lansdale and Brooks-Gunn (2014) to reflect the specifics of adolescent mothers' developmental needs and milestones in LAMICs. The diagram aims to highlight key ingredients and pathways to long-term health and economic stability for this generation, and the next.

Naturally, the specifics of the content as well as the delivery mechanisms will need to be adapted to the demands of a particular context. For instance, approaches may differ substantially depending on the geographic location (rural vs. urban), or if the adolescent girl is married or not. However, several of the pathways are reflective of self-regulatory functioning, a basic competence that permeates several if not all domains of life, and has applicability across contexts. While targeting self-regulation could be useful for adults at any age, we believe this to be a key ingredient in any youth development program.

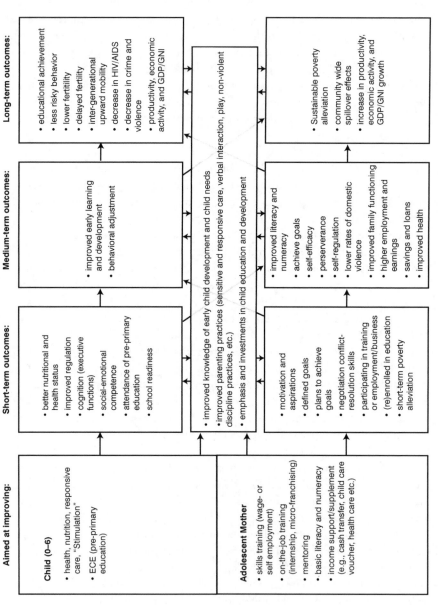

FIGURE 13.1 Dual-Generation Program Model for Adolescent Mothers in Low- and Middle-Income Countries

Targeting Self-Regulation

Some of the selection criteria for Career*Advance®* as well as *Year Up* tap into behavioral and regulatory competencies that may be insufficiently developed in the most disadvantaged adolescent girls grappling with the realities of early motherhood. Effective self-regulation plays a central role in various life domains, from educational achievement, holding gainful employment, having stable and positive relationships, and being a responsive and sensitive parent. In fact, research suggests that self-regulatory competence serves as a good indicator of adolescent resilience and a promising target for intervention strategies aimed at improving adolescent adjustment in the face of adversity (Dishion & Connell, 2006). Even though developmental science has enabled us to understand the relevance of self-regulation in healthy and productive development, much of the prevention science has focused on specific problem behaviors, rather than identifying shared risk, protective, and promotive factors (Guerra & Bradshaw, 2008). In other words, identifying self-regulation as a core competence would improve our understanding of how to best support adolescent mothers in ways that will spill over into other domains of life, including parenting. There has been some investigation into how self-regulation ("core competencies") can be fostered with regards to interventions targeting adolescent high-risk sexual behaviors (Charles & Blum, 2008), violence (Sullivan, Farrell, Bettencourt, & Helms, 2008), and substance use (Haegerich & Tolan, 2008). These approaches need yet to be integrated into programs targeting a range of behaviors and skills, including parenting and employability, and adapted to and tested in LAMIC contexts.

Dual-Generation Programs for Adolescent Mothers during Crises

Dual-generation programs with features of the models reviewed may help mitigate the effects of economic shocks on particularly vulnerable populations of parents such as adolescent mothers and their children in LAMICs. The existing evaluations of programs like the *Yale Child Welfare Project*, *New Chance*, and *Project Redirection* are too few to examine such a pattern. However, considering each of the main components of a dual-generation program – support for parents' human capital development; and support for children's early learning through early childhood care and education – these separate literatures have on occasion examined effects on subgroups that differed in levels of economic disadvantage. This is not entirely comparable to the context of economic crises, but does give some indication of variability in impacts based on family-level risk.

Re-analysis of the US welfare-to-work experiments of the 1990s showed that effects of efforts to increase employment on employment itself were strongest among those with moderate and high levels of economic disadvantage (among samples that were entirely poor, generally below the federal poverty threshold;

economic disadvantage was measured through a combination of prior low education and income and lack of employment). However, positive impacts on children's achievement accrued only among those families with moderate levels of disadvantage (Alderson, Gennetian, Dowsett, Imes, & Huston, 2008). Effects of the income-increasing employment programs similarly showed positive impacts concentrated on those families with moderate levels of disadvantage (Yoshikawa, Magnuson, Bos, & Hsueh, 2003).

Turning to early childhood care and education, we can consider the 0–3 period separately from the preschool age period. Relatively few evaluations have examined the impact of high-quality child care differentially by levels of economic disadvantage. Dearing, McCartney, and Taylor (2009) showed in the National Institute of Child Health and Human Development (NICHD) Early Child Care and Youth Development study that higher-quality child care's positive associations with later math and literacy were stronger for the more disadvantaged families. The Infant Health and Development Program provided both home visits in the first year to parents of moderate and severe low birth weight babies, and then center-based care for their children starting at age 1 and extending to age 3. Effects on long-term achievement were concentrated on the low-income families in the sample (the overall sample was mixed socioeconomically and included middle-class families). In addition, decomposing effects of the home visit vs. center-based components indicated that these positive long-term effects were attributable to the center-based care, but not the home visits (Duncan & Sojourner, 2013). The preschool evaluation literature is generally concentrated on disadvantaged and small samples. The relatively few evaluations of mixed-income and larger samples show that effects on cognitive outcomes are generally stronger for more disadvantaged subgroups (Gormley, Gayer, Phillips, & Dawson, 2005; Weiland & Yoshikawa, 2013).

How this literature informs programs and policies in low-income countries, and in particular in times of economic crises, remains largely unclear. Wuermli, Hempel, Aber, and Lundberg (2012a) have reviewed policies and programs to mitigate the effects of economic crises on young people's development. Aside from short-term poverty alleviation programs such as unconditional cash transfers and public works programs, most programs that have proven effective at improving youth's labor market outcomes (e.g., comprehensive skills training programs) or young children's development (e.g., conditional cash transfers) require substantial administrative and physical infrastructure to be in place long before an economic crisis happens. The need for an immediate response to a situation of emergency does not allow for the careful configuration and design of complex program structures. Moreover, most successful comprehensive training programs for youth rely on a strong and growing private sector to provide training and employment opportunities (Ibarrarán & Rosas Shady, 2009). Nevertheless, it is worth building the structures and systems needed to implement successful dual-generation programs with a focus on the long-run that could be scaled up to reach larger segments of the population during economic crises.

Conclusions

While in an ideal world adolescent pregnancy, particularly unwanted pregnancy, would not exist, the reality is less than ideal. Adolescent pregnancy rates remain high, in some countries at epidemic levels. And in many places these high incidence rates coincide with poor developmental outcomes, persistently high rates of extreme poverty, and substantial gender inequality. Given the prevalence of stunting, and suboptimal cognitive, socioemotional development and learning in many low-income populations in LAMICs, looking into stress, mental health, and self-regulatory capacity of adolescent mothers as a locus of change makes sense.

Similarly, economic boom and bust cycles seem to be the norm, rather than the exception. However, natural disasters and political and social crises are much more frequent than financial crises, and large positive economic shocks are three times as likely as negative shocks (Wuermli et al., 2012b). Crises may exacerbate risk processes that transmit the effects of adolescent motherhood to lower health and well-being of the parent, less optimal parenting, and lower levels of child learning, well-being, and development. However, crises may also provide opportunities for redefining social norms more generally, and gender norms and gender relations more specifically, as economic necessity may demand deviations from the status quo. This could open up labor market opportunities to women, providing them with economic and social resources and power. It is therefore just as much an opportunity to promote the development of adolescent mothers and their children, as it is an imperative to protect their development from the negative consequences of shocks.

Conclusive evidence on dual-generation programs, and dual-generation research on single-generation programs, is still lacking. Dual-generation programs show promise – however, the larger-scale evaluations in the literature showed variable results. Recent efforts are too early in their evaluations. The components of dual-generation programs – livelihoods and job skills focused programs and early childhood care and education – generally show stronger effects among the more disadvantaged, suggesting that when each of these components is of high quality, they may together mitigate some of the risks conferred by household-level economic disadvantage. This may extend to the effects of economic crises, which generally increase household disadvantage.

Rigorous evaluations, such as randomized controlled trials, are needed to identify causal effects of such programs on parenting youth's and their children's outcomes. There needs to be a concerted effort at understanding the developmental needs of youth, in particular in their role as parents. Existing youth programs such as *Year Up* need to be scrutinized to uncover the mechanisms and processes through which these programs effect change. In addition, much work needs to be done to understand how to better serve high-risk adolescents with children. Adolescent mothers, for instance, may encounter difficulty succeeding in programs such as *Year Up* due to deeply rooted self-regulatory deficiencies or a lack of high-quality child care, factors increasing the risks to their children's healthy development. Going forward, systematic inquiry will need to utilize interdisciplinary and cross-professional collaboration, mixed methods, and high-quality implementation science approaches.

Human development and behavior are embedded within and shaped by local cultures which have implications for the interpretation of research findings (LeVine, 2010; Weisner, 2002). Yet practically all social and behavioral science has been conducted on a very small and homogenous population, grossly unrepresentative of the world's people (Henrich, Heine, & Norenzayan, 2010). Future investigations into the effects of adolescent motherhood across different country contexts will need to take a sociocultural perspective in analyzing the social and emotional consequences of early marriage and childbearing. As mentioned earlier, most adolescent pregnancies in low-income countries occur within marriages. A stress and self-regulation paradigm might unveil information about the effects of early marriage and childbearing, and how such cultural traditions may or may not be undermining young women's development, or the development of their children.

There remains much room for debate around the cultural relevance of a stress and self-regulation paradigm to explain human development in low-income countries. As with poverty, stress is relative and context specific. As a simple example, where adolescent pregnancy carries a lot of stigma, girls may experience more social stress in forms of bullying and being ostracized. Nevertheless, as the physiological stress response is intricately and dynamically interlinked with immune, cognitive, socioemotional, and behavioral functioning, one may want to consider a stress paradigm as it relates to persistent and new epidemiological challenges, including the rise in non-communicable diseases.

Recent studies, predominantly from the United States and Europe, have begun to investigate the role of fathers in their children's development. This topic is now also surfacing in the international child development arena. Moving forward, however, it will be of great importance to consider young fathers' roles as parents and providers. Recent research is revealing the importance of fathers' involvement in their children's life (Cabrera, Shannon, & Tamis-LeMonda, 2007). However, so far there has been very little work on this topic in LAMICs, especially with very young children, mainly because many cultures adhere to traditional gender roles. However, the father could be a second source of nurturing for the child. In cases where the adolescent mother lives with the father of the child, he could be a source of support or a source of stress. It will be important to consider such relationship dynamics when designing services and working with adolescent mothers in diverse cultural contexts.

The prevalence of adolescent motherhood, the large numbers of children that fail to reach their developmental potential, and the sustained deep poverty that seems to be transmitted from one generation to the next in many parts of this world warrant closer investigation of comprehensive dual-generation approaches for adolescent mothers and their children. Redirecting resources toward adolescent mothers may meet political resistance. It is the responsibility of applied human developmentalists and funders alike to produce rigorous evidence in order to effectively convey the importance and the cost-effectiveness of dual-generation intervention approaches tailored to the developmental needs of very young mothers. Dual-generation programs can provide the developmental support for today's children, while continued efforts to curb adolescent fertility will improve development of future generations.

Acknowledgments

Funding for this project was made possible in part by grant number 1H79AE000100-1 to the UC Davis Center for Poverty Research from the US Department of Health and Human Services, Office of the Assistant Secretary for Planning and Analysis (ASPE), which was awarded by the Substance Abuse and Mental Health Services Administration (SAMHSA); and NYU Abu Dhabi Research Institute for core support to the research center, Global TIES for Children, which provides intramural support for research activities that directly contributed to this chapter. The views expressed are those of the authors and do not necessarily reflect the official policies of the Department of Health and Human Services or NYU Abu Dhabi Institute. We also thank Dr. Paul Hastings (UC Davis), Dr. Ross Thompson (UC Davis), and Dr. Shubha Chakravarty (The World Bank) who provided invaluable comments on drafts of this manuscript and background writings which informed this chapter; and all other colleagues from research and practice who have offered nuanced insights into the challenges in effectively serving adolescent mothers and their children in low- and middle-income countries.

References

Adato, M., de la Brière, B., Mindek, D., & Quisumbing, A. (2000). *The impact of PROGRESA on women's status and intrahousehold relations*. Final report, International Food Policy Research Institute, Washington DC.

Adoho, F., Chakravarty, S., Korkoyah, D. T. J., Lundberg, M., & Tasneem, A. (2014). The impact of an adolescent girls employment program: The EPAG project in Liberia. *Policy Research Working Paper 6832*. Washington, DC: The World Bank.

Agarwal, B. (1997). "Bargaining" and gender relations: Within and beyond the household. *Feminist Economics, 3*, 1–51.

Aguiar, M., Hurst, E., & Karabarbounis, L. (2013). Time use during the great recession. *The American Economic Review, 103*, 1664–1696.

Aizer, A. (2010). The gender wage gap and domestic violence. *The American Economic Review, 100*, 1847–1859.

Alderman, H., & King, E. M. (1998). Gender differences in parental investment in education. *Structural Change and Economic Dynamics, 9*, 453–468.

Alderson, D. P., Gennetian, L. A., Dowsett, C. J., Imes, A., & Huston, A. C. (2008). Effects of employment-based programs on families by prior levels of disadvantage. *Social Service Review, 82*, 361–394.

Baird, S., Chirwa, E., McIntosh, C., & Ozler, B. (2010). The short-term impacts of a schooling conditional cash transfer program on the sexual behavior of young women. *Health Economics, 19 Suppl*, 55–68.

Baumeister, R. F., & Vohs, K. D. (2007). Self-regulation, ego depletion, and motivation. *Social and Personality Psychology Compass, 1*, 115–128.

Beegle, K., Frankenberg, E., & Thomas, D. (2001). Bargaining power within couples and use of prenatal and delivery care in Indonesia. *Studies in Family Planning, 32*, 130–146.

Behrman, J. R., Foster, A. D., Rosenweig, M. R., & Vashishtha, P. (1999). Women's schooling, home teaching, and economic growth. *Journal of Political Economy, 107*, 682–714.

Bell, M. A., & Deater-Deckard, K. (2007). Biological systems and the development of self-regulation: Integrating behavior, genetics, and psychophysiology. *Journal of Developmental and Behavioral Pediatrics, 28*, 409–420.

Benería, L. (2003). *Gender, development, and globalization: Economics as if all people mattered.* New York: Routledge.

Benería, L., & Roldan, M. (1987). *The crossroads of class and gender: Industrial homework, subcontracting, and household dynamics in Mexico City.* Chicago, IL: University of Chicago Press.

Berlinski, S., & Galiani, S. (2007). The effect of a large expansion of pre-primary school facilities on preschool attendance and maternal employment. *Labour Economics, 14*, 665–680.

Berlinski, S., Galiani, S., & McEwan, P. J. (2009). Preschool and maternal labor market outcomes: Evidence from a regression discontinuity design. *IFS Working Paper W09/05.* London: Institute for Fiscal Studies.

Best, J. R., Miller, P. H., & Naglieri, J. A. (2011). Relations between executive function and academic achievement from ages 5 to 17 in a large, representative national sample. *Learning and Individual Differences, 21*, 327–336.

Brooks-Gunn, J., & Furstenberg Jr, F. F. (1986). The children of adolescent mothers: Physical, academic, and psychological outcomes. *Developmental Review, 6*, 224–251.

Brooks-Gunn, J., & Petersen, A. C. (1991). Studying the emergence of depression and depressive symptoms during adolescence. *Journal of Youth and Adolescence, 20*, 115–119.

Cabrera, N. J., Shannon, J. D., & Tamis-LeMonda, C. (2007). Fathers' influence on their children's cognitive and emotional development: From toddlers to pre-K. *Applied Developmental Science, 11*, 208–213.

Card, D., Kluve, J., & Weber, A. (2009). Active labor market policy evaluations: A meta-analysis. IZA *Discussion Paper Series*, No 4002.

Casey, B. J., Jones, R. M., & Hare, T. A. (2008). The adolescent brain. *Annals of the New York Academy of Sciences, 1124*, 111–126.

Charles, V. E., & Blum, R. W. (2008). Core competencies and the prevention of high-risk sexual behavior. *Core Competencies to Prevent Problem Behaviors and Promote Positive Youth Development, 122*, 61–74.

Chase-Lansdale, P. L., & Brooks-Gunn, J. (2014). Two-generation programs in the twenty-first century. *The Future of Children: Helping Parents, Helping Children – Two-Generation Mechanisms, 24*, 13–39.

Chatterji, M., Murray, N., London, D., & Anglewicz, P. (2005). The factors influencing transactional sex among young men and women in 12 sub Saharan African countries. *Social Biology, 52*, 56–72.

Coley, R. L., & Chase-Lansdale, P. L. (1998). Adolescent pregnancy and parenthood. Recent evidence and future directions. *American Psychologist, 53*, 152–166.

Conde-Agudelo, A., Belizan, J. M., & Lammers, C. (2005). Maternal-perinatal morbidity and mortality associated with adolescent pregnancy in Latin America: Cross-sectional study. *American Journal of Obstetrics & Gynecology, 192*, 342–349.

Cunha, F., & Heckman, J. J. (2008). Formulating, identifying and estimating the technology of cognitive and noncognitive skill formation. *Journal of Human Resources, 43*, 738–782.

Dearing, E., McCartney, K., & Taylor, B. A. (2009). Does higher quality early child care promote low-income children's math and reading achievement in middle childhood? *Child Development, 80*, 1329–1349.

Dishion, T. J., & Connell, A. (2006). Adolescents' resilience as a self-regulatory process: promising themes for linking intervention with developmental science. *Annals of the New York Academy of Sciences, 1094*, 125–138.

Duncan, G. J., & Sojourner, A. J. (2013). Can intensive early childhood intervention programs eliminate income-based cognitive and achievement gaps? *Journal of Human Resources, 48*, 945–968.

Duncan, G. J., Bos, H., Gennetian, L. A., & Hill, H. (2009). New hope: A thoughtful and effective approach to "make work pay". *Northwestern Journal of Law and Social Policy, 4*, 101–115.

Elder Jr, G. H. (1999). *Children of the Great Depression: Social change in life experience.* Boulder, CO: Westview Press.

Elder Jr, G. H., Van Nguyen, T., & Caspi, A. (1985). Linking family hardship to children's lives. *Child Development, 56*, 361–375.

Elster, A. B. (1984). The effect of maternal age, parity, and prenatal care on perinatal outcome in adolescent mothers. *American Journal of Obstetrics and Gynecology, 149*, 845–847.

Erulkar, A., Ferede, A., Girma, W., & Ambelu, W. (2013). Evaluation of "Biruh Tesfa" (Bright Future) program for vulnerable girls in Ethiopia. *Vulnerable Children and Youth Studies, 8*, 182–192.

Esquivel, V. (2006). What else do we have to cope with? Gender, paid and unpaid work during Argentina's last crisis. *The International Working Group on Gender, Macroeconomics, and International Economics (GEM-IWG) Working Paper Series,* 06-06.

Fraser, A. M., Brockert, J. E., & Ward, R. H. (1995). Association of young maternal age with adverse reproductive outcomes. *New England Journal of Medicine, 332*, 1113–1117.

Garcia Coll, C., Vohr, B. R., Hoffman, J., & Oh, W. (1986). Maternal and environmental factors affecting developmental outcome of infants of adolescent mothers. *Journal of Developmental and Behavioral Pediatrics, 7*, 230–236.

Gassman-Pines, A., Gibson-Davis, C. M., & Ananat, E. O. (2015). How economic downturns affect children's development: An interdisciplinary perspective on pathways of influence. *Child Development Perspectives, 9*, 233–238.

Ge, X., Conger, R. D., & Elder, G. H. (2001). Pubertal transition, stressful life events, and the emergence of gender differences in adolescent depressive symptoms. *Developmental Psychology, 37*, 404–417.

Ge, X., Brody, G. H., Conger, R. D., & Simons, R. L. (2006). Pubertal maturation and African American children's internalizing and externalizing symptoms. *Journal of Youth and Adolescence, 35*, 531–540.

Geronimus, A. T., & Korenman, S. (1993). The socioeconomic costs of teenage childbearing: Evidence and interpretation. *Demography, 30*, 281–290.

Gillibrand, E., Robinson, P., Brawn, R., & Osborn, A. (1999). Girls' participation in physics in single sex classes in mixed schools in relation to confidence and achievement. *International Journal of Science Education, 21*, 349–362.

Glick, P., & Sahn, D. E. (2000). Schooling of girls and boys in a West African country: The effects of parental education, income, and household structure. *Economics of Education Review, 19*, 63–87.

Goldin, C. (1994). *Labor markets in the twentieth century*. Cambridge, MA: National Bureau of Economic Research.

Goldin, C. (1998). America's graduation from high school: The evolution and spread of secondary schooling in the twentieth century. *The Journal of Economic History, 58*, 345–374.

Goldin, C. (1999). Egalitarianism and the returns to education during the great transformation of American education. *Journal of Political Economy, 107*, S65–S94.

Gomez, C. J. (2016). *Negotiating motherhood and education: Low-income mothers' motivation for attending school while parenting a young child* (Dissertation). Cambridge, MA: Harvard University.

Gormley, W. T., Gayer, T., Phillips, D., & Dawson, B. (2005). The effects of universal pre-K on cognitive development. *Developmental Psychology, 41*, 872–884.

Grantham-McGregor, S. M., Fernald, L. C. H., Kagawa, R. M. C., & Walker, S. (2014). Effects of integrated child development and nutrition interventions on child development and nutritional status. *Annals of the New York Academy of Sciences, 1308*, 11–32.

Guerra, N. G., & Bradshaw, C. P. (2008). Linking the prevention of problem behaviors and positive youth development: Core competencies for positive youth development and risk prevention. *New Directions for Child and Adolescent Development, 2008*, 1–17.

Haddad, L., Hoddinott, J., & Alderman, H. E. (1997). *Intrahousehold resource allocation in developing countries: Models, methods, and policy*. Baltimore, MD: Johns Hopkins University Press for the International Food Policy Research Institute.

Haegerich, T. M., & Tolan, P. H. (2008). Core competencies and the prevention of adolescent substance use. *Core Competencies to Prevent Problem Behaviors and Promote Positive Youth Development, 122*, 47–60.

Heckman, J. J., & Rubinstein, Y. (2001). The importance of noncognitive skills: Lessons from the GED testing program. *American Economic Review, 91*, 145–149.

Heckman, J. J., Stixrud, J., & Urzua, S. (2006). The effects of cognitive and noncognitive abilities on labor market outcomes and social behavior. *NBER Working Paper*, No. 12006.

Henrich, J., Heine, S. J., & Norenzayan, A. (2010). The weirdest people in the world? *Behavioral and Brain Sciences, 33*, 61–83; discussion 83–135.

Hoddinott, J., & Haddad, L. (1995). Does female income share influence household expenditures? Evidence from Cote D'Ivoire. *Oxford Bulletin of Economics and Statistics, 57*, 77–96.

Ibarrarán, P., & Rosas Shady, D. (2009). Evaluating the impact of job training programmes in Latin America: Evidence from IDB funded operations. *Journal of Development Effectiveness, 1*, 195–216.

Jaffee, S., Caspi, A., Moffitt, T. E., Belsky, J., & Silva, P. (2001). Why are children born to teen mothers at risk for adverse outcomes in young adulthood? Results from a 20-year longitudinal study. *Development and Psychopathology, 13*, 377–397.

Jensen, R., & Thornton, R. (2003). Early female marriage in the developing world. *Gender & Development, 11*, 9–19.

Juster, R. P., McEwen, B. S., & Lupien, S. J. (2010). Allostatic load biomarkers of chronic stress and impact on health and cognition. *Neuroscience & Biobehavioral Reviews, 35*, 2–16.

Kabeer, N. (1997). Women, wages and intra-household power relations in urban Bangladesh. *Development and Change, 28*, 261–302.

Kalil, A. (2013). Effects of the Great Recession on child development. *Annals of the American Academy of Political and Social Science, 650*, 232–249.

Kalil, A., & Ziol-Guest, K. (2011). *The Great Recession and married parents' use of time.* Paper presented at the Society for Research in Child Development Biennial Meeting. Montreal, Quebec, Canada.

Kapil, U. (2002). Integrated Child Development Services (ICDS) scheme: a program for holistic development of children in India. *The Indian Journal of Pediatrics, 69*, 597–601.

Karatoreos, I. N., & McEwen, B. S. (2013). Annual research review: The neurobiology and physiology of resilience and adaptation across the life course. *Journal of Child Psychology and Psychiatry, 54*, 337–347.

Karlan, D., & Valdivia, M. (2011). Teaching entrepreneurship: Impact of business training on microfinance clients and institutions. *Review of Economics and Statistics, 93*, 510–527.

Katz, E. (2008). *Programs promoting young women's employment: What works.* Paper presented at the Launch of the Adolescent Girls Initiative, Washington, DC.

Khandker, S. R. (2005). Microfinance and poverty: Evidence using panel data from Bangladesh. *The World Bank Economic Review, 19*, 263–286.

Lee, C., & Gramotnev, H. (2006). Predictors and outcomes of early motherhood in the Australian Longitudinal Study on Women's Health. *Psychology Health and Medicine, 11*, 29–47.

Leerlooijer, J. N., Bos, A. E., Ruiter, R. A., van Reeuwijk, M. A., Rijsdijk, L. E., Nshakira, N., & Kok, G. (2013). Qualitative evaluation of the Teenage Mothers Project in Uganda: A community-based empowerment intervention for unmarried teenage mothers. *BMC Public Health, 13*, 816.

LeVine, R. A. (2010). The six cultures study: Prologue to a history of a landmark project. *Journal of Cross-Cultural Psychology, 41*, 513–521.

Levitt-Dayal, M., Motihar, R., Kanani, S., & Mishra, A. (2003). Adolescent girls in India choose a better future: an impact assessment of an educational programme. New Delhi, India: The Centre for Development and Population Activities (CEDPA).

Lundberg, M., & Wuermli, A. J. (Eds) (2012). *Children and youth in crisis: Protecting and promoting human development in times of economic shocks.* Washington, DC: World Bank.

Lundberg, S., & Pollak, R. A. (1996). Bargaining and distribution in marriage. *The Journal of Economic Perspectives, 10*, 139–158.

Lupien, S. J., McEwen, B. S., Gunnar, M. R., & Heim, C. (2009). Effects of stress throughout the lifespan on the brain, behaviour and cognition. *Nature Reviews Neuroscience, 10*, 434–445.

Martinez, S., Naudeau, S., & Pereira, V. (2012). *The promise of preschool in Africa: A randomized impact evaluation of early childhood development in rural Mozambique.* Washington, DC: World Bank Group & Save the Children.

McQueston, K., Silverman, R., & Glassman, A. (2012). Adolescent fertility in low-and middle-income countries: effects and solutions. *Center for Global Development Working Paper, 295.*

Mead, N. L., Baumeister, R. F., Gino, F., Schweitzer, M. E., & Ariely, D. (2009). Too tired to tell the truth: Self-control resource depletion and dishonesty. *Journal of Experimental Social Psychology, 45*, 594–597.

Mensch, B. S., & Lloyd, C. B. (1998). Gender differences in the schooling experiences of adolescents in low-income countries: The case of Kenya. *Studies in Family Planning, 29*, 167–184.

Miller, B., & Sollie, D. (1986). Normal stresses during the transition to parenthood. In R. Moos (Ed.), *Coping with life crises* (pp. 129–138). New York: Springer.

Moore, M. R., & Brooks-Gunn, J. (2002). Adolescent parenthood. *Handbook of Parenting, 3*, 173–214.

Morris, P., Duncan, G. J., & Clark-Kauffman, E. (2005). Child well-being in an era of welfare reform: the sensitivity of transitions in development to policy change. *Developmental Psychology, 41*, 919–932.

Paranjothy, S., Broughton, H., Adappa, R., & Fone, D. (2009). Teenage pregnancy: who suffers? *Archives of Disease in Childhood, 94*, 239–245.

Paul Schultz, T. (2002). Why governments should invest more to educate girls. *World Development, 30*, 207–225.

Petersen, A. C., Compas, B. E., Brooks-Gunn, J., Stemmler, M., Ey, S., & Grant, K. E. (1993). Depression in adolescence. *American Psychologist, 48*, 155–168.

Pianta, R. C., Barnett, W. S., Burchinal, M., & Thornburg, K. R. (2009). The effects of preschool education: What we know, how public policy is or is not aligned with the evience base, and what we need to know. *Psychological Science in the Public Interest, 10*, 49–88.

Pinquart, M., & Silbereisen, R. K. (2004). Human development in times of social change: Theoretical considerations and research needs. *International Journal of Behavioral Development, 28*, 289–298.

Polit, D. F. (1988). *The Challenge of Serving Teenage Mothers. Lessons from Project Redirection.* New York: Manpower Demonstration Research Corporation.

Polit, D. F. (1989). Effects of a comprehensive program for teenage parents: Five years after Project Redirection. *Family Planning Perspectives, 21*, 164–187.

Posner, M. I., & Rothbart, M. K. (2000). Developing mechanisms of self-regulation. *Development and Psychopathology, 12*, 427–441.

Quint, J. C., Bos, J., & Polit, D. F. (1997). *New chance: Final report on a comprehensive program for young mothers in poverty and their children.* New York: MDRC.

Quisumbing, A. R., & de La Brière, B. (2000). *Women's assets and intrahousehold allocation in rural Bangladesh: Testing measures of bargaining power.* Washington, DC: International Food Policy Research Institute.

Raver, C. C., Garner, P. W., & Smith-Donald, R. (2007). The roles of emotion regulation and emotion knowledge for children's academic readiness: Are the links causal? In R. C. Pianta, M. J. Cox, & K. Snow (Eds), *School readiness and the transition to kindergarten in the era of accountability* (pp. 121–147). Baltimore, MD: Paul H. Brookes Publishing.

Richards, E., Theobald, S., George, A., Kim, J. C., Rudert, C., Jehan, K., & Tolhurst, R. (2013). Going beyond the surface: Gendered intra-household bargaining as a social determinant of child health and nutrition in low and middle income countries. *Social Science & Medicine, 95*, 24–33.

Roder, A., & Elliott, M. (2014). *Sustained gains: Year Up's continued impact on young adults' earnings.* New York: Economic Mobility Corporation.

Rossi, A. S. (1968). Transition to parenthood. *Journal of Marriage and Family, 30*, 26–39.

Sabol, T. J., Sommer, T. E., Chase-Lansdale, P. L., Brooks-Gunn, J., Yoshikawa, H., King, C. T., Kathawalla, U., Alamuddin, R., Gomez, C. J., & Ross, E. C. (2015). Parents' persistence and certification in a two-generation education and training program. *Children and Youth Services Review, 58*, 1–10.

Sebastian, C., Viding, E., Williams, K. D., & Blakemore, S. J. (2010). Social brain development and the affective consequences of ostracism in adolescence. *Brain and Cognition, 72*, 134–145.

Seitz, V., & Apfel, N. H. (1994). Parent focused intervention: Diffusion effects on siblings. *Child Development, 65*, 677–683.

Seitz, V., Rosenbaum, L. K., & Apfel, N. H. (1985). Effects of family support intervention: A ten-year follow-up. *Child Development, 56*, 376–391.

Shonkoff, J. P. (2012). Leveraging the biology of adversity to address the roots of disparities in health and development. *Proceedings of the National Academy of Sciences of the United States of America, 109 Suppl 2*, 17302–17307.

Shonkoff, J. P., & Phillips, D. A. (Eds). (2000). *From neurons to neighborhoods: The science of early childhood development.* Washington, DC: National Academy Press

Skoufias, E., & Parker, S. W. (2006). Job loss and family adjustments in work and schooling during the Mexican peso crisis. *Journal of Population Economics, 19*, 163–181.

Sommer, T. E., Chase-Lansdale, P. L., Brooks-Gunn, J., Gardner, M., Rauner, D. M., & Freel, K. (2012). Early childhood education centers and mothers' postsecondary attainment: A new conceptual framework for a dual-generation education intervention. *Teachers College Record, 114*, 1–40.

Sullivan, T. N., Farrell, A. D., Bettencourt, A. F., & Helms, S. W. (2008). Core competencies and the prevention of youth violence. *Core Competencies to Prevent Problem Behaviors and Promote Positive Youth Development, 122*, 33–46.

Taylor, J. L. (2009). Midlife impacts of adolescent parenthood. *Journal of Family Issues, 30*, 484–510.

Tomasik, M. J., & Silbereisen, R. K. (2009). Demands of social change as a function of the political context, institutional filters, and psychosocial resources. *Social Indicators Research, 94*, 13–28.

Ventura, S. J., & Bachrach, C. A. (2000). Nonmarital childbearing in the United States, 1940–99. *National Vital Statistics Reports, 48*, n16, 2–46.

Vohs, K. D., Baumeister, R. F., Schmeichel, B. J., Twenge, J. M., Nelson, N. M., & Tice, D. M. (2008). Making choices impairs subsequent self-control: a limited-resource account of decision making, self-regulation, and active initiative. *Journal of Personality and Social Psychology, 94*, 883–898.

Walker, S. P., Wachs, T. D., Meeks Gardner, J., Lozoff, B., Wasserman, G. A., Pollitt, E., & Carter, J. A. (2007). Child development: risk factors for adverse outcomes in developing countries. *The Lancet, 369*, 145–157.

Walker, S. P., Wachs, T. D., Grantham-McGregor, S., Black, M. M., Nelson, C. A., Huffman, S. L., Baker-Henningham, H., Chang, S. M., Hamadani, J. D., Lozoff,

B., Gardner, J. M. M., Powell, C. A., Rahman, A., & Richter, L. (2011). Inequality in early childhood: Risk and protective factors for early child development. *The Lancet, 378,* 1325–1338.

Weiland, C., & Yoshikawa, H. (2012). The effects of large scale economic change and policies on children's developmental contexts and developmental outcomes. *Child Development Perspectives, 6,* 342–350.

Weiland, C., & Yoshikawa, H. (2013). Impacts of a prekindergarten program on children's mathematics, language, literacy, executive function, and emotional skills. *Child Development, 84,* 2112–2130.

Weisner, T. S. (2002). Ecocultural understanding of children's developmental pathways. *Human Development, 45,* 275–281.

WHO (2008). MPS notes: Adolescent pregnancy. *Department of Making Pregnancy Safer, Vol. 1, No. 1.* Geneva, CH: World Health Organization.

WHO (2014). Adolescent pregnancy. *Fact sheet No. 364.* Retrieved Jan 10, 2015, from www.who.int/mediacentre/factsheets/fs364/en/

Wuermli, A. J., Hempel, K., Aber, J. L., & Lundberg, M. (2012a). Policies to protect and promote young people's development during crisis. In M. Lundberg & A. J. Wuermli (Eds), *Children and youth in crisis: Protecting and promoting human development in times of economic shocks* (pp. 229–277). Washington, DC: World Bank.

Wuermli, A. J., Silbereisen, R. K., Lundberg, M., Lamont, M., Behrman, J., & Aber, J. L. (2012b). A conceptual framework. In M. Lundberg & A. J. Wuermli (Eds), *Children and youth in crisis: Protecting and promoting human development in times of economic shocks* (pp. 29–101). Washington, DC: World Bank.

Yoshikawa, H., Aber, J. L., & Beardslee, W. R. (2012). The effects of poverty on the mental, emotional, and behavioral health of children and youth implications for prevention. *American Psychologist, 67,* 272–284.

Yoshikawa, H., Rosman, E. A., & Hsueh, J. (2001). Variation in teenage mothers' experiences of child care and other components of welfare reform: Selection processes and developmental consequences. *Child Development, 72,* 299–317.

Yoshikawa, H., Magnuson, K. A., Bos, J. M., & Hsueh, J. (2003). Effects of earnings-supplement policies on adult economic and middle-childhood outcomes differ for the "hardest to employ". *Child Development, 74,* 1500–1521.

Zafar, S., Sikander, S., Haq, Z., Hill, Z., Lingam, R., Skordis-Worrall, J., Hafeez, A., Kirkwood, B., & Rahman, A. (2014). Integrating maternal psychosocial well-being into a child-development intervention: the five-pillars approach. *Annals of the New York Academy of Sciences, 1308,* 107–117.

14

THE DEVELOPMENT OF AN INTERVENTION BASED ON POSITIVE PSYCHOLOGY FOR CHILDREN INVOLVED IN BULLYING

*Juliana Pureza, Carolina Lisboa,
and Angela Helena Marin*

Introduction

Several studies in the field of clinical psychology that focus on child development support the positive impact of preventive interventions. The economic rationality of prevention predicts that social assistance towards mental health could be optimized if there was more investment in the promotion of interpersonal development and positive behaviors of children, reinforcing the relevance of investigations that focus on the development of interventions (Del Prette & Del Prette, 2005a). Hence, the psychological treatment of children should be considered not only as a therapeutic focus for interventions, but also as a form of mental illness prevention and health promotion (Petersen & Wainer, 2011).

One of the research topics in the child development field concerns the identification and understanding of the bullying process. The absence of data or public attention when it comes to bullying in Brazil does not allow us to conclude whether this process is a contemporary phenomenon or not, however, due to its serious consequences, there is an increase in scientific interest on this subject in order to better understand and prevent it (Kuhn, Lyra, & Tosi, 2011; Lisboa, Braga, & Ebert, 2009). Several researchers in Latin America have examined predictors of school climate (Aron, Milicic, & Armijo, 2012; Bear, et al., 2016; Berger, Alcalay, Torretti & Milicic, 2011; Guerra, Castro, & Vargas, 2011; Preiss, Calcagni & Grau, 2015). These studies provide evidence of bullying and cyberbullying as predictors of a negative school climate, thus justifying the need and urgency for interventions towards these processes (Bear et al., 2016).

Bullying happens when a child or adolescent is systematically attacked, without apparent motivation by one or more aggressors, resulting in social exclusion (Olweus, 1993). This kind of aggression may consist of a set of either direct aggressive (physical and verbal) or indirect acts (indifference, isolation, exclusion, defamation, provocation related to a disability, among others) that occur without apparent motivation, but in an intentional manner (Lisboa et al., 2009). In order to identify this phenomenon, it is important to consider the establishment of relations characterized by power imbalance, intending social exclusion. Therefore, conflicts faced by children in specific situations cannot be considered bullying, as well as jokes performed in a playful way (Craig & Harel, 2004). Currently, results from the World Health Report show bullying as a global issue that affects one third of the children around the world (Craig & Harel, 2004), a proportion that is also found in Brazil (Francisco & Libório, 2009; Malta et al., 2010).

There is an established relationship between bullying and gender. Studies have demonstrated greater involvement of boys in bullying phenomena which may be related to the type of aggressiveness they use to express: physical violence. In other words, as boys tend to express more physical acts of aggression which are more explicit and easily identified maybe this fact explains why studies evidenced boys as aggressors and victims of bullying more than girls. Girls tend to express more relational aggression, behaviors that use to be more implicit and even more difficult to identify (Kuhn et al., 2011; Lisboa, 2005; Lisboa et al., 2009). It is also observed that younger children tend to be more involved in bullying situations because, as they grow older, they become not only more developed physically but also emotionally and therefore are less likely to be victimized by their peers (Craig & Harel, 2004; Lisboa et al., 2009; Malta et al., 2010; Olweus, 1993). Some studies demonstrate that students up to 12 years of age engage more frequently in cases of bullying when compared to older students (Cross et al., 2011; Rigby, 1997; Whitney & Smith, 1993). Similarly, interventions that aim to reduce bullying in schools have achieved greater success when they focus on this younger age group (Cross et al., 2011).

There are several negative consequences of bullying on children. Bullying results in various types of damage to a child's development that may aggravate existing problems or trigger psychological disorders and learning disabilities (Binsfeld & Lisboa, 2010; Caballo, Calderero, Carrillo, Salazar, & Irurtia, 2011a). For example, studies reveal that children who are victims or perpetrators may show low self-esteem and depression symptoms (Binsfeld & Lisboa, 2010; Lopes Neto, 2005) that may be long lasting and have an important impact into adulthood (Zwierzynska, Wolke, & Lereya, 2013). In addition, an association between severe depression disorder and bullying can lead victims to commit suicide, which tends to be widely reported by the media (Binsfeld & Lisboa, 2010). However, a study conducted in southern Brazil has shown that bullies tend to be more depressed than victims (Binsfeld & Lisboa, 2010). In this sense, it is observed that depression can be considered as a cause and/or as a consequence of bullying, being an important variable for its identification and crucial for the development of interventions.

Given the fact that bullying is a process that occurs during an interaction between peers, the involvement of a child in this phenomenon may also have implications on their social relationships with their classmates making it difficult for the youth involved to establish friendship bonds (Lisboa et al., 2009). In this sense, many authors have connected the bullying experience with the development of social skills (Castro, Melo, & Silvares, 2003; Crawford & Manassis, 2011; Kristensen, Schaefer, Rigoli, Busnello, & Calbo, 2009; Larke & Beran, 2006). Social skills (SS) are behaviors that express feelings, attitudes, opinions, or rights in a contextually appropriate and effective manner, respecting other people's behavior, solving problems, and reducing the probability of emergence of future problems (Caballo, 2003).

Direct and indirect involvement in bullying seem to be related to a low SS repertoire (Larke & Beran, 2006). In addition, victimization and exclusion of peer group may constitute the beginning of a vicious cycle for the development of SS, in which the rejected child starts to bond only with other peers who are also rejected and who may have his/her risky behaviors reinforced by this new group (Castro et al., 2003). Just as with depression, it is possible to identify that a deficit in SS also could be associated as cause and consequence of bullying situations.

Given the crucial role of the development of social skills in coping with bullying, some intervention studies on coping and treatment of bullying have been conducted using SS training (Caballo et al., 2011b; Joronen, Konu, Rankin, & Stedt-Kurki, 2011; Karna et al., 2011a, 2011b). In a systematic review of literature, of the 18 international studies about interventions focusing on bullying in childhood that were identified, half of them mentioned using the training of SS (Pureza, Marin, & Lisboa, submitted). Such interventions have shown an increase in children's SS and a decrease in interpersonal violence rates among peers (Caballo et al., 2011b; Joronen et al., 2011; Karna et al., 2011a, 2011b). It is important to address that the theoretical framework of these interventions is not clear and most of all, not presented in the papers reviewed. The importance of placing the intervention and techniques in a theoretical framework is crucial not only to replicate studies, but also to guarantee the ethics of all intervention strategies (Pureza et al., submitted).

In general, bullying interventions show a preventive focus and are directed at students, teachers and other school professionals on the premise that these individuals constitute the social context in which bullying emerges and remains. Bullying is considered as a group phenomenon, derived from dysfunctional relationships established between students (Caballo et al., 2011b). Bullying prevention interventions should focus on groups, once bullying is a group phenomena. Group interventions focusing on bullying issues show more efficacy than individual intervention strategies. Furthermore, a group activity may be capable of generating a new repertoire and provides opportunities for behavior modeling through observation (Bieling, McCabe, & Antony, 2008; Binsfeld & Lisboa, 2010; White & Freeman, 2003). Also, the development of group interventions enables a larger number of participants to benefit in a short period of time since it is cost effective (fewer trained professionals for many patients), and easier to replicate owing to a smaller infrastructure. It is important to emphasize that bullying is a group phenomenon that not only emerges but it is also reinforced by the group, justifying the possibility that a collective intervention may be more effective than individual focus strategies (Caballo et al., 2011b). Additionally, interventions that aim to change school climate tend to increase intolerance with the phenomenon and seem to be more effective than those directed only at teachers or students involved (Ttofi & Farrington, 2011).

Despite the social and scientific relevance of the study on bullying, the already documented results of interventions in literature are inexpressive or inconclusive. There is no consensus about theoretical frameworks and techniques/methods to intervene on this phenomenon (Merrell, Gueldner, Ross, & Isava, 2008; Ttofi & Farrington, 2011). Furthermore, clinical, systematic and effective interventions for the treatment of children involved in bullying are also scarce (Allen, 2010; Caballo et al., 2011b; Neme, Mello, Gazzola, & Justi, 2008).

One of the areas of psychology that has sought to develop interventions focused on health promotion is positive psychology (Del Prette & Del Prette, 2005a; Roffey, 2012; Segrin & Taylor, 2007; Seligman, 2011), which studies the psychological fundamentals of well-being and happiness, as well as strengths and human virtues that can be fostered (Paludo & Koller, 2007; Seligman, 2011). It is important to underscore the difference between studies based on positive psychology, interventions in positive psychology, and positive development programs. Studies that aim to understand, discuss, or promote positive aspects connected to the human being's health are based on the perspective of positive psychology. Moreover, positive psychology interventions aim to foster positive emotions and well-being among individuals (Seligman, 2011; Sousa, 2010). Positive development programs, in turn, can be defined as broader interventions that focus on promoting positive aspects of development, such as SS (Sousa, 2010). These interventions and programs in positive psychology, although recent, have presented satisfactory results not only in the clinical context but also in schools and other social contexts (Pureza, Kuhn, Castro, & Lisboa, 2012a; Seligman, 2011; Sousa, 2010). Considering these issues and evidence, the positive psychology paradigm was chosen as a background for the present study to develop an intervention for children to cope with bullying. In addition, as positive psychology adopts an evidence-based theoretical approach, some studies based on this approach are also associated with cognitive-behavioral therapy – CBT (Knapp & Beck, 2008; Seligman, 2011; Seligman, Steen, Park,

& Peterson, 2005). The clinical background and professional experience of the researchers – authors of this chapter – in CBT justified the adoption of the clinical approach together with positive psychology as a framework for the developed intervention. In fact, studies that integrate positive psychology and CBT already exist in literature (Duckworth, Steen, & Seligman, 2005; Hamilton, Kitzman, & Guyotte, 2006; Karwoski, Garratt, & Ilardi, 2006).

CBT has been, ever since its creation, heavily influenced by the medical model of diagnosis and treatment. Its structure is based on problem solving and focused on making the patient–therapist pairing concentrate only on pathology and in what is dysfunctional (Bannink, 2013). Even though its primary purpose is to reduce symptoms, there are several CBT techniques that are congruent with the positive psychology's objective of assessing and promoting the patient's potential to improve its own well-being (Karwoski, Garratt, & Ilardi, 2006).

There are also proposals for CBT's association with positive psychology as a distinct paradigm, referred to in literature as positive CBT. Positive CBT aims to deactivate patients' problems and activate their psychological resources, changing the focus of what is dysfunctional for what is healthy and positive (Bannink, 2013). Thus, positive psychology can be an important tool to improve CBT's effectiveness, as well as to enhance the long-term benefits of this therapeutic approach (Karwoski et al., 2006).

Positive psychology is an expanding field, even though it is still recent in the national and international contexts (Paludo & Koller, 2007; Pureza et al., 2012a). Although some interventions referred SS training as one of the ways to cope and intervene with bullying (Pureza et al., submitted), there is a paucity of studies with systematic interventions on positive psychology and CBT with a focus on bullying. Against this backdrop, this chapter presents the development and implementation of an intervention associating positive psychology and cognitive-behavioral therapy on Brazilian children involved in bullying. The study also aimed to demonstrate differences about the involvement in bullying situations, depression indicators, and SS repertoire pre-and post-intervention.

Method

Design

A quantitative and quasi-experimental design was adopted, with pre-and post-intervention assessment (Creswell, 2007).

Participants

Brazilian students from two schools from a city in South Brazil were invited to participate in the study. Approximately 150 5th and 6th graders were invited. Only

71 of the children invited presented parent consent forms to participate in the study. Students who gave their consent were divided, randomly, in two groups: intervention group (IG) and comparison group (CG). However, 31 children missed some intervention meetings or were absent in the days of the pre- or post-test, and thus were not included in the final sample for analysis. Two schools were contacted and chosen by convenience, and the groups were initially equal in number of participants. Due to the high dropout rate during the intervention, the post-test was held with 40 children: 26 (IG) and 14 (CG). Mean age was 11.37 (SD = 1.07) and 20 participants were boys (50%). The IG comprised 12 girls (46.2%) and 14 boys (53.8%) with a mean age of 11.50 (SD = 0.98). The CG included eight girls (57.1%) and six boys (42.9%) with a mean age of 11.14 (SD = 1.23).

Measures

*   Cuestionario Multimodal de Interação Escolar – CMIE-II (Caballo, Arias, Calderero, Salazar, & Irurtia, 2011a): this questionnaire was self-administered, comprising 64 items, divided into five subscales relating to the different roles involved in bullying (bully, victimization, bystander, severe victimization, and active observer), and answered in a four-points Likert scale (from 1 = never to 4 = many times). Cronbach's alpha in the original study was .90. In the present study, Cronbach's alpha was .79.
*   Social Skills Rating System – SSRS (Bandeira, Del Prette, Del Prette, & Magalhães, 2009): in this study, only the self-assessment form for children was used, containing 34 items divided into six subscales: empathy, assertiveness, responsibility, problem avoidance, expression of feelings, and emotions control, answered in a three-points Likert scale (1 = never to 3 = very often). The measure is validated in Brazil. Cronbach's alpha was .81 in the present study.
*   Children's Depression Inventory – CDI (Kovacs, 1983): this assessment was derived from an adaptation of the Beck Depression Inventory (BDI) for adults. Its purpose is to verify the existence and the severity of depressive symptoms among children and adolescents from 7 to 17 years old. A 27-item self-report scale describes depression symptoms in a three-points Likert scale. The CDI demonstrates satisfactory psychometric properties in Brazil (Hutz & Giacomoni, 2000), and the Cronbach's alpha reached was .80 in the original study, where as in this research it was .81.

Ethical Procedures and Data Collection

According to the Ethical Guidelines and Norms involving research with human subjects, provided by the National Board of Health on Resolution n° 466, this study followed all necessary ethical care and was approved by the Vale do Rio dos Sinos University Research Ethics Committee (Protocol n° 128/2009).

Initial contact was made with the selected-by-convenience public schools that would be invited to take part in the study. Once schools accepted to participate, fifth and sixth graders were invited to engage in the intervention. Students interested in participating were asked for their parent's consent by signing the informed consent form (ICF). After parents' agreement, measures were applied to the subjects collectively. All parents who returned the consent form agreed to have their children participate in the intervention, but 53.33% parents did not return the consent forms. This can be accounted for due to the poor relation between the parents and the school authorities, high dropout rate, and high absenteeism among children.

Subsequently, children from the intervention group participated in meetings coordinated by three researchers. There were children in IG and the CG in both schools, to avoid school bias in the data analysis. Meetings were structured in the group cognitive-behavioral therapy format (Bieling et al., 2008), having techniques based on positive psychology, integrating both paradigms (Bannink, 2013; Karwoski et al., 2006; Ruini & Fava, 2009).

The group intervention lasted 10 weeks totaling eight weekly meetings of 50 minutes each, aside from two meetings for the pre- and post-test. The meeting with children involved psychoeducation on bullying and SS training (Pureza et al., submitted). Techniques based on positive psychology as well as CBT were included in the intervention: the initial session's (session 1) goal was bullying's psychoeducation, and the techniques used were expository lectures and group discussions, as well as homework assignments, in which participants were to report their own experience with bullying situations. The intermediated sessions (sessions 2 to 6) were based on positive psychology with activities focusing on well-being, strengths, and virtues in addition to SS training (Del Prette & Del Prette, 2005b; Seligman, Ernst, Gillham, Reivicha, & Linkins, 2009). The techniques used were the "box of emotions" (children were to identify situations in their lives that aroused different emotions), analysis of the strengths and virtues (group discussions based on movies and children's books characters), and social skills training (conducting role-playing based in school situations with passive, aggressive, and assertive behaviors). Final sessions (sessions 7 and 8) aimed at bullying contents through techniques addressed in previous sessions (Murphy, Yaruss, & Quesal, 2007). The techniques used in these meetings were group discussions and role-playing focusing on coping strategies for bullying (such as, by the end of the meeting children made a movie showing a positive resolution for a bullying situation, and the movie premiere was presented to the families and schools' staff). Description of the sessions along with their goals and activities is presented in Table 14.1.

At the end of the intervention, children provided qualitative feedback and their impressions of the group intervention. Similarly, as a control measure, implementation and transmission of speech information measures were used

TABLE 14.1   Description of the Intervention Meetings Regarding their Goals and Activities

Session	Goal	Activities
Pre- test	Administer Questionnaires	CMIE-III, SSRS, CDI
Session 1	Bullying Psychoeducation	What is it?; myths about bullying; characteristics and social roles in bullying
Session 2	Positive Psychology	Psychoeducation about positive emotions - "Emotions Box" and "Emotions Gym"
Session3	Positive Psychology	Psychoeducation about strengths and virtues (characters); cartoon discussion
Session 4	Positive Psychology	Positive introduction and personal strengths analysis
Session 5	Positive Psychology	Psychoeducation about empathy; role-play and "Empathy Bingo"
Session 6	Positive Psychology	Psychoeducation about assertiveness; role-play and discussion about bullying through videos
Session 7	Bullying Intervention	Rain of ideas: "What to do?"; role-play and recording of students interventions
Session 8	Bullying Intervention	Movie Premiere: presentation of videos to guests and discussion
Post- test	Readminister Questionnaires	CMIE-III, SSRS, CDI

(Remor & Gómez, 2012) to evaluate the clarity and understanding of the contents in each session. At the end of each session, children responded to two questions concerning the clarity and understanding of the work content in the meeting. To evaluate the clarity, the question asked was "were the contents covered in the meeting today clear to you?", and to evaluate the understanding, the question was "did you understand the contents and activities covered in the meeting today?"

It should be stressed that feedback on the study's results were shared with the children, their parents and school authorities. In the case of high indicators of depression, specific individual feedback was given to the parents and referrals to individual psychotherapy were performed.

Results

A comparison between the IG and CG pre- and post-intervention through the Mann-Whitney U Test for independent samples showed that groups differed in pre-test when it came to assertiveness ($Z = -2.70$, $p < 0.01$), problems avoidance ($Z = -2.13$, $p < 0.03$), SS total score ($Z = -2.24$, $p < 0.02$), and depression indicators ($Z = -2.89$, $p < 0.00$). Prior to the intervention, the CG showed higher assertiveness ($M = 10.92$, $SD = 2.73$), problems avoidance ($M = 8.35$, $SD = 2.70$), and SS total score ($M = 53.14$, $DP = 17.27$) than the IG (assertiveness: $M = 8.11$, $SD = 2.81$; problems avoidance: $M = 6.69$, $SD = 2.13$; SS total score: $M = 42.03$, $SD = 10.13$). In contrast, the IG showed higher means of depression indicators ($M = 11.76$; $SD = 7.06$) than the CG ($M = 6.00$, $SD = 4.33$). This initial difference found between the groups, and the high dropout rate of intervention, shows that a non-clinical sample of children in public schools have, in fact, clinical symptoms that may be underestimated or undiagnosed. This fact generates considerable difficulty to perform evidence-based research or investigations about intervention's efficacy or effectiveness at the school ecological environment. The implementation of experimental and quasi-experimental methodologies in Brazil, considering the diversity of contexts may be very complex when it is not performed in a lab setting. It is important to address as a bias the differences between groups at pre-test, but it is also important to emphasize that to intervene and to evaluate these interventions in Brazilian school contexts is a challenge and so researchers have to address approaches to deal with this potential bias in the ecology of the school context.

Such differences did not remain significant in the evaluation conducted after the intervention, suggesting that groups were more homogeneous considering variables assessed at the end of the study, which can be an effect of the intervention but also a result of the human development process itself, because of some confounding variables that were not controlled, as you can see in the description in Table 14.2. Only a significant difference was observed regarding the witness role in bullying ($Z = -2.77$; $p < 0.001$), inferring that the IG showed more behaviors associated with the witness role (M = 9.19, SD = 6.03) than the CG (M = 5.78, SD = 1.67) after the intervention. It is important to mention that a comparison between the IG pre- and post-intervention through the Mann-Whitney U Test was also done. A within group comparison of the CG pre- and post-intervention was also done. These analyses also explain the differences in the values of the Z scores. Three different analysis and comparisons were done: IG and CG pre- and post-test, IG pre- and post-test, and CG pre and post-test.

IG showed no differences considering SS or depression indicators pre- and post-test (within group comparison). However, there was a significant difference in the sub-category of the witness role (Z = –2.69, p < 0.01), having its score increased after the intervention (pre-test: M = 6.61, SD = 1.81; post-test: M = 9.19, SD = 6.03). In the post-test, there was a decrease in SS scores in problem avoidance (pre-test: M = 8.35, SD = 2.70; post-test: M = 7.00, SD = 2.88) and SS total score (pre-test: M = 53.14, SD = 17.27; post-test: M = 46.14, SD = 11.34). In contrast, for the CG (within group comparison), no significant differences were identified among variables related to bullying, although a decrease in problem avoidance was noted (Z = –2.06, p < 0.03), as well as a decrease in SS total score (Z = –1.86, p < 0.06). These results can be seen in more detail in Table 14.3.

TABLE 14.2 Intervention Group ($n=26$) and Comparison Group ($n=14$) Pre- and Post-Intervention

	IG ($n=26$)		CG ($n=14$)	
	Z	p	Z	p
Aggressiveness	–1.08	0.28	–1.73	0.08
Vitimization	–0.34	0.73	–0.43	0.67
Severe victimizations	–0.10	0.92	–1.30	0.19
Active observation	–0.01	0.99	–0.41	0.68
Bystander	–0.48	0.63	–2.77	<0.01
Responsibility	–1.43	0.15	–0.11	0.91
Empathy	–0.04	0.89	–1.67	0.09
Assertiveness	–2.70	<0.01	–1.48	0.14
Self-control	–1.45	0.15	–0.22	0.83
Problems avoidance	–2.13	<0.03	–0.06	0.95
Expressing feelings	–1.65	0.10	–0.64	0.52
SS total score	–2.24	<0.02	–0.62	0.53
Depression indicators	–2.89	<0.00	–1.72	0.08

TABLE 14.3 Comparison between Intervention Group ($n=26$) and Comparison Group ($n=14$) Pre- and Post-intervention

	IG (n=26)		CG (n=14)	
	Z	p	Z	p
Aggressiveness	−1.37	0.17	−0.04	0.97
Vitimization	−0.26	0.80	−0.40	0.69
Severe victimizations	−0.16	0.87	−1.50	0.13
Active observation	−0.34	0.73	−0.63	0.53
Bystander	−2.69	<0.01	−1.74	0.08
Responsibility	−0.19	0.85	−1.70	0.09
Empathy	−0.62	0.53	−1.31	0.19
Assertiveness	−0.20	0.84	−1.85	0.07
Self-control	−0.12	0.90	−1.22	0.22
Problems avoidance	−0.42	0.67	−2.06	<0.03
Expressing feelings	−0.44	0.66	−1.04	0.30
SS total score	−0.80	0.42	−1.86	<0.06
Depression indicators	−0.81	0.42	−0.94	0.35

Finally, the sample was divided into groups according to bullying roles. Categories relating to bullying roles have been defined according to the Bullying Questionnaire cut-off. The CG was not considered in this analysis because the N in each subgroup (bullying roles) was too small. For the IG, only the severe victims ($n = 13$) were considered in the analysis. Roles of witness ($n = 3$), offender ($n = 6$), victim ($n = 5$), and active observer ($n = 7$) were also not included due to the small number of participants in each subgroup.

The Wilcoxon test for paired samples showed that the severe victims group presented an increase in witness behaviors ($Z = –2.65$, $p < 0.01$), as well as a tendency to an improvement on assertiveness ($Z = –1.70$, $p < 0.08$), and on SS total score ($Z = -1.71$, $p < 0.08$), as can be seen by the results described in Table 14.4. Similarly, this group also presented a decrease in depression indicators ($Z =–2.32$, $p < 0.02$).

Discussion

Studies that aim to evaluate interventions for children and adolescents based on positive psychology, show results that point to an improvement in happiness, social skills, and academic performance, in contrast to a decrease in depressive

TABLE 14.4 Comparison of Pre and Post-intervention Results for Severe Victims Group
(*n*=13)

	Severe Victims *n=13*	
	Z	p
Aggressiveness	–0.97	0.33
Vitimization	–0.35	0.72
Severe victimizations	–0.89	0.37
Active observation	–0.77	0.44
Bystander	–2.66	<0.01
Responsibility	–0.77	0.44
Empathy	–0.97	0.33
Assertiveness	–1.71	<0.08
Self-control	–0.99	0.32
Problems avoidance	–1.25	0.21
Expressing feelings	–1.69	0.09
SS total score	–1.71	<0.08
Depression indicators	–2.32	<0.02

symptoms (Seligman et al., 2009; Seligman et al., 2005; Sin & Lyubomirsky, 2009). Similarly, studies that propose an integration between CBT and positive psychology suggest a positive impact on SS and in the decrease of depressive symptoms (Karwoski et al., 2006; Seligman, Steen, Park, & Peterson, 2005).

In this study, the proposed intervention based on positive psychology and CBT for children involved in bullying showed some interesting results. Even though the IG showed more depression indicators and less SS than the CG in the pre-test, both groups did not differ in the post-test, showing an improvement of the IG. Though this may count as a modest result, it could also suggest an impact of the intervention in social skills and depressive symptoms.

Moreover, the IG showed an increase in witness behaviors when compared to the CG. This result suggests that their participation in the intervention may have provided these children more awareness and allowed them to identify bullying situations that they could not identify earlier. However, the same effect was not found in the CG. Therefore, one can hypothesize that the intervention may have created greater awareness among students concerning bullying since they were psychoeducated about the different ways that this process can be expressed.

Despite the general increase in bullying situations in schools being a worrisome matter, the identification of this phenomenon is of utmost importance for the development of prevention strategies. In this sense, bullying awareness can help to avoid underestimation of this phenomenon expressed by judgments like "bullying doesn't exist" or "everything is bullying."

The severe victims group presented a decrease in depression indicators, and an increase in SS and witness behavior. Such data suggests that the intervention may have a positive effect on severe bullying that involves physical aggression, threats, and lower academic performance. Studies suggest that interventions based on strengths, virtues, well-being, and happiness can also increase variables like self-esteem, self-efficacy, and self-reliance (Diener, Oishi, & Lucas, 2002; Lyubomirsky, Sheldon, & Schkade, 2005; Park, 2004). It is likely that the intervention based on positive psychology has resulted in the empowerment of children by making them feel stronger and less vulnerable, which may have increased their sense of self-efficacy, perceiving themselves as more able to identify severe situations of bullying and activate their support network. It is possible to find in literature evidence that indicates the negative association of self-efficacy with some bullying roles (Thornberg & Jungert, 2013). Similarly, this increase in self-efficacy could be related to the decrease in depression indicators that was observed after the intervention in this severe victims group. This study did not measure self-efficacy, but self-efficacy is related to awareness and self-confidence, and we infer that maybe the awareness and knowledge about what is and what causes bullying has increased.

The intervention did not confirm what was expected. In other words, the intervention did not lead to substantial improvements in SS and a decrease in indicators of depression and bullying behaviors. However, the intervention may have improved the awareness of bullying, and that is an important result and a first step to a micro- and macro-system change. An important limitation of this study was the fact that the IG and the CG were not homogeneous in the pretest. An intervention that embraced the entire school instead of only a subgroup would boost these results extending the impact to other bullying dimensions, therefore having a greater impact in the group as a whole (Salmivalli, 2010).

Considering methodological difficulties, this study may be considered as a pilot. Its main contribution was the development of an innovative intervention combining CBT and positive psychology to the bullying phenomenon. Such association has only recently been documented in literature and it is essential for future research.

In conclusion, it is important to highlight that this study has allowed the identification and the discussion of possibilities of intervention for bullying in the school context, going beyond clinical interventions with victims and perpetrators individually in traditional clinical settings, considering the school environment. Despite the difficulty of planning and the execution of research on bullying, researchers who propose clinical interventions, especially in childhood, should consider the social context, thus, creating new possibilities for psychotherapeutic intervention and better relationship between clinical and social context. However, these studies are multi-faceted, pointing to the need to develop new skills adapted to the Brazilian reality in order to discuss practical interventions.

In this sense, positive psychology is as an innovative theoretical approach, which aims to keep up with the expansion movement of psychology, using the evidence-based therapy approach to innovation and research. Regarding the limitations, such as the heterogeneity and sample size, and the need to contemplate other social roles in bullying as active observer and professors or others school members, it is believed that this study has contributed to the construction of knowledge about interventions about the bullying phenomenon and new possibilities for interventions based on the integration of CBT and positive psychology. The study points to the challenges of intervention studies in Brazil allowing interested researchers to discuss and improve methods to better cover the demands of this area. In addition, this study integrates the CBT and positive psychology and shows its adequacy to support school intervention to cope with bullying. All the conceptual ideas and techniques seem to work and were well accepted by the children. Despite several obstacles to conducting evidence-based intervention research, ethical concerns, and institutional resistance difficulties, we need to open this debate to questions and comments to move forward. Sharing experiences may be the best way. Collecting data is important, but changing the ecological system in order to understand the context and intervene to promote health is the social compromise of psychology researchers.

References

Allen, K. P. A. (2010). Bullying intervention system: Reducing risk and creating support for aggressive students. *Preventing School Failure, 54*(3), 199–209.

Aron, A. M., Milicic, N., & Armijo, I. (2012). Clima social escolar: Una escala de evaluación – Escala de Clima Social Escolar, ECLIS. *Universitas Psychologica, 11*(3), 803–813.

Bandeira, M., Del Prette, Z. A. P., Del Prette, A., & Magalhães, T. (2009). Validação das escalas de habilidades sociais, comportamentos problemáticos e competência acadêmica (SSRS-BR) para o ensino fundamental. *Psicologia: Teoria e Pesquisa, 25*(2), 271–282.

Bannink, F. P. (2013). Positive CBT: From reducing distress to building success. *Journal of Contemporary Psychotherapy, 43*(2), 1–8.

Bear, G. G., Holst, B., Lisboa, C. S. M., Chen, D., Yang, C., & Chen, F. F. (2016) A Brazilian Portuguese survey of school climate: Evidence of validity and reliability. *International Journal of School & Educational Psychology, 4*(3), 1–14.

Berger, C., Alcalay, L., Torretti, A., & Milicic, N. (2011). Socioemotional wellbeing and academic achievement: Evidence from a multilevel approach. *Psicologia, Reflexao e Critica, 24*(2), 344–351.

Bieling, P. J., McCabe, R. E., & Antony, M. M. (2008). *Terapia cognitivo-comportamental em grupos.* Porto Alegre: Artmed.

Binsfeld, A. R., & Lisboa, C. S. M. (2010). Bullying: Um estudo sobre papéis sociais, ansiedade e depressão no contexto escolar do sul do Brazil. *Interpersona, 4*(1), 74–105.

Caballo, V. E. (2003). *Manual de avaliação e treinamento das habilidades sociais.* São Paulo: Santos.

Caballo, V. E., Arias, B., Calderero, M., Salazar, I. C., & Irurtia, M. J. (2011a). Acoso escolar y ansiedad social en niños (I): Análisis de su relación y desarrollo de nuevos instrumentos de evaluación. *Psicología Conductual, 19*(3), 591–609.

Caballo, V. E., Calderero, M., Carrillo, G. B., Salazar, I. C., & Irurtia, M. J. (2011b). Acoso escolar y ansiedad social en niños (II): Una propuesta de intervención en formato lúdico. *Psicología Conductual, 19*(3), 611–626.

Castro, R. E. F., Melo, M. H. S., & Silvares, E. F. M. (2003). O julgamento de pares de crianças com dificuldades interativas após um modelo ampliado de intervenção. *Psicologia: Reflexão e Crítica, 16*(2), 309–318.

Craig, W. M., & Harel, Y. (2004). Bullying, physical fighting and victimization. In C. Currie, C. Roberts, A. Morgan, R. Smith, W. Settertobulte, & O. Samdal (Eds), *Young people's health in context: International report from the HBSC 2001/02 survey. WHO policy series: Health policy for children and adolescents, 4.* Copenhagen: WHO Regional Office for Europe, 133–144.

Crawford, A. M., & Manassis, K. (2011). Anxiety, social skills, friendship quality, and peer victimization: An integrated model. *Journal of Anxiety Disorders, 25*(7), 924–931.

Creswell, J. W. (2007). *Projeto de pesquisa: Métodos qualitativo, quantitativo e misto.* Porto Alegre: Artmed.

Cross, D., Monks, H., Hall, M., Shaw, T., Pintabona, Y., Erceg. E., Hamilton, G., Roberts, C., Waters, S., & Lester, L. (2011). Three-year results of the friendly schools whole of school intervention on children's bullying behavior. *British Educational Research Journal, 37*(1), 105–129.

Del Prette, Z. A. P., & Del Prette, A. (2005a). A importância das habilidades sociais na infância. In Z. A. P. Del Prette, & A. Del Prette (Eds), *Psicologia das habilidades sociais na infância: Teoria e prática* (p. 270). Petrópolis: Vozes, 15–29.

Del Prette, Z. A. P., & Del Prette, A. (2005b). Parte III – Habilidades sociais relevantes: Análise e intervenção. In Z. A. P. Del Prette, & A. Del Prette (Eds), *Psicologia das habilidades sociais na infância: Teoria e prática* (p. 270). Petrópolis: Vozes, 113–190.

Diener, E., Oishi, S., & Lucas, R. E. (2002). Subjective well-being: The science of happiness and life satisfaction. In C.R. Snyder, & S.J. Lopez (Eds), *Handbook of positive psychology* (pp. 63–73). Oxford: Oxford University Press.

Duckworth, A. L., Steen, T. A., & Seligman, M. E. P. (2005). Positive psychology in clinical practice, Annual Review of Clinical Psychology, *1*(1), 629–651.

Francisco, M. V., & Libório, R. M. C. (2009). Um estudo sobre *bullying* entre escolares do ensino fundamental. *Psicologia: Reflexão e Crítica, 22*(2), 200–207.

Guerra, V. C., Castro, A. L., & Vargas, C. J. (2011). Psychometric examination of the School Social Climate Questionnaire in Chilean students. *Psicothema, 23*(1), 140–145.

Hamilton, N. A., Kitzman, H., & Guyotte, S. (2006). Enhancing health and emotion: Mindfulness as a missing link between cognitive therapy and positive psychology. Journal of Cognitive Psychotherapy, *20*(2), 123–134.

Hutz, C. S., & Giacomoni, C. H. (2000). *Adaptação Brazileira do Inventário de Depressão Infantil* (CDI). Manuscrito não publicado. Curso de Pós-Graduação em Psicologia do Desenvolvimento, Universidade Federal do Rio Grande do Sul. Porto Alegre, RS.

Joronen, K., Konu, A., Rankin, H. S., & Stedt-Kurki, P. (2011). An evaluation of a drama program to enhance social relationships and anti-bullying at elementary school: A controlled study. *Health Promotion International, 27*(1), 5–14.

Karna, A., Voeten, M., Little, T., Poskiparta, E., Kaljonen, A., & Salmivalli, C. (2011a). A large-scale evaluation of the KiVa antibullying program: Grades 4–6. *Child Development, 82*(1), 311–330.

Karna, A., Voeten, M., Little, T. D., Poskiparta, E., Alanen, E., & Salmivalli, C. (2011b). Going to scale: A nonrandomized nationwide trial of the KiVa antibullying program for grades 1–9. *Journal of Consulting and Clinical Psychology, 79*(6), 796–805.

Karwoski, L., Garratt, G. M., & Ilardi, S. S. (2006). On the integration of cognitive-behavioral therapy for depression and positive psychology, *Journal of Cognitive Psychotherapy, 20*(2), 159–170.

Knapp, P., & Beck, A. T. (2008). Fundamentos, modelos conceituais, aplicações e pesquisa da terapia cognitiva. *Revista Brasileira de Psiquiatria, 30*(2), 54–64.

Kovacs, M. (1983). *The Children's Depression Inventory: A self-rated depression scale for school age youngsters*. Pittsburgh, PA: University of Pittsburgh, School of Medicine.

Kristensen, C. H., Schaefer, L. S., Rigoli, M. M., Busnello, F. B., & Calbo, A. S. (2009). Bullying na escola: Comportamento agressivo, vitimização e conduta pró-social entre pares. *Contextos Clínicos, 2*(2), 73–80.

Kuhn, Q. L., Lyra, R. L., & Tosi, P. C. S. (2011). Bullying em contextos escolares. *Unoesc & Ciência – ACHS, 2*(1), 49–62.

Larke, I. D., & Beran, T. N. (2006). The relationship between bullying and social skills in primary school students. *Issues in Educational Research, 16*(1), 38–51.

Lisboa, C. S. M. (2005). *Comportamento agressivo, relações de amizade e vitimização em crianças em idade escolar: Fatores de risco e proteção*. Tese de Doutorado não publicada, PPG em Psicologia, Universidade Federal do Rio Grande do Sul, Porto Alegre.

Lisboa, C., Braga, L. L., & Ebert, G. (2009). O fenômeno bullying ou vitimização entre pares na atualidade: Definições, formas de manifestação e possibilidades de intervenção. *Contextos Clínicos, 2*(1), 59–71.

Lopes Neto, A. (2005). Bullying: Comportamento agressivo entre estudantes. *Jornal de Pediatria, 81*(5), 164–172.

Lyubomirsky, S., Sheldon, K. M., & Schkade, D. (2005). Pursuing happiness: The architecture of sustainable change. *Review of General Psychology Copyright, 9*(2), 111–131.

Malta, D. C., Silva, M. A. I., Mello, F. C. M., Monteiro, R. A., Sardinha, L. M. V., Crespo, C., Carvalho, M. G. O., Silva, M. M. A., & Porto, D. L. (2010). Bullying nas escolas Brazileiras: Resultados da Pesquisa Nacional de Saúde do Escolar (PeNSE), 2009. *Ciência & Saúde Coletiva, 15*(2), 3065–3076.

Merrell, K. W., Gueldner, B. A., Ross, S. W., & Isava, D. M. (2008). How effective are school bullying intervention programs? A meta-analysis of intervention research. *School Psychology Quarterly, 23*(1), 26–42.

Murphy, W. P., Yaruss, J. S., & Quesal, R. W. (2007). Enhancing treatment for school-age children who stutter, II: Reducing bullying through role-playing and self-disclosure. *Journal of Fluency Disorders, 32,*139–162.

Neme, C. M. B., Mello, L. C. de, Gazzola, R. A., & Justi, M. M. (2008). Fenômeno bullying: análise de pesquisas em Psicologia publicadas no período de 2000 a 2006. *Pediatria Moderna, 4*, 200–204.

Olweus, D. (1993). *Bullying at school: What we know and what we can do*. London: Blackwell.

Paludo, S. S., & Koller, S. H. (2007). Psicologia positiva: Uma nova abordagem para antigas questões. *Paidéia, 17*(36), 9–20.

Park, N. (2004). The role of subjective well-being in positive youth development. *The ANNALS of the American Academy of Political and Social Science, 591*(1), 25–39.

Petersen, C. S., & Wainer, R. (2011). *Terapias cognitivo-comportamentais para crianças e adolescentes: Ciência e arte*. Porto Alegre: Artmed.

Preiss, D. D., Calcagni, E., & Grau, V. (2015). Classroom research and child and adolescent development in South America. *New Directions for Child and Adolescent Development, 147*, 85–92.

Pureza, F. R., Marin, A. H., & Lisboa, C. S. M. (submitted for publication) Intervenções para o fenômeno bullying na infância: Uma revisão sistemática da literatura.

Pureza, J. R., Kuhn, C. H. C., Castro, E. K., & Lisboa, C. S. M. (2012a). Psicologia positiva no Brasil: Uma revisão sistemática da literatura. *Revista Brasileira de Terapias Cognitivas, 8*(2), 109–117.

Pureza, J. R., Rusch, S. G. S., Wagner, M. F., & Oliveira, M. S. (2012b). Treinamento de habilidades sociais em universitários: Uma proposta de intervenção. *Revista Brasileira de Terapias Cognitivas, 8*(1), 2–9.

Remor, E., & Amorós Gómez, M. (2012). Efecto de un programa de intervención para la potenciación de las fortalezas y los recursos psicológicos sobre el estado de ánimo, optimismo, quejas de salud subjetivas y la satisfacción con la vida en Estudiantes universitarios. *Acta Colombiana de Psicología, 15*(2), 75–85

Rigby, K. (1997). What children tell us about bullying in schools? *Children Australia, 22*(2), 28–34.

Roffey, S. (2012). Introduction to positive relationships: Evidence based-practice across the world. In S. Roffey (Ed.), *Positive relationships: Evidence based-practice across the world* (pp.1–16). London: Springer.

Ruini, C., & Fava, G. A. (2009) Well-being therapy for generalized anxiety disorder. *Journal of Clinical Psychology: In Session, 65*(5), 510–519.

Salmivalli, C. (2010). Bullying and the peer group: A review. *Aggression and Violent Behavior, 15*(2), 112–120.

Segrin, C., & Taylor, M. (2007). Positive interpersonal relationships mediate the association between social skills and psychological well-being. *Personality and Individual Diferences, 43*(4), 637–646.

Seligman, M. E. P. (2011). O que é bem-estar? In M. E. P. Seligman, *Florescer*. Rio de Janeiro: Objetiva, 15–40.

Seligman, M. E. P., Steen, T. A., Park, N., & Peterson, C. (2005). Positive psychology in progress: Empirical validation of interventions. *American Psychologist, 60*(5), 410–421.

Seligman, M. E. P., Ernst, R. M., Gillham, J., Reivicha, K., & Linkins, M. (2009). Positive education: Positive psychology and classroom interventions. *Oxford Review of Education, 35*(3), 293–311.

Sin, N. L., & Lyubomirsky, S. (2009). Enhancing well-being and alleviating depressive symptoms with positive psychology interventions: A practice-friendly meta-analysis. *Journal of Clinical Psychology: In Session, 65*(5), 467–487.

Sousa, I. A. (2010). *A avaliação do impacto de uma conjugação de exercícios da Psicologia Positiva.* Tese de Mestrado não publicada, Faculdade de Psicologia, Universidade de Lisboa, Lisboa.

Thornberg R., & Jungert, T. (2013) Bystander behavior in bullying situations: Basic moral sensitivity, moral disengagement and defender self-efficacy. *Journal of Adolescence, 36*(3), 475–483.

Ttofi, M. M., & Farrington, D. P. (2011). Effectiveness of school-based programs to reduce bullying: A systematic and meta-analytic review. *Journal of Experimental Criminology,* 7(1), 27–56.

White, J. R., & Freeman, A. S. (2003). *Terapia cognitivo-comportamental em grupo para populações e problemas específicos.* São Paulo: Roca.

Whitney, I., & Smith, P. K. (1993). A survey of the nature and extent of bullying in junior/ middle and secondary schools. *Educational Research, 35*(1), 34–39.

Zwierzynska, K., Wolke, D., & Lereya, T. S. (2013). Peer victimization in childhood and internalizing problems in adolescence: A prospective longitudinal study. *Journal of Abnormal Child Psychology, 41*(2), 309–323.

15

LESSONS LEARNED FOR POLICY IMPACT FROM RESEARCH AND INTERVENTIONS

Christiane Spiel and Barbara Schober

Classic theories and approaches in developmental psychology (in the Rousseau–Piaget tradition) often focus on deficiencies which indicate what children cannot yet do, in comparison to adults, and most of them are retrospective, starting with the "end point" as reference (Koops, 2004). Children cannot, for example, think in a formal operational way. Around 2000, a new vision and vocabulary emerged (e.g., Larson, 2000; Lerner, Dowling, & Anderson, 2003). Youth are considered as resources to be developed. The main focus shifted to young persons' potential for successful, healthy, and positive development (Lerner et al., 2003; see also Fisher & Lerner, 2005; Lerner, Jacobs, & Wertlieb, 2005). Representatives of "positive development" describe problem solving, emotional regulation, and physical safety as foundational strengths for well-being. These foundational strengths constitute the positive underpinnings of early child health and development, as well as ongoing well-being throughout the life course (see e.g., Bornstein, Davidson, Keyes, & Moore, 2003; Mueller, et al., 2011). The approach on "positive youth development" is based on the understanding that all young people need support, guidance, and opportunities. With this support, they can develop self-assurance in four central areas that are considered as decisive for a happy, healthy, and successful life (National Clearinghouse on Families & Youth [NCFY], n.d.):

- a sense of competence: being able to do something well;
- a sense of usefulness: having something to contribute;
- a sense of belonging: being part of a community;
- a sense of power: having control over one's future.

Consequently, this new vision has an explicit applied perspective with direct implications on what families, practitioners, and policy makers do and should do to promote positive development in youth. There is high agreement among researchers, policy makers, and practitioners that kindergarten and school are the places to foster positive development and to apply evidence-based intervention. As pointed out by Kratochwill (2007, p. 829), "… schools provide unique opportunities to target children's mental health, their academic performance, and the important relationship between the two; … school practice provides a unique opportunity to follow children, developmentally, across the years (typically kindergarten through 12th grade)". In addition, psychologists working in schools have an extraordinary access to children in families and can focus on prevention and promotion at multiple levels and with multiple targets (Kratochwill, 2007).

As a consequence of this new vision, evidence-based intervention programs in educational contexts have become highly important in recent years (Kratochwill & Shernoff, 2003). But transferring these programs into practice and into the wider field of public policy often fails (Fixsen, Blase, Metz, & van Dyke, 2013). It is the intention of this chapter (1) to discuss reasons for the poor transfer, (2) to make recommendations how successful and sustainable transfer can be realized, and finally (3) to propose a six-step procedure for policy impact from research.

Reasons for Poor Transfer of Research Findings

An important factor for the success of prevention and intervention programs is the quality of their implementation (Berkel, Mauricio, Schoenfelder, & Sandler, 2011; Durlak, & DuPre, 2008; Fixsen, Blase, Naoom, & Wallace, 2009; Metz & Albers, 2014). Empirical research on implementation in general, and on the implementation of prevention and intervention programs in particular, show that the key factor for success is to involve an intensive cooperation between researchers, policy makers, and practitioners (see Roland 2000; Spiel & Strohmeier, 2007, 2011) within a mutually respectful, collaborative process (Shonkoff, & Bales, 2011). Datnow (2002, 2005) showed that reform adoption, implementation, and sustainability are the result of the interrelations between and across groups in different contexts, at various points in time (Datnow & Stringfield, 2000). Spoth and Greenberg (2011) provided similar findings. According to them, practitioner–scientist partnerships and supporting infrastructures can support the local adoption of evidence-based interventions, and produce community-level reductions in youth problem behaviors and concomitant positive youth development (see also Crowley, Greenberg, Feinberg, Spoth, & Redmond, 2012).

However, the establishment of a high-quality and fruitful cooperation of researchers, practitioners, and policy makers is difficult for various reasons. In the following, we specify these reasons, based on insights from intervention and prevention projects, in which we aimed an implementation into practice explicitly involving policy makers and practitioners (see Spiel, Schober, Strohmeier, & Finsterwald, 2011; Spiel & Strohmeier, 2012; Spiel, Wagner, & Strohmeier, 2012). In fact, there seem to be reasons for poor transfer on the part of all parties involved.

Researchers more often explore general mechanisms than practical actions in concrete situations. They tend to disregard translational research in comparison to basic research, which has higher impact in the scientific community (Fixsen, Blase, & van Dyke, 2011). Consequently, they often have a lack of knowledge about field conditions.

Practitioners usually have not very much knowledge about standards, criteria, and methods of research which causes difficulties in communication. As they are busy with many other concrete challenges and tasks, they are often not highly motivated to increase their knowledge by means of research findings.

Policy makers, similar to practitioners, commonly have poor knowledge about standards, criteria, and methods of research, which causes very comparable problems. As a consequence, the consideration of scientific findings into political argumentation often is missed. Furthermore, research results might contradict political programs and ideologies.

However, besides these general problems for transferring research evidence into practice, there are specific ones in the field of education. In recent years there was a general movement to develop and disseminate evidence-based interventions and programs in practical settings. But there are considerable differences in implementation both among countries – Anglo-American countries are more evidence oriented – and among various public service areas (Nutley, Walter, & Davies, 2007). Especially in the field of education, the adoption of instructional programs and practices has been driven more by ideology than by evidence, in contrast to other areas of public service (Slavin, 2008; see also Spiel, 2009a).

There are several reasons for the specific situation in the field of education (see Spiel, 2009b; Spiel & Strohmeier, 2012). It often takes a lot of time to see the results of interventions in the field of education, which contrasts with politicians' needs to score quick wins with the next elections in mind. So far, no clear standards of evidence have been established in the area of education. There are important differences in the way in which research is understood, created, and synthesized, which supports the influence of ideologies on political decisions.

The transfer of scientific knowledge to practice is costly and risky. There are many possible interferences when transferring prevention or intervention programs into practice such as teacher and parent attitudes, and their ability to learn and to transfer what they have learned to everyday life. The demand to change established attitudes and behavior provokes resistance not only because of the investment in changes but also because it signals a need to improve the hitherto existing behavior. Resistance against change, therefore, also protects self-worth. And last but not least, in most European countries formal structures providing a systematic transfer from research to policy and practice are lacking.

Conditions for Successful and Sustainable Transfer of Research Findings

In this section we make some recommendations on how successful and sustainable transfer can be realized despite all the obstacles described above. Again, we explicitly focus on all three groups: researchers, practitioners, and policy makers.

The main demand for *researchers* is that their studies are conducted in accordance with standards of evidence (see e.g., Spiel, Lösel, & Wittmann, 2009). As part of the evidence-based movement, various efforts have been made to define standards of evidence. Such standards are provided from several societies and organizations, and are more and more accepted and applied in scientific research. For example, the Society for Prevention Research (Flay et al., 2005) has provided standards to assist practitioners, policy makers, and administrators in determining which interventions are efficacious, which are effective, and which are ready for dissemination (for details, see Flay et al., 2005). While efficacy is the extent to which an intervention does more good than harm when delivered under optimal conditions, effectiveness refers to program effects when delivered under more real-world conditions (Flay et al., 2005, p. 1). Other standards are provided by, for instance, the Campbell Collaboration (see www.campbellcollaboration.org), the Best Evidence Encyclopedia (see www.bestevidence.org), the What Works Clearinghouse (see www.whatworks. ed.gov), and the Evidence for Policy and Practice Information and Co-ordinating Centre (see http://eppi.ioe.ac.uk/cms). Common to these standards is the fact that evidence-based programs are defined by the research methodology used to evaluate them, and randomized trials are defined as the gold standard for defining evidence (Fixsen et al., 2009). Prevention and intervention programs have to be theoretically based, evaluated using state-of-the-art methods under real-world conditions, should show consistent positive effects (including one long-term), are carefully documented (manuals etc.), and provide clear information about target groups and costs, monitoring, and evaluation tools.

However, if transfer should work, researchers are also forced to communicate their research findings in the language of practitioners and politicians. Consequently, researchers have to consider the perspective of practitioners and policy makers and meet them as equals. In order to implement prevention and intervention research into public policy, stable alliances both with policy makers and practitioners as well as with the relevant institutions, e.g. schools, are needed. Respective networks should be built in advance. We recommend also including people from the media in such networks.

Additionally, researchers, research institutions, the scientific community as a whole as well as policy makers are asked to reconsider the already established quality criteria for success which are more oriented to basic research using experiments than on longitudinal intervention studies involving evaluation and implementation.

There are also several demands on *practitioners* which are necessary preconditions for successful and sustainable transfer of research findings (see e.g., Beelmann, 2011). Some requirements concern attitudes and knowledge. Interventions can only work in the field if practitioners see and can accept the necessity of changes. As mentioned above this requirement is not easy to fulfill. The demand to change established attitudes and behavior provokes resistance not only because of the investment in changes but also because it signals a need to improve the hitherto existing behavior. Resistance against change, therefore, also protects self-worth. Practitioners need to require knowledge about research in general and research findings related to the intended interventions and programs specifically. But demands on practitioners go beyond change of attitudes and knowledge acquisition: Practitioners also need to prepare themselves and their institutions for an intervention. For example, in schools, it is of high importance that the principal has high respected educational leadership and that there is high consensus among the teachers about education, teaching, and achievement and that teachers are cooperatively planning these issues (see e.g., Scheerens, 1990). Furthermore, readiness for intervention also requires high responsibility and willingness for engagement both on the school and the single teacher level. Working teams have to be established with a majority of consensus in the institution and with administrative support (see e.g., Spiel & Strohmeier, 2011). Furthermore, supportive community networks are required and have to be established. Promotable conditions for success are the establishment of basic evaluation attitudes in teachers and a school culture where failures are seen as learning opportunities.

Accordingly, there are also demands on *policy makers* to meet the requirements for successful and sustainable transfer of research findings (Beelmann, 2011). Again, the demands concern changes in attitudes but also measures to provide a transfer supportive context. Policy makers should advocate for evidence in policy. That means, for example, that policy decisions about programs are based on evaluations and cost-benefit analyses. Incentive systems must be established in institutions such as schools to encourage compliance with policy decisions. Furthermore, policy makers have to provide for the opportunities to make institutions and practitioners ready for intervention and programs. Important prerequisites to make schools ready for interventions are evidence-based teacher education, leadership training for principals, and the establishment of quality assurance systems in schools (see e.g., Senge et al., 2000; Schober, Klug, Finsterwald, Wagner, & Spiel, 2012). Last but not least, policy makers are forced to promote the acceptance of evidence-based prevention and intervention programs in the public.

In the following section we reconsider the described demands and recommendations in a more process-oriented manner specifying a concrete procedure for bringing them into action in the field of positive youth development.

A Six-Step Procedure for Policy Impact from Research

Based on the explanations in the two sections above, we propose a six-step procedure for policy impact from research (see Spiel, Schober, & Strohmeier, in press; Schober & Spiel, in press). This procedure is also based on theoretical and empirical knowledge from prior research (e.g., Glasgow, Vogt, & Boles, 1999; Greenhalgh, Robert, MacFarlane, Bate, & Kyriakidou, 2004) and our own experience in intervention and implementation research (e.g., Finsterwald, Wagner, Schober, Lüftenegger, & Spiel, 2013; Gradinger, Yanagida, Strohmeier, & Spiel, 2015; Schober, Lüftenegger, Wagner, Finsterwald, & Spiel, 2013; Schultes, Stefanek, van de Schoot, Strohmeier, & Spiel, 2014). The six steps together should be considered as parts of a dynamic process with many sub-processes, feedback loops, and interdependencies.

Step 1: Identify Where Support is Needed

Researchers are used to identify scientific problems and wishes for new insights. The "positive youth development" approach is predicated on the understanding that all young people need support, guidance, and opportunities. Therefore, the focus is not only on problems arising in basic research but also on policy impact of research and on intervention and prevention programs. Consequently, researchers must not only be curiosity-driven but also mission-driven, combining the quest for fundamental understanding with a consideration of practical use (Stokes, 1997). In other words, if scientists intend to contribute to positive youth development and the transfer of research findings, the first step requires socio-political responsibility as a basic mindset.

Step 2: Ensure Availability of Robust Knowledge

The availability of robust and sound scientific knowledge and evidence is a fundamental precondition for giving support or guidance. Moreover, it is a prerequisite for any kind of transfer (Spiel, Lösel, & Wittmann, 2009). Consequently, researchers have to be experts in the relevant field with excellent knowledge of theory, methods, empirical findings, and limitations. This also includes the political dimension of research in the sense of defining and financing corresponding research topics. Obviously, within the positive youth development research a large body of theoretical and empirical knowledge and findings have been produced so far.

Step 3: Identify Reasonable Starting Points for Action

A wide body of research has made it clear that many intervention programs and measures do not work everywhere and at all times (Meyers, Durlak, & Wandersmann, 2012). As a consequence, researchers do not only need high expertise in the relevant scientific field: It must be combined with a differentiated view of prevailing cultural and political conditions. Researchers need knowledge and experience in the relevant practical field and its contextual conditions. As mentioned above, schools have been identified as key contexts to foster positive development. Researchers need to know whether the respective institutions are ready for intervention and if not, how to prepare them.

Step 4: Establish a Cooperation Process with Policy Makers

This step is a very crucial one. Successful development and implementation of evidence-based intervention in practical settings not only requires cooperation, persistence, and time, but also money. As research often follows its own, very intrinsic logic, which clearly differs from political thinking, a very deliberate process of establishing cooperation and building alliances is necessary. Researchers have to be aware of policy makers' scope of action and have to consider that there are other influences on government and policy, beyond evidence (Davies, 2004, 2012). They have to keep in mind that policy making is highly embedded in a bureaucratic culture and is forced to respond quickly to everyday contingencies. Finally, researchers have to consider that policy making is always a matter of what works at what costs and with what outcomes (Davies, 2004, 2012). Therefore, researchers are forced to integrate evidence with all these factors. Consequently, the establishment of such a cooperation process with policy makers requires that researchers make their voice heard, and that they are sometimes very insistent (see also Spiel et al., in press). Here, the orientation on positive development preparing the fundament for ongoing well-being throughout the life course might be helpful for establishing such a cooperation.

Step 5: Coordinate Development of Intervention and Implementation

So far, intervention and implementation research have not yet been systematically connected. Different research groups with different research traditions are usually involved in intervention research and in implementation research. Implementation researchers are mostly given mandates by policy makers to take on the implementation of already existing interventions (Fixsen et al., 2011). This might be a key reason why translating interventions into widespread community practice is so difficult (Spoth et al., 2013). Therefore, we strongly recommend a systematic integration of intervention and implementation research (Spiel et al., in press; Schober & Spiel, in press). The whole conceptualization of an intervention as well as its evaluation and implementation should systematically consider the needs of the field (Spiel et al., 2011) in an integrated way (Beelmann & Karing, 2014).

Step 6: Transfer of Program Implementation

For this final scaling-up step, several models and guidelines have been proposed by implementation science. Implementation science emerged in the early eighties of the last century (Rossi & Wright, 1984) and has been defined as "the scientific study of methods to promote the systemic uptake of research findings and evidence-based practices into professional practice and public policy" (Forman et al., 2013, p. 80; see also Eccles & Mittman, 2006). In the last decade, many implementation studies have been conducted and several conceptual models and implementation frameworks have been presented. In 2012, Meyers and colleagues provided a review consisting 25 frameworks. They found 14 dimensions that were common to many of these frameworks and grouped them into six areas: (a) assessment strategies, (b) decisions about adaptation, (c) capacity-building strategies, (d) creating a structure for implementation, (e) ongoing implementation support strategies, and (f) improving future applications. According to their synthesis, the implementation process consists of a temporal series of these interrelated steps, which are critical to quality implementation (see also Spiel et al., in press). When implementing programs in the field of positive youth development, we strongly recommend picking up the findings provided by implementation science and applying respective implementation frameworks (e.g., Fixsen et al., 2013; Meyers et al., 2012; Spoth et al., 2013).

Conclusions

So far, the positive youth development approach has been very successful. A large body of theoretical, empirical, and methodological papers are published based on this vision (see e.g., Bowers et al., 2010; Larson, 2000; Lerner et al., 2003; Lippman, Moore, & McIntosh, 2011; Mueller et al., 2011), and several workshops and conferences targeting this approach have been organized. However as, for example, shown by the papers presented at the Society of Research in Child Development (SRCD) Special Topic Meeting in Prague, 2014, knowledge and findings are mostly isolated, often coming from cross-sectional studies, are very seldom replicated and systematically connected. Furthermore, interventions and programs are mostly conducted by researchers as pilot studies, are often not replicated, and large-scale implementation is mostly missed.

Therefore, we strongly recommend to put findings together to an integrative–holistic framework, and to describe the positive youth approach and its findings in the language of politicians and practitioners by considering regional and local cultures and traditions. Last but not least, we encourage researchers to apply the proposed six-steps procedure for getting policy impact from research and interventions.

References

Beelmann, A. (2011). The scientific foundation of prevention. The status quo and future challenges of developmental crime prevention. In T. Bliesener, A. Beelmann & M. Stemmler (Eds), *Antisocial behavior and crime: Contributions of developmental and evaluation research to prevention and intervention* (pp. 137–164). Cambridge, MA: Hogrefe International.

Beelmann, A., & Karing, C. (2014). Implementationsfaktoren und -prozesse in der Präventionsforschung: Strategien, Probleme, Ergebnisse, Perspektiven [Implementation factors and processes in prevention research: Strategies, problems, findings, prospects]. *Psychologische Rundschau, 65*(3), 129–139. doi:10.1026/0033-3042/a000215

Berkel, C., Mauricio, A. M., Schoenfelder, E., & Sandler, I. N. (2011). Putting the pieces together: An integrated model of program implementation. *Prevention Science, 12*(1), 23–33. doi:10.1007/s11121-010-0186-1

Bornstein, M. H., Davidson, L., Keyes, C. L. M., & Moore, K. A. (2003). *Well-being: Positive development throughout the life course.* Mahwah, NJ: Lawrence Erlbaum Associates, Inc.

Bowers, E. P., Li, Y., Kiely, M. K., Brittian, A., Lerner, J. V., & Lerner, R. M. (2010). The five Cs model of positive youth development: A longitudinal analysis of confirmatory factor structure and measurement invariance. *Journal of Youth and Adolescence, 39*(7), 720–735. http://doi.org/10.1007/s10964-010-9530-9

Crowley, D. M., Greenberg, M.T., Feinberg, M.E., Spoth, R.L., & Redmond, C.R. (2012). The effect of the PROSPER partnership model on cultivating local stakeholder knowledge of evidence-based programs: A five-year longitudinal study of 28 communities. *Prevention Science,* 13(1), 96–105. doi:10.1007/s11121-011-0250-5

Datnow, A. (2002). Can we transplant educational reform, and does it last? *Journal of Educational Change 3*(3), 215–239. doi:10.1023/A:1021221627854

Datnow, A. (2005). The sustainability of comprehensive school reform models in changing district and state contexts. *Educational Administration Quarterly, 41*(1), 121–153. doi:10.1177/0013161X04269578

Datnow, A., & Stringfield, S. (2000). Working together for reliable school reform. *Journal of Education for Students Placed at Risk (JESPAR), 5*(1–2), 183–204. doi:10.1080/10824 669.2000.9671386

Davies, P. (2004, February). *Is evidence-based government possible? Jerry Lee lecture 2004.* Paper presented at the 4th Annual Campbell Collaboration Colloquium, Washington, DC.

Davies, P. (2012). The state of evidence-based policy evaluation and its role in policy formation. *National Institute Economic Review, 219*(1), 41–52. doi:10.1177/002795011221900105

Durlak, J. A., & DuPre, E. P. (2008). Implementation matters: A review of research on the influence of implementation on program outcomes and the factors affecting implementation. *American Journal of Community Psychology, 41*(3–4), 327–350. doi:10.1007/s10464-008-9165-0

Eccles, M. P., & Mittman, B. S. (2006). Welcome to implementation science. *Implementation Science, 1*(1). doi:10.1186/1748-5908-1-1

Finsterwald, M., Wagner, P., Schober, B., Lüftenegger, M., & Spiel, C. (2013). Fostering lifelong learning: Evaluation of a training teacher education program for professional teachers. *Teaching and Teacher Education, 29*(1), 144–155. doi:10.1016/j.tate.2012.08.009

Fisher, C. B., & Lerner, R. M. (2005). *Applied developmental science: An encyclopedia of research, policies, and programs.* Thousand Oaks, CA: Sage.

Fixsen, D., Blase, K., Metz, A., & Van Dyke, M. (2013). Statewide implementation of evidence-based programs. *Exceptional Children, 79*(2), 213–230. doi: 10.1177/001440291307900206

Fixsen, D. L., Blase, K. A., Naoom, S. F., & Wallace, F. (2009). Core implementation components. *Research on Social Work Practice, 19*(5), 531–540. doi:10.1177/1049731509335549

Fixsen, D. L., Blase, K. A., & Van Dyke, M. K. (2011). Mobilizing communities for implementing evidence-based youth violence prevention programming: A commentary. *American Journal of Community Psychology, 48*(1–2), 133–137. doi: 10.1007/s10464-010-9410-1

Flay, B. R., Biglan, A., Boruch, R. F., Castro, F. G., Gottfredson, D., Kellam, S., ... & Ji, P. (2005). Standards of evidence: Criteria for efficacy, effectiveness and dissemination. *Prevention Science, 6*(3), 151–175. doi:10.1007/s11121-005-5553-y

Forman, S. G., Shapiro, E. S., Codding, R. S., Gonzales, J. E., Reddy, L. A., Rosenfield, S. A., ... & Stoiber, K. C. (2013). Implementation science and school psychology. *School Psychology Quarterly, 28*(2), 77–100. doi:10.1037/spq0000019

Glasgow, R. E., Vogt, T. M., & Boles, S. M. (1999). Evaluating the public health impact of health promotion interventions: the RE-AIM framework. *American Journal of Public Health, 89*(9), 1322–1327. doi:10.2105/AJPH.89.9.1322

Gradinger, P., Yanagida, T., Strohmeier, D., & Spiel, C. (2015). Prevention of cyberbullying and cyber victimization: Evaluation of the ViSC Social Competence program. *Journal of School Violence, 14*(1), S.87–110. doi:10.1080/15388220.2014.963231.

Greenhalgh, T., Robert, G., MacFarlane, F., Bate, P., & Kyriakidou, O. (2004). Diffusion of innovations in service organizations: systematic review and recommendations. *The Milbank Quarterly, 82*(4), 581–629. doi:10.1111/j.0887-378X.2004.00325.x

Koops, W. (2004). Imaging childhood in European history and developmental psychology. *European Journal of Developmental Psychology, 1*(1), 1–18. doi:10.1080/17405620444000067

Kratochwill, T. R. (2007). Preparing psychologists for evidence-based school practice: Lessons learned and challenges ahead. *American Psychologist, 62*(8), 829–843. doi:10.1037/0003-066X.62.8.829

Kratochwill, T. R., & Shernoff, E. S. (2003). Evidence-based practice: Promoting evidence-based interventions in school psychology. *School Psychology Quarterly, 18*(4), 389–408. doi:10.1521/scpq.18.4.389.27000

Larson, R. W. (2000). Toward a psychology of positive youth development. *American Psychologist, 55*(1), 170–183. doi:10.1037/0003-066X.55.1.170

Lerner, R. M., Dowling, E. M., & Anderson, P. M. (2003). Positive youth development: Thriving as the basis of personhood and civil society. *Applied Developmental Science*, 7(3), 172–180. doi: 10.1207/S1532480XADS0703_8

Lerner, R. M., Jacobs, F., & Wertlieb, D. (2005). *Applied developmental science: An advanced textbook*. Thousand Oaks, CA: Sage Publications.

Lippman, L. H., Moore, K. A., & McIntosh, H. (2011). Positive indicators of child well-being: A conceptual framework, measures, and methodological issues. *Applied Research in Quality of Life*, 6(4), 425–449. doi:10.1007/s11482-011-9138-6

Metz, A., & Albers, B. (2014). What does it take? How federal initiatives can support the implementation of evidence-based programs to improve outcomes for adolescents. *Journal of Adolescent Health*, 54(3), 92–96. doi:10.1016/j.jadohealth.2013.11.025

Meyers, D. C., Durlak, J. A., & Wandersmann, A. (2012). The quality implementation framework: A synthesis of critical steps in the implementation process. *American Journal of Community Psychology*, 50(3–4), 462–480. doi:10.1007/s10464-012-9522-x

Mueller, M. K., Phelps, E., Bowers, E. P., Agans, J. P., Urban, J. B., & Lerner, R. M. (2011). Youth development program participation and intentional self-regulation skills: Contextual and individual bases of pathways to positive youth development. *Journal of Adolescence*, 34(6), 1115–1125. doi:10.1016/j.adolescence.2011.07.010

National Clearinghouse on Families & Youth. (n.d.). *Promoting positive youth development: An investment in youth & communities* [Brochure]. (Available from: www.ncfy.com/publications/pdf/promote-pyd.pdf – retrieved 10 September 2008).

Nutley, S. M., Walter, I., & Davies, H. T. O. (2007). *Using evidence: How research can inform public services*. Bristol, UK: The Policy Press.

Roland, E. (2000). Bullying in school: Three national innovations in Norwegian schools in 15 years. *Aggressive Behavior*, 26(1), 135–143. doi: 10.1002/(SICI)1098-2337

Rossi, P. H., & Wright, J. D. (1984). Evaluation research: An assessment. *Annual Review of Sociology*, 10, 331–352. doi:10.1146/annurev.so.10.080184.001555

Scheerens, J. (1990). School effectiveness and the development of process indicators of school functioning. *School Effectiveness and School Improvement*, 1(1), 61–80. doi: 10.1080/0924345900010106.

Schober, B., & Spiel, C. (in press). Enabling improvements: Combining intervention and implementation research. In R.A. Scott, S. M. Kosslyn, & M. Buchmann (Eds), *Emerging Trends in the Social and Behavioral Sciences*. Hoboken, NJ: John Wiley & Sons.

Schober, B., Klug, J., Finsterwald, M., Wagner, P., & Spiel, C. (2012). Ergebnisorientierte Qualitätsentwicklung von Schule: Spezifische Kompetenzen von Lehrkräften, Schulleiterinnen und Schulleitern [Output-oriented quality development of schools: Specific competences of teachers and administrators.]. In M. Bruneforth, B. Herzog-Punzenberger & L. Lassnigg (Eds), *Nationaler Bildungsbericht Österreich: Indikatoren und Themen im Überblick* (pp. 111–142). Graz, Austria: Leykam.

Schober, B., Lüftenegger, M., Wagner, P., Finsterwald, M., & Spiel, C. (2013). Facilitating lifelong learning in school-age learners: Programs and recommendations. *European Psychologist, 18*(2), 114–125. doi:10.1027/1016-9040/a000129

Schultes, M.-T., Stefanek, E., van de Schoot, R., Strohmeier, D., & Spiel, C. (2014). Measuring implementation of a school-based violence prevention program: Fidelity and teachers' responsiveness as predictors of proximal outcomes. *Zeitschrift für Psychologie, 222*(1), 49–57. doi: 10.1027/2151-2604/a000165

Senge, P., Cambron-McCabe, N., Lucas, T., Smith, B., Dutton, J., & Kleiner, A. (2000). *Schools that learn*. London: Nicholas Brealey Publishing.

Shonkoff, J. P., & Bales S. N. (2011). Science does not speak for itself: translating child development research for the public and its policymakers. *Child Development, 82*(1), 17–32. doi:10.1111/j.1467-8624.2010.01538.x.

Slavin, R. E. (2008). Perspectives on evidence-based research in education – What works? Issues in synthesizing educational program evaluations. *Educational Researcher, 37*(1), 5–14. doi:10.3102/0013189X08314117

Spiel, C. (2009a). Evidence-based practice: A challenge for European developmental psychology. *European Journal of Developmental Psychology, 6*(1), 11–33. doi:10.1080/17405620802485888

Spiel, C. (2009b). Evidenzbasierte Bildungspolitik und Bildungspraxis – eine Fiktion? Problemaufriss, Thesen, Anregungen [Evidence-based education policy and educational practice: A fiction? Problem, theses, and suggestions]. *Psychologische Rundschau, 60*(4), 255–256. doi:10.1026/0033-3042.60.4.255

Spiel, C., & Strohmeier, D. (2007). Generalstrategie zur Gewaltprävention an Österreichischen Schulen und Kindergärten "Gemeinsam gegen Gewalt" [General strategy for violence prevention in Austrian school and kindergarten "Together against violence"]. *Projektbericht für das Bundesministerium für Unterricht, Kunst und Kultur*. Vienna: Universität Wien.

Spiel, C., & Strohmeier, D. (2011). National strategy for violence prevention in the Austrian public school system: Development and implementation. *International Journal of Behavioral Development, 35*(5), 412–418. doi:10.1177/0165025411407458

Spiel, C., & Strohmeier, D. (2012). Evidence-based practice and policy: When researchers, policy makers, and practitioners learn how to work together. *European Journal of Developmental Psychology, 9*(1), 150–162. doi:10.1080/17405629.2011.616776

Spiel, C., Lösel, F., & Wittmann, W. W. (2009). Transfer psychologischer Erkenntnisse – eine notwendige, jedoch schwierige Aufgabe [Transfer of psychological knowledge – an essential, but complex task]. *Psychologische Rundschau, 60*(4), 241–242.

Spiel, C., Schober, B., & Strohmeier, D. (in press). Implementing intervention research into public policy – the "I3-Approach". *Prevention Science*.

Spiel, C., Wagner, P., & Strohmeier, D. (2012). Violence prevention in Austrian schools: Implementation and evaluation of a national strategy. *International Journal of Conflict and Violence, 6*(2), 176–186.

Spiel, C., Schober, B., Strohmeier, D., & Finsterwald, M. (2011). Cooperation among researchers, policy makers, administrators, and practitioners: Challenges and recommendations. *ISSBD Bulletin 2011, 2*(60), 11–14.

Spoth, R., & Greenberg, M. (2011). Impact challenges in community science-with-practice: Lessons from PROSPER on transformative practitioner-scientist partnerships and prevention infrastructure development. *American Journal of Community Psychology, 48*(1), 106–119. doi:10.1007/s10464-010-9417-7

Spoth, R., Rohrbach, L. A., Greenberg, M., Leaf, P., Brown, C. H., Fagan, A., ... & Hawkins, J. D. (2013). Addressing core challenges for the next generation of type 2 translation research and systems: The translation science to population impact (TSci Impact) framework. *Prevention Science, 14*(4), 319–351. doi:10.1007/s11121-012-0362-6

Stokes, D. E. (1997). *Pasteur's Quadrant: Basic science and technological innovation*. Washington, D. C.: Brookings Institution Press.

16

HOW YOUTH DEVELOPMENT DEMANDS GREATER COMMITMENT TO RESEARCH, INTERVENTION, AND SOCIAL POLICY

The Example of Adolescent Health in India

Suman Verma

Introduction

Adolescence marks the developmental transition period into adulthood. This is a time when puberty and brain maturation lead to new sets of behaviors as well as capacities that enable transitions in family, peer, and educational domains, and in health behaviors. These transitions modify childhood trajectories towards health and well-being (Viner et al., 2012). The adolescent period is also characterized by plasticity, a fundamental strength that has the potential for systematic changes that may result in positive functioning (Lerner, 2009). Fostering developmental transactions between the plastic, developing young person and the contextual setting increases the chances that young people may manifest healthy and positive developmental changes across the adolescent years (Lerner et al., 2012). The nature and quality of young people's future lives – as well as a country's future social and economic development – depend largely on how well adolescents navigate this transition.

The world is home to 1.8 billion young people between ages 10–24 years with 9 in 10 of the world's young population living in low-income countries. With 356 million 10–24 year olds, India has the world's largest youth population (UNFPA State of World Population Report, 2014). A developing country like

India could see its economy soar, provided it invests heavily in young people's health and education as well as protects their rights. India provides a good case example to examine the extent to which this demographic dividend is being harnessed to achieve inclusive growth and offer opportunity and well-being for the young people. My focus is on critical youth investments in the area of health and well-being. One of the social determinants for poor health is inequality that results in lack of access to resources and opportunities for development. This chapter highlights how both the perception and the experience of inequality negatively impacts health outcomes among young people in India.

In India, social, economic, and health factors may undermine the ability of adolescents to lead full and productive lives. This is of particular concern given the sheer number of young people in India – an estimated 31% of national population is between 10–24 years of age and almost 22% are 10–19 year olds (Office of the Registrar General and Census Commissioner of India, 2011). It is well recognized that India's progress in achieving the Millennium Development Goals (MDGs) and now the Sustainable Development Goals (SDGs) are related to its success in achieving its population stabilization goals and, to a large extent, to the investment made in its young people (Population Council and UNICEF, 2013).

The government made a political commitment to meet the specific needs of the adolescent population. Policies are in place to ensure access to equitable education, reproductive health services, and information targeted especially at adolescents; programs have been initiated to provide nutrition to adolescents, and laws were enacted to protect the young from exploitation in the workplace and through trafficking. Today's adolescents are healthier, better educated, and more aware; their age at marriage has increased, and gender disparities in education have declined.

Yet, adolescents are still at a disadvantage. Access to education, employment opportunities, and reproductive health and care services remain limited. Adolescents, particularly females, face social barriers that limit their agency and autonomy in decision making and restrict their ability to make informed choices about their lives.

A key challenge in addressing these issues is the lack of a universal definition for this population. The Ministry of Health and Family Welfare, Government of India (GOI) adopts the UNICEF definition of adolescents as those aged 10–19 years. However, various agencies in the government continue to use different definitions and age groups. For instance, the Ministry of Youth Affairs and Sports (2003) in the National Youth Policy 2003 includes 13–35 year olds as youth but recognizes adolescents aged 13–19 as a special group and advocates specialized programs for them which are different from those aimed at youth aged 20—25 years. Further, the Child Marriage Restraint Act defines a child as men who are under 21 and women who are under 18, while the Immoral Traffic Prevention Act considers those below 16 years of age as a child, or the Juvenile

Justice Act considers any individual who is below 18 as a child (Jejeebhoy & Santhya, 2011). The lack of consensus on the age group makes it difficult to form policies, provide legal protection, and create health, education, and social welfare services for this population.

For the purposes of this examination, I will refer to adolescents as those aged between 10–19 years. In cases where youth programs overlap, I will include those between the age group of 10–24 years. In this chapter, I (i) examine the government's investment in adolescent health in India while looking at demographic indicators that characterize their specific vulnerabilities; (ii) review existing programs and policies for adolescents and identify gaps and challenges to their optimum growth and development; and (iii) provide recommendations for future areas of research, intervention, and evidence-based policies for positive youth development. I draw from articles and reports (Population Council and UNICEF, 2013); GOI reports and publications; large national and sub-national surveys, including the National Family Health Survey (NFHS); Youth in India study by the International Institute of Population Sciences (IIPS) and Population Council (2010); the Annual Status of Education Report (ASER, 2014); and current policy and strategy documents pertaining to protection of adolescents implemented by various departments of the GOI. India is a diverse country with significant regional, gender, religious, and caste differences. This chapter is an overview; it may not be able to comprehensively capture the differences in these sub-groups. Please note that it is beyond the scope of this chapter to cover some of the excellent initiatives undertaken by the non-government organizations or the public sector in reaching out to the needs of the disadvantaged youth in India.

The limited information available to assess certain adolescent health determinants highlights data gaps and priorities for additional data collection. Few studies focus on adolescents 10–19 years of age. Additionally, adolescents are not a homogeneous group; their situations and needs vary by age, sex, socioeconomic and sociocultural context, marital status, level of education, residence, employment status, migration status, sexual activity, and religion. Limited evidence was available on adolescents in the age group of 10–14 years, especially with regard to sexual and reproductive health (Population Council and UNICEF, 2013). Also, NFHS has limited disaggregated data on 15–19-year-olds on various health indicators.

The report of the Commission on Social Determinants of Health (WHO, 2008) drew attention to the crucial role of living conditions for preventing morbidity and mortality, improving health status, and dictating inequalities in health outcomes and utilization of health services. Key recommendations made were to measure the problem, evaluate action, and expand the knowledge base. Using the framework outlined in the report, Cowling, Dandona & Dandona (2014) examined the status of and inequities in social determinants of health (SDH) in India. The multidimensional poverty index (MPI) – a composite measure of health, education, and standard of living – was calculated for all three rounds of the National Family Health Survey, adjusting the methodology to generate comparable findings from the three data sets. Data from government agencies was analyzed to assess voting patterns, political participation, and air and water pollution. Changes in the MPI demonstrate progress in each domain over time, but high rates persist in important areas such as the majority of households use indoor biomass fuel and have unimproved sanitation, and more than one-third of households with a child under the age of three years have undernourished children. There are large, but narrowing, gender gaps in education indicators, but no measurable change in women's participation in governance or labor force participation. Less than 25% of workers have job security and fewer than 15% have any social security benefit. Alarming rates of air pollution are observed, with particulate matter concentration persistently above the critical level. The authors (Cowling, Dandona & Dandona (2014) conclude that these are priority areas for public policy related to SDH in India. Against this ecological backdrop of the country and its impact on the health of its future human resource, the following section examines some demographic indicators of adolescent health in India.

Demographic Indicators of Adolescent Health and Development

This section addresses key aspects of adolescents' lives, including education, nutrition, sexual and reproductive health (SRH), and challenges they face such as child work, abuse and violence, substance misuse, trafficking, and mental health. These vulnerabilities impact adolescents' health and well-being and create obstacles to their positive development.

Education

Access to educational attainment is a basic right and one of the key structural factors in adolescent health. According to the Annual Status of Education Report (ASER, 2014) the primary school enrollment has increased significantly over the last decade, and India has almost met target 3 of MDG 2 in 2015 with 96.7% of children in the age group of 6–14 years enrolled. In the rural areas, there was a decline in the percent of 11–14-year-old girls not enrolled in school from 10.5% in 2006 to 5.5% in 2014. School enrollment of children in private schools (6–14-year-olds) in the rural areas has been rising over the years from 18.7% in 2006 to 30.8% in 2014. This is accounted for as being due to the improvement in school facilities overtime (2010 vs. 2014), such as availability of library books, computers, drinking water, and toilets (ASER, 2014).

However, young people continue to be challenged when it comes to completing their education. There is a steep dropout rate after completion of elementary education – and subsequently at secondary and higher secondary levels – suggesting that gains at the elementary level have not had an impact on the school sector as a whole (UNICEF, 2012). According to government estimates, the dropout rates at the elementary level are 40.3% for boys, 44% for girls and 49.5% for children from backward castes such as scheduled caste (SC) and scheduled tribes (ST). These figures further increase at the secondary school level with the dropout rates being 47.9% for boys, 50.4% for girls, and 63.45% for adolescents from SC/ST groups. The literacy rates for the 15+ age group is 76.7% for males (compared to 57.05% for SC/ST males), and 54.9% for females (compared to 27.6% for SC/ST females) (Ministry of Human Resource Development, 2013).

India has made marked progress in improving access to education, with the mean number of years of schooling for the working population (15 years and above) having increased from 4.19 years in 2000 to 5.12 years in 2010. Secondary school enrollment also increased from 4.3% per year during the 1990s to 6.27% per year in the decade ending 2009–10 (Planning Commission, Twelfth Five Year Plan, 2012–2017, GOI). Data from the NFHS 3 show that 22% of girls aged 15–19 reported having no education, compared to 7% of boys in the same age group. Further, 74% of adolescent girls aged 15–19 years reported they could read and write, compared to 89% of boys of the same age. The gender gap widens further at the secondary level, where more young girls drop out of school. Only 18% of the girls (15–19 years) had completed 10+ years of education, compared to 25% of boys in the same age group (IIPS & Macro International, 2007).

For accessing education, religious and caste differences remain a concern. A sub-national study among youth aged 15–24 years undertaken in six states of India showed that as many as 32% Muslim girls and 13% of Muslim boys aged 15–24 had not received an education; this is compared to 25% of Hindu girls and 8% of Hindu boys. Further, 21% of Muslim girls and 31% of Muslim boys compared to 31% of Hindu girls and 43% of Hindu boys had completed Class 10. Caste differences also exist in the level of education attainment with youth from the scheduled caste/scheduled tribes less likely to have completed 10 years of education than general caste young males (27% vs. 54%) and females (18% vs. 45%) (IIPS & Population Council, 2010).

Studies also show that 8.1 million (4.3%) children aged 6–13 years, out of an estimated 190 million, were out-of-school with greater numbers of rural vs. urban, girls vs. boys, and backward castes vs. general castes being out-of-school (Population Council and UNICEF, 2013; UNICEF, 2012).

Non-enrollment or withdrawal from school takes place for various reasons, including economic barriers (Bandyopadhyaya & Subrahmanian, 2008), the need to undertake household chores, parental concerns about girls' safety, and poor quality of teaching in schools (Rani, 2011; Sharma, Shubhangna & Shipra, 2007). Among young women who discontinued their education, one in seven in Classes 7–9 and one in four in Classes 10–11 reported marriage as the main reason for dropping out of school (IIPS & Population Council, 2010).

School-level barriers include a lack of secondary schools, limited geographic access, and absence of adequate water and toilet facilities within the school, especially separate toilets for girls (Rani, 2011). Poor-quality education and limited vocational training further prevent young people from continuing their education. The learning levels in elementary education in both scholastic and co-scholastic areas are far below the corresponding levels in other countries (Planning Commission, Twelfth Five Year Plan, 2012–2017, GOI).

Nutrition

Good nutrition during childhood and adolescence is essential for growth and development, health and well-being, and for the prevention of some chronic diseases in adulthood. It helps in reducing susceptibility to infections and enhances lifelong learning capacities and adult productivity. Poverty combined with low levels of awareness of nutritional needs among parents results in high rates of malnutrition among children. There is high prevalence of anemia among the young, particularly among girls from marginalized communities. Some studies show obesity as an emerging problem in India and an increase in irregular dietary habits among the young.

In India, 33% of adolescent girls between 11–18 years of age are undernourished. Their health and nutritional status is further compromised by early marriage and early childbearing (Planning Commission, Twelfth Five Year Plan, 2012–2017, GOI). Findings from the NFHS 3 indicate that as many as 56% of females and 30% of males in the 15–19 age group are anemic (IIPS & Macro International, 2007). The high prevalence of anemia among females in India, particularly in the rural areas, is of great concern, as it is directly associated with increased risk of maternal and perinatal mortality. Teenaged and anemic mothers are more prone to deliver low birth weight or premature babies, have inadequate iron stores for the newborn, and lower physical activity and productivity (Population Council and UNICEF, 2013).

The situation is no different in the urban areas with Mane et al. (2012) reporting prevalence of anemia in 51% of girls residing in Pune city when compared to 13% in boys. Gender bias further aggravates the situation: socioeconomic variables such as father's occupational status, per capita income, and number of siblings are predictors of undernutrition among girls (but not boys). This discrepancy is indicative of gender discrimination against female children resulting in them suffering from chronic undernutrition (Mondala, Biswasb & Boseb, 2012). Apart from malnutrition and anemia, studies also point to high prevalence of micronutrient deficiencies among adolescents (Kapil & Bhavna, 2002).

Recent studies also address the growing concern about obesity and being overweight among adolescents in India. According to the NFHS 3 data on the 15–19-year age group, 47% of females and 58% of males are thin and 2.4%

of females and 2% of males are obese (IIPS & Macro International, 2007). Among school-going adolescents (12–18 years), being overweight was found to be higher for boys (14%) than girls (9%) and obesity was 2.9% among boys and 1.5% among girls. The authors (Goyal, Shah & Saboo, 2010) also found a positive correlation between high socioeconomic status and obesity among adolescents. Intervention studies addressing nutritional needs of adolescents suggest that preventive supplementation coupled with nutrition education may be an effective strategy for combating iron and other micronutrients deficiencies in growing children and adolescents (Ahluwalia, 2002).

Sexual and Reproductive Health

Adolescents face a number of challenges with regard to their sexual and reproductive health (SRH) at the individual, familial, and the system level. Early marriage, early and unsafe initiation into sexual activities (and consequently early childbearing (Santhya & Jejeebhoy, 2012)), limited knowledge of and access to contraception, unwanted pregnancies and lack of access to safe abortion services (Singh, Rai, Alagarajan & Singh, 2012), exposure to sexually transmitted infections, and lack of autonomy and gender-based power imbalances exacerbate young people's vulnerabilities (Population Council and UNICEF, 2013).

According to the NFHS 3, more than one-quarter (27%) of women were married before age 15 and more than half (58%) were married before the minimum legal age of 18 years. Among girls aged 15–19 years, 27% are currently married (15% of urban women and 33% of rural women). However, very few men in this age group are currently married (1% of urban and 4% of rural men).

The strong correlation between early marriage and school dropout is noteworthy. Only 13% of women who completed at least ten years of education were married by 18 years, as compared to more than 72% who had no education at all (IIPS and Macro International, 2007). As a consequence of marriage, childbearing is also initiated early for many women in this age group. Apart from high risk of pregnancy complication because of physiological immaturity, inexperience with child care practices and early initiation into adult roles also influences child and maternal health. The risk of maternal death is about three times higher in girls aged 15–19 years and five times higher in those younger than 15 years, compared to women in their twenties (Barua, Apte & Pradeep, 2007). The proportion of women aged 15–19 who have begun childbearing is more than twice as high in the rural areas as in urban areas (19% and 9% respectively; IIPS and Macro International, 2007).

On the one hand, today's adolescents are exposed to a wide range of media messages. They're given new unorthodox ideas about their roles and rights, yet they're expected to conform to traditional norms that do not permit formation of romantic relationships or intermixing with the opposite sex among the unmarried.

Higher-risk sexual behavior (such as unprotected sex or sex with n re than one partner) is of particular concern in this age group, as it is associated with the risk of sexually transmitted infections (STIs). The Youth Study findings indicate that among young men and women aged 15–19 years who reported experiencing premarital sex – 21% and 25% respectively – reported engaging in sex with more than one partner (IIPS & Population Council, 2010).

The proportion of never-married youth who report having had sex is higher in rural areas among both men and women, with a significant proportion not using condoms to protect against disease and unwanted pregnancy (Parasuraman et al., 2009). The unmarried are particularly vulnerable to unwanted pregnancies and they delay accessing safe abortion services. The obstacles reported by the unmarried in accessing abortion services included delay in recognizing pregnancy, unsuccessful previous attempts to terminate pregnancy, the need for assured confidentiality in selecting the abortion facility, and a lack of partner support (Jejeebhoy et al., 2010).

At the family or household level, barriers related to SRH issues include lack of family support in taking independent decisions, unequal gender norms (more constraints for females), and limited communication between parents and adolescents. Barua and Kurz (2001) report that young women do not have the autonomy to delay the first pregnancy, as the family members do not want to delay the birth of a grandchild in the family. Limited autonomy in the marital home implies limited access to healthcare and contraception indicating that, though a significant proportion of married adolescents want to delay their first pregnancy, they are unable to do so; there is family pressure to not use contraceptives for fear of a negative impact on future health and childbearing. The decision to access healthcare services is also vastly limited for young married women, and more so for adolescents, as the main decision makers continue to be the husbands or mothers-in-law (Santhya & Jejeebhoy, 2003).

There is a culture of silence between parents and their adolescents in talking about matters related to topics such as romantic relationships and reproductive health matters. Findings from the Youth Study indicate that romantic relationships and reproductive processes were rarely discussed with parents (0–2% of young men, 1–6% of young women). Young women were more comfortable in talking to their mothers about menstruation (77%) and more urban women than their rural counterparts were likely to have discussed growing up matters related to SRH with their mothers (IIPS & Population Council, 2010).

The existing health system does not recognize the diverse needs of youth, and it is not conducive to or supportive of providing unbiased services to adolescents, particularly to those who are unmarried. Most of the reproductive healthcare services provided in the public sector cater to the needs of the married, but even with these the young people shy away from seeking services due to embarrassment at discussing SRH issues. The unmarried are at a greater disadvantage and may not access services because of lack of confidentiality, an inability to pay for the services, the need for parental approval, and insensitive attitude of the providers (Nath & Garg, 2008).

Child Work

Early initiation into work is a complex issue with a varied set of factors that push young people to work. Conditions of extreme poverty and economic distress, a view that earning an income is more valuable than spending time in school, and pressure to stay at home to complete household chores and take care of younger siblings – especially for girls – are among the factors that result in children leaving school at an early age. These children have to forgo educational opportunities and take up jobs in the organized or the unorganized sector wherein they are often underpaid and have to work in hazardous conditions.

With estimates ranging from 12.6 million (GOI) to 44 million (International Labour Organization: ILO), to as high as 70–80 million (civil society estimates), India has the world's largest population of working children (Save the Children, 2009). Data from the NFHS 3 indicates that nearly one in every eight children (12%) aged 5–14 years either works for their own household or for someone else. Rates increase from 5% among boys aged 5–7 years to 15% among boys aged 12–14 years. The latter group is mainly engaged in paid work or family work, whereas girls in this age group are responsible for household chores or family work (Ministry of Statistics and Programme Implementation, 2012).

The problem of child labor is largely a rural one, with many children employed in agriculture and farms in the rural areas. Many of those who migrate to urban areas to supplement the family's income start work in service establishments, restaurants and on the streets as ragpickers, porters, vendors, and domestic workers among others (Population Council and UNICEF, 2013). Work participation rates are also higher among the minority religious communities, when compared to Hindu groups (Ministry of Statistics and Programme Implementation, 2012).

Child laborers face multiple challenges, including working long hours in hazardous conditions, exposure to physical abuse at the workplace, malnutrition, susceptibility to infections and ailments, and low wages (Verma, 1999; Verma & Saraswathi, 2002). In many cases, exposure to harmful chemicals or pollutants results in visual impairment, deformities, malnutrition, diseases such as tuberculosis, respiratory infections, and cancer from exposure to harmful chemicals (Ministry of Statistics and Programme Implementation, 2012).

Child Abuse

Child and sexual abuse is prevalent in India in various forms. There has been a significant increase in the number of reported crimes against young people.

According to the National Crimes Records Bureau (2014), there was an increase in the crime rate against children from 13.2% in 2013 to 20.1% in 2014. A total of 18,763 children were sexually assaulted during 2014.

Physical and sexual abuse among the young can occur at home, school, the workplace, or on the streets. A national level study undertaken by the Ministry of Women and Child Development (2007) reported high incidence of physical abuse among children (50%) with 69% being victims of either physical, mental, or emotional abuse. Most sexual abuse is perpetrated by family members or persons known to the family. In a study of high school adolescents, Patel and Gracy (2001) found that one-third (33%) of students reported some form of sexual abuse, along with physical and verbal violence in the 12 months preceding the interview. The study also reported significantly poorer academic performance, poorer mental and physical health, greater substance abuse, poorer parental relations, and a high risk of consensual sexual behaviors among the abused students. Another study on street children reported that 9% were sexually abused, 4% had STIs, and 1% were HIV positive (Bal et al., 2010).

Maximum prevalence of pediatric STIs has been reported by Dhawan, Gupta and Kumar (2010) in the age group of 11–14 years with nearly two-thirds of the cases in this age group. Most of these children with STIs were illiterate and belonged to low socioeconomic groups, with a few from remand homes for juvenile delinquents. This finding also highlights the early onset of voluntary or consensual sexual activity occurring in this group. This study also reports that homosexual and bisexual behavior among adolescents further increases the chances of acquiring STDs at an early age. HIV-infected adolescents face considerable physical challenges, including delayed growth and development, late puberty, stunting, wasting, and malnutrition (Mothi, 2012).

Trafficking for sex is another form of abuse that requires urgent attention and action by the government. Sex work in India takes different forms. Available evidence suggests that the majority of trafficked persons are young women or children who have been forced into sex work as a result of poverty, often before they were 18 years old (Joffres et al., 2008). Sex tourism related to the sexual exploitation of young boys and girls by national and international tourists is widespread, and street children are particularly vulnerable to this type of exploitation (Ministry of Women and Child Development, 2007).

Substance Misuse

Adolescence and early adulthood are the most susceptible periods for initiation of tobacco use. The Global Youth Tobacco Survey is a school-based cross-sectional survey carried out with students aged 13–15 years in randomly selected schools that was conducted in all six regions of India in 2006 and 2009. The 2009 survey results reveal that 14.6% of this age group are using tobacco in the country. Of those, 8.1% of students smoked tobacco. As many as 11% of all male students were users of smoking or smokeless tobacco, while 6% of female students used smokeless tobacco and 3.7% smoked tobacco (Ministry of Health and Family Welfare and WHO, 2009). Smoking behaviour among adolescents is positively associated with high use of tobacco among friends and parental tobacco use (Sinha, Gupta & Pednekar, 2003).

Several studies document use of other addictive substances among adolescents in school, out of school, and those living on the streets. Substances include inhalants (petrol, glue, correction fluids, and adhesives), non-prescription drugs (pain killers, cough syrups), and injected drugs and opioids. Few studies examine alcohol use, and cocaine use is limited to higher socioeconomic groups. Curiosity, peer pressure, depression, a desire to overcome shyness, and being tricked by others are some of the factors pushing adolescents to use drugs (Childline India Foundation, 2008; Sarangi, Acharya & Panigrahi, 2008).

Mental Health

According to recent reviews, mental disorders that begin in adolescence place a significant burden of both physical and mental illness in adulthood (Patel, Flisher, Hetrick & McGorry, 2007; WHO, 2012). Yet, population-level studies on mental health and the prevalence and incidence of psychiatric disorders in adolescence remain hard to find.

Evidence from studies on children and adolescents point to a prevalence rate of psychiatric disorders ranging from 7% to 20% (Reddy, Gupta, Lohiya & Kharya, 2013; Srinath et al., 2005). A meta-analysis of five psychiatric epidemiological studies yielded an estimated prevalence of mental morbidity of 22.2 per 1,000 population among 15–24 year olds (Sunitha & Gururaj, 2014). Reasons for this wide range are variations in sources of information, method of elicitation, case definition, and lower sensitivity to certain disorders.

Studies also show prevalence of severe and extreme grade of depression in 11.2% of school dropouts and 3% among school-going adolescents aged 13–19 years (Bansal, Goyal & Srivastava, 2009; Nair, Paul & John, 2004). Poor mental health is related to other concerns among the youth, including poor educational achievement, substance abuse, violence, and poor sexual health (Patel et al., 2007).

Suicide is a leading public health concern in the country, especially for young people. Based on the first national survey of causes of death conducted in 2001–3 by the Registrar General of India, Patel (2012) reports that close to 60% of all suicide deaths in Indian women occur between 15 and 29 years; for men, it's just 40%. High risk of suicidal behavior among young people is likely to be related to the risk-taking and impulsivity that characterizes this stage of life. There is need for promoting adolescent-friendly mental health care and counseling services in the communities in order to respond to the growing problems among young people.

Social Policies and Programs for Adolescent Health and Development

Based on the unique needs of the adolescent population, the GOI has initiated a number of policies and programs that consider marital status, nature of work, place of residence, and gender. The report of the Population Council and UNICEF (2013) summarizes some of these initiatives undertaken by the government while critically examining existing gaps.

In the education sector, the government has put in place a number of policies and programs aimed at increasing enrollment and retention in school, and providing technical and vocational education training for those who are unable to pursue secondary education. These programs, implemented by the Ministry of Human Resource Development, the Directorate of Education, and Ministry of Youth Affairs and Sports also reiterate the government's commitment to reducing gender disparities in access to education among adolescents and youth.

The National Youth Policy, 1988 and revised in 2003 and 2012, the National Education Policy, 1986 and revised in 1992, the Program of Action towards Universalization of Elementary Education of 1992, the Sarv Shiksha Abhiyan launched in 2001, the Rashtriya Madhyamik Shiksha Abhiyan launched in 2008–9, and the more recent Right of Children to Free and Compulsory Education (RTE) Act of 2010 (Ministry of Law and Justice, 2009) are some examples of government initiatives to ensure education for all. In order to provide education to girls who drop out of school, the government has launched two programs – namely, the National Program for Girls Education at the Elementary Level (Class 8) and the Kasturba Gandhi BalikaVidyalaya, for concerted efforts to improve girls' participation at the upper primary level (Classes 5 to 8).

There is increasing recognition of the need for education to be culturally relevant to the needs of the adolescents and to provide them with skills that make them employable and financially independent. The government launched the National Skills Development Initiative in 2009 (Ministry of Labour and Employment, 2009), providing adolescents, women, and school dropouts with opportunities to acquire vocational skills. The Saakshar Bharat Scheme 2009 (Ministry of Human Resource Development, 2009) is yet another government initiative geared towards providing functional literacy and numeracy for 15–35 year olds who have never attended school. It also enables neo-literates to continue their learning, acquire education equivalent to formal education, and learn relevant skills that would create employment opportunities (Population Council and UNICEF, 2013).

There are several policies and programs aimed at improving nutritional status among adolescents, specifically girls. The National Nutritional Policy 1993 was instrumental in setting nutrition goals to control and prevent malnutrition in the country. The policy sought to create a balance between the short-term direct nutrition interventions and long-term institutional and structural changes to improve the nutritional status for all sections of the society. In the year 2000, to give impetus to nutrition among adolescent girls, Kishori Shakti Yojana (KSY) was made a part of the Integrated Child Development Services (ICDS) program. KSY reaches out to girls who are school dropouts (11–18 year olds) and provides take-home rations, a health package, and non-formal education along with home-based and vocational skills development (ICDS and Planning Commission, 2011).

Additionally, the GOI also launched the Nutrition Program for Adolescent Girls (NPAG) in 2002 in 51 districts for adolescent girls and pregnant/lactating women. Beneficiaries were weighed once every three months to identify those who weighed less than 35 kg, and then provided 6 kg of food grain per month for the next three months at no cost. In 2010, the Ministry of Women and Child Development merged the above two programs (KSY and NPAG) to start the Rajiv Gandhi Scheme for Empowerment of Adolescent Girls (RGSEAG), called the SABLA program to provide supplementary nutrition to adolescent girls (11–18 years). Out-of-school girls are also provided two adult folic acid tablets per week along with nutrition and health education (Implementation Guidelines for SABLA program, Ministry of Women and Child Development, 2010; Population Council and UNICEF, 2013). The widespread Mid-Day Meal Scheme for children from Classes 1–8 in government and aided schools and those in alternative and innovative education centers provides a cooked mid-day meal where 300 calories and 8–12 grams of protein is given to each beneficiary.

For the first time, the National Population Policy 2000 (Ministry of Health and Family Welfare, 2000) recognized adolescents as an underserved group that need access to SRH-related information, counseling, and services that are affordable and easily accessible. The National AIDS Prevention and Control Policy 2002 reiterates the need to provide detailed information on HIV and to promote safe sex at the school and college level through curricular and extracurricular activities (National AIDS Control Organisation, 2002). The Exposure Draft National Youth Policy 2012 recognizes the need for an integrated and collaborative approach to youth development programs and the need to provide a distinct framework to all concerned ministries and departments (Ministry of Youth Affairs and Sports, 2012).

Other laws and policies are also in place that address the issue of early marriage, and promote gender equity and empowerment. Programs under the Reproductive and Child Health Program II (RCH II) recognize the need for specific services for adolescents and provide adolescent reproductive and sexual health (ARSH) services including outreach, information and counseling, management of RTI/STI, and communication activities and mass media campaigns to promote utilization of ARSH services to delay age at marriage and improve health outcomes (Ministry of Health and Family Welfare, 2006).

The Adolescence Education Program (AEP) was launched as early as 1993 as an introduction to sex education and was repeated in the National Curriculum Framework in 2005, and subsequently launched in 2005 by the Ministry of Human Resource Development and the National AIDS Control Organisation (NACO). The widespread University Talk AIDS Program has not been evaluated to assess their effectiveness in imparting information and their acceptability by the young (Santhya & Jejeebhoy, 2012).

While there are several government-initiated programs to raise adolescents' awareness of SRH matters, most of these cater to school-going adolescents, thus leaving out a large number of out-of-school adolescents, dropouts, the poor, or the socially excluded. The existing programs for the out-of-school population are more likely to reach young men, and not young women – as the latter do not have the freedom of mobility (Santhya & Jejeebhoy, 2012). A major challenge facing the country is the gap between policy including laws and their implementation. Laws that aim to protect the young such as the prevention of early marriage, sexual harassment, rape, sex selection, and prohibition of dowry are not implemented to their fullest extent; however, regional variations exist.

There has been a declining trend in the prevalence of child labor in the country in the past two decades with provisions in the Constitution of India that imposes on the state the primary responsibility of ensuring that the rights of children are protected. The Commission for the Protection of Child Rights Act was set up in 2005 and provides for national and state-level commissions to protect the rights of children, specifically by examining and reviewing legal safeguards, to initiate inquiries for any violations of child rights, to spread awareness about child rights, and to establish Children's Courts for speedy trials of offences against children or violations of child rights (Ministry of Statistics and Programme Implementation, 2012). The National Policy on Child Labor 1987 covers issues related to the problem of child labor.

The National Child Labor Projects, launched in 1988, include time-bound projects such as special schools to provide informal education, vocational training, supplementary nutrition, stipends, and health care to children withdrawn from employment. The National Plan of Action for Children 2005 aims to secure for all children legal and social protection from all kinds of abuse, exploitation, and neglect (Population Council and UNICEF, 2013).

To deal with the growing prevalence of substance use, the GOI rolled out the Cable Television Network (Regulation) Amendment Bill in 2000, prohibiting cigarette and alcohol advertisements on television. Since 2008, smoking in India has been prohibited in public places and the sale of tobacco products within 100 yards of educational institutions is banned. The Department of AIDS Control implements harm reduction services for injection drug users across the country through the Targeted Intervention Program and Oral Substitution Therapy.

However, neither is designed to address the needs of adolescent injection drug users (Population Council and UNICEF, 2013).

The National Mental Health Policy of India was rolled out in 2014. The policy is inclusive in nature and incorporates an integrated, participatory, rights, and evidence-based approach. The strategic areas identified for action are effective governance and accountability, promotion of mental health, prevention of mental disorders and suicide, universal access, enhanced availability of human resources, community participation, research, monitoring, and evaluation (Ministry of Health and Family Welfare, 2014).

Gaps and Challenges in Meeting Unmet Needs of Adolescents

The story of adolescent health in India is one of growth, gains, and gaps with impending challenges. The economy is growing, and it can benefit from an expanding work force, but the largest democracy of the world is also home to the greatest number of children and youth in the world. With nearly half a billion children and young people aged 0–25 in the country, much remains to be done to ensure the survival, growth, and healthy development of this asset: its children and youth. Stubbornly high rates of out-of-school adolescents, malnutrition, child labor, gender-based inequities, poor sanitation, dangerous levels of air and water pollutants, and persistent social disparities in access to quality services are just some of the obstacles we face in ensuring that those in need are reached, particularly children, youth, and women from the marginalized groups.

These challenges persist in spite of relevant (and, in some cases long-term) public policies, indicating that analytical studies are needed to understand the impact of interventions related to a variety of social determinants of health (Cowling, et al., 2014). While many policies addressing adolescent needs are in place in the country, there is fragmentation in the provision of services and the deleterious implications of failing to see the "whole" child/adolescent for meeting their needs and rights.

Further, gaps exist in policy implementation due to several factors such as state vs. central government responsibility in program implementation, budgetary allocations and utilization, delay in release of funds from the center, lack of effective outreach to needy beneficiaries, poor monitoring and evaluation of the efficacy of the program, and lack of a holistic approach using the rights framework. Proactive government support and intervention is required for stronger enforcement of youth protection policies and legislation (Human Rights Watch, 2003; Population Council and UNICEF, 2013).

Implication for Research, Social Policy, and Programs for Greater Investment in Youth Development

Research

To improve adolescent health, we must first improve young people's quality of life with families, peers, and in schools; we must address risk and protective factors in the social milieu at a population level; we must focus on factors that are protective across various health outcomes (Viner et al., 2012). Additionally, we need more data about vulnerable groups of young people, where the problem is most acute and deeper understanding of resilience enhancing factors to plan need-based preventive interventions to promote healthy behaviors (Verma, Sta. Maria & Morojele, 2011).

We need common conceptual frameworks such as the Social Determinants of Health (WHO, 2008) for guiding studies of the major influences on equity in health. Such frameworks enhance the likelihood that the results of research studies can be interpreted in a policy framework. Equity studies require well-defined variables with a validated method of measurement. Further, causal pathways from determinants to health vary in different population groups such as children, youth, adults, or the elderly (Starfield, 2001). We need studies on equity that separately examine these different pathways in sub-groups to feed into the need for different approaches to interventions.

By increasing partnerships among universities, governments, international organizations, and the private sector, we can promote research that examines public health programs that are close to the supply of and demand for health services (Verma & Petersen, 2015).

Social Policy and Programs

Positive youth development requires eliminating health inequities among young people while adopting a holistic approach whereby the health impacts of all government policies and societal practices are recognized and addressed. Health inequities are often a result of human rights violations, and often public health systems are both a cause of and a solution to health inequities. Available, accessible, acceptable, and quality primary health care should be within the reach of all people, including the youth.

Governments need to ensure universal access to evidence-based public health interventions for all and allocate health resources according to need. Accurate health information should be available to all so that everyone, particularly women, young people, and the most vulnerable, can make informed decisions about their health.

Civil society organizations need to scale up their activities to bring prevention, treatment, care, and support to those who are left out of the formal health system – children, female adolescents, and women who have the least access to appropriate health services. Civil society should expand their reach by encouraging health-seeking behaviors among young people, as well as fostering social inclusion. Representatives from civil society, the private sector, and academia should play a greater role in helping the government in putting health inequity issues high on the development agenda.

Investment in a comprehensive, multi-sectoral, integrated health approach is the only way forward. Standalone programs have a limited impact (International Federation of Red Cross and Red Crescent Societies, 2011). Interventions for young people should therefore go beyond health to address social and economic determinants – education, malnutrition, gender, alcohol/substance misuse, work opportunities, poor housing, indoor/outdoor air pollution, and poverty.

Health spending is an investment that yields returns in individual and population health, education, and economic growth. The government policies need to align commitments with identified gaps and encourage skilled human resources for health, the coverage of mother, child and youth health interventions, and integration with other SDGs to bridge gaps.

Finally, for the future of sustainable communities, we need to engage young people in equity and justice efforts (Petersen, Koller, Motti & Verma, 2016) so their lives are stories of opportunities in realizing their rights in a way that is equitable and non-discriminatory.

Conclusion

For sustainable progress, India needs to invest in empowering its youth. The key to transforming the demographic dividend into economic growth lies not just in having more young people, but having greater numbers of healthier, educated, better trained, and more productive young people (Rajendram, 2013). India must harness the advantage of its youth by building on their strengths, improving the overall health and well-being, equipping youth with quality education and skills training, and putting in place a policy framework where they can be empowered. With a Human Development Indicators ranking of 137 out of 187 countries, India has a long way to go, and must swiftly invest in developing the potential of its enormous human capital (World Bank, 2014).

Both now and in the coming decades, the fight against poverty, inequality, and gender discrimination will be incomplete in the country, and its effectiveness compromised, without a stronger focus on youth development and participation. Poor educational levels and corresponding skill deficits among young people is contributing to bleak youth employment trends. The global economic crisis has produced a large cohort of unemployed youth in the country. For those who are employed, decent work is scarce. Positive youth investment can result in improvement of capacities and enable the aspirations of youth so that they can contribute to and benefit from more stable, democratic, and prosperous communities.

For India, this large youth population can be both an opportunity and a challenge. Development can be accelerated when the majority of youth in the country are able to make significant contributions to economic, social, and political life in a way that lifts the country out of poverty, ensures greater stability, and promotes healthier societies. Alternatively, progress and prosperity will be limited if the country is unable to meet the basic needs of their youth. As a nation, India can become stronger by investing in its youth potential and by trying out unconventional approaches and looking for creative solutions to accelerate progress towards a future in which all young people gain access to the services and opportunities that are theirs by right – but not always in reality.

References

Ahluwalia, N. (2002). Intervention strategies for improving iron status of young children and adolescents, *India Nutrition Reviews*, 60(Issue Supplement s5), S115–S117.

ASER (2014). Annual Status of Education Report. Accessed on January 29, 2016, available at http://img.asercentre.org/docs/Publications/ASER%20Reports/ASER%202014/National%20PPTs/aser2014indiaenglish.pdf

Bal, B., Mitra, R., Mallick, A.H., Chakraborti, S. & Sarkar, K. (2010). Nontobacco substance use, sexual abuse, HIV, and sexually transmitted infection among street children in Kolkata, India, *Substance Use and Misuse*, 45(10), 1668–1682.

Bandyopadhyay, M. & Subrahmanian, R. (2008). *Gender equity in education: A review of trends and factors. Consortium for Research on Educational Access, Transitions & Equity (CREATE)*. Research Monograph No. 18. Sussex: CREATE and New Delhi: National University of Educational Planning and Administration.

Bansal, V., Goyal, S. & Srivastava, K. (2009). Study of prevalence of depression in adolescent students of a public school, *Indian Psychiatry Journal*, 18(1), 43–46.

Barua, A. & Kurz, K. (2001). Reproductive health-seeking by married adolescent girls in Maharashtra, India, *Reproductive Health Matters*, 9(17), 53–62.

Barua, A., Apte, H. & Pradeep, K. (2007). Care and support of unmarried adolescent girls in Rajasthan, *Economic and Political Weekly*, 42(44), 54–62.

Childline India Foundation (2008). *Lost in the haze: A study on substance abuse among children*. Mumbai: Childline India Foundation.

Cowling, K., Dandona, R. & Dandona, L. (2014). Social determinants of health in India: progress and inequities across states, *International Journal of Equity in Health*, 13(88). DOI: 10.1186/s12939-014-0088-0

Dhawan, J., Gupta, S. & Kumar, B. (2010). Sexually transmitted diseases in children in India, *Indian Journal of Dermatology, Venereology, and Leprology*, 76(5), 489–493.

Goyal, R.K., Shah, V.N. & Saboo, B.D. (2010). Prevalence of overweight and obesity in Indian adolescent school going children: Its relationship with socioeconomic status and associated lifestyle factors, *Journal of Association of Physicians, India*, 58, 151–158.

Human Rights Watch (2003). World Report 2003. Accessed on March 4, 2016, available at https://www.hrw.org/legacy/wr2k3/asia.html

ICDS and Planning Commission (2011). Evaluation study on Integrated Child Development Services Schemes. Accessed on March 3, 2016, available at http://planningcommission.nic.in/reports/peoreport/peoevalu/peo_icds_v1.pdf

International Federation of Red Cross and Red Crescent Societies (2011). Eliminating health inequities: Every women and every child counts. Accessed on February 17, 2016, available at http://www.ifrc.org/Global/Publications/Health/1208600-Health%20inequities%20advocacy%20report-EN-LR%20FINAL.pdf

International Institute for Population Sciences (IIPS) and Macro International (2007). *National Family Health Survey (NFHS-3), India, 2005–2006.* Mumbai: IIPS.

International Institute for Population Sciences (IIPS) and Population Council (2010). *Youth in India: Situation and needs 2006–2007.* Mumbai: IIPS.

Jejeebhoy, S.J., Kalyanwala, S., Zavier, A.J. F., Kumar, R. & Jha, N. (2010). Experience seeking abortion among unmarried young women in Bihar and Jharkhand, India: Delays and disadvantages, *Reproductive Health Matters*, 18(35), 163–174.

Jejeebhoy, S.J. & Santhya, K.G. (2011). *Parent–child communication on sexual and reproductive health matters: Perspectives of mothers and fathers of youth in India.* New Delhi: Population Council.

Joffres, C., Mills, E., Joffres, M., Khanna, T., Walia, H. & Grund, D. (2008). Sexual slavery without borders: Trafficking for commercial sexual exploitation in India, *International Journal for Equity in Health*, 7(22). doi: 10.1186 /1475-9276-7-22

Kapil, U. & Bhavna, A. (2002). Adverse effects of poor micronutrient status during childhood and adolescence, *Nutrition Reviews*, 60(5), S84–S90.

Lerner, J.V., Bowers, E., Minor, K., Boyd, M.J., Mueller, M.K., Schmid, K.L., Napolitano, C.M., Lewin-Bizan, S. & Lerner, R.M. (2012). Positive youth development: Processes, philosophies, and programs. In I.B. Weiner, R.M. Lerner, M.A. Easterbrooks & J. Mistry (Eds), *Handbook of psychology: Developmental psychology* (vol. 6, 2nd ed., p. 365). Hoboken, NJ: Wiley.

Lerner, R.M. (2009). The positive youth development perspective: Theoretical and empirical bases of a strength-based approach to adolescent development. In C.R. Snyder & S.J. Lopez (Eds), *Oxford handbook of positive psychology* (2nd ed., pp. 149–163). Oxford, UK: Oxford University Press.

Mane, S.V., Agarkhedkar, S.R., Karwa, D.S., Pande, V., Singhania, S.S. &Karambelkar, G.R. (2012). Study of risk factors for lifestyle diseases among adolescents in Western India, *International Journal of Pharmaceutical and Biomedical Sciences*, 3(4), 224–228.

Ministry of Health and Family Welfare (2000). *National population policy 2000.* New Delhi: GOI.

Ministry of Health and Family Welfare (2006). *Implementation Guide on RCH II: Adolescent Reproductive and Sexual Health Strategy for State and District Programme Managers.* New Delhi: MoHFW,

Ministry of Health and Family Welfare (2014). The mental health policy of India. Accessed on January 14, 2016, available at http://www.nhp.gov.in/sites/default/files/pdf/national%20mental%20health%20policy%20of%20india%202014.pdf

Ministry of Health and Family Welfare and WHO (2009). Tobacco use among students and teachers: Findings from the Global Youth Tobacco Survey (GYTS) and Global School Personnel Survey (GSPS). Accessed on March 20, 2016 www.searo.who.int/india/tobacco/GYTS_India_report_2003-09.pdf

Ministry of Human Resource Development (2009). Saakshar Bharat. Accessed on February 22, 2016.

Ministry of Human Resource Development (2013). *Educational statistics at a glance.* New Delhi: GOI. Accessed on March 20, 2016 http://mhrd.gov.in/sites/upload_files/mhrd/files/statistics/EAG_2013.pdf

Ministry of Labour and Employment (2009). *National skills development initiative.* New Delhi: GOI.

Ministry of Law and Justice (2009). The Right of Children to Free and Compulsory Education Act 2009. No. 35, *The Gazette of India.* New Delhi: GOI.

Ministry of Statistics and Programme Implementation (2012). *Children in India: 2012 – A statistical appraisal.* New Delhi: GOI. Accessed on January 25, 2016, available at https://www.scribd.com/document/127921445/Mospi-nic-in-Mospi-New-Upload-Children-in-India-2012-Rev

Ministry of Women and Child Development (2007). *Study on child abuse in India: 2007.* New Delhi: GOI.

Ministry of Women and Child Development (2010). *Implementation guidelines for SABLA programme.* Accessed on December, 10 2015 www.wcd.nic.in/sites/default/files/2-sablaguidemar11.pdf

Ministry of Youth Affairs and Sports (2003). *The National Youth Policy 2003.* New Delhi: MOYAS, Government of India.

Ministry of Youth Affairs and Sports (2012). *Exposure draft national youth policy 2012.* New Delhi: GOI.

Mondala, P., Biswasb, R.S. & Boseb, K. (2012). Gender discrimination in undernutrition with mediating factors among Bengalee school children from Eastern India, *Journal of Comparative Human Biology,* 63(2), 126–135.

Mothi, S.N. (2012). Adolescents living with HIV in India: the clock is ticking, *Indian Journal of Paediatrics,* 79(12), 1642–1647.

Nair, M.K., Paul, M.K. & John, R. (2004). Prevalence of depression among adolescents, *Indian Journal of Pediatrics,* 71(6), 523–524.

Nath, A. & Garg, S. (2008). Adolescent-friendly health services in India: A need of the hour, *Indian Journal of Medical Sciences,* 62(11), 465–472.

National AIDS Control Organisation (2002). *National AIDS prevention and control policy.* New Delhi: NACO.

National Crimes Records Bureau (2014). *Crimes against children.* New Delhi: NCRB. Accessed on February 13, 2016, available at http://ncrb.nic.in/StatPublications/CII/CII2014/Compendium%202014.pdf

Office of the Registrar General and Census Commissioner of India (2011). Population enumeration data. Accessed on November, 2015, available at http://www.censusindia.gov.in/2011census/population_enumeration.html

Parasuraman, S. S., Kishor, S., Singh, K. & Vaidehi, Y. (2009). *A profile of youth in India 2005–2006: National Family Health Survey (NFHS-3).* Mumbai: IIPS.

Patel. V. (2012). Dying young, *The Hindu,* June 23, 2012. Accessed on January 10, 2016, available at http://www.thehindu.com/opinion/op-ed/invisible-health-risk-that-stalks-indias-youth/article3555531.ece

Patel, V. & Gracy, A. (2001). Gender, sexual abuse and risk behaviours in adolescents: A cross-sectional survey in schools in Goa, *The National Medical Journal of India,* 14(5), 263–267.

Patel, V., Flisher, A.J., Hetrick, S. & McGorry, P. (2007). Mental health of young people: a global public health challenge, *The Lancet,* 369(9569), 1302–1313.

Petersen, A.C., Koller, S.H., Motti-Stefanidi, F., & Verma, S. (2016). Global equity and justice issues for young people during the first three decades of life. In S.S. Horn, M. Ruck, & L. Liben (Eds), Equity and Justice in Developmental Science: Implications for Young People, Families and Communities (Vol. 2), *Advances in Child Development and Behavior*, 51: 289–320. NY: Elsevier, doi: 10. 1016/bs.acdb,2016.05.006

Planning Commission, Twelfth Five Year Plan (2012–2017) *Social sectors volume III.* New Delhi: Planning Commission, Government of India. Accessed Volume 3 on February 5, 2016, available at http://planningcommission.gov.in/plans/planrel/12thplan/pdf/12fyp_vol3.pdf

Population Council and UNICEF (2013). *Adolescents in India: A desk review of existing evidence and behaviours, programmes and policies.* New Delhi: Population Council and UNICEF.

Rajendram, D. (2013). The promise and peril of India's youth bulge. *The Diplomat*, March, 2013. Accessed on March 10, 2016 http://thediplomat.com/2013/03/the-promise-and-peril-of-indias-youth-bulge/1/

Rani, U. R. (2011). Reasons for rising school dropout rates of rural girls in India: An analysis using soft computing approach, *International Journal of Current Research*, 3(9), 140–143.

Reddy, V.B., Gupta, A., Lohiya, A. & Kharya, P. (2013). Mental health issues and challenges in India: A review, *International Journal of Scientific and Research Publications*, 3(2), 1–3.

Santhya, K.G. & Jejeebhoy, S.J. (2003). Sexual and reproductive health needs of married adolescent girls, *Economic and Political Weekly*, 38(41), 4370–4377.

Santhya, K.G. & Jejeebhoy, S.J. (2012). *The sexual and reproductive health and rights of young people in India: A review of the situation.* New Delhi: Population Council.

Sarangi, L., Acharya, H.P. & Panigrahi, O.P. (2008). Substance abuse among adolescents in urban slums of Sambalpur, *Indian Journal of Community Medicine*, 33(4), 265–267.

Save the Children (2009). *Child labour: The child labour doesn't work!* Position paper. New Delhi: Save the Children. Accessed on December 20, 2015, available at https://www.savethechildren.in/resource-centre/position-papers/position-on-child-labour

Sharma, R., Shubhangna, S. & Shipra, N. (2007). Extent of female school dropouts in Kangra District of Himachal Pradesh, *Journal of Social Sciences*, 15(3), 201–204.

Singh, P.K., Rai, R.K., Alagarajan, M. & Singh, L. (2012). Determinants of maternity care services utilization among married adolescents in rural India, *PLoS ONE*, 7(2), e31666.

Sinha, D.N., Gupta, P.C. & Pednekar, M.S. (2003). Tobacco use among students in the eight Northeastern states of India, *Indian Journal of Cancer*, 40(2), 43–59.

Srinath, S., Girimaji, S.S., Gururaj, G., Seshadri, S., Subbakrishna, D.K. & Bhola, P. (2005). Epidemiological study of child and adolescent psychiatric disorders on urban and rural areas of Bangalore, India, *Indian Journal of Medical Research,* 122(1), 67–79.

Starfield, B. (2001). Improving equity in health: A research agenda, *International Journal of Health Services,* 31(3), 545–566.

Sunitha, S. & Gururaj, G. (2014). Health behaviors and problems among young people in India: Cause for concern and call for action, *Indian Journal of Medical Research*, 140(2), 185–208.

UNFPA State of World Population Report (2014). *The power of 1.8 billion: Adolescents, youth and the transformation of the future.* Accessed on March 11, 2016, available at http://eeca.unfpa.org/publications/state-world-population-2014-report

UNICEF (2012). *A national vision for girls' education in India: Roadmap to 2015.* New Delhi: UNICEF.

Verma, S. (1999). Socialization for survival: Developmental issues among working street children in India. In M. Raffaelli and R. Larson (Eds). *Developmental issues among homeless and working street youth* (pp. 5–18). San Francisco, CA: Jossey-Bass.

Verma, S. & Petersen, A. (2015). Global concerns in adolescent health with a case study of India. In L.A. Jensen (Ed.). *The Oxford handbook of human development and culture* (pp. 355–376). New York: Oxford University Press.

Verma, S. & Saraswathi, T.S. (2002). Adolescence in India: Street urchins or Silicon valley millionaires? In B. B.Brown, R. W. Larson & T. S.Saraswathi (Eds), *The World's Youth*. Cambridge University Press.

Verma, S., Sta. Maria, M. & Morojele, N. (2011). A cross-cultural view to the study of resilience among street children, *ISSBD Bulletin*, 1(59), 11–14.

Viner, R.M., Ozer, E.M., Denny, S., Marmot, M., Resnick, M., Fatusi, A. & Currie, C. (2012). Adolescence and the social determinants of health, *The Lancet*, 379(9826), 1641–1651.

WHO (2008). *Commission on social determinants of health: Closing the gap in a generation – Health equity through action on the social determinants of health.* Geneva: WHO.

WHO (2012). *Adolescent mental health: Mapping actions of nongovernment organizations and other international organizations.* Accessed on February 11, 2016 www.who.int/mental_health/publications/adolescent_mental_health/en/

World Bank (2014). *World development indicators.* Accessed on March 11, 2016, available at http://hdl.handle.net/10986/18237

17

ACHIEVING POSITIVE DEVELOPMENT FOR YOUTH GLOBALLY

How Far Have We Come and What Is Yet Needed?

Sílvia H. Koller, Frosso Motti-Stefanidi, Anne C. Petersen, and Suman Verma

Review of Volume Goals

This volume aims to gather research being conducted globally whose focus is on achieving positive development for youth. The sample from which we drew contributions for the volume was the invited and submitted presentations from the Society for Research in Child Development (SRCD) conference in Prague, Czech Republic in Fall 2014. A few outstanding presenters at that conference were unable to prepare a chapter for this volume; despite their absence, we hope that we have captured something from their work.

We especially wanted to gather research on (1) the processes through which significant social change, such as the economic recession, affects the development of youth, and (2) what social contexts, both structural and proximal, help support better outcomes. Further, we wanted to learn how to help youth become engines of hope and change in their communities and countries. We recognized that context matters for conducting research as well as for youth development, and drew researchers who represented the global research community so that they could bring the richness of their experiences to the volume. We aimed to learn about effective programs and policy to help youth adapt well to social change, and when possible, transform these changes into opportunity.

This chapter aims to review the key themes that emerged from the chapters of the volume. In addition, we identify areas and topics that have not been addressed but that are necessary in order to advance research and knowledge as well as effective programs and policy in this area.

Review of Contributions from this Volume

Each chapter of the volume helps us to draw an interesting world map. From the levels of individuals, families, neighborhoods, youth organizations, mentoring programs, communities, and networks, both challenges and opportunities are diversely presented. The expression "it takes a village to raise a child" comes from an African proverb that emphasizes an idea that it takes multiple adults to assist in the development of a single youngster. This concept is demonstrated by the chapter by Hamilton and colleagues with their focus on the importance of non-parental adults in the lives of youth.

The dominant conceptual perspective for development in context that guides the research presented in these chapters is that of Bronfenbrenner (1979). Indeed, most chapters (e.g., Schoon) demonstrated that individual development is closely related to context, from the family microsystem to the broader community and cultural systems. For example, Buchmann found that youth in Switzerland who did well with worsening job markets were from families where parents had higher educational levels, thus amplifying social inequality for those with lower educational levels. Taking a different perspective on the link among cultural systems, families, and individual development, Abubakar and colleagues found that for youth in four distinct cultures and countries, family connectedness mattered for their psychological well-being.

This volume integrates research findings on positive youth development from a wide range of countries including Albania, Brazil, Bulgaria, Chile, Finland, former Soviet Union, Germany, Greece, India, Italy, Kenya, Kosovo, Romania, Spain, Switzerland, the Czech Republic, Turkey, and USA. Diversity within each country was also considered. For example, Silbereisen contrasted gradual and rapid political and economic change experienced by youth in the former East Germany (and Poland) with that of youth in West Germany.

The world economic downturn and recession, which impeded labor market entry for youth, has created a collection of risks to development, especially for youth who are in transition from school to work. Most chapters focused on economic issues such as poverty and impoverishment, economic resources, or on disadvantaged populations more generally. For example, the study of non-parental adult relationships for youth mentioned above (Hamilton and colleagues) used samples of low-income youth from four countries. The effect of family economic hardship on youth unemployment was discussed in the chapters by Silbereisen, Buchmann, and Upadyaya and Salmela-Aro. Buchmann provided a good summary of these effects: the effect of adverse economic change or stress was amplified for youth already economically disadvantaged.

Some chapters focused on identity issues, such as ethnic and national identities. For example, the chapter by Dimitrova and colleagues studied Roma minority youth from six countries to determine whether Roma or national identity dominated for the youth, and whether either identity mattered for self-esteem.

Intergenerational relationships including parenting provided another focus for chapters. For example, Lansford examined the global research literature for effects of parenting style on positive youth development, and concluded that parenting mediates the effect of socioeconomic status on PYD. Abubakar and colleagues studied youth from four countries and found that family connectedness was related to better psychological well-being. And we mentioned the emphasis by Hamilton and colleagues on non-parental adult relationships.

Gender inequality was a special focus in the chapters of Verma and Wuermli and Yoshikawa. Verma focused on India, with the largest youth population globally. She emphasized the role that gender plays in amplifying social inequity. Girls have more limited access to education and services such as health care, and are expected due to cultural norms to marry young and begin childbearing early. Wuermli and Yoshikawa focused on the need for dual-generation interventions serving adolescent mothers and their children in low- and middle-income countries, especially during economic and other crises, to prevent the downward and long-term cycle adversely affecting the health and economic well-being of both mother and child.

School and neighborhood contexts featured in many chapters in the volume as the locus for research and especially interventions. Bullying in these contexts is the focus of the chapter by Pureza and colleagues; they present an intervention program to address this problem combining positive psychology and cognitive behavior therapy. The chapter by Ozer and colleagues described several novel intervention programs based in schools or neighborhoods with a focus on enhancing positive development and good health outcomes.

Effects of societal changes on youth considered over developmental time as well as cumulative risk factors was a central focus of the chapters, in the context of ecological, cultural, political, and individual factors. Each chapter discussed different challenges. A major finding in several chapters was that risk factors often intensify over time (e.g., Schoon). Most chapters examined group and individual differences in the context of a systemic economic adversity that negatively affected countries, families, and individuals, and focused on identifying personal and contextual resources that promote youth's positive adaptation under these circumstances. For example, Motti-Stefanidi and colleagues examined the effects of the economic crisis on youth in Greece, both migrant and native, using a resilience framework for understanding why some youth do well and others do not. They found that family and other social contexts could either increase the risk for adaptation and mental health or buffer the effect of the crisis. Similarly, stronger emotional stability buffered effects for some youth while weaker emotional stability amplified risk.

Most authors focused on positive outcomes and predictors. On a broader level, disadvantaged youth in health and educational systems, early adolescent parenthood, and political unrest were studied to learn how youth achieve positive results as well as what interventions can help stressed youth follow positive trajectories.

The authors (e.g., Silbereisen; Motti-Stefanidi and colleagues) presented data with some case examples, demonstrating that some youth adapt well in high-risk situations, while other youth do not. The Jena Model (Silbereisen) found that greater capacity to explore led to better outcomes for youth experiencing significant change. More generally, belief systems, faith, openness to change, constructive life experiences, sense of well-being, satisfaction in life, and fruitful engagement to life projects may lead youth to overcome the odds, thrive, and strive for a better life in spite of adversity.

Similarly, a number of authors described proximal contexts that support youth adaptation and development during times of economic downturn compared to contexts that actually place youth at greater risk. For example, Buchmann found that Swiss youth whose parents were better educated had better outcomes in finding meaningful work, thus amplifying social inequality. Motti-Stefanidi and colleagues reported evidence for amplifying and buffering effects from both contextual and individual factors.

Interventions and policies were mentioned in most chapters, often as the primary focus, and grounded in the appropriate culture. Several lessons emerge from the chapters. First, the authors combine theory with practice. There is no good practice without a good theory behind it. Second, methodological and innovative technologies were also presented, for both research and intervention. Voelkle's chapter presented new approaches for analyzing longitudinal data. Ozer and colleagues presented interventions from four interdisciplinary teams working in three countries that used technology in ways that effectively engaged youth to achieve positive development. Further, the measures used in this volume were culturally sensitive and highly important for valid research across diverse populations. For example, Abubakar and colleagues carefully calibrated their measures for their study comparing four cultures. Third, every individual and community has its own needs to be identified and understood before implementing a clinical plan or an intervention. What works for youth in some contexts may well not work for others, a point emphasized in the chapter by Wuermli and Yoshikawa. Fourth, evidence-based research and policies should be synchronized by design, to assure that the research implications can be effectively implemented in programs and policy, a point powerfully made in the Spiel and Schober chapter.

Notably, these chapters suggested positive outcomes of empowerment, innovation, and strengthening youth development. Participation of youth is engaged as a change strategy in some chapters of this volume, demonstrating the importance of making youth's voices heard. A related principle that is recurrent in these chapters emphasizes the importance that youth be the authors of their own lives. Offering them opportunities to do something worthy may result in positive self-esteem. Young people who do not have such opportunities may become involved in negative outcomes (Raffaelli, Koller, & Cerqueira Santos, 2012). Authorship promotes self-regulatory capacities. They also may be exemplars and models in their own communities. Community activation is an important strategy to build and have strong emotional, social, and cultural support networks.

Finally, these chapters leave us with a large array of new possibilities. Several positive pathways for youth are suggested which involve companionship, positive relationships, responsibility, and room for personal growth. One of these is civic engagement, where the youth voice is heard and opinions are debated and discussed for bettering their own communities and legislation. For example, the chapter by Hamilton and colleagues demonstrates that youth benefit and develop more positively when they have opportunities to engage in meaningful ways with their communities. Developmental processes are affected by the wider social context that draws attention to the role of public policies and practices that influence the nature of the environment in which youth live. Decision making, leadership, political efficacy, and opportunities for reflection are outcomes that youth find while engaging in civic opportunities.

Youth organizations are also spaces that provide constructive experiences, which build relationships with adults outside the family boundaries. This promotes potential sources of adult relationships for youth and greater access to positive role models. To be effective, interventions should be community based and provide integrated service delivery, building up resources and sustainable relationships from inside the community, thereby strengthening the social fabric of youth's lives.

This volume demonstrates that positive youth development is a major topic of interest among researchers and practitioners around the world. Further, each of the authors brought us new perspectives and novel solutions. Further, there is an urgent need for a clear global agenda for children, adolescents, and adults that takes cultural perspectives and diverse contexts into account. It is never too early or too late to intervene.

The Way Forward: Next Steps for Research, Programs, and Policy

What was missing from the research in this volume, and in the field more generally? Several major areas stand out:

1   More research is needed with majority world populations/communities conducted by, possibly in partnership with, majority world researchers.

2   More research must be conducted with full engagement of the communities and/or populations it is intended to benefit.
3   More research is needed that is designed to have impact on programs (sometimes called practice or interventions) and policy.
4   More research is needed that focuses on positive, instead of on problematic, outcomes.
5   More research is needed that engages youth as designers, leaders, and implementers in the work.

While many of these points are addressed in the chapters in this volume, the authors repeatedly noted that more work is necessary. Next, we will develop each of these points in turn.

Majority World Youth, Communities, and Researchers

While the number of majority world researchers and studies is increasing, their paucity was apparent in this effort from the beginning. Half of the co-editors represent middle-income countries while the other half represent countries classified as upper income. Such representation of other than minority world countries (upper income) is far too unusual. The neglect of majority world researchers is not simply selection bias on the part of majority world researchers, selecting those they know best, though this is surely a factor. Rather, the route to becoming a researcher from the majority world is much more challenging, as it is with attaining success in any field. In spite of limited resources, young researchers in the majority world may have mentors who can support the development of a research program. However, a challenge that majority world researchers may face involves working in a language other than their mother tongue and learning the dominant scientific culture of their field.

Steadily many majority world researchers have become part of the global research community, as evidenced by the authors in this volume. Many have managed to successfully overcome some obstacles and to become researchers. But what would bring these too infrequent successes to scale? How can existing majority world researchers be supported to conduct more research on majority world youth development? One approach would be to support research collaborations, bringing the resources of the minority world to the majority world. Funders in the US, for example, now have mechanisms to support this approach, albeit on a small scale, primarily focused on significant global scientific issues such as global disease threats, global climate change, and the like. Unfortunately, the opportunities for global investment in youth have received scant attention by comparison. A case could surely be made of the importance of investing in youth for the future economic and social good of nations. And the results, if approached in this collaborative way – achieving mutual benefit – would help build majority world infrastructure, train majority world early career scholars, and yield world-class science, programs, and policy. The investment is surely worth.

Community-Engaged Research

As the chapters in this volume have demonstrated, research in which the intended beneficiaries are engaged, results in more valid, culturally sensitive results, and yields benefit to communities, or specific youth populations. Such community-engaged research is ethical, yields sustainable programs, and eases the path to policy in most communities and nations. Such an approach stands in distinct contrast to extractive science in which the research results are obtained with no consent from, or participation of, the intended beneficiaries. Extractive science is unethical but remains dominant in most fields in the minority world.

Integrated Research, Programs, and Policy

This volume includes much exemplary intervention research yet current practice globally does not yet embrace the most recent evidence-based practice. Increasingly, program or intervention research, now termed intervention science, is integrated with developmental science (e.g., Wuermli et al., 2015). Bandura's self-efficacy theory (e.g., Bandura, 1977) is one of the precursors to current positive youth development perspectives (e.g., Motti-Stefanidi, Asendorpf, & Masten, 2012). Self-efficacy theory posited that self-efficacy beliefs determine the initiation of coping behavior, specifically the degree of effort and duration under conditions of challenge or stress. Bandura's theory is inherently one that integrates science and intervention, with hypotheses tested through experimentation or programmatic interventions. It seems especially appropriate to integrate developmental science with intervention science since their goals for positive development of young people are so similar. Yet much developmental research globally continues to be observational. Intervention programs that are implemented should be integrated with research designs. If research populations are engaged with the design, implementation, and use of the research, ethical issues are moot because the "subjects" of the research are fully engaged, and yielding what everyone hopes will be benefits. Such research seems appropriate everywhere but especially where the secondary benefits are so great.

Focus on Positive Development for Youth

Studies conducted in the majority world or focused on ethnic minorities in the minority world still focus on negative behavior more often than positive behavior (e.g., Garcia-Coll, 2013; Verma & Petersen, 2015.) We want good outcomes for young people but we are undermining this goal when we focus on negative behavior of youth such as bullying and underachievement, rather than their positive counterparts (the behavior we hope to see) such as prosocial behavior and achievement. As we noted in the introductory chapter (Petersen et al.), research has demonstrated that interventions focusing on fixing or changing negative behavior do not work. Effective interventions focus on promoting the behavior that we hope to see youth developing (Catalano et al., 2012). It is a tremendous disservice to youth to fail to help them achieve their goals. And as the chapters in this volume have demonstrated, it is not difficult to focus positively with our interventions and research. Similarly, it follows from this volume that it would be effective for researchers and all interested in youth to redirect global policy toward positive development.

Engaging Youth as Actors in their own Development

As many chapters noted, one of the most effective ways to help youth develop positively is to engage them in defining their futures, often by engaging them in our research or programs. The results of such efforts speak for themselves (Hamilton et al.). And the youth who are engaged in this way feel respected and efficacious, just as Bandura's theory predicted.

Gender Equity

In order to advance the discourse on gender in the context of PYD, a larger framework is needed which links empowerment, rights, and mainstreaming of girls and women in all social spaces. As researchers and practitioners, it is also crucial to consider the realities of women's daily lives. In a low- or middle-income country context, gender relations are influenced by poverty, insecurity, impunity, and patriarchy. Achieving gender equity requires a stronger and diverse but unified voice for change, greater accountability, and increased targeted resources. Women and girls' empowerment also requires increase in opportunities and competencies, as well as mainstreaming the gender equality agenda in institutions and processes in a way that transforms social values that have sustained gender inequality.

While all adolescents deserve our attention, the needs of adolescent girls in low- and middle-income countries are particularly pressing. Current research needs to widen its lens and focus on the social and economic contexts in which their lives are embedded, such as home, school, and work, as well as to investigate adolescent reproductive health, marriage, and childbearing. We need to accelerate radically all efforts to broaden the types of data collected on adolescents and to contextualize their experience. We lack a significant body of research in low-income countries on the social and economic consequences of early childbearing, inside or outside of marriage. Such data would greatly strengthen the arguments both against early childbearing and in favor of desirable policies outside the health sector that help to delay childbearing – namely, those promoting education and livelihood opportunities for girls (Diniz, Volling, & Koller, 2014).

Research in the area of violence and health suggests links with gender and social inequalities that place large sections of the population at increased risk. Different types of violence often co-occur and lead to similar problematic outcomes. Unfortunately, research and prevention activities for the various types of violence have often been developed in isolation from one another. If this fragmentation can be overcome, the scope and effectiveness of interventions is likely to be enhanced.

Global Policy

Youth policies and positive programming approaches have to respond to the specific conditions and circumstances faced by young people in each country, in some cases in parts of countries, given the diverse nature of socioeconomic and cultural conditions in larger countries. Simplistic and universal strategies are unlikely to work.

Many of the existing intervention programs are taking a vertical approach addressing isolated symptoms. Narrowly focused programs often do not work. There is a need for more inter-sectoral approaches to address issues affecting youth worldwide, such as unemployment, protection, and health. A cross-sectoral approach to complex problems can help identify innovative solutions (Verma & Petersen, 2015).

Effective approaches have to address the real issues youth are facing. They have to be based on robust research, thorough analysis, and good quality data. There is need for greater recognition and better understanding of the psychosocial factors in youth development. This needs to include a meaningful dialogue with them on questions affecting their lives and open debate on sensitive areas, such as sexual and reproductive health. Large amounts of public resources are wasted on youth programs that do not work, that address problems not relevant for youth, or that are poorly designed. There is also a need to evaluate existing programs and policies to identify why they are not working in order to learn from experience and to identify the strengths and weaknesses of existing approaches (Koller et al., 2015).

As many chapters in this volume have reiterated, there is a general lack of data about youth, their situation, their opinions, and behaviors. There is an urgent need for a wide range of data, disaggregated by gender and age from countries, particularly the low- and middle-income country regions in order to base programs and policies for youth on a sound basis of knowledge.

References

Bandura, A. (1977). Self-efficacy: Toward a unifying theory of behavioral change. *Psychological Review, 84*(2), 191–215. doi: 10.1037/0033-295X.84.2.191.

Bronfenbrenner, U. (1979). *The ecology of human development: Experiments by nature and design.* Cambridge, MA: Harvard University Press.

Catalano, R. F., Fagan, A. A., Gavin, L. E., Greenberg, M. T., Irwin, C. E., Jr., Ross, D. A., & Shek, D. T. (2012). Worldwide application of prevention science in adolescent health. *The Lancet, 379* (9826), 1653–1664. doi: 10.1016/S0140-6736(12)60238-4.

Diniz, E., Volling. B., & Koller, S H. (2014). Social support and maternal depression from pregnancy to postpartum: The association with positive maternal behaviours among Brazilian adolescent mothers. *Early Child Development and Care, 185*(7), 1053–1066. doi: 10.1080/03004430.2014.978309.

Garcia-Coll, C. (2013). Minority children: The future majority of the USA. *Social Policy Report, 27*(2), 23. doi: 23. 10.1111/1467-8624.00344.

Koller, S.H., Dutra-Thomé, L., Nieto Silva, C.J., Morais, N. A., & Santana, J.P. (2015). Work in adolescence: home, villages, streets, and armies. In L. A. Jensen (Ed.), *Oxford handbook of human development and culture: An interdisciplinary perspective.* doi: 10.1093/oxfordhb/9780199948550.013.28.

Motti-Stefanidi, F., Asendorpf, J. B., & Masten, A. S. (2012). The adaptation and well-being of adolescent immigrants in Greek schools: A multilevel, longitudinal study of risks and resources. *Development and Psychopathology, 24*(2), 451–473. doi:10.1017/S0954579412000090.

Raffaelli, M., Koller, S. H., & Cerqueira-Santos, E.(2012). Protective factors moderate between risk exposure and behavioral adjustment among low income Brazilian adolescents and young adult. *British Journal of Educational Psychology, 9*, 74–92.

Verma, S. & Petersen, A. C. (2015). Global concerns with adolescent health with a case study of India. In L.A. Jensen (Ed.), *Oxford handbook of human development and culture: An interdisciplinary perspective.* New York: Oxford University Press. doi: 10.1093/oxfordhb/9780199948550.013.22.

Wuermli, A.J., Tubbs, C.C., Petersen, A.C., & Aber, J.L (2015). Children and youth in low- and middle-income countries: Toward an integrated developmental and intervention science. *Child Development Perspectives, 9*(1), 1–6. doi: 10.1111/cdep.12108.

INDEX

Page references in *italic* indicate figures and tables. The abbreviation PYD stands for positive youth development.